Exploring Ethics

Exploring Ethics
An Introductory Anthology

THIRD EDITION

Edited by

STEVEN M. CAHN
The City University of New York Graduate Center

New York   Oxford
OXFORD UNIVERSITY PRESS

Oxford University Press is a department of the University of Oxford.
It furthers the University's objective of excellence in research, scholarship,
and education by publishing worldwide.

Oxford   New York
Auckland   Cape Town   Dar es Salaam   Hong Kong   Karachi
Kuala Lumpur   Madrid   Melbourne   Mexico City   Nairobi
New Delhi   Shanghai   Taipei   Toronto

With offices in
Argentina   Austria   Brazil   Chile   Czech Republic   France   Greece
Guatemala   Hungary   Italy   Japan   Poland   Portugal   Singapore
South Korea   Switzerland   Thailand   Turkey   Ukraine   Vietnam

Copyright © 2014, 2011, 2009 by Oxford University Press.

For titles covered by Section 112 of the US Higher Education Opportunity
Act, please visit www.oup.com/us/he for the latest information about
pricing and alternate formats.

Published by Oxford University Press.
198 Madison Avenue, New York, NY 10016
www.oup.com

Oxford is a registered trademark of Oxford University Press

Library of Congress Cataloging-in-Publication Data

Exploring ethics : an introductory anthology / Steven M. Cahn.—Third edition
       pages cm
Includes index.
Summary: "Exploring Ethics: An Introductory Anthology, Third Edition, is
a concise, affordable and engaging introduction to moral philosophy. Steven
M. Cahn brings together a rich, balanced, and wide-ranging collection of
fifty-one readings on ethical theory and contemporary moral issues. Message:
Remarkable, accessible, concise, and engaging introduction to moral
philosophy"—Provided by publisher.
ISBN 978-0-19-994658-7 (pbk.)
1. Ethics.   I. Cahn, Steven M.
BJ1012.E97 2013
170—dc23   2013022320

Printing number: 9 8 7 6 5 4

Printed in the United States of America
on acid-free paper

To my wife,
Marilyn Ross, M.D.

Contents

PART III: MORAL PROBLEMS

A. ABORTION

B. EUTHANASIA

C. WORLD HUNGER

D. TERRORISM

E. TORTURE

F. CAPITAL PUNISHMENT

G. ANIMAL RIGHTS

H. THE ENVIRONMENT

Preface

Most anthologies in ethics contain far more material than can be covered in one course, and the readings are often daunting in their complexity. The few simpler and more concise collections usually stress moral problems while deemphasizing discussion of the concepts and methods of ethics.

This book can be completed in a single semester, and the readings have been edited, wherever appropriate, to enhance their accessibility. Moral theory is given its due alongside a selection of contemporary moral issues.

The first part, Challenges to Morality, considers questionable assumptions sometimes brought to the study of ethics. The second part, Moral Theories, focuses on competing explanations of why certain actions are right and others wrong. The third part, Moral Problems, features opposing readings on a variety of controversial issues, such as abortion, euthanasia, terrorism, and affirmative action.

Those who wish to learn more about any particular subject can consult the *Encyclopedia of Ethics*, second edition (Routledge, 2001), edited by Lawrence C. Becker and Charlotte B. Becker. It contains detailed entries with bibliographies on every significant topic in the field.

New to This Edition

- Articles have been added on euthanasia, capital punishment, animal rights, affirmative action, moral issues in academia, the trolley problem, and the meaning of life.
- The Arnulf Zweig translation of Kant's *Groundwork for the Metaphysics of Morals* replaces the translation by Mary Gregor, and more of Kant's work is included.
- The articles by Don Marquis and Carl Cohen have been re-edited.

Readings Added to This Edition

- Bonnie Steinbock, "The Intentional Termination of Life"
- Walter Berns, "The Morality of Capital Punishment"
- Stephen Nathanson, "The Death Penalty as a Symbolic Issue"
- Mary Anne Warren, "Speaking of Animal Rights"
- Tom L. Beauchamp, "Truth in Advertising"
- Leslie Pickering Francis, "Consensual Sex on Campus"
- George Sher, "The Letter Writer's Dilemma"
- Judith Jarvis Thomson, "The Trolley Problem" and "Turning the Trolley"
- Susan Wolf, "Meaning in Life"
- Christine Vitrano, "Meaningful Lives?"

An essay by Thomas D. Sullivan from the previous edition is omitted.

Instructor and Student Resources

The **Instructor's Manual** on a **Companion Website (www.oup.com/ us/cahn),** which accompany the text, have been updated for the Third Edition. The instructor's materials, available on the Companion Website, include a Testbank of objective questions, key terms with definitions, reading summaries, and PowerPoint-based lecture slides. On the Companion Website, students will find summaries that provide brief overviews, flashcards that highlight key terms, and essay questions that reaffirm the main ideas and arguments.

Acknowledgments

I am grateful to Robert Miller, executive editor at Oxford University Press, for his encouragement and guidance, and to editorial assistants Kristin Maffei and Emily Krupin for their generous help. I also wish to thank the staff of Oxford University Press for their assistance throughout production.

I would also like to express my appreciation to those reviewers, chosen by the publisher, who suggested changes for the Third Edition: Kristofer Arca, Miami Dade College; Thomas Atchison, Metropolitan State University; Jeff Behrends, University of Wisconsin–Madison; Andrew Fitz-Gibbon, SUNY Cortland; Rebecca S. Hertsgaard, College of the Desert; Joseph Kirkland, The University of Michigan, Dearborn; John Mizzoni, Neumann University; David Phillips,

University of Houston; Deborah White, University of Massachusetts Lowell and Middlesex Community College, Lowell.

Note

Some of the selections were written when the custom was to use the noun "man" and the pronoun "he" to refer to all persons regardless of sex, and I have retained the authors' original wording. With this proviso, we begin our readings.

Introduction

CHAPTER 1

Morality and Moral Philosophy

William K. Frankena

The terms "ethics" and "moral philosophy" may be used interchangeably. "Ethics" is derived from the Greek work *ethos* meaning "character"; "moral" is from the Latin *moralis*, relating to "custom." But what is the nature of the subject referred to as "ethics" or "moral philosophy"? That question is addressed here by William K. Frankena (1908–1994), who was Professor of Philosophy at the University of Michigan.

Suppose that all your life you have been trying to be a good person, doing your duty as you see it and seeking to do what is for the good of your fellowmen. Suppose, also, that many of your fellowmen dislike you and what you are doing and even regard you as a danger to society, although they cannot really show this to be true. Suppose, further, that you are indicted, tried, and condemned to death by a jury of your peers, all in a manner which you correctly consider to be quite unjust. Suppose, finally, that while you are in prison awaiting execution, your friends arrange an opportunity for you to escape and go into exile with your family. They argue that they can afford the necessary bribes and will not be endangered by your escaping; that if you escape, you will enjoy a longer life; that your wife and children will be better off; that your friends will still be able to see you; and that people generally will think that you should escape. Should you take the opportunity?

This is the situation Socrates, the patron saint of moral philosophy, is in at the opening of Plato's dialogue, the *Crito*. The dialogue gives us his answer to our question and a full account of his reasoning in arriving at it. It will, therefore, make a good beginning for our study.

From William K. Frankena, *Ethics*, 2nd edition. Copyright © 1973. Reprinted by permission of Pearson Education, Inc., Upper Saddle River, NJ.

Socrates first lays down some points about the approach to be taken. To begin with, we must not let our decision be determined by our emotions, but must examine the question and follow the best reasoning. We must try to get our facts straight and to keep our minds clear. Questions like this can and should be settled by reason. Secondly, we cannot answer such questions by appealing to what people generally think. They may be wrong. We must try to find an answer we ourselves can regard as correct. We must think for ourselves. Finally, we ought never to do what is morally wrong. The only question we need to answer is whether what is proposed is right or wrong, not what will happen to us, what people will think of us, or how we feel about what has happened.

Having said this, Socrates goes on to give, in effect, a threefold argument to show that he ought not to break the laws by escaping. First: we ought never to harm anyone. Socrates' escaping would harm the state, since it would violate and show disregard for the state's laws. Second: if one remains living in a state when one could leave it, one tacitly agrees to obey its laws; hence, if Socrates were to escape he would be breaking an agreement, which is something one should not do. Third: one's society or state is virtually one's parent and teacher, and one ought to obey one's parents and teachers.

In each of these arguments Socrates appeals to a general moral rule or principle which, upon reflection, he and his friend Crito accept as valid: (1) that we ought never to harm anyone, (2) that we ought to keep our promises, and (3) that we ought to obey or respect our parents and teachers. In each case he also uses another premise which involves a statement of fact and applies the rule or principle to the case in hand: (1a) if I escape I will do harm to society, (2a) if I escape I will be breaking a promise, and (3a) if I escape I will be disobeying my parent and teacher. Then he draws a conclusion about what he should do in his particular situation. This is a typical pattern of reasoning in moral matters. . . .

At some point you . . . will almost inevitably raise the question of how ethical judgments and principles . . . are to be justified . . . ; and this is likely to lead to the further question of what is meant by saying that something is right, good, virtuous, just, and the like. . . .

When this happens the discussion has developed into a full-fledged philosophical one. Ethics is a branch of philosophy; it is *moral philosophy* or philosophical thinking about morality, moral problems, and moral judgments. What this involves is illustrated by the sort of thinking Socrates was doing in the *Crito*. . . .

Moral philosophy arises when, like Socrates, we pass beyond the stage in which we are directed by traditional rules and even beyond the stage in which these rules are so internalized that we can be said to be inner-directed, to the stage in which we think for ourselves. . . . We may . . . distinguish three kinds of thinking that relate to morality in one way or another.

1. There is descriptive empirical inquiry, historical or scientific, such as is done by anthropologists, historians, psychologists, and sociologists. Here, the goal is to describe or explain the phenomena of morality or to work out a theory of human nature which bears on ethical questions.

2. There is normative thinking of the sort that Socrates was doing in the *Crito* or that anyone does who asks what is right, good, or obligatory. This may take the form of asserting a normative judgment like
"I ought not to try to escape from prison,"
"Knowledge is good," or
"It is always wrong to harm someone,"
and giving or being ready to give reasons for this judgment. Or it may take the form of debating with oneself or with someone else about what is good or right in a particular case or as a general principle, and then forming some such normative judgment as a conclusion.

3. There is also "analytical," "critical," or "meta-ethical" thinking. This is the sort of thinking we imagined that Socrates would have come to if he had been challenged to the limit in the justification of his normative judgments. . . . It does not consist of empirical or historical inquiries and theories, nor does it involve making or defending any normative or value judgments. It does not try to answer either particular or general questions about what is good, right, or obligatory. It asks and tries to answer . . . questions like the following: What is the meaning or use of the expressions "(morally) right" or "good"? How can ethical and value judgments be established or justified? Can they be justified at all? . . .

We shall take ethics to include meta-ethics as just described, but as also including normative ethics or thinking of the second kind. . . . In fact, we shall take ethics to be primarily concerned with . . . answering problems about what is right or ought to be done, and as being interested in meta-ethical questions mainly because it seems necessary to answer such questions before one can be entirely satisfied with one's normative theory (although ethics is also interested in meta-ethical questions for their own sakes). However, since certain psychological and anthropological theories are considered to have a bearing on the answers to normative and meta-ethical questions, as we shall see in discussing egoism . . . and relativism, we shall also include some descriptive or empirical thinking of the first kind.

Study Questions

1. What is a typical pattern of reasoning in moral matters?
2. In answering moral questions, do we need factual knowledge?
3. What are the differences among descriptive morality, normative ethics, and meta-ethics?
4. How does moral reasoning differ from mathematical reasoning?

CHAPTER 2

Crito

Plato

Here is the *Crito*, discussed in the previous selection. Plato (c. 428–347 B.C.E.), the famed Athenian philosopher, authored a series of such dialogues, most of which feature his teacher Socrates (469–399 B.C.E.), who himself wrote nothing but in conversation was able to befuddle the most powerful minds of his day.

SOCRATES: Why have you come at this hour, Crito? It's still very early, isn't it?

CRITO: Yes, very.

SOCRATES: About what time?

CRITO: Just before daybreak.

SOCRATES: I'm surprised the prison-warder was willing to answer the door.

CRITO: He knows me by now, Socrates, because I come and go here so often; and besides, I've done him a small favour.

SOCRATES: Have you just arrived, or have you been here for a while?

CRITO: For quite a while.

SOCRATES: Then why didn't you wake me up right away instead of sitting by me in silence?

CRITO: Well *of course* I didn't wake you, Socrates! I only wish I weren't so sleepless and wretched myself. I've been marvelling all this time as I saw how peacefully you were sleeping, and I deliberately

---

kept from waking you, so that you could pass the time as peacefully as possible. I've often admired your disposition in the past, in fact all your life; but more than ever in your present plight, you bear it so easily and patiently.

SOCRATES: Well, Crito, it really would be tiresome for a man of my age to get upset if the time has come when he must end his life.

CRITO: And yet others of your age, Socrates, are overtaken by similar troubles, but their age brings them no relief from being upset at the fate which faces them.

SOCRATES: That's true. But tell me, why *have* you come so early?

CRITO: I bring painful news, Socrates—not painful for you, I suppose, but painful and hard for me and all your friends—and hardest of all for me to bear, I think.

SOCRATES: What news is that? Is it that the ship has come back from Delos,[1] the one on whose return I must die?

CRITO: Well no, it hasn't arrived yet, but I think it will get here today, judging from reports of people who've come from Sunium,[2] where they disembarked. That makes it obvious that it will get here today; and so tomorrow, Socrates, you will have to end your life.

SOCRATES: Well, may that be for the best, Crito. If it so please the gods, so be it. All the same, I don't think it will get here today.

CRITO: What makes you think that?

SOCRATES: I'll tell you. You see, I am to die on the day after the ship arrives, am I not?

CRITO: At least that's what the authorities say.

SOCRATES: Then I don't think it will get here on the day that is just dawning, but on the next one. I infer that from a certain dream I had in the night—a short time ago, so it may be just as well that you didn't wake me.

CRITO: And what was your dream?

SOCRATES: I dreamt that a lovely, handsome woman approached me, robed in white. She called me and said, "Socrates, Thou shalt reach fertile Phthia upon the third day."[3]

CRITO: What a curious dream, Socrates.

SOCRATES: Yet its meaning is clear, I think, Crito.

CRITO: All too clear, it would seem. But please, Socrates, my dear friend, there is still time to take my advice, and make your escape—because if you die, I shall suffer more than one misfortune: not only shall I lose such a friend as I'll never find again, but it will look to many people, who hardly know you or me, as if I'd abandoned you—since I could have rescued you if I'd been willing to put up the money. And yet what could be more shameful than a reputation for valuing money more highly than friends? Most people won't believe that it was you who refused to leave this place yourself, despite our urging you to do so.

SOCRATES: But why should we care so much, my good Crito, about what most people believe? All the most capable people, whom we should take more seriously, will think the matter has been handled exactly as it has been.

CRITO: Yet surely, Socrates, you can see that one must heed popular opinion too. Your present plight shows by itself that the populace can inflict not the least of evils, but just about the worst, if someone has been slandered in their presence.

SOCRATES: Ah Crito, if only the populace *could* inflict the worst of evils! Then they would also be capable of providing the greatest of goods, and a fine thing that would be. But the fact is that they can do neither: they are unable to give anyone understanding or lack of it, no matter what they do.

CRITO: Well, if you say so. But tell me this, Socrates: can it be that you are worried for me and your other friends, in case the blackmailers[4] give us trouble, if you escape, for having smuggled you out of here? Are you worried that we might be forced to forfeit all our property as well, or pay heavy fines, or even incur some further penalty? If you're afraid of anything like that, put it out of your mind. In rescuing you we are surely justified in taking that risk, or even worse if need be. Come on, listen to me and do as I say.

SOCRATES: Yes, those risks do worry me, Crito—amongst many others.

CRITO: Then put those fears aside—because no great sum is needed to pay people who are willing to rescue you and get you out of here. Besides, you can surely see that those blackmailers are cheap, and it wouldn't take much to buy them off. My own means are available to you and would be ample, I'm sure. Then again, even if—out of concern on my behalf—you think you shouldn't be spending my money, there are visitors here who are ready to spend theirs. One of them, Simmias from Thebes, has actually brought enough money for this very purpose, while Cebes and quite a number of others are also prepared to contribute. So, as I say, you shouldn't hesitate to save yourself on account of those fears.

And don't let it trouble you, as you were saying in court, that you wouldn't know what to do with yourself if you went into exile. There will be people to welcome you anywhere else you may go: if you want to go to Thessaly,[5] I have friends there who will make much of you and give you safe refuge, so that no one from anywhere in Thessaly will trouble you.

Next, Socrates, I don't think that what you propose—giving yourself up, when you could be rescued—is even just. You are actually hastening to bring upon yourself just the sort of thing which your enemies would hasten to bring upon you—indeed, they have done so—in their wish to destroy you.

What's more, I think you're betraying those sons of yours. You will be deserting them, if you go off when you could be raising and educating them: as far as you're concerned, they will fare as best they may. In all likelihood, they'll meet the sort of fate which usually befalls orphans once they've lost their parents. Surely, one should either not have children at all, or else see the toil and trouble of their upbringing and education through to the end; yet you seem to me to prefer the easiest path. One should rather choose the path that a good and resolute man would choose, particularly if one professes to cultivate goodness all one's life. Frankly, I'm ashamed for you and for us, your friends: it may appear that this whole predicament of yours has been handled with a certain feebleness on our part. What with the bringing of your case to court when that could have been avoided, the actual conduct of the trial, and now, to crown it all, this absurd outcome of the business, it may seem that the problem has eluded us through some fault or feebleness on our part—in that we failed to save you, and you failed to save yourself, when that was quite possible and feasible, if we had been any use at all.

Make sure, Socrates, that all this doesn't turn out badly, and a disgrace to you as well as us. Come now, form a plan—or rather, don't even plan, because the time for that is past, and only a single plan remains. Everything needs to be carried out during the coming night; and if we go on waiting around, it won't be possible or feasible any longer. Come on, Socrates, do all you can to take my advice, and do exactly what I say.

SOCRATES: My dear Crito, your zeal will be invaluable if it should have right on its side; but otherwise, the greater it is, the harder it makes matters. We must therefore consider whether or not the course you urge should be followed—because it is in my nature, not just now for the first time but always, to follow nothing within me but the principle which appears to me, upon reflection, to be best.

I cannot now reject the very principles that I previously adopted, just because this fate has overtaken me; rather, they appear to me much the same as ever, and I respect and honour the same ones that I did before. If we cannot find better ones to maintain in the present situation, you can be sure that I won't agree with you—not even if the power of the populace threatens us, like children, with more bogeymen than it does now, by visiting us with imprisonment, execution, or confiscation of property.

What, then, is the most reasonable way to consider the matter? Suppose we first take up the point you make about what people will think. Was it always an acceptable principle that one should pay heed to some opinions but not to others, or was it not? Or was it acceptable before I had to die, while now it is exposed as an idle assertion made for the sake of talk, when it is really childish nonsense? For my part, Crito, I'm eager to look into this together with you, to see whether the principle is to be viewed any differently, or in the same way, now that I'm in this position, and whether we should disregard or follow it.

As I recall, the following principle always used to be affirmed by people who thought they were talking sense: the principle, as I was just saying, that one should have a high regard for some opinions held by human beings, but not for others. Come now, Crito: don't you think that was a good principle? I ask because you are not, in all foreseeable likelihood, going to die tomorrow, and my present trouble shouldn't impair your judgement. Consider, then: don't you think it a good principle, that one shouldn't respect all human opinions, but only some and not others; or, again, that one shouldn't respect everyone's opinions, but those of some people, and not those of others? What do you say? Isn't that a good principle?

CRITO: It is.

SOCRATES: And one should respect the good ones, but not the bad ones?

CRITO: Yes.

SOCRATES: And good ones are those of people with understanding, whereas bad ones are those of people without it?

CRITO: Of course.

SOCRATES: Now then, once again, how were such points established? When a man is in training, and concentrating upon that, does he pay heed to the praise or censure or opinion of each and every man, or only to those of the individual who happens to be his doctor or trainer?

CRITO: Only to that individual's.

SOCRATES: Then he should fear the censures, and welcome the praises of that individual, but not those of most people.

CRITO: Obviously.

SOCRATES: So he must base his actions and exercises, his eating and drinking, upon the opinion of the individual, the expert supervisor, rather than upon everyone else's.

CRITO: True.

SOCRATES: Very well. If he disobeys that individual and disregards his opinion, and his praises, but respects those of most people, who are ignorant, he'll suffer harm, won't he?

CRITO: Of course.

SOCRATES: And what is that harm? What does it affect? What element within the disobedient man?

CRITO: Obviously, it affects his body, because that's what it spoils.

SOCRATES: A good answer. And in other fields too, Crito—we needn't go through them all, but they surely include matters of just and unjust, honourable and dishonourable, good and bad, the subjects of our present deliberation—is it the opinion of most people that we should follow and fear, or is it that of the individual authority—assuming that some expert exists who should be respected and feared above all others? If we don't follow that person, won't we corrupt and impair the element which (as we agreed) is made better by what is just, but is spoilt by what is unjust? Or is there nothing in all that?

CRITO: I accept it myself, Socrates.

SOCRATES: Well now, if we spoil the part of us that is improved by what is healthy but corrupted by what is unhealthy, because it is not expert opinion that we are following, are our lives worth

living once it has been corrupted? The part in question is, of
course, the body, isn't it?

CRITO: Yes.

SOCRATES: And are our lives worth living with a poor or corrupted
body?

CRITO: Definitely not.

SOCRATES: Well then, are they worth living if the element which is
impaired by what is unjust and benefited by what is just has been
corrupted? Or do we consider the element to which justice or
injustice belongs, whichever part of us it is, to be of less value
than the body?

CRITO: By no means.

SOCRATES: On the contrary, it is more precious?

CRITO: Far more.

SOCRATES: Then, my good friend, we shouldn't care all that much
about what the populace will say of us, but about what the expert
on matters of justice and injustice will say, the individual authority, or Truth. In the first place, then, your proposal that we should
care about popular opinion regarding just, honourable, or good
actions, and their opposites, is mistaken.

"Even so," someone might say, "the populace has the power to
put us to death."

CRITO: *That's* certainly clear enough; one might say that, Socrates.

SOCRATES: You're right. But the principle we've rehearsed, my dear
friend, still remains as true as it was before—for me at any rate.
And now consider this further one, to see whether or not it still
holds good for us. We should attach the highest value, shouldn't
we, not to living, but to living well?

CRITO: Why yes, that still holds.

SOCRATES: And living well is the same as living honourably or justly?
Does that still hold or not?

CRITO: Yes, it does.

SOCRATES: Then in the light of those admissions, we must ask the
following question: is it just, or is it not, for me to try to get out
of here, when Athenian authorities are unwilling to release me?
Then, if it does seem just, let us attempt it; but if it doesn't, let us
abandon the idea.

As for the questions you raise about expenses and reputation
and bringing up children, I suspect they are the concerns of those

who cheerfully put people to death, and would bring them back to life if they could, without any intelligence, namely, the populace. For us, however, because our principle so demands, there is no other question to ask except the one we just raised: shall we be acting justly—we who are rescued as well as the rescuers themselves—if we pay money and do favours to those who would get me out of here? Or shall we in truth be acting unjustly if we do all those things? And if it is clear that we shall be acting unjustly in taking that course, then the question whether we shall have to die through standing firm and holding our peace, or suffer in any other way, ought not to weigh with us in comparison with acting unjustly.

CRITO: I think that's finely *said*, Socrates; but do please consider what we should *do*.

SOCRATES: Let's examine that question together, dear friend; and if you have objections to anything I say, please raise them, and I'll listen to you—otherwise, good fellow, it's time to stop telling me, again and again, that I should leave here against the will of Athens. You see, I set great store upon persuading you as to my course of action, and not acting against your will. Come now, just consider whether you find the starting point of our inquiry acceptable, and try to answer my questions according to your real beliefs.

CRITO: All right, I'll try.

SOCRATES: Do we maintain that people should on no account whatever do injustice willingly? Or may it be done in some circumstances but not in others? Is acting unjustly in no way good or honourable, as we frequently agreed in the past? Or have all those former agreements been jettisoned during these last few days? Can it be, Crito, that men of our age have long failed to notice, as we earnestly conversed with each other, that we ourselves were no better than children? Or is what we then used to say true above all else? Whether most people say so or not, and whether we must be treated more harshly or more leniently than at present, isn't it a fact, all the same, that acting unjustly is utterly bad and shameful for the agent? Yes or no?

CRITO: Yes.

SOCRATES: So one must not act unjustly at all.

CRITO: Absolutely not.

SOCRATES: Then, even if one is unjustly treated, one should not return injustice, as most people believe—given that one should act not unjustly at all.

CRITO: Apparently not.

SOCRATES: Well now, Crito, should one ever ill-treat anybody or not?

CRITO: Surely not, Socrates.

SOCRATES: And again, when one suffers ill-treatment, is it just to return it, as most people maintain, or isn't it?

CRITO: It is not just at all.

SOCRATES: Because there's no difference, I take it, between ill-treating people and treating them unjustly.

CRITO: Correct.

SOCRATES: Then one shouldn't return injustice or ill-treatment to any human being, no matter how one may be treated by that person. And in making those admissions, Crito, watch out that you're not agreeing to anything contrary to your real beliefs. I say that because I realize that the belief is held by few people, and always will be. Those who hold it share no common counsel with those who don't; but each group is bound to regard the other with contempt when they observe one another's decisions. You too, therefore, should consider very carefully whether you share that belief with me, and whether we may begin our deliberations from the following premise: neither doing nor returning injustice is ever right, nor should one who is ill-treated defend himself by retaliation. Do you agree? Or do you dissent and not share my belief in that premise? I've long been of that opinion myself, and I still am now; but if you've formed any different view, say so, and explain it. If you stand by our former view, however, then listen to my next point.

CRITO: Well, I do stand by it and share that view, so go ahead.

SOCRATES: All right, I'll make my next point—or rather, ask a question. Should the things one agrees with someone else be done, provided they are just, or should one cheat?

CRITO: They should be done.

SOCRATES: Then consider what follows. If we leave this place without having persuaded our city, are we or are we not ill-treating certain people, indeed people whom we ought least of all to be ill-treating? And would we be abiding by the things we agreed, those things being just, or not?

CRITO: I can't answer your question, Socrates, because I don't understand it.

SOCRATES: Well, look at it this way. Suppose we were on the point of running away from here, or whatever else one should call it. Then the Laws, or the State of Athens, might come and confront us, and they might speak as follows:

"Please tell us, Socrates, what do you have in mind? With this action you are attempting, do you intend anything short of destroying us, the Laws and the city as a whole, to the best of your ability? Do you think that a city can still exist without being overturned, if the legal judgments rendered within it possess no force, but are nullified or invalidated by individuals?"

What shall we say, Crito, in answer to that and other such questions? Because somebody, particularly a legal advocate,[6] might say a great deal on behalf of the law that is being invalidated here, the one requiring that judgements, once rendered, shall have authority. Shall we tell them, "Yes, that is our intention, because the city was treating us unjustly, by not judging our case correctly"? Is that to be our answer, or what?

CRITO: Indeed it is, Socrates.

SOCRATES: And what if the Laws say, "And was that also part of the agreement between you and us, Socrates? Or did you agree to abide by whatever judgments the city rendered?"

Then, if we were surprised by their words, perhaps they might say, "Don't be surprised at what we are saying, Socrates, but answer us, seeing that you like to use question-and-answer. What complaint, pray, do you have against the city and ourselves, that you should now attempt to destroy us? In the first place, was it not we who gave you birth? Did your father not marry your mother and beget you under our auspices? So will you inform those of us here who regulate marriages whether you have any criticism of them as poorly framed?"

"No, I have none," I should say.

"Well then, what of the laws dealing with children's upbringing and education, under which you were educated yourself? Did those of us Laws who are in charge of that area not give proper direction, when they required your father to educate you in the arts and physical training?"[7]

"They did," I should say.

"Very good. In view of your birth, upbringing, and education, can you deny, first, that you belong to us as our offspring and slave, as your forebears also did? And if so, do you imagine that you are on equal terms with us in regard to what is just, and that whatever treatment we may accord to you, it is just for you to do the same thing back to us? You weren't on equal terms with your father, or your master (assuming you had one), making it just for you to return the treatment you received—answering back when you were scolded, or striking back when you were struck, or doing many other things of the same sort. Will you then have licence against your fatherland and its Laws, if we try to destroy you, in the belief that that is just? Will you try to destroy us in return, to the best of your ability? And will you claim that in doing so you are acting justly, you who are genuinely exercised about goodness? Or are you, in your wisdom, unaware that, in comparison with your mother and father and all your other forebears, your fatherland is more precious and venerable, more sacred and held in higher esteem among gods, as well as among human beings who have any sense; and that you should revere your fatherland, deferring to it and appeasing it when it is angry, more than your own father? You must either persuade it, or else do whatever it commands; and if it ordains that you must submit to certain treatment, then you must hold your peace and submit to it: whether that means being beaten or put in bonds, or whether it leads you into war to be wounded or killed, you must act accordingly, and that is what is just; you must neither give way nor retreat, nor leave your position; rather, in warfare, in court, and everywhere else, you must do whatever your city or fatherland commands, or else persuade it as to what is truly just; and if it is sinful to use violence against your mother or father, it is far more so to use it against your fatherland."

What shall we say to that, Crito? That the Laws are right or not?

CRITO: I think they are.

SOCRATES: "Consider then, Socrates," the Laws might go on, "whether the following is also true: in your present undertaking you are not proposing to treat us justly. We gave you birth, upbringing, and education, and a share in all the benefits we could provide for you along with all your fellow citizens. Nevertheless, we proclaim, by the formal granting of permission, that any Athenian who wishes, once he has been admitted to adult status,[8] and has observed the conduct of city business and ourselves, the Laws, may—if he is dissatisfied with us—go wherever he pleases and take his property. Not one of us Laws hinders or forbids that: whether any of you wishes to emigrate to a colony, or to go and live as an alien elsewhere, he may go wherever he pleases and keep his property, if we and the city fail to satisfy him.

"We do say, however, that if any of you remains here after he has observed the system by which we dispense justice and otherwise manage our city, then he has agreed with us by his conduct to obey whatever orders we give him. And thus we claim that anyone who fails to obey is guilty on three counts: he disobeys us as his parents; he disobeys those who nurtured him; and after agreeing to obey us he neither obeys nor persuades us if we are doing anything amiss, even though we offer him a choice, and do not harshly insist that he must do whatever we command. Instead, we give him two options: he must either persuade us or else do as we say; yet he does neither. Those are the charges, Socrates, to which we say you too will be liable if you carry out your intention; and among Athenians, you will be not the least liable, but one of the most."

And if I were to say, "How so?" perhaps they could fairly reproach me, observing that I am actually among those Athenians who have made that agreement with them most emphatically.

"Socrates," they would say, "we have every indication that you were content with us, as well as with our city, because you would never have stayed home here, more than is normal for all other Athenians, unless you were abnormally content. You never left our city for a festival—except once to go to the Isthmus[9]—nor did you go elsewhere for other purposes, apart from military service. You never travelled abroad, as other people do; nor were you eager for acquaintance with a different city or different laws: we and our city sufficed for you. Thus, you emphatically opted for us, and agreed to be a citizen on our terms. In particular, you fathered children in our city, which would suggest that you were content with it.

"Moreover, during your actual trial it was open to you, had you wished, to propose exile as your penalty; thus, what you are now attempting to do without the city's consent, you could have done with it. On that occasion, you kept priding yourself that it would not trouble you if you had to die: you would choose death ahead of exile, so you said. Yet now you dishonour those words, and show no regard for us, the Laws, in your effort to destroy us. You are acting as the meanest slave would act, by trying to run away in spite of those compacts and agreements you made with us, whereby you agreed to be a citizen on our terms.

"First, then, answer us this question: are we right in claiming that you agreed, by your conduct if not verbally, that you would be a citizen on our terms? Or is that untrue?"

What shall we say in reply to that, Crito? Mustn't we agree?

CRITO: We must, Socrates.

SOCRATES: "Then what does your action amount to," they would say, "except breaking the compacts and agreements you made with us? By your own admission, you were not coerced or tricked into making them, or forced to reach a decision in a short time: you had seventy years in which it was open to you to leave if you were not happy with us, or if you thought those agreements unfair. Yet you preferred neither Lacedaemon nor Crete[10]—places you often say are well governed—nor any other Greek or foreign city: in fact, you went abroad less often than the lame and the blind or other cripples. Obviously, then, amongst Athenians you were exceptionally content with our city and with us, its Laws— because who would care for a city apart from its laws? Won't you, then, abide by your agreements now? Yes you will, if you listen to us, Socrates; and then at least you won't make yourself an object of derision by leaving the city.

"Just consider: if you break those agreements, and commit any of those offences, what good will you do yourself or those friends of yours? Your friends, pretty obviously, will risk being exiled themselves, as well as being disenfranchised or losing their property. As for you, first of all, if you go to one of the nearest cities, Thebes or Megara[11]—they are both well governed—you will arrive as an enemy of their political systems, Socrates: all who are concerned for their own cities will look askance at you, regarding you as a subverter of laws. You will also confirm your jurors in their judgment, making them think they decided your case correctly: any subverter of laws, presumably, might well be thought to be a corrupter of young, unthinking people.

"Will you, then, avoid the best-governed cities and the most respectable of men? And if so, will your life be worth living? Or will you associate with those people, and be shameless enough to converse with them? And what will you say to them, Socrates? The things you used to say here, that goodness and justice are most precious to mankind, along with institutions and laws? Don't you think that the predicament of Socrates will cut an ugly figure? Surely you must.

"Or will you take leave of those spots, and go to stay with those friends of Crito's up in Thessaly? That, of course, is a region of the utmost disorder and licence; so perhaps they would enjoy hearing from you about your comical escape from jail, when you dressed up in some outfit, wore a leather jerkin or some other runaway's garb, and altered your appearance. Will no one observe that you, an old man with probably only a short time left to live, had the nerve to cling so greedily to life by violating the most important laws? Perhaps not, so long as you don't trouble anyone. Otherwise, Socrates, you will hear a great deal to your own discredit. You will live as every person's toady and lackey; and what will you be doing—apart from living it up in Thessaly, as if you had travelled all the way to Thessaly to have dinner? As for those principles of yours about justice and goodness in general—tell us, where will they be then?

"Well then, is it for your children's sake that you wish to live, in order to bring them up and give them an education? How so? Will you bring them up and educate them by taking them off to Thessaly and making foreigners of them, so that they may gain that advantage too? Or if, instead of that, they are brought up here, will they be better brought up and educated just because you are alive, if you are not with them? Yes, you may say, because those friends of yours will take care of them. Then will they take care of them if you travel to Thessaly, but not take care of them if you travel to Hades? Surely if those professing to be your friends are of any use at all, you must believe that they will.

"No, Socrates, listen to us, your own nurturers: do not place a higher value upon children, upon life, or upon anything else, than upon what is just, so that when you leave for Hades, this may be your whole defence before the authorities there: to take that course seems neither better nor more just or holy, for you or for any of your friends here in this world. Nor will it be better for you when you reach the next. As things stand, you will leave this world (if you do) as one who has been treated unjustly not by us Laws, but by human beings; whereas if you go into exile, thereby shamefully returning injustice for injustice and ill-treatment for ill-treatment, breaking the agreements and compacts you made with us, and inflicting harm upon the people you should least harm—yourself, your friends, your fatherland, and ourselves—then we shall be angry with you in your lifetime; and our brother Laws in Hades will not receive you kindly there, knowing that you tried, to the best of your ability, to destroy us too. Come then, do not let Crito persuade you to take his advice rather than ours."

That, Crito, my dear comrade, is what I seem to hear them saying, I do assure you. I am like the Corybantic revellers[12] who think they are still hearing the music of pipes: the sound of those arguments is ringing loudly in my head, and makes me unable to hear the others. As far as these present thoughts of mine go, then, you may be sure that if you object to them, you will plead in vain. Nonetheless, if you think you will do any good, speak up.

CRITO: No, Socrates, I've nothing to say.

SOCRATES: Then let it be, Crito, and let us act accordingly, because that is the direction in which God is guiding us.

Notes

1. The small island of Delos was sacred to the god Apollo. A mission sailed there annually from Athens to commemorate her deliverance by Theseus from servitude to King Minos of Crete. No executions could be carried out in Athens until the sacred ship returned.
2. The headland at the southeastern extremity of Attica, about 50 kilometres from Athens. The winds were unfavourable at the time; so the ship may have been taking shelter at Sunium when the travellers left it there.
3. In Homer's *Iliad* (ix. 363) Achilles says, "on the third day I may return to fertile Phthia," meaning that he can get home in three days.
4. Athens had no public prosecutors. Prosecutions were undertaken by private citizens, who sometimes threatened legal action for personal, political, or financial gain.
5. The region of northern Greece, lying 200–300 kilometres northwest of Attica.
6. It was customary in Athens to appoint a public advocate to defend laws which it was proposed to abrogate.

7. The standard components of traditional Athenian education.
8. Admission to Athenian citizenship was not automatic, but required formal registration by males at the age of 17 or 18, with proof of age and parental citizenship.
9. The Isthmus was the strip of land linking the Peloponnese with the rest of Greece. Socrates may have attended the Isthmian Games, which were held every two years at Corinth.
10. Lacedaemon was the official name for the territory of Sparta. Sparta and Crete were both authoritarian and "closed" societies, which forbade their citizens to live abroad.
11. Thebes was the chief city in Boeotia, the region lying to the northwest of Attica; Megara was on the Isthmus. Both lay within easy reach of Athens.
12. The Corybantes performed orgiastic rites and dances to the sound of pipe and drum music. Their music sometimes induced a state of frenzy in emotionally disordered people, which was followed by a deep sleep from which the patients awoke cured.

Study Questions

1. According to Socrates, should one heed popular opinion about moral matters?
2. If you reside in a country, do you implicitly agree to abide by its laws?
3. Does Socrates accept the fairness of the laws under which he was tried and convicted?
4. Do you believe Socrates would have been wrong to escape?

CHAPTER 3

Phaedo

Plato

The *Phaedo*, one of Plato's greatest and most complex works, is set in the Athenian prison on the day of Socrates's death. The discussion focuses on Plato's attempts to prove the immortality of the soul. Near the end of the dialogue, Socrates utters his last thoughts, drinks poison, and dies. This scene, reprinted here, has had an enormous impact on the conscience of countless succeeding generations.

When he'd spoken, Crito said: "Very well, Socrates: what instructions have you for these others or for me, about your children or about anything else? What could we do, that would be of most service to you?"

"What I'm always telling you, Crito," said he, "and nothing very new: if you take care for yourselves, your actions will be of service to me and mine, and to yourselves too, whatever they may be, even if you make no promises now; but if you take no care for yourselves, and are unwilling to pursue your lives along the tracks, as it were, marked by our present and earlier discussions, then even if you make many firm promises at this time, you'll do no good at all."

"Then we'll strive to do as you say," he said; "but in what fashion are we to bury you?"

"However you wish," said he: "provided you catch me, that is, and I don't get away from you." And with this he laughed quietly, looked towards us and said: "Friends, I can't persuade Crito that I am

From *Phaedo*, translated by David Gallop. Copyright © 1975 by Oxford University Press. Reprinted by permission of the publisher. The notes are by Andrea Tschemplik and are used with her permission.

Socrates here, the one who is now conversing and arranging each of the things being discussed; but he imagines I'm that dead body he'll see in a little while, so he goes and asks how he's to bury me! But as for the great case I've been arguing all this time, that when I drink the poison[1], I shall no longer remain with you, but shall go off and depart for some happy state of the blessed, this, I think, I'm putting to him in vain, while comforting you and myself alike. So please stand surety for me with Crito, the opposite surety to that which he stood for me with the judges: his guarantee was that I *would* stay behind, whereas you must guarantee that, when I die, I shall *not* stay behind, but shall go off and depart; then Crito will bear it more easily, and when he sees the burning or interment of my body, he won't be distressed for me, as if I were suffering dreadful things, and won't say at the funeral that it is Socrates they are laying out or bearing to the grave or interring. Because you can be sure, my dear Crito, that misuse of words is not only troublesome in itself, but actually has a bad effect on the soul. Rather, you should have confidence, and say you are burying my body; and bury it however you please, and think most proper."

After saying this, he rose and went into a room to take a bath, and Crito followed him but told us to wait. So we waited, talking among ourselves about what had been said and reviewing it, and then again dwelling on how great a misfortune had befallen us, literally thinking of it as if we were deprived of a father and would lead the rest of our life as orphans. After he'd bathed and his children had been brought to him—he had two little sons and one big one—and those women of his household had come, he talked with them in Crito's presence, and gave certain directions as to his wishes; he then told the women and children to leave, and himself returned to us.

By now it was close to sunset, as he'd spent a long time inside. So he came and sat down, fresh from his bath, and there wasn't much talk after that. Then the prison official came in, stepped up to him and said: "Socrates, I shan't reproach you as I reproach others for being angry with me and cursing, whenever by order of the rulers I direct them to drink the poison. In your time here I've known you for the most generous and gentlest and best of men who have ever come to this place; and now especially, I feel sure it isn't with me that you're angry, but with others, because you know who are responsible. Well now, you know the message I've come to bring: good-bye, then, and try to bear the inevitable as easily as you can." And with this he turned away in tears, and went off.

Socrates looked up at him and said: "Goodbye to you too, and we'll do as you say." And to us he added: "What a civil man he is! Throughout my time here he's been to see me, and sometimes talked with me, and been the best of fellows; and now how generous of him to weep for me! But come on, Crito, let's obey him: let someone bring in the poison, if it has been prepared; if not, let the man prepare it."

Crito said: "But Socrates, I think the sun is still on the mountains and hasn't yet gone down. And besides, I know of others who've taken the draught long after the order had been given them, and after dining well and drinking plenty, and even in some cases enjoying themselves with those they fancied. Be in no hurry, then: there's still time left."

Socrates said: "It's reasonable for those you speak of to do those things—because they think they gain by doing them; for myself, it's reasonable not to do them; because I think I'll gain nothing by taking the draught a little later: I'll only earn my own ridicule by clinging to life, and being sparing when there's nothing more left. Go on now; do as I ask, and nothing else."

Hearing this, Crito nodded to the boy who was standing nearby. The boy went out, and after spending a long time away he returned, bringing the man who was going to administer the poison, and was carrying it ready-pounded in a cup. When he saw the man, Socrates said: "Well, my friend, you're an expert in these things: what must one do?"

"Simply drink it," he said, "and walk about till a heaviness comes over your legs; then lie down, and it will act of itself." And with this he held out the cup to Socrates.

He took it perfectly calmly, Echecrates, without a tremor, or any change of colour or countenance; but looking up at the man, and fixing him with his customary stare, he said: "What do you say to pouring someone a libation from this drink? Is it allowed or not?"

"We only prepare as much as we judge the proper dose, Socrates," he said.

"I understand," he said: "but at least one may pray to the gods, and so one should, that the removal from this world to the next will be a happy one; that is my own prayer: so may it be." With these words he pressed the cup to his lips, and drank it off with good humour and without the least distaste.

Till then most of us had been fairly well able to restrain our tears; but when we saw he was drinking, that he'd actually drunk it, we could do so no longer. In my own case, the tears came pouring out in spite of myself, so that I covered my face and wept for myself—not for him, no, but for my own misfortune in being deprived of such a man for a companion. Even before me, Crito had moved away, when he was unable to restrain his tears. And Apollodorus, who even earlier had been continuously in tears, now burst forth into such a storm of weeping and grieving, that he made everyone present break down except Socrates himself.

But Socrates said: "What a way to behave, my strange friends! Why, it was mainly for this reason that I sent the women away, so that they shouldn't make this sort of trouble; in fact, I've heard one should die in silence. Come now, calm yourselves and have strength."

When we heard this, we were ashamed and checked our tears. He walked about, and when he said that his legs felt heavy he lay down on his back—as the man told him—and then the man, this one who'd given him the poison, felt him, and after an interval examined his feet and legs; he then pinched his foot hard and asked if he could feel it, and Socrates said not.

After that he felt his shins once more; and moving upwards in this way, he showed us that he was becoming cold and numb. He went on feeling him, and said that when the coldness reached his heart, he would be gone.

By this time the coldness was somewhere in the region of his abdomen, when he uncovered his face—it had been covered over—and spoke; and this was in fact his last utterance: "Crito," he said, "we owe a cock to Asclepius: please pay the debt, and don't neglect it."[2]

"It shall be done," said Crito; "have you anything else to say?"

To this question he made no answer, but after a short interval he stirred, and when the man uncovered him his eyes were fixed; when he saw this, Crito closed his mouth and his eyes.

And that, Echecrates, was the end of our companion, a man who, among those of his time we knew, was—so we should say—the best, the wisest too, and the most just.

Notes

1. The poison was hemlock, frequently used in ancient executions.
2. Asclepius was the hero or god of healing. A provocative, but disputed, interpretation of Socrates's final instruction is that he considers death the cure for life and, therefore, wishes to make an offering in gratitude to the god of health.

Study Questions

1. According to Socrates, how could Crito be of most service?
2. Why, according to Socrates, will he have to be caught in order to be buried?
3. What lessons can be drawn from the equanimity with which Socrates faced death?
4. Is death an evil?

Letter from a Birmingham Jail

Martin Luther King, Jr.

In 1963 Dr. Martin Luther King, Jr., was imprisoned in Birmingham, Alabama, for participating in a civil rights demonstration. While in jail, he wrote a letter justifying his actions. Referring several times to Socrates, Dr. King explained that because he believed that the laws that enforced racial segregation were unjust, he refused to act as the government required but had willingly accepted the legal punishment for his actions, thus indicating his respect for democratic procedure. He insisted that such disobedience be nonviolent, that all laws except the unjust ones be obeyed, and that such breaking of the laws be resorted to only when fundamental moral principles were at stake. In 1964 he was awarded the Nobel Peace Prize. In 1968 he was assassinated.

My dear Fellow Clergymen,

While confined here in the Birmingham city jail, I came across your recent statement calling our present activities "unwise and untimely." Seldom, if ever, do I pause to answer criticism of my work and ideas. If I sought to answer all of the criticisms that cross my desk, my secretaries would be engaged in little else in the course of the day, and I would have no time for constructive work. But since I feel that you are men of genuine good will and your criticisms are sincerely set forth, I would like to answer your statement in what I hope will be patient and reasonable terms.

I think I should give the reason for my being in Birmingham, since you have been influenced by the argument of "outsiders coming in."

From James M. Washington, ed., *A Testament of Hope: The Essential Writings of Martin Luther King, Jr.* Copyright © 1963 by Martin Luther King, Jr. Renewed © 1991 by Coretta Scott King. Reprinted by arrangement with The Heirs to the Estate of Martin Luther King, Jr., c/o Writers House as agent for the proprietor New York, NY.

I have the honor of serving as president of the Southern Christian Leadership Conference, an organization operating in every southern state, with headquarters in Atlanta, Georgia. We have some eighty-five affiliate organizations all across the South—one being the Alabama Christian Movement for Human Rights. Whenever necessary and possible we share staff, educational and financial resources with our affiliates. Several months ago our local affiliate here in Birmingham invited us to be on call to engage in a nonviolent direct-action program if such were deemed necessary. We readily consented and when the hour came we lived up to our promises. So I am here, along with several members of my staff, because we were invited here. I am here because I have basic organizational ties here.

Beyond this, I am in Birmingham because injustice is here. Just as the eighth century prophets left their little villages and carried their "thus saith the Lord" far beyond the boundaries of their hometowns; and just as the Apostle Paul left his little village of Tarsus and carried the gospel of Jesus Christ to practically every hamlet and city of the Graeco-Roman world, I too am compelled to carry the gospel of freedom beyond my particular hometown. Like Paul, I must constantly respond to the Macedonian call for aid.

Moreover, I am cognizant of the interrelatedness of all communities and states. I cannot sit idly by in Atlanta and not be concerned about what happens in Birmingham. Injustice anywhere is a threat to justice anywhere. We are caught in an inescapable network of mutuality, tied in a single garment of destiny. Whatever affects one directly affects all indirectly. Never again can we afford to live with the narrow, provincial "outside agitator" idea. Anyone who lives in the United States can never be considered an outsider anywhere in this country.

You deplore the demonstrations that are presently taking place in Birmingham. But I am sorry that your statement did not express a similar concern for the conditions that brought the demonstrations into being. I am sure that each of you would want to go beyond the superficial social analyst who looks merely at effects, and does not grapple with underlying causes. I would not hesitate to say that it is unfortunate that so-called demonstrations are taking place in Birmingham at this time, but I would say in more emphatic terms that it is even more unfortunate that the white power structure of this city left the Negro community with no other alternative.

In any nonviolent campaign there are four basic steps: (1) collection of the facts to determine whether injustices are alive, (2) negotiation, (3) self-purification, and (4) direct action. We have gone through all of these steps in Birmingham. There can be no gainsaying of the fact that racial injustice engulfs this community.

Birmingham is probably the most thoroughly segregated city in the United States. Its ugly record of police brutality is known in every section of this country. Its unjust treatment of Negroes in the courts is a notorious reality. There have been more unsolved bombings of Negro homes and churches in Birmingham than any city in this nation. These are the hard, brutal and unbelievable facts. On the basis of these conditions Negro leaders sought to negotiate with the city fathers. But the political leaders consistently refused to engage in good faith negotiation.

Then came the opportunity last September to talk with some of the leaders of the economic community. In these negotiating sessions certain promises were made by the merchants—such as the promise to remove the humiliating racial signs from the stores. On the basis of these promises Rev. Shuttlesworth and the leaders of the Alabama Christian Movement for Human Rights agreed to call a moratorium on any type of demonstrations. As the weeks and months unfolded we realized that we were the victims of a broken promise. The signs remained. Like so many experiences of the past we were confronted with blasted hopes, and the dark shadow of a deep disappointment settled upon us. So we had no alternative except that of preparing for direct action, whereby we would present our very bodies as a means of laying our case before the conscience of the local and national community. We were not unmindful of the difficulties involved. So we decided to go through a process of self-purification. We started having workshops on nonviolence and repeatedly asked ourselves the questions, "Are you able to accept blows without retaliating?" "Are you able to endure the ordeals of jail?" We decided to set our direct-action program around the Easter season, realizing that with the exception of Christmas, this was the largest shopping period of the year. Knowing that a strong economic withdrawal program would be the by-product of direct action, we felt that this was the best time to bring pressure on the merchants for the needed changes. Then it occurred to us that the March election was ahead and so we speedily decided to postpone action until after election day. When we discovered that Mr. Connor was in the run-off, we decided again to postpone action so that the demonstrations could not be used to cloud the issues. At this time we agreed to begin our nonviolent witness the day after the run-off.

This reveals that we did not move irresponsibly into direct action. We too wanted to see Mr. Connor defeated; so we went through postponement after postponement to aid in this community need. After this we felt that direct action could be delayed no longer.

You may well ask, "Why direct action? Why sit-ins, marches, etc.? Isn't negotiation a better path?" You are exactly right in your call for negotiation. Indeed, this is the purpose of direct action. Nonviolent direct action seeks to create such a crisis and establish such creative tension that a community that has constantly refused to negotiate is forced to confront the issue. It seeks so to dramatize the issue that it can no longer be ignored. I just referred to the creation of tension as a part of the work of the nonviolent resister. This may sound rather shocking. But I must confess that I am not afraid of the word tension. I have earnestly worked and preached against violent tension, but there is a type of constructive nonviolent tension that is necessary for growth. Just as Socrates felt that it was necessary to create a tension in the mind so that individuals could rise from the bondage of myths and half-truths to the unfettered realm of creative analysis and objective appraisal, we must see the need of having nonviolent gadflies to create the kind of tension in society that will help men to rise from the dark depths of prejudice and racism to the majestic heights of understanding and brotherhood. So the purpose of the direct action is to create a situation so crisis-packed that it will inevitably open the door to negotiation. We, therefore, concur with you in your call for negotiation. Too long has our beloved Southland been bogged down in the tragic attempt to live in monologue rather than dialogue.

One of the basic points in your statement is that our acts are untimely. Some have asked, "Why didn't you give the new administration time to act?" The only answer that I can give to this inquiry is that the new administration must be prodded about as much as the outgoing one before it acts. We will be sadly mistaken if we feel that the election of Mr. Boutwell will bring the millennium to Birmingham. While Mr. Boutwell is much more articulate and gentle than Mr. Connor, they are both segregationists, dedicated to the task of maintaining the status quo. The hope I see in Mr. Boutwell is that he will be reasonable enough to see the futility of massive resistance to desegregation. But he will not see this without pressure from the devotees of civil rights. My friends, I must say to you that we have not made a single gain in civil rights without determined legal and nonviolent pressure. History is the long and tragic story of the fact that privileged groups seldom give up their privileges voluntarily.

Individuals may see the moral light and voluntarily give up their unjust posture; but as Reinhold Niebuhr has reminded us, groups are more immoral than individuals.

We know through painful experience that freedom is never voluntarily given by the oppressor; it must be demanded by the oppressed. Frankly, I have never yet engaged in a direct action movement that was "well-timed," according to the timetable of those who have not suffered unduly from the disease of segregation. For years now I have heard the words "Wait!" It rings in the ear of every Negro with a piercing familiarity. This "Wait" has almost always meant "Never." It has been a tranquilizing thalidomide, relieving the emotional stress for a moment, only to give birth to an ill-formed infant of frustration. We must come to see with the distinguished jurist of yesterday that "justice too long delayed is justice denied." We have waited for more than 340 years for our constitutional and God-given rights. The nations of Asia and Africa are moving with jet-like speed toward the goal of political independence, and we still creep at horse and buggy pace toward the gaining of a cup of coffee at the lunch counter. I guess it is easy for those who have never felt the stinging darts of segregation to say, "Wait." But when you have seen vicious mobs lynch your mothers and fathers at will and drown your sisters and brothers at whim; when you have seen hatefilled policemen curse, kick, brutalize and even kill your black brothers and sisters with impunity; when you see the vast majority of your twenty million Negro brothers smothering in an airtight cage of poverty in the midst of an affluent society; when you suddenly find your tongue twisted and your speech stammering as you seek to explain to your six-year-old daughter why she can't go to the public amusement park that has just been advertised on television, and see tears welling up in her little eyes when she is told that Funtown is closed to colored children, and see the depressing clouds of inferiority begin to form in her little mental sky, and see her begin to distort her little personality by unconsciously developing a bitterness toward white people; when you have to concoct an answer for a five-year-old son asking in agonizing pathos: "Daddy, why do white people treat colored people so mean?"; when you take a crosscountry drive and find it necessary to sleep night after night in the uncomfortable corners of your automobile because no motel will accept you; when you are humiliated day in and day out by nagging signs reading "white" and "colored"; when your first name becomes "nigger" and your middle name becomes "boy" (however old you are) and your last name becomes "John," and when your wife and mother are never given the respected tide "Mrs."; when you are harried by day and haunted by night by the fact that you are a Negro, living constantly at tiptoe stance never quite knowing what to expect next, and plagued with inner fears and outer resentments; when you are forever fighting a degenerating sense of "nobodiness"; then you will understand why we find it difficult to wait. There comes a time when the cup of endurance runs over, and men are no longer willing to be plunged into an abyss of injustice where they experience the blackness of corroding despair. I hope, sirs, you can understand our legitimate and unavoidable impatience.

You express a great deal of anxiety over our willingness to break laws. This is certainly a legitimate concern. Since we so diligently urge people to obey the Supreme Court's decision of 1954 outlawing segregation in the public schools, it is rather strange and paradoxical to find us consciously breaking laws. One may well ask, "How can you advocate breaking some laws and obeying others?" The answer is found in the fact that there are two types of laws: there are *just* and there are *unjust* laws. I would agree with Saint Augustine that "An unjust law is no law at all."

Now what is the difference between the two? How does one determine when a law is just or unjust? A just law is a man-made code that squares with the moral law or the law of God. An unjust law is a code that is out of harmony with the moral law. To put it in the terms of Saint Thomas Aquinas, an unjust law is a human law that is not rooted in eternal and natural law. Any law that uplifts human personality is just. Any law that degrades human personality is unjust. All segregation statutes are unjust because segregation distorts the soul and damages the personality. It gives the segregator a false sense of superiority, and the segregated a false sense of inferiority. To use the words of Martin Buber, the great Jewish philosopher, segregation substitutes an "I-it" relationship for the "I-thou" relationship, and ends up relegating persons to the status of things. So segregation is not only politically, economically and sociologically unsound, but it is morally wrong and sinful. Paul Tillich has said that sin is separation. Isn't segregation an existential expression of man's tragic separation, an expression of his awful estangement, his terrible sinfulness? So I can urge men to disobey segregation ordinances because they are morally wrong.

Let us turn to a more concrete example of just and unjust laws. An unjust law is a code that a majority inflicts on a minority that is not binding on itself. This is difference made legal. On the other hand a just law is a code that a majority compels a minority to follow that it is willing to follow itself. This is sameness made legal.

Let me give another explanation. An unjust law is a code inflicted upon a minority which that minority had no part in enacting or creating because they did not have the unhampered right to vote. Who can say that the legislature of Alabama which set up the segregation laws was democratically elected? Throughout the state of Alabama all types of conniving methods are used to prevent Negroes from becoming registered voters and there are some counties without a single Negro registered to vote despite the fact that the Negro constitutes a majority of the population. Can any law set up in such a state be considered democratically structured?

These are just a few examples of unjust and just laws. There are some instances when a law is just on its face and unjust in its application. For instance, I was arrested Friday on a charge of parading without permit. Now there is nothing wrong with an ordinance which requires a permit for a parade, but when the ordinance is used to preserve segregation and to deny citizens the First Amendment privilege of peaceful assembly and peaceful protest, then it becomes unjust.

I hope you can see the distinction I am trying to point out. In no sense do I advocate evading or defying the law as the rabid segregationist would do. This would lead to anarchy. One who breaks an unjust law must do it *openly, lovingly* (not hatefully as the white mothers did in New Orleans when they were seen on television screaming, "nigger, nigger, nigger"), and with a willingness to accept the penalty. I submit that an individual who breaks law that conscience tells him is unjust, and willingly accepts the penalty by staying in jail to arouse the conscience of the community over its injustice, is in reality expressing the very highest respect for law.

Of course, there is nothing new about this kind of civil disobedience. It was seen sublimely in the refusal of Shadrach, Meshach and Abednego to obey the laws of Nebuchadnezzar because a higher moral law was involved. It was practiced superbly by the early Christians who were willing to face hungry lions and the excruciating pain of chopping blocks, before submitting to certain unjust laws of the Roman Empire. To a degree academic freedom is a reality today because Socrates practiced civil disobedience.

We can never forget that everything Hitler did in Germany was "legal" and everything the Hungarian freedom fighters did in Hungary was "illegal." It was "illegal" to aid and comfort a Jew in Hitler's Germany. But I am sure that if I had lived in Germany during that time I would have aided and comforted my Jewish brothers even though it was illegal. If I lived in a Communist country today where certain principles dear to the Christian faith are suppressed, I believe I would openly advocate disobeying these anti-religious laws. I must make two honest confessions to you, my Christian and Jewish brothers. First, I must confess that over the last few years I have been gravely disappointed with the white moderate. I have almost reached the regrettable conclusion that the Negro's great stumbling block in the stride toward freedom is not the White Citizen's Counciler or the Ku Klux Klanner, but the white moderate who is more devoted to "order" than to justice; who prefers a negative peace which is the absence of tension to a positive peace which is the presence of justice; who constantly says, "I agree with you in the goal you seek, but I can't agree with your methods of direct action"; who paternalistically feels that he can set the timetable for another man's freedom; who lives by the myth of time and who constantly advised the Negro to wait until a "more convenient season." Shallow understanding from people of good will is more frustrating than absolute misunderstanding from people of ill will. Lukewarm acceptance is much more bewildering than outright rejection.

I had hoped that the white moderate would understand that law and order exist for the purpose of establishing justice, and that when they fail to do this they become dangerously structured dams that block the flow of social progress. I had hoped that the white moderate would understand that the present tension of the South is merely a necessary phase of the transition from an obnoxious negative peace, where the Negro passively accepted his unjust plight, to a substance-filled positive peace, where all men will respect the dignity and worth of human personality. Actually, we who engage in nonviolent direct action are not the creators of tension. We merely bring to the surface the hidden tension that is already alive. We bring it out in the open where it can be seen and dealt with. Like a boil that can never be cured as long as it is covered up but must be opened with all its pus-flowing ugliness to the natural medicines of air and light, injustice must likewise be exposed, with all of the tension its exposing creates, to the light of human conscience and the air of national opinion before it can be cured.

In your statement you asserted that our actions, even though peaceful, must be condemned because they precipitate violence. But can this assertion be logically made? Isn't this like condemning the robbed man because his possession of money precipitated the evil act of robbery? Isn't this like condemning Socrates because his unswerving commitment to truth and his philosophical delvings precipitated the misguided popular mind to make him drink the hemlock? Isn't this like condemning Jesus because His unique God-consciousness and never-ceasing devotion to his will precipitated the evil act of crucifixion? We must come to see, as federal courts have consistently affirmed, that it is immoral to urge an individual to withdraw his efforts to gain his basic constitutional rights because the quest precipitates violence. Society must protect the robbed and punish the robber.

I had also hoped that the white moderate would reject the myth of time. I received a letter this morning from a white brother in Texas which said: "All Christians know that the colored people will receive equal rights eventually, but it is possible that you are in too great of a religious hurry. It has taken Christianity almost two thousand years to accomplish what it has. The teachings of Christ take time to come to earth." All that is said here grows out of a tragic misconception of time. It is the strangely irrational notion that there is something in the very flow of time that will inevitably cure all ills. Actually time is neutral. It can be used either destructively or constructively. I am coming to feel that the people of ill will have used time much more effectively than the people of good will. We will have to repent in this generation not merely for the vitriolic words and actions of the bad people, but for the appalling silence of the good people. We must come to see that human progress never rolls in on wheels of inevitability. It comes through the tireless efforts and persistent work of men willing to be co-workers with God, and without this hard work time itself becomes an ally of the forces of social stagnation. We must use time creatively, and forever realize that the time is always ripe to do right. Now is the time to make real the promise of democracy, and transform our pending national elegy into a creative psalm of brotherhood. Now is the time to lift our national policy from the quicksand of racial injustice to the solid rock of human dignity.

You spoke of our activity in Birmingham as extreme. At first I was rather disappointed that fellow clergymen would see my nonviolent efforts as those of the extremist. I started thinking about the fact that I stand in the middle of two opposing forces in the Negro community. One is a force of complacency made up of Negroes who, as a result of long years of oppression, have been so completely drained of self-respect and a sense of "somebodiness" that they have adjusted to segregation, and, of a few Negroes in the middle class who, because of a degree of academic and economic security, and because at points they profit by segregation, have unconsciously become insensitive to the problems of the masses. The other force is one of bitterness and hatred, and comes perilously close to advocating violence. It is expressed in the various black nationalist groups that are springing up over the nation, the largest and best known being Elijah Muhammad's Muslim movement. This movement is nourished by the contemporary frustration over the continued existence of racial discrimination. It is made up of people who have lost faith in America, who have absolutely repudiated Christianity, and who have concluded that the white man is an incurable "devil." I have tried to stand between these two forces, saying that we need not follow the "donothingism" of the complacent or the hatred and despair of the black nationalist. There is the more excellent way of love and nonviolent protest. I'm grateful to God that, through the Negro church, the dimension of nonviolence entered our struggle. If this philosophy had not emerged, I am convinced that by now many streets of the South would be flowing with floods of blood. And I am further convinced that if our white brothers dismiss as "rabble-rousers" and "outside agitators" those of us who are working through the channels of nonviolent direct action and refuse to support our nonviolent efforts, millions of Negroes, out of frustration and despair, will seek solace and security in black nationalist ideologies, a development that will lead inevitably to a frightening racial nightmare.

Oppressed people cannot remain oppressed forever. The urge for freedom will eventually come. This is what happened to the American Negro. Something within has reminded him of his birthright of freedom; something without has reminded him that he can gain it. Consciously and unconsciously, he has been swept in by what the Germans call the *Zeitgeist*, and with his black brothers of Africa, and his brown and yellow brothers of Asia, South America and the Caribbean, he is moving with a sense of cosmic urgency toward the promised land of racial justice. Recognizing this vital urge that has engulfed the Negro community, one should readily understand public demonstrations. The Negro has many pent-up resentments and latent frustrations. He has to get them out. So let him march sometime; let him have his prayer pilgrimages to the city hall; understand why he must have sit-ins and freedom rides. If his repressed emotions do not come out in these nonviolent ways, they will come out in ominous expressions of violence. This is not a threat; it is a fact of history. So I have not said to my people "get rid of your discontent."

But I have tried to say that this normal and healthy discontent can be channelized through the creative outlet of nonviolent direct action. Now this approach is being dismissed as extremist. I must admit that I was initially disappointed in being so categorized.

But as I continued to think about the matter I gradually gained a bit of satisfaction from being considered an extremist. Was not Jesus an extremist in love—"Love your enemies, bless them that curse you, pray for them that despitefully use you." Was not Amos an extremist for justice—"Let justice roll down like waters and righteousness like a mighty stream." Was not Paul an extremist for the gospel of Jesus Christ—"I bear in my body the marks of the Lord Jesus." Was not Martin Luther an extremist—"Here I stand; I can do none other so help me God." Was not John Bunyan an extremist—"I will stay in jail to the end of my days before I make a butchery of my conscience." Was not Abraham Lincoln an extremist—"This nation cannot survive half slave and half free." Was not Thomas Jefferson an extremist—"We hold these truths to be self-evident, that all men are created equal." So the question is not whether we will be extremist but what kind of extremist will we be. Will we be extremists for hate or will we be extremists for love? Will we be extremists for the preservation of injustice—or will we be extremists for the cause of justice? In that dramatic scene on Calvary's hill, three men were crucified, We must not forget that all three were crucified for the same crime—the crime of extremism. Two were extremists for immorality, and thusly fell below their environment. The other, Jesus Christ, was an extremist for love, truth and goodness, and thereby rose above his environment. So, after all, maybe the South, the nation and the world are in dire need of creative extremists.

I had hoped that the white moderate would see this. Maybe I was too optimistic. Maybe I expected too much. I guess I should have realized that few members of a race that has oppressed another race can understand or appreciate the deep groans and passionate yearnings of those that have been oppressed and still fewer have the vision to see that injustice must be rooted out by strong, persistent and determined action. I am thankful, however, that some of our white brothers have grasped the meaning of this social revolution and committed themselves to it. They are still all too small in quantity, but they are big in quality. Some like Ralph McGill, Lillian Smith, Harry Golden and James Dabbs have written about our struggle in eloquent, prophetic and understanding terms. Others have marched with us down nameless streets of the South. They have languished in filthy roach-infested jails, suffering the abuse and brutality of angry policemen who see them as "dirty nigger-lovers." They, unlike so many of their moderate brothers and sisters, have recognized the urgency of the moment and sensed the need for powerful "action" antidotes to combat the disease of segregation.

Let me rush on to mention my other disappointment. I have been so greatly disappointed with the white church and its leadership. Of course, there are some notable exceptions. I am not unmindful of the fact that each of you has taken some significant stands on this issue. I commend you, Rev. Stallings, for your Christian stance on this past Sunday, in welcoming Negroes to your worship service on a non-segregated basis. I commend the Catholic leaders of this state for integrating Springhill College several years ago.

But despite these notable exceptions I must honestly reiterate that I have been disappointed with the church. I do not say that as one of the negative critics who can always find something wrong with the church. I say it as a minister of the gospel, who loves the church; who was nurtured in its bosom; who has been sustained by its spiritual blessings and who will remain true to it as long as the cord of life shall lengthen.

I had the strange feeling when I was suddenly catapulted into the leadership of the bus protest in Montgomery several years ago that we would have the support of the white church. I felt that the white ministers, priests and rabbis of the South would be some of our strongest allies. Instead, some have been outright opponents, refusing to understand the freedom movement and misrepresenting its leaders; all too many others have been more cautious than courageous and have remained silent behind the anesthetizing security of the stained-glass windows.

In spite of my shattered dreams of the past, I came to Birmingham with the hope that the white religious leadership of this community would see the justice of our cause, and with deep moral concern, serve as the channel through which our just grievances would get to the power structure. I had hoped that each of you would understand. But again I have been disappointed. I have heard numerous religious leaders of the South call upon their worshippers to comply with a desegregation decision because it is the *law*, but I have longed to hear white ministers say, "Follow this decree because integration is morally *right* and the Negro is your brother." In the midst of blatant injustices inflicted upon the Negro, I have watched white churches stand on the sideline and merely mouth pious irrelevancies and sanctimonious trivialities. In the midst of a mighty struggle to rid our nation of racial and economic injustice, I have heard so many ministers say, "Those are social issues with which the gospel has no real concern," and I have watched so many churches commit themselves to a completely otherworldly religion which made a strange distinction between body and soul, the sacred and the secular.

So here we are moving toward the exit of the twentieth century with a religious community largely adjusted to the status quo, standing as a taillight behind other community agencies rather than a headlight leading men to higher levels of justice.

I have traveled the length and breadth of Alabama, Mississippi and all the other southern states. On sweltering summer days and crisp autumn mornings I have looked at her beautiful churches with their lofty spires pointing heavenward. I have beheld the impressive outlay of her massive religious education buildings. Over and over again I have found myself asking: "What kind of people worship here? Who is their God? Where were their voices when the lips of Governor Barnett dripped with words of interposition and nullification? Where were they when Governor Wallace gave the clarion call for defiance and hatred? Where were their voices of support when tired, bruised and weary Negro men and women decided to rise from the dark dungeons of complacency to the bright hills of creative protest?"

Yes, these questions are still in my mind. In deep disappointment, I have wept over the laxity of the church. But be assured that my tears have been tears of love. There can be no deep disappointment where there is not deep love. Yes, I love the church; I love her sacred walls. How could I do otherwise? I am in a rather unique position of being the son, the grandson and the great-grandson of preachers. Yes, I see the church as the body of Christ. But, oh! How we have blemished and scarred that body through social neglect and fear of being nonconformists.

There was a time when the church was very powerful. It was during that period when the early Christians rejoiced when they were deemed worthy to suffer for what they believed. In those days the church was not merely a thermometer that recorded the ideas and principles of popular opinion; it was a thermostat that transformed the mores of society. Wherever the early Christians entered a town the power structure got disturbed and immediately sought to convict them for being "disturbers of the peace" and "outside agitators." But they went on with the conviction that they were "a colony of heaven," and had to obey God rather than man. They were small in number but big in commitment. They were too God-intoxicated to be "astronomically intimidated." They brought an end to such ancient evils as infanticide and gladiatorial contest.

Things are different now. The contemporary church is often a weak, ineffectual voice with an uncertain sound. It is so often the arch-supporter of the status quo. Far from being disturbed by the presence of the church, the power structure of the average community is consoled by the church's silent and often vocal sanction of things as they are.

But the judgment of God is upon the church as never before. If the church of today does not recapture the sacrificial spirit of the early church, it will lose its authentic ring, forfeit the loyalty of millions, and be dismissed as an irrelevant social club with no meaning for the twentieth century. I am meeting young people every day whose disappointment with the church has risen to outright disgust.

Maybe again, I have been too optimistic. Is organized religion too inextricably bound to the status quo to save our nation and the world? Maybe I must turn my faith to the inner spiritual church, the church within the church, as the true *ecclesia* and the hope of the world. But again I am thankful to God that some noble souls from the ranks of organized religion have broken loose from the paralyzing chains of conformity and joined us as active partners in the struggle for freedom. They have left their secure congregations and walked the streets of Albany, Georgia, with us. They have gone through the highways of the South on tortuous rides for freedom. Yes, they have gone to jail with us. Some have been kicked out of their churches, and lost support of their bishops and fellow ministers. But they have gone with the faith that right defeated is stronger than evil triumphant. These men have been the leaven in the lump of the race. Their witness has been the spiritual salt that has preserved the true meaning of the gospel in these troubled times. They have carved a tunnel of hope through the dark mountain of disappointment.

I hope the church as a whole will meet the challenge of this decisive hour. But even if the church does not come to the aid of justice, I have no despair about the future. I have no fear about the outcome of our struggle in Birmingham, even if our motives are presently misunderstood. We will reach the goal of freedom in Birmingham and all over the nation, because the goal of America is freedom. Abused and scorned though we may be, our destiny is tied up with the destiny of America. Before the Pilgrims landed at Plymouth we were here. Before the pen of Jefferson etched across the pages of history the majestic words of the Declaration of Independence, we were here. For more than two centuries our foreparents labored in this country without wages; they made cotton king; and they built the homes of their masters in the midst of brutal injustice and shameful humiliation—and yet out of a bottomless vitality they continued to thrive and develop. If the inexpressible cruelties of slavery could not stop us, the opposition we now face will surely fail. We will win our freedom because the sacred heritage of our nation and the eternal will of God are embodied in our echoing demands.

I must close now. But before closing I am impelled to mention one other point in your statement that troubled me profoundly. You warmly commended the Birmingham police force for keeping "order" and "preventing violence." I don't believe you would have so warmly commended the police force if you had seen its angry violent dogs literally biting six unarmed, nonviolent Negroes. I don't believe you would so quickly commend the policemen if you would observe their ugly and inhuman treatment of Negroes here in the city jail; if you would watch them push and curse old Negro women and young Negro girls; if you would see them slap and kick old Negro men and young boys; if you will observe them, as they did on two occasions, refuse to give us food because we wanted to sing our grace together. I'm sorry that I can't join you in your praise for the police department.

It is true that they have been rather disciplined in their public handling of the demonstrators. In this sense they have been rather publicly "nonviolent." But for what purpose? To preserve the evil system of segregation. Over the last few years I have consistently preached that nonviolence demands that the means we use must be as pure as the ends we seek. So I have tried to make it clear that it is wrong to use immoral means to attain moral ends. But now I must affirm that it is just as wrong, or even more so, to use moral means to preserve immoral ends. Maybe Mr. Connor and his policemen have been rather publicly nonviolent, as Chief Pritchett was in Albany, Georgia, but they have used the moral means of nonviolence to maintain the immoral end of flagrant racial injustice. T. S. Eliot has said that there is no greater treason than to do the right deed for the wrong reason.

I wish you had commended the Negro sit-inners and demonstrators of Birmingham for their sublime courage, their willingness to suffer and their amazing discipline in the midst of the most inhuman provocation. One day the South will recognize its real heroes.

They will be the James Merediths, courageously and with a majestic sense of purpose facing jeering and hostile mobs and the agonizing loneliness that characterizes the life of the pioneer. They will be old, oppressed, battered Negro women, symbolized in a seventy-two-year-old woman of Montgomery, Alabama, who rose up with a sense of dignity and with her people decided not to ride the segregated buses, and responded to one who inquired about her tiredness with ungrammatical profundity: "My feet is tired, but my soul is rested." They will be the young high school and college students, young ministers of the gospel and a host of their elders courageously and nonviolently sitting-in at lunch counters and willingly going to jail for conscience's sake. One day the South will know that when these disinherited children of God sat down at lunch counters they were in reality standing up for the best in the American dream and the most sacred values in our Judeo-Christian heritage, and thusly, carrying our whole nation back to those great walls of democracy which were dug deep by the Founding Fathers in the formulation of the Constitution and the Declaration of Independence.

Never before have I written a letter this long (or should I say a book?). I'm afraid that it is much too long to take your precious time. I can assure you that it would have been much shorter if I had been writing from a comfortable desk, but what else is there to do when you are alone for days in the dull monotony of a narrow jail cell other than write long letters, think strange thoughts, and pray long prayers?

If I have said anything in this letter that is an overstatement of the truth and is indicative of an unreasonable impatience, I beg you to forgive me. If I have said anything in this letter that is an understatement of the truth and is indicative of my having a patience that makes me patient with anything less than brotherhood, I beg God to forgive me.

I hope this letter finds you strong in the faith. I also hope that circumstances will soon make it possible for me to meet each of you, not as an integrationist or a civil rights leader, but as a fellow clergyman and a Christian brother. Let us all hope that the dark clouds of racial prejudice will soon pass away and the deep fog of misunderstanding will be lifted from our fear-drenched communities and in some not too distant tomorrow the radiant stars of love and brotherhood will shine over our great nation with all of their scintillating beauty.

Yours for the cause of Peace and Brotherhood, Martin Luther King, Jr.

Study Questions

1. What is civil disobedience?
2. How does civil disobedience differ from mere lawbreaking?
3. Is every unjust law an appropriate target for civil disobedience?
4. How do the arguments of Dr. King differ from those of Socrates in Plato's *Crito*?

Challenges to Morality

CHAPTER 5

How Not to Answer Moral Questions

Tom Regan

Faced with an ethical issue, some people challenge the supposition that the problem can be resolved through reasoned discussion. They claim that moral judgments are merely expressions of personal preference, matters of individual opinion, reflections of majority will, or commands of a supposed higher authority, such as God. In any of these cases, reasoning about ethics is useless. All we can do is express our feelings, reiterate our beliefs, consult polls, or perhaps seek divine guidance. In the following selection Tom Regan, Professor Emeritus of Philosophy at North Carolina State University, argues that none of these ways of dealing with moral questions is appropriate.

Moral Judgements and Personal Preferences

Some people like New Age music; others do not. Some people think bourbon is just great; others detest its taste. Some people will go to a lot of trouble to spend an afternoon in the hot sun at the beach; others can think of nothing worse. In all these cases disagreement in preference exists. Someone likes something; someone else does not. Are moral disagreements, disagreements over whether something is morally right or wrong, good or bad, just or unjust, the same as disagreements in preference?

It does not appear so. For one thing, when a person (say, Jack) says he likes something, he is not denying what another person (Jill) says if she says she does not like it. Suppose Jack says, "I (Jack) like the

From Tom Regan, *Matters of Life and Death: New Introductory Essays in Moral Philosophy,* 3rd edition. Copyright © 1993 by McGraw-Hill. Reprinted by permission of The McGraw-Hill Companies.

Grateful Dead," and Jill says, "I (Jill) do not like the Grateful Dead."
Then clearly Jill does not deny what Jack says. To deny what Jack says,
Jill would have to say, "You (Jack) do not like the Grateful Dead,"
which is not what she says. So, in general, when two people express
different personal preferences, the one does not deny what the other
affirms. It is perfectly possible for two opposing expressions of personal preference to be true at the same time.

When two people express conflicting judgements about the morality of something, however, the disagreement is importantly different.
Suppose Jack says, "All wars are unjust," while Jill says, "Some wars
are just." Then Jill *is* denying what Jack affirms; she is *denying* that
wars are unjust, so that if what she said were true, what Jack said
would have to be false. Some philosophers have denied this. They
have maintained that moral judgements should be understood as
expressions of personal preferences. Though this view deserves to be
mentioned with respect, it is doubtful that it is correct. When people
say that something is morally right or wrong, it is always appropriate to ask them to give reasons to justify their judgement, reasons for
accepting their judgement as *correct*. In the case of personal preferences, however, such requests are inappropriate. If Jack says he likes
to go to the beach, it hardly seems apt to press him to give reasons to
justify what he says. If he says abortion is always wrong, however, it is
highly relevant to test Jack's judgement by examining the reasons he
gives for thinking what he does. In this case we want to know whether
Jack's judgement is correct, not merely what Jack likes or dislikes.

This difference between expressions of differing personal preference and conflicting moral judgements points to one way not to
answer moral questions. Given that moral judgements are not just
expressions of personal preference, it follows that moral right and
wrong cannot be determined just by finding out about someone's
personal preferences. This is true even in the case of our own preferences. Our personal preferences are certainly important, but we do
not answer moral questions just by saying that we like some things
and dislike others.

Why Thinking It So Does Not Make It So

The same is true about what someone thinks. Quite aside from her
personal preferences, Bonnie, if she is sincere, does think that we who
are well off ought to make sacrifices to help feed the many starving
people in the world if she says that we ought to do so. Nevertheless,

if her judgement is a *moral* judgement, what she means cannot be "I (Bonnie) think we who are well off ought to make sacrifices to help feed the many starving people in the world." If it were, then she would not be affirming something that Clyde denies, when *he* says, "We who are well off ought not to make such sacrifices." Each would merely be stating that each thinks something, and it is certainly possible for it *both* to be true that Bonnie thinks that we ought to make sacrifices for those who are starving *and*, at the same time, that Clyde thinks we ought not. So if Clyde is denying what Bonnie affirms, he cannot merely be stating that *he* thinks that we ought not to make sacrifices for these people. Clearly, Clyde believes that *what* he says is *correct*; and whether it *is* correct is independent of his thinking that it is. Thus, the fact that Clyde happens to think what he does is just as irrelevant to establishing whether we ought or ought not to make sacrifices to help those who are starving as Jack's feelings about war. And the same is true concerning what *we* happen to think. Our thinking something right or wrong does not make it so.

The Irrelevance of Statistics

Someone might think that though what one person thinks or feels about moral issues does not settle matters, what all or most people think or feel does. A single individual is only one voice; what most or all people think or feel is a great deal more. There is strength in numbers. Thus, the correct method for answering questions about right and wrong is to find out what most or all people think or feel. Opinion polls should be conducted, statistics compiled. That will reveal the truth.

This approach to moral questions is deficient. All that opinion polls can reveal is what all or most people think or feel about various controversial questions—for example, "Should convicted murderers be executed?" Twenty years ago most Americans believed that capital punishment should be abolished; today most Americans believe it should be retained. This is an important, interesting change in public opinion. . . . Clearly, however, merely establishing that most Americans today favor the death penalty or, to take another example, that most favor the legalization of euthanasia, is not to establish that the majority opinion is *correct*. In times past, virtually everyone believed that the world is flat, yet this consensus did not settle the correct description of its shape. There is no compelling reason to assume that the answers to moral questions differ in this respect.

Questions of moral right and wrong, in short, cannot be answered just by taking a vote and seeing what the majority favors.

The Appeal to a Moral Authority

Suppose it is conceded that we cannot answer moral questions just by finding out what Jack or Jill or Bonnie and Clyde happen to think or feel, or by finding out what all or most people happen to think or feel. After all, single individuals like Jack or Jill, or most or all people like them, might think or feel one way when they should think or feel differently. We ordinary mortals, after all, are fallible. But now suppose there is someone who *never is mistaken* when it comes to moral questions: If this person judges that something is morally right, it *is* morally right; if it is judged wrong, it is wrong. No mistakes are made. Let us call such a person a moral authority. Might appealing to the judgements of a moral authority be the correct method for answering moral questions?

Most people who think there is a moral authority think this authority is not an ordinary mortal but a god. This causes problems immediately. Whether there is a god (or gods) is a very controversial question, and to rest questions of right and wrong on what an alleged god says (or the gods say) is already to base morality on an intellectually unsettled foundation. The difficulties go deeper than this, however, since even if there is a god who is a moral authority, very serious questions arise concerning whether people always understand what this authority says. The difficulties that exist when Jews and Christians consult the Bible are illustrative. Problems of interpretation abound. Some who think that we were created to be vegetarians think they find evidence in the Bible that God thinks so too; others think they find evidence that God does not. Some who think that God allows us to exploit nature without regard to its values cite what they think are supporting chapters and verses; others cite other chapters and verses they think show that God does not allow this, or they cite the same passages and argue that they should be interpreted differently. The gravity of these and kindred problems of interpretation should not be underestimated. Even if there is a moral authority, and even if the God Jews and Christians worship should happen to be this authority, that would not make it easy to find out what is right and wrong. The problem of finding out what God thinks on these matters would still remain and would be especially acute in areas where the Bible offers very little, if any, direct guidance—on the ethics of the use of life-sustaining technology for the irreversibly comatose, for example.

Problems of interpretation aside, it is clear that the correct method for answering moral questions cannot consist merely in discovering what some alleged moral authority says. Even if there is a moral authority, those who are not moral authorities can have no good reason for thinking that there is one unless the judgements of this supposed authority can be checked for their truth or reasonableness, and it is not possible to do this unless what is true or reasonable regarding right and wrong can be known independently of what this supposed authority says. An example from another quarter might make this point clearer. A plumber proves his "authority as a plumber" not merely by what he says but by the quality of his work, which can be verified independently of what he says in any particular case. *After* we have come to know, on independent grounds, that a particular plumber's judgement is reliable, *then* we have reason to rely on his judgement in the future. The same is true of the authority of one's judgement in, say, science, economics, the law, and morality: One's "credentials" can be established in the case of moral judgements only if there are independent ways of testing the truth or reasonableness of moral judgements. Thus, because there must be some independent way of knowing what judgements are true or reasonable in order to test for the authority of another's moral judgements, to appeal to this or that "moral authority" cannot itself be the method that we seek for answering moral questions.

Study Questions

1. Are moral judgments merely personal preferences?
2. Can moral disagreements ever be resolved by statistics?
3. Can moral questions be decided by appealing to a moral authority?
4. If you firmly believe an action is moral, might you be wrong?

CHAPTER 6

God and Morality

Steven M. Cahn

The widespread view that morality depends on religious commitment
deserves additional consideration. The next selection by Steven M. Cahn,
editor of this book and Professor of Philosophy at the City University of
New York Graduate Center, focuses on some problems with the claim that
a theological conception of right and wrong suffices as a basis for moral
reasoning.

According to many religions, although not all, the world was created by God, an all-powerful, all-knowing, all-good being. Although
God's existence has been doubted, let us for the moment assume its
truth. What implications of this supposition would be relevant to
our lives?

Some people would feel more secure in the knowledge that the
world had been planned by an all-good being. Others would feel
insecure, realizing the extent to which their existence depended on a
decision of this being. In any case, most people, out of either fear or
respect, would wish to act in accord with God's will.

Belief in God by itself, however, provides no hint whatsoever which
actions God wishes us to perform or what we ought to do to please
or obey God. We may affirm that God is all-good, yet have no way of
knowing the highest moral standards. All we may presume is that,
whatever these standards, God always acts in accordance with them.
We might expect God to have implanted the correct moral standards
in our minds, but this supposition is doubtful in view of the conflicts
among people's intuitions. Furthermore, even if consensus prevailed,

it might be only a means by which God tests us to see whether we have the courage to dissent from popular opinion.

Some would argue that if God exists, then murder is immoral, because it destroys what God with infinite wisdom created. This argument, however, fails on several grounds. First, God also created germs, viruses, and disease-carrying rats. Because God created these things, ought they not be eliminated? Second, if God arranged for us to live, God also arranged for us to die. By killing, are we assisting the work of God? Third, God provided us with the mental and physical potential to commit murder. Does God wish us to fulfill this potential?

Thus God's existence alone does not imply any particular moral precepts. We may hope our actions are in accord with God's standards, but no test is available to check whether what we do is best in God's eyes. Some seemingly good people suffer great ills, whereas some seemingly evil people achieve happiness. Perhaps in a future life these outcomes will be reversed, but we have no way of ascertaining who, if anyone, is ultimately punished and who ultimately rewarded.

Over the course of history, those who believed in God's existence typically were eager to learn God's will and tended to rely on those individuals who claimed to possess such insight. Diviners, seers, and priests were given positions of great influence. Competition among them was severe, however, for no one could be sure which oracle to believe.

In any case prophets died, and their supposedly revelatory powers disappeared with them. For practical purposes what was needed was a permanent record of God's will. This requirement was met by the writing of holy books in which God's will was revealed to all.

But even though many such books were supposed to embody the will of God, they conflicted with one another. Which was to be accepted? Belief in the existence of God by itself yields no answer.

Let us suppose, however, that an individual becomes persuaded that a reliable guide to God's will is contained in the Ten Commandments. This person, therefore, believes it wrong to commit adultery, steal, or murder.

But why is it wrong? Is it wrong because God says it is wrong, or does God say it is wrong because it *is* wrong?

This crucial issue was raised more than two thousand years ago in Plato's remarkable dialogue, the *Euthyphro*. Plato's teacher,

Socrates, who in most of Plato's works is given the leading role, asks the overconfident Euthyphro whether actions are right because God says they are right, or whether God says actions are right because they are right.

In other words, Socrates was inquiring whether actions are right because of God's fiat or whether God is subject to moral standards. If actions are right because of God's command, then anything God commands would be right. Had God commanded adultery, stealing, and murder, then adultery, stealing, and murder would be right— surely an unsettling and to many an unacceptable conclusion.

Granted, some may be willing to adopt this discomforting view, but then they face another difficulty. If the good is whatever God commands, to say that God's commands are good amounts to saying that God's commands are God's commands, a mere tautology or repetition of words. In that case, the possibility of meaningfully praising the goodness of God would be lost.

The lesson here is that might does not make right, even if the might is the infinite might of God. To act morally is not to act out of fear of punishment; it is not to act as one is commanded to act. Rather, it is to act as one ought to act, and how one ought to act is not dependent on anyone's power, even if the power be divine.

Thus actions are not right because God commands them; on the contrary, God commands them because they are right. What is right is independent of what God commands, for what God commands must conform to an independent standard in order to be right.

We could act intentionally in accord with this independent standard without believing in the existence of God; therefore morality does not rest on that belief. Consequently, those who do not believe in God can be highly moral (as well as immoral) people, and those who do believe in the existence of God can be highly immoral (as well as moral) people. This conclusion should come as no surprise to anyone who has contrasted the benevolent life of the inspiring teacher, the Buddha, an atheist, with the malevolent life of the monk Torquemada, who devised and enforced the boundless cruelties of the Spanish Inquisition.

In short, believing in the existence of God does not by itself imply any specific moral principles, and knowing God's will does not provide any justification for morality. Thus regardless of our religious commitments, the moral dimension of our lives remains to be explored.

Study Questions

1. If God exists, is murder immoral?
2. Is murder wrong because God prohibits it, or does God prohibit murder because it is wrong?
3. Can those who do not believe in God be highly moral people?
4. Can people who practice different religions agree about how to resolve a moral disagreement?

CHAPTER 7

The Challenge of Cultural Relativism

James Rachels

The search for universal answers to moral questions is often said to be futile because morality differs from one culture to another. This view, known as cultural relativism, maintains that while we can seek understanding of a particular culture's moral system, we have no basis for judging it.

In the next section James Rachels (1941–2003), who was Professor of Philosophy at the University of Alabama at Birmingham, examines cultural relativism and finds that it has serious shortcomings.

How Different Cultures Have Different Moral Codes

Darius, a king of ancient Persia, was intrigued by the variety of cultures he encountered in his travels. He had found, for example, that the Callatians (a tribe of Indians) customarily ate the bodies of their dead fathers. The Greeks, of course, did not do that—the Greeks practiced cremation and regarded the funeral pyre as the natural and fitting way to dispose of the dead. Darius thought that a sophisticated understanding of the world must include an appreciation of such differences between cultures. One day, to teach this lesson, he summoned some Greeks who happened to be present at his court and asked them what they would take to eat the bodies of their dead fathers. They were shocked, as Darius knew they would be, and replied that no amount of money could persuade them to do such a thing. Then Darius called in some Callatians, and while the Greeks listened asked them what they would take to burn their dead fathers' bodies. The Callatians were horrified and told Darius not even to mention such a dreadful thing.

This story, recounted by Herodotus in his *History*, illustrates a recurring theme in the literature of social science: different cultures have different moral codes. What is thought right within one group may be utterly abhorrent to the members of another group, and vice versa. Should we eat the bodies of the dead or burn them? If you were a Greek, one answer would seem obviously correct; but if you were a Callatian, the opposite would seem equally certain.

It is easy to give additional examples of the same kind. Consider the Eskimos. They are a remote and inaccessible people. Numbering only about 25,000, they live in small, isolated settlements scattered mostly along the northern fringes of North America and Greenland. Until the beginning of this century, the outside world knew little about them. Then explorers began to bring back strange tales.

Eskimo customs turned out to be very different from our own. The men often had more than one wife, and they would share their wives with guests, lending them for the night as a sign of hospitality. Moreover, within a community, a dominant male might demand—and get—regular sexual access to other men's wives. The women, however, were free to break these arrangements simply by leaving their husbands and taking up with new partners—free, that is, so long as their former husbands chose not to make trouble. All in all, the Eskimo practice was a volatile scheme that bore little resemblance to what we call marriage.

But it was not only their marriage and sexual practices that were different. The Eskimos also seemed to have less regard for human life. Infanticide, for example, was common. Knud Rasmussen, one of the most famous early explorers, reported that he met one woman who had borne twenty children but had killed ten of them at birth. Female babies, he found, were especially liable to be destroyed, and this was permitted simply at the parents' discretion, with no social stigma attached to it. Old people also, when they became too feeble to contribute to the family, were left out in the snow to die. So there seemed to be, in this society, remarkably little respect for life.

To the general public, these were disturbing revelations. Our own way of living seems so natural and right that for many of us it is hard to conceive of others living so differently. And when we do hear of such things, we tend immediately to categorize those other peoples as "backward" or "primitive." But to anthropologists and sociologists, there was nothing particularly surprising about the Eskimos. Since the time of Herodotus, enlightened observers have been accustomed to the idea that conceptions of right and wrong differ from culture to culture. If we assume that *our* ideas of right and wrong will be shared by all peoples at all times, we are merely naive.

Cultural Relativism

To many thinkers, this observation—"Different cultures have different moral codes"—has seemed to be the key to understanding morality. The idea of universal truth in ethics, they say, is a myth. The customs of different societies are all that exist. These customs cannot be said to be "correct" or "incorrect," for that implies we have an independent standard of right and wrong by which they may be judged. But there is no such independent standard; every standard is culture-bound. The great pioneering sociologist William Graham Sumner, writing in 1906, put the point like this:

> The "right" way is the way which the ancestors used and which has been handed down. The tradition is its own warrant. It is not held subject to verification by experience. The notion of right is in the folkways. It is not outside of them, of independent origin, and brought to test them. In the folkways, whatever is, is right. This is because they are traditional, and therefore contain in themselves the authority of the ancestral ghosts. When we come to the folkways we are at the end of our analysis.

This line of thought has probably persuaded more people to be skeptical about ethics than any other single thing. *Cultural Relativism,* as it has been called, challenges our ordinary belief in the objectivity and universality of moral truth. It says, in effect, that there is no such thing as universal truth in ethics; there are only the various cultural codes, and nothing more. Moreover, our own code has no special status; it is merely one among many.

As we shall see, this basic idea is really a compound of several different thoughts. It is important to separate the various elements of the theory because, on analysis, some parts of the theory turn out to be correct, whereas others seem to be mistaken. As a beginning, we may distinguish the following claims, all of which have been made by cultural relativists:

1. Different societies have different moral codes.
2. There is no objective standard that can be used to judge one societal code better than another.

3. The moral code of our own society has no special status; it is merely one among many.
4. There is no "universal truth" in ethics—that is, there are no moral truths that hold for all peoples at all times.
5. The moral code of a society determines what is right within that society; that is, if the moral code of a society says that a certain action is right, then that action *is* right, at least within that society.
6. It is mere arrogance for us to try to judge the conduct of other peoples. We should adopt an attitude of tolerance toward the practices of other cultures.

Although it may seem that these six propositions go naturally together, they are independent of one another, in the sense that some of them might be true even if others are false. In what follows, we will try to identify what is correct in Cultural Relativism, but we will also be concerned to expose what is mistaken about it.

The Cultural Differences Argument

Cultural Relativism is a theory about the nature of morality. At first blush it seems quite plausible. However, like all such theories, it may be evaluated by subjecting it to rational analysis; and when we analyze Cultural Relativism we find that it is not so plausible as it first appears to be.

The first thing we need to notice is that at the heart of Cultural Relativism there is a certain *form of argument*. The strategy used by cultural relativists is to argue from facts about the differences between cultural outlooks to a conclusion about the status of morality. Thus we are invited to accept this reasoning:

1. The Greeks believed it was wrong to eat the dead, whereas the Callatians believed it was right to eat the dead.
2. Therefore, eating the dead is neither objectively right nor objectively wrong. It is merely a matter of opinion, which varies from culture to culture.

Or, alternatively:

1. The Eskimos see nothing wrong with infanticide, whereas Americans believe infanticide is immoral.
2. Therefore, infanticide is neither objectively right nor objectively wrong. It is merely a matter of opinion, which varies from culture to culture.

Clearly, these arguments are variations of one fundamental idea. They are both special cases of a more general argument, which says,

1. Different cultures have different moral codes.
2. Therefore, there is no objective "truth" in morality. Right and wrong are only matters of opinion, and opinions vary from culture to culture.

We may call this the *Cultural Differences Argument.* To many people, it is very persuasive. But from a logical point of view, is it a *sound* argument?

It is not sound. The trouble is that the conclusion does not really follow from the premise—that is, even if the premise is true, the conclusion still might be false. The premise concerns what people *believe*: in some societies, people believe one thing; in other societies, people believe differently. The conclusion, however, concerns *what really is the case.* The trouble is that this sort of conclusion does not follow logically from this sort of premise.

Consider again the example of the Greeks and Callatians. The Greeks believed it was wrong to eat the dead; the Callatians believed it was right. Does it follow, *from the mere fact that they disagreed,* that there is no objective truth in the matter? No, it does not follow; for it *could* be that the practice was objectively right (or wrong) and that one or the other of them was simply mistaken.

To make the point clearer, consider a very different matter. In some societies, people believe the earth is flat. In other societies, such as our own, people believe the earth is (roughly) spherical. Does it follow, *from the mere fact that they disagree,* that there is no "objective truth" in geography? Of course not; we would never draw such a conclusion because we realize that, in their beliefs about the world, the members of some societies might simply be wrong. There is no reason to think that if the world is round everyone must know it. Similarly, there is no reason to think that if there is a moral truth everyone must know it. The fundamental mistake in the Cultural Differences Argument is that it attempts to derive a substantive conclusion about a subject (morality) from the mere fact that people disagree about it.

It is important to understand the nature of the point that is being made here. We are *not* saying (not yet, anyway) that the conclusion of the argument is false. Insofar as anything being said here is concerned, it is still an open question whether the conclusion is true. We *are* making a purely logical point and saying that the conclusion does not *follow from* the premise. This is important, because in order to determine whether the conclusion is true, we need arguments in its support. Cultural Relativism proposes this argument, but unfortunately the argument turns out to be fallacious. So it proves nothing.

The Consequences of Taking Cultural Relativism Seriously

Even if the Cultural Differences Argument is invalid, Cultural Relativism might still be true. What would it be like if it were true?

In the passage quoted above, William Graham Sumner summarizes the essence of Cultural Relativism. He says that there is no measure of right and wrong other than the standards of one's society: "The notion of right is in the folkways. It is not outside of them, of independent origin, and brought to test them. In the folkways, whatever is, is right."

Suppose we took this seriously. What would be some of the consequences?

1. *We could no longer say that the customs of other societies are morally inferior to our own.* This, or course, is one of the main points stressed by Cultural Relativism. We would have to stop condemning other societies merely because they are "different." So long as we concentrate on certain examples, such as the funerary practices of the Greeks and Callatians, this may seem to be a sophisticated, enlightened attitude.

However, we would also be stopped from criticizing other, less benign practices. Suppose a society waged war on its neighbors for the purpose of taking slaves. Or suppose a society was violently anti-Semitic and its leaders set out to destroy the Jews. Cultural Relativism would preclude us from saying that either of these practices was wrong. We would not even be able to say that a society tolerant of Jews is *better* than the anti-Semitic society, for that would imply some sort of transcultural standard of comparison. The failure to condemn *these* practices does not seem "enlightened": on the contrary, slavery and anti-Semitism seem wrong *wherever* they occur. Nevertheless, if we took Cultural Relativism seriously, we would have to admit that these social practices also are immune from criticism.

2. *We could decide whether actions are right or wrong just by consulting the standards of our society.* Cultural Relativism suggests a simple test for determining what is right and what is wrong: all one has to do is ask whether the action is in accordance with the code of one's

society. Suppose a resident of South Africa is wondering whether his country's policy of *apartheid*—rigid racial segregation—is morally correct. All he has to do is ask whether this policy conforms to his society's moral code. If it does, there is nothing to worry about, at least from a moral point of view.

This implication of Cultural Relativism is disturbing because few of us think that our society's code is perfect—we can think of ways it might be improved. Yet Cultural Relativism would not only forbid us from criticizing the codes of *other* societies; it would stop us from criticizing our *own*. After all, if right and wrong are relative to culture, this must be true for our own culture just as much as for others.

3. *The idea of moral progress is called into doubt.* Usually, we think that at least some changes in our society have been for the better. (Some, of course, may have been changes for the worse.) Consider this example: Throughout most of Western history the place of women in society was very narrowly circumscribed. They could not own property; they could not vote or hold political office; with a few exceptions, they were not permitted to have paying jobs; and generally they were under the almost absolute control of their husbands. Recently much of this has changed, and most people think of it as progress.

If Cultural Relativism is correct, can we legitimately think of this as progress? Progress means replacing a way of doing things with a *better* way. But by what standard do we judge the new ways as better? If the old ways were in accordance with the social standards of their time, then Cultural Relativism would say it is a mistake to judge them by the standards of a different time. Eighteenth-century society was, in effect, a different society from the one we have now. To say that we have made progress implies a judgment that present-day society is better, and that is just the sort of transcultural judgment that, according to Cultural Relativism, is impermissible.

Our idea of social *reform* will also have to be reconsidered. A reformer, such as Martin Luther King, Jr., seeks to change his society for the better. Within the constraints imposed by Cultural Relativism, there is one way this might be done. If a society is not living up to its own ideals, the reformer may be regarded as acting for the best: the ideals of the society are the standard by which we judge his or her proposals as worthwhile. But the "reformer" may not challenge the ideals themselves, for those ideals are by definition correct. According to Cultural Relativism, then, the idea of social reform makes sense only in this very limited way.

These three consequences of Cultural Relativism have led many thinkers to reject it as implausible on its face. It does make sense, they say, to condemn some practices, such as slavery and anti-Semitism, wherever they occur. It makes sense to think that our own society has made some moral progress, while admitting that it is still imperfect and in need of reform. Because Cultural Relativism says that these judgments make no sense, the argument goes, it cannot be right.

Why There Is Less Disagreement Than It Seems

The original impetus for Cultural Relativism comes from the observation that cultures differ dramatically in their views of right and wrong. But just how much do they differ? It is true that there are differences. However, it is easy to overestimate the extent of those differences. Often, when we examine what *seems* to be a dramatic difference, we find that the cultures do not differ nearly as much as it appears.

Consider a culture in which people believe it is wrong to eat cows. This may even be a poor culture, in which there is not enough food; still, the cows are not to be touched. Such a society would *appear* to have values very different from our own. But does it? We have not yet asked why these people will not eat cows. Suppose it is because they believe that after death the souls of humans inhabit the bodies of animals, especially cows, so that a cow may be someone's grandmother. Now do we want to say that their values are different from ours? No; the difference lies elsewhere. The difference is in our belief systems, not in our values. We agree that we shouldn't eat Grandma; we simply disagree about whether the cow *is* (or could be) Grandma.

The general point is this: Many factors work together to produce the customs of a society. The society's values are only one of them. Other matters, such as the religious and factual beliefs held by its members and the physical circumstances in which they must live, are also important. We cannot conclude, then, merely because customs differ, that there is a disagreement about *values*. The difference in customs may be attributable to some other aspect of social life. Thus there may be less disagreement about values than there appears to be.

Consider the Eskimos again. They often kill perfectly normal infants, especially girls. We do not approve of this at all; a parent who did this in our society would be locked up. Thus there appears to be a great difference in the values of our two cultures. But suppose we ask *why* the Eskimos do this. The explanation is not that they have less affection for their children or less respect for human life. An Eskimo family will always protect its babies if conditions permit. But they live in a harsh environment, where food is often in short supply. A fundamental postulate to Eskimo thought is, "Life is hard, and the margin of safety small." A family may want to nourish its babies but be unable to do so.

As in many "primitive" societies, Eskimo mothers will nurse their infants over a much longer period of time than mothers in our culture. The child will take nourishment from its mother's breast for four years, perhaps even longer. So even in the best of times there are limits to the number of infants that one mother can sustain. Moreover, the Eskimos are a nomadic people—unable to farm, they must move about in search of food. Infants must be carried, and a mother can carry only one baby in her parka as she travels and goes about her outdoor work. Other family members can help, but this is not always possible.

Infant girls are more readily disposed of because, first, in this society the males are the primary food providers—they are the hunters, according to the traditional division of labor—and it is obviously important to maintain a sufficient number of food gatherers. But there is an important second reason as well. Because the hunters suffer a high casualty rate, the adult men who die prematurely far outnumber the women who die early. Thus if male and female infants survived in equal numbers, the female adult population would greatly outnumber the male adult population. Examining the available statistics, one writer concluded that "were it not for female infanticide . . . there would be approximately one-and-a-half times as many females in the average Eskimo local group as there are food-producing males."

So among the Eskimos, infanticide does not signal a fundamentally different attitude toward children. Instead, it is a recognition that drastic measures are sometimes needed to ensure the family's survival. Even then, however, killing the baby is not the first option considered. Adoption is common; childless couples are especially happy to take a more fertile couple's "surplus." Killing is only the last resort. I emphasize this in order to show that the raw data of the anthropologists can be misleading; it can make the differences in values between cultures appear greater than they are. The Eskimos' values are not all that different from our values. It is only that life forces upon them choices that we do not have to make.

How All Cultures Have Some Values in Common

It should not be surprising that, despite appearance, the Eskimos are protective of their children. How could it be otherwise? How could a group survive that did *not* value its young? This suggests a certain argument, one which shows that all cultural groups must be protective of their infants:

1. Human infants are helpless and cannot survive if they are not given extensive care for a period of years.
2. Therefore, if a group did not care for its young, the young would not survive, and the older members of the group would not be replaced. After a while the group would die out.
3. Therefore, any cultural group that continues to exist must care for its young. Infants that are *not* cared for must be the exception rather than the rule.

Similar reasoning shows that other values must be more or less universal. Imagine what it would be like for a society to place no value at all on truth telling. When one person spoke to another, there would be no presumption at all that he was telling the truth—for he could just as easily be speaking falsely. Within that society, there would be no reason to pay attention to what anyone says. (I ask you what time it is, and you say, "Four o'clock." But there is no presumption that you are speaking truly; you could just as easily have said the first thing that came into your head. So I have no reason to pay attention to your answer—in fact, there was no point in my asking you in the first place!) Communication would then be extremely difficult, if not impossible. And because complex societies cannot exist without regular communication among their members, society would become impossible. It follows that in any complex society there must be presumption in favor of truthfulness. There may of course be exceptions to this rule: there may be situations in which it is thought to be permissible to lie. Nevertheless, these will be exceptions to a rule that is in force in the society.

Let me give one further example of the same type. Could a society exist in which there was no prohibition on murder? What would this be like? Suppose people were free to kill other people at will, and no one thought there was anything wrong with it. In such a "society," no one could feel secure. Everyone would have to be constantly on guard. People who wanted to survive would have to avoid other people as much as possible. This would inevitably result in individuals trying to become as self-sufficient as possible—after all, associating with others would be dangerous. Society on any large scale would collapse. Of course, people might band together in smaller groups with others that they *could* trust not to harm them. But notice what this means: they would be forming smaller societies that *did* acknowledge a rule against murder. The prohibition of murder, then, is a necessary feature of all societies.

There is a general theoretical point here, namely, that *there are some moral rules that all societies will have in common, because those rules are necessary for society to exist.* The rules against lying and murder are two examples. And in fact, we do find these rules in force in all viable cultures. Cultures may differ in what they regard as legitimate exceptions to the rules, but this disagreement exists against a background of agreement on the larger issues. Therefore, it is a mistake to overestimate the amount of difference between cultures. Not *every* moral rule can vary from society to society.

What Can Be Learned From Cultural Relativism

At the outset, I said that we were going to identify both what is right and wrong in Cultural Relativism. Thus far I have mentioned only its mistakes: I have said that it rests on an invalid argument, that it has consequences that make it implausible on its face, and that the extent of cultural disagreement is far less than it implies. This all adds up to a pretty thorough repudiation of the theory. Nevertheless, it is still a very appealing idea, and the reader may have the feeling that all this is a little unfair. The theory *must* have something going for it, or else why has it been so influential? In fact, I think there *is* something right about Cultural Relativism, and now I want to say what that is. There are two lessons we should learn from the theory, even if we ultimately reject it.

1. Cultural Relativism warns us, quite rightly, about the danger of assuming that all our preferences are based on some absolute rational standard. They are not. Many (but not all) of our practices are merely peculiar to our society, and it is easy to lose sight of that fact. In reminding us of it, the theory does a service.

Funerary practices are one example. The Callatians, according to Herodotus, were "men who eat their fathers"—a shocking idea, to us at least. But eating the flesh of the dead could be understood as a sign of respect. It could be taken as a symbolic act that says, We wish this person's spirit to dwell within us. Perhaps this was the understanding of the Callatians. On such a way of thinking, burying the dead could be seen as an act of rejection, and burning the corpse as positively scornful. If this is hard to imagine, then we may need to have our imaginations stretched. Of course we may feel a visceral repugnance at the idea of eating human flesh in any circumstances. But what of it? This repugnance may be, as the relativists say, only a matter of what is customary in our particular society.

There are many other matters that we tend to think of in terms of objective right and wrong, but that are really nothing more than social conventions. Should women cover their breasts? A publicly exposed breast is scandalous in our society, whereas in other cultures it is unremarkable. Objectively speaking, it is neither right nor wrong—there is no objective reason why either custom is better. Cultural Relativism begins with the valuable insight that many of our practices are like this—they are only cultural products. Then it goes wrong by concluding that, because *some* practices are like this, *all* must be.

2. The second lesson has to do with keeping an open mind. In the course of growing up, each of us has acquired some strong feelings: we have learned to think of some types of conduct as acceptable, and others we have learned to regard as simply unacceptable. Occasionally, we may find those feelings challenged. We may encounter someone who claims that our feelings are mistaken. For example, we may have been taught that homosexuality is immoral, and we may feel quite uncomfortable around gay people and see them as alien and "different." Now someone suggests that this may be a mere prejudice; that there is nothing evil about homosexuality; that gay people are just people, like anyone else, who happen, through no choice of their own, to be attracted to others of the same sex. But because we feel so strongly about the matter, we may find it hard to take this seriously. Even after we listen to the arguments, we may still have the unshakable feeling that homosexuals *must*, somehow, be an unsavory lot.

Cultural Relativism, by stressing that our moral views can reflect the prejudices of our society, provides an antidote for this kind of dogmatism. When he tells the story of the Greeks and Callatians, Herodotus adds,

> For if anyone, no matter who, were given the opportunity of choosing from amongst all the nations of the world the set of beliefs which

he thought best, he would inevitably, after careful consideration of their relative merits, choose that of his own country. Everyone without exception believes his own native customs, and the religion he was brought up in, to be the best.

Realizing this can result in our having more open minds. We can come to understand that our feelings are not necessarily perceptions of the truth—they may be nothing more than the result of cultural conditioning. Thus when we hear it suggested that some element of our social code is *not* really the best and we find ourselves instinctively resisting the suggestion, we might stop and remember this. Then we may be more open to discovering the truth, whatever that might be.

We can understand the appeal of Cultural Relativism, then, even though the theory has serious shortcomings. It is an attractive theory because it is based on a genuine insight—that many of the practices and attitudes we think so natural are really only cultural products. Moreover, keeping this insight firmly in view is important if we want to avoid arrogance and have open minds. These are important points, not to be taken lightly. But we can accept these points without going on to accept the whole theory.

Study Questions

1. What is the cultural differences argument?
2. According to Rachels, why is that argument unsound?
3. If the cultural differences argument is unsatisfactory, might cultural relativism still be true?
4. According to Rachels, what can be learned from cultural relativism?

CHAPTER 8

Right and Wrong

Thomas Nagel

Another challenge to morality claims that we have no good reason to care about others. In the next selection Thomas Nagel, who is Professor of Philosophy and of Law at New York University, responds that, as a matter of consistency, if you agree that another person has a reason not to harm you, then in similar circumstances you have a reason not to harm that other person.

Suppose you work in a library, checking people's books as they leave, and a friend asks you to let him smuggle out a hard-to-find reference work that he wants to own.

You might hesitate to agree for various reasons. You might be afraid that he'll be caught, and that both you and he will then get into trouble. You might want the book to stay in the library so that you can consult it yourself.

But you may also think that what he proposes is wrong—that he shouldn't do it and you shouldn't help him. If you think that, what does it mean, and what, if anything, makes it true?

To say it's wrong is not just to say it's against the rules. There can be bad rules which prohibit what isn't wrong—like a law against criticizing the government. A rule can also be bad because it requires something that *is* wrong—like a law that requires racial segregation in hotels and restaurants. The ideas of wrong and right are different from the ideas of what is and is not against the rules. Otherwise they couldn't be used in the evaluation of rules as well as of actions.

If you think it would be wrong to help your friend steal the book, then you will feel uncomfortable about doing it: in some way you won't want to do it, even if you are also reluctant to refuse help to a friend. Where does the desire not to do it come from; what is its motive, the reason behind it?

There are various ways in which something can be wrong, but in this case, if you had to explain it, you'd probably say that it would be unfair to other users of the library who may be just as interested in the book as your friend is, but who consult it in the reference room, where anyone who needs it can find it. You may also feel that to let him take it would betray your employers, who are paying you precisely to keep this sort of thing from happening.

These thoughts have to do with effects on others—not necessarily effects on their feelings, since they may never find out about it, but some kind of damage nevertheless. In general, the thought that something is wrong depends on its impact not just on the person who does it but on other people. They wouldn't like it, and they'd object if they found out.

But suppose you try to explain all this to your friend, and he says, "I know the head librarian wouldn't like it if he found out, and probably some of the other users of the library would be unhappy to find the book gone, but who cares? I want the book; why should I care about them?"

The argument that it would be wrong is supposed to give him the reason not to do it. But if someone just doesn't care about other people, what reason does he have to refrain from doing any of the things usually thought to be wrong, if he can get away with it: what reason does he have not to kill, steal, lie, or hurt others? If he can get what he wants by doing such things, why shouldn't he? And if there's no reason why he shouldn't, in what sense is it wrong? . . .

There is no substitute for a direct concern for other people as the basis of morality. But morality is supposed to apply to everyone: and can we assume that everyone has such a concern for others? Obviously not: some people are very selfish, and even those who are not selfish may care only about the people they know, and not about everyone. So where will we find a reason that everyone has not to hurt other people, even those they don't know?

Well, there's one general argument against hurting other people which can be given to anybody who understands English (or any other language), and which seems to show that he has *some* reason to care about others, even if in the end his selfish motives are so strong that he persists in treating other people badly anyway. It's an argument that I'm sure you've heard, and it goes like this: "How would you like it if someone did that to you?"

It's not easy to explain how this argument is supposed to work. Suppose you're about to steal someone else's umbrella as you leave a restaurant in a rainstorm, and a bystander says, "How would you like it if someone did that to you?" Why is it supposed to make you hesitate, or feel guilty?

Obviously the direct answer to the question is supposed to be, "I wouldn't like it at all!" But what's the next step? Suppose you were to say, "I wouldn't like it if someone did that to me. But luckily no one *is* doing it to me. I'm doing it to someone else, and I don't mind that at all!"

This answer misses the point of the question. When you are asked how you would like it if someone did that to you, you are supposed to think about all the feelings you would have if someone stole your umbrella. And that includes more than just "not liking it"—as you wouldn't "like it" if you stubbed your toe on a rock. If someone stole your umbrella you'd *resent* it. You'd have feelings about the umbrella thief, not just about the loss of the umbrella. You'd think, "Where does he get off, taking my umbrella that I bought with my hard-earned money and that I had the foresight to bring after reading the weather report? Why didn't he bring his own umbrella?" and so forth.

When our own interests are threatened by the inconsiderate behavior of others, most of us find it easy to appreciate that those others have a reason to be more considerate. When you are hurt, you probably feel that other people should care about it: you don't think it's no concern of theirs, and that they have no reason to avoid hurting you. That is the feeling that the "How would you like it?" argument is supposed to arouse.

Because if you admit that you would *resent* it if someone else did to you what you are now doing to him, you are admitting that you think he would have a reason not to do it to you. And if you admit that, you have to consider what that reason is. It couldn't be just that it's *you* that he's hurting, of all the people in the world. There's no special reason for him not to steal *your* umbrella, as opposed to anyone else's. There's nothing so special about you. Whatever the reason is, it's a reason he would have against hurting anyone else in the same way. And it's a reason anyone else would have too, in a similar situation, against hurting you or anyone else.

But if it's a reason anyone would have not to hurt anyone else in this way, then it's a reason *you* have not to hurt someone else in this way (since *anyone* means *everyone*). Therefore it's a reason not to steal the other person's umbrella now.

This is a matter of simple consistency. Once you admit that another person would have a reason not to harm you in similar circumstances, and once you admit that the reason he would have is very general and doesn't apply only to you, or to him, then to be consistent you have to admit that the same reason applies to you now. You shouldn't steal the umbrella, and you ought to feel guilty if you do.

Someone could escape from this argument if, when he was asked, "How would you like it if someone did that to you?" he answered, "I wouldn't resent it at all. I wouldn't *like* it if someone stole my umbrella in a rainstorm, but I wouldn't think there was any reason for him to consider my feelings about it." But how many people could honestly give that answer? I think most people, unless they're crazy, would think that their own interests and harms matter, not only to themselves, but in a way that gives other people a reason to care about them too. We all think that when we suffer it is not just bad *for us* but *bad, period.*

The basis of morality is a belief that good and harm to particular people (or animals) is good or bad not just from their point of view, but from a more general point of view, which every thinking person can understand. That means that each person has a reason to consider not only his own interests but the interests of others in deciding what to do. And it isn't enough if he is considerate only of some others—his family and friends, those he specially cares about. Of course he will care more about certain people, and also about himself. But he has some reason to consider the effect of what he does on the good or harm of everyone. If he's like most of us, that is what he thinks others should do with regard to him, even if they aren't friends of his.

Study Questions

1. Can a duly enacted law be morally wrong?
2. Do you have any reason to care about others?
3. Do others have any reason to care about you?
4. Does consistency require that your answers to questions 2 and 3 be the same?

CHAPTER 9

Egoism and Moral Scepticism

James Rachels

Morality involves taking into account interests apart from our own. Do we ever do so? According to psychological egoism, we don't because all human behavior is motivated only by self-interest. According to ethical egoism, even if we could act in the interest of others, we ought not do so but should be concerned only with ourselves. In the selection that follows, James Rachels, whose work we read previously, considers both psychological and ethical egoism, concluding that neither is acceptable.

1. Our ordinary thinking about morality is full of assumptions that we almost never question. We assume, for example, that we have an obligation to consider the welfare of other people when we decide what actions to perform or what rules to obey; we think that we must refrain from acting in ways harmful to others, and that we must respect their rights and interests as well as our own. We also assume that people are in fact capable of being motivated by such considerations, that is, that people are not wholly selfish and that they do sometimes act in the interests of others.

Both of these assumptions have come under attack by moral sceptics, as long ago as by Glaucon in Book II of Plato's *Republic*. Glaucon recalls the legend of Gyges, a shepherd who was said to have found a magic ring in a fissure opened by an earthquake. The ring would make its wearer invisible and thus would enable him to go anywhere and do anything undetected. Gyges used the power of the ring to gain entry to the Royal Palace, where he seduced the Queen, murdered the King, and subsequently seized the throne. Now Glaucon asks us to imagine that there are two such rings, one given to a man of virtue and one given to a rogue. The rogue, of course, will use his ring unscrupulously and do anything necessary to increase his own wealth and power. He will recognize no moral constraints on his conduct, and, since the cloak of invisibility will protect him from discovery, he can do anything he pleases without fear of reprisal. So, there will be no end to the mischief he will do. But how will the so-called virtuous man behave? Glaucon suggests that he will behave no better than the rogue: "No one, it is commonly believed, would have such iron strength of mind as to stand fast in doing right or keep his hands off other men's goods, when he could go to the market-place and fearlessly help himself to anything he wanted, enter houses and sleep with any woman he chose, set prisoners free and kill men at his pleasure, and in a word go about among men with the powers of a god. He would behave no better than the other; both would take the same course."[1] Moreover, why shouldn't he? Once he is freed from the fear of reprisal, why shouldn't a man simply do what he pleases, or what he thinks is best for himself? What reason is there for him to continue being "moral" when it is clearly not to his own advantage to do so?

These sceptical views suggested by Glaucon have come to be known as *psychological egoism* and *ethical egoism*, respectively. Psychological egoism is the view that all men are selfish in everything that they do, that is, that the only motive from which anyone ever acts is self-interest. On this view, even when men are acting in ways apparently calculated to benefit others, they are actually motivated by the belief that acting in this way is to their own advantage, and if they did not believe this, they would not be doing that action. Ethical egoism is, by contrast, a normative view about how men *ought* to act. It is the view that, regardless of how men do in fact behave, they have no obligation to do anything except what is in their own interests. According to ethical egoists, a person is always justified in doing whatever is in his own interests, regardless of the effect on others.

Clearly, if either of these views is correct, then "the moral institution of life" (to use Butler's well-turned phrase) is very different than what we normally think. The majority of mankind is grossly deceived about what is, or ought to be, the case, where morals are concerned.

2. Psychological egoism seems to fly in the face of the facts. We are tempted to say, "Of course people act unselfishly all the time. For

example, Smith gives up a trip to the country, which he would have enjoyed very much, in order to stay behind and help a friend with his studies, which is a miserable way to pass the time. This is a perfectly clear case of unselfish behavior, and if the psychological egoist thinks that such cases do not occur, then he is just mistaken." Given such obvious instances of "unselfish behavior," what reply can the egoist make? There are two general arguments by which he might try to show that all actions, including those such as the one just outlined, are in fact motivated by self-interest. Let us examine these in turn:

a. The first argument goes as follows: If we describe one person's action as selfish, and another person's action as unselfish, we are overlooking the crucial fact that in both cases, assuming that the action is done voluntarily, *the agent is merely doing what he most wants to do.* If Smith stays behind to help his friend, that only shows that he wanted to help his friend more than he wanted to go to the country. And why should he be praised for his "unselfishness" when he is only doing what he most wants to do? So, since Smith is only doing what he wants to do, he cannot be said to be acting unselfishly.

This argument is so bad that it would not deserve to be taken seriously except for the fact that so many otherwise intelligent people have been taken in by it. First, the argument rests on the premise that people never voluntarily do anything except what they want to do. But this is patently false; there are at least two classes of actions that are exceptions to this generalization. One is the set of actions which we may not want to do, but which we do anyway as a means to an end which we want to achieve, for example, going to the dentist in order to stop a toothache, or going to work every day in order to be able to draw our pay at the end of the month. These cases may be regarded as consistent with the spirit of the egoist argument, however, since the ends mentioned are wanted by the agent. But the other set of actions are those which we do, not because we want to, nor even because there is an end which we want to achieve, but because we feel ourselves *under an obligation* to do them. For example, someone may do something because he has promised to do it, and thus feels obligated, even though he does not want to do it. It is sometimes suggested that in such cases we do the action because, after all, we want to keep our promises; so, even here, we are doing what we want. However, this dodge will not work: if I have promised to do something, and if I do not want to do it, then it is simply false to say that I want to keep my promise. In such cases we feel a conflict precisely because we do *not* want to do what we feel obligated to do. It is reasonable to think that Smith's action falls roughly into this second category: he might stay behind, not because he wants to, but because he feels that this friend needs help.

But suppose we were to concede, for the sake of the argument, that all voluntary action is motivated by the agent's wants, or at least that Smith is so motivated. Even if this were granted, it would not follow that Smith is acting selfishly or from self-interest. For if Smith wants to do something that will help his friend, even when it means forgoing his own enjoyments, that is precisely what makes him *un*selfish. What else could unselfishness be, if not wanting to help others? Another way to put the same point is to say that it is the *object* of a want that determines whether it is selfish or not. The mere fact that I am acting on *my* wants does not mean that I am acting selfishly; that depends on *what it is* that I want. If I want only my own good, and care nothing for others, then I am selfish; but if I also want other people to be well-off and happy, and if I act on *that* desire, then my action is not selfish. So much for this argument.

b. The second argument for psychological egoism is this: Since so-called unselfish actions always produce a sense of self-satisfaction in the agent,[2] and since this sense of satisfaction is a pleasant state of consciousness, it follows that the point of the action is really to achieve a pleasant state of consciousness, rather than to bring about any good for others. Therefore, the action is "unselfish" only at a superficial level of analysis. Smith will feel much better with himself for having stayed to help his friend—if he had gone to the country, he would have felt terrible about it—and that is the real point of the action. According to a well-known story, this argument was once expressed by Abraham Lincoln:

> Mr. Lincoln once remarked to a fellow-passenger on an old-time mud-coach that all men were prompted by selfishness in doing good. His fellow-passenger was antagonizing this position when they were passing over a corduroy bridge that spanned a slough. As they crossed this bridge they espied an old razor-backed sow on the bank making a terrible noise because her pigs had got into the slough and were in danger of drowning. As the old coach began to climb the hill, Mr. Lincoln called out, "Driver, can't you stop just a moment?" Then Mr. Lincoln jumped out, ran back, and lifted the little pigs out of the mud and water and placed them on the bank. When he returned, his companion remarked: "Now, Abe, where does selfishness come in on this little episode?" "Why, bless your soul, Ed, that was the very essence

of selfishness. I should have had no peace of mind all day had I gone on and left that suffering old sow worrying over those pigs. I did it to get peace of mind, don't you see?"[3]

This argument suffers from defects similar to the previous one. Why should we think that merely because someone derives satisfaction from helping others this makes him selfish? Isn't the unselfish man precisely the one who *does* derive satisfaction from helping others, while the selfish man does not? If Lincoln "got peace of mind" from rescuing the piglets, does this show him to be selfish, or, on the contrary, doesn't it show him to be compassionate and good-hearted? (If a man were truly selfish, why should it bother his conscience that *others* suffer—much less pigs?) Similarly, it is nothing more than shabby sophistry to say, because Smith takes satisfaction in helping his friend, that he is behaving selfishly. If we say this rapidly, while thinking about something else, perhaps it will sound all right; but if we speak slowly, and pay attention to what we are saying, it sounds plain silly.

Moreover, suppose we ask *why* Smith derives satisfaction from helping his friend. The answer will be, it is because Smith cares for him and wants him to succeed. If Smith did not have these concerns, then he would take no pleasure in assisting him; and these concerns, as we have already seen, are the marks of unselfishness, not selfishness. To put the point more generally: if we have a positive attitude toward the attainment of some goal, then we may derive satisfaction from attaining that goal. But the *object* of our attitude is *the attainment of that goal*; and we must want to attain the goal *before* we can find any satisfaction in it. We do not, in other words, desire some sort of "pleasurable consciousness" and then try to figure out how to achieve it; rather, we desire all sorts of different things—money, a new fishing boat, to be a better chess player, to get a promotion in our work, etc.—and because we desire these things, we derive satisfaction from attaining them. And so, if someone desires the welfare and happiness of another person, he will derive satisfaction from that; but this does not mean that this satisfaction is the object of his desire, or that he is in any way selfish on account of it.

It is a measure of the weakness of psychological egoism that these insupportable arguments are the ones most often advanced in its favor. Why, then, should anyone ever have thought it a true view? Perhaps because of a desire for theoretical simplicity: In thinking about human conduct, it would be nice if there were some simple formula that would unite the diverse phenomena of human behavior under a single explanatory principle, just as simple formulae in physics bring together a great many apparently different phenomena. And since it is obvious that self-regard is an overwhelmingly important factor in motivation, it is only natural to wonder whether all motivation might not be explained in these terms. But the answer is clearly No; while a great many human actions are motivated entirely or in part by self-interest, only by a deliberate distortion of the facts can we say that all conduct is so motivated. This will be clear, I think, if we correct three confusions which are commonplace. The exposure of these confusions will remove the last traces of plausibility from the psychological egoist thesis.

The first is the confusion of selfishness with self-interest. The two are clearly not the same. If I see a physician when I am feeling poorly, I am acting in my own interest but no one would think of calling me "selfish" on account of it. Similarly, brushing my teeth, working hard at my job, and obeying the law are all in my self-interest but none of these are examples of selfish conduct. This is because selfish behavior is behavior that ignores the interests of others, in circumstances in which their interests ought not to be ignored. This concept has a definite evaluative flavor; to call someone "selfish" is not just to describe his action but to condemn it. Thus, you would not call me selfish for eating a normal meal in normal circumstances (although it may surely be in my self-interest); but you would call me selfish for hoarding food while others about are starving.

The second confusion is the assumption that every action is done *either* from self-interest or from other-regarding motives. Thus, the egoist concludes that if there is no such thing as genuine altruism then all actions must be done from self-interest. But this is certainly a false dichotomy. The man who continues to smoke cigarettes, even after learning about the connection between smoking and cancer, is surely not acting from self-interest, not even by his own standards— self-interest would dictate that he quit smoking at once—and he is not acting altruistically either. He *is*, no doubt, smoking for the pleasure of it, but all that this shows is that undisciplined pleasure-seeking and acting from self-interest are very different. This is what led Butler to remark that "the thing to be lamented is, not that men have so great regard to their own good or interest in the present world, for they have not enough."[4]

The last two paragraphs show (*a*) that it is false that all actions are selfish, and (*b*) that it is false that all actions are done out of self-interest. And it should be noted that these two points can be made, and were, without any appeal to putative examples of altruism.

The third confusion is the common but false assumption that a concern for one's own welfare is incompatible with any genuine concern for the welfare of others. Thus, since it is obvious that everyone (or very nearly everyone) does desire his own well-being, it might be thought that no one can really be concerned with others. But again, this is false. There is no inconsistency in desiring that everyone, including oneself *and* others, be well-off and happy. To be sure, it may happen on occasion that our own interests conflict with the interests of others, and in these cases we will have to make hard choices. But even in these cases we might sometimes opt for the interests of others, especially when the others involved are our family or friends. But more importantly, not all cases are like this: sometimes we are able to promote the welfare of others when our own interests are not involved at all. In these cases not even the strongest self-regard need prevent us from acting considerately toward others.

Once these confusions are cleared away, it seems to me obvious enough that there is no reason whatever to accept psychological egoism. On the contrary, if we simply observe people's behavior with an open mind, we may find that a great deal of it is motivated by self-regard, but by no means all of it; and that there is no reason to deny that "the moral institution of life" can include a place for the virtue of beneficence.[5]

3. The ethical egoist would say at this point, "Of course it is possible for people to act altruistically, and perhaps many people do act that way—but there is no reason why they *should* do so. A person is under no obligation to do anything except what is in his own interests."[6] This is really quite a radical doctrine. Suppose I have an urge to set fire to some public building (say, a department store) just for the fascination of watching the spectacular blaze: according to this view, the fact that several people might be burned to death provides no reason whatever why I should not do it. After all, this only concerns *their* welfare, not my own, and according to the ethical egoist the only person I need think of is myself.

Some might deny that ethical egoism has any such monstrous consequences. They would point out that it is really to my own advantage not to set the fire—for, if I do that I may be caught and put into prison (unlike Gyges, I have no magic ring for protection). Moreover, even if I could avoid being caught it is still to my advantage to respect the rights and interests of others, for it is to my advantage to live in a society in which people's rights and interests are respected. Only in such a society can I live a happy and secure life; so, in acting kindly toward

others, I would merely be doing my part to create and maintain the
sort of society which it is to my advantage to have.[7] Therefore, it is
said, the egoist would not be such a bad man; he would be as kindly
and considerate as anyone else, because he would see that it is to his
own advantage to be kindly and considerate.

This is a seductive line of thought, but it seems to me mistaken.
Certainly it is to everyone's advantage (including the egoist's) to preserve a stable society where people's interests are generally protected.
But there is no reason for the egoist to think that merely because
he will not honor the rules of the social game, decent society will
collapse. For the vast majority of people are not egoists, and there
is no reason to think that they will be converted by his example—
especially if he is discreet and does not unduly flaunt his style of life.
What this line of reasoning shows is not that the egoist himself must
act benevolently, but that he must encourage *others* to do so. He must
take care to conceal from public view his own self-centered method
of decision making, and urge others to act on precepts very different
from those on which he is willing to act.

The rational egoist, then, cannot advocate that egoism be universally adopted by everyone. For he wants a world in which his own
interests are maximized; and if other people adopted the egoistic
policy of pursuing their own interests to the exclusion of his interests, as he pursues his interests to the exclusion of theirs, then such
a world would be impossible. So he himself will be an egoist, but he
will want others to be altruists.

This brings us to what is perhaps the most popular "refutation" of
ethical egoism current among philosophical writers—the argument
that ethical egoism is at bottom inconsistent because it cannot be universalized.[8] The argument goes like this:

To say that any action or policy of action is *right* (or that it *ought*
to be adopted) entails that it is right for *anyone* in the same sort of
circumstances. I cannot, for example, say that it is right for me to lie
to you, and yet object when you lie to me (provided, of course, that
the circumstances are the same). I cannot hold that it is all right for
me to drink your beer and then complain when you drink mine. This
is just the requirement that we be consistent in our evaluations; it
is a requirement of logic. Now it is said that ethical egoism cannot
meet this requirement because, as we have already seen, the egoist
would not want others to act in the same way that he acts. Moreover,
suppose he *did* advocate the universal adoption of egoistic policies:
he would be saying to Peter, "You ought to pursue your own interests

even if it means destroying Paul"; and he would be saying to Paul, "You ought to pursue your own interests even if it means destroying Peter." The attitudes expressed in these two recommendations seem clearly inconsistent—he is urging the advancement of Peter's interest at one moment, and countenancing their defeat at the next. Therefore, the argument goes, there is no way to maintain the doctrine of ethical egoism as a consistent view about how we ought to act. We will fall into inconsistency whenever we try.

What are we to make of this argument? Are we to conclude that ethical egoism has been refuted? Such a conclusion, I think, would be unwarranted; for I think that we can show, contrary to this argument, how ethical egoism can be maintained consistently. We need only to interpret the egoist's position in a sympathetic way: we should say that he has in mind a certain kind of world which he would prefer over all others; it would be a world in which his own interests were maximized, regardless of the effects on the other people. The egoist's primary policy of action, then, would be to act in such a way as to bring about, as nearly as possible, this sort of world. Regardless of however morally reprehensible we might find it, there is nothing *inconsistent* in someone's adopting this as his ideal and acting in a way calculated to bring it about. And if someone did adopt this as his ideal, then he would not advocate universal egoism; as we have already seen, he would want other people to be altruists. So, if he advocates any principles of conduct for the general public, they will be altruistic principles. This could not be inconsistent; on the contrary, it would be perfectly consistent with his goal of creating a world in which his own interests are maximized. To be sure, he would have to be deceitful; in order to secure the good will of others, and a favorable hearing for his exhortations to altruism, he would have to pretend that he was himself prepared to accept altruistic principles. But again, that would be all right; from the egoist's point of view, this would merely be a matter of adopting the necessary means to the achievement of his goal—and while we might not approve of this, there is nothing inconsistent about it. Again, it might be said, "He advocates one thing, but does another. Surely *that's* inconsistent." But it is not; for what he advocates and what he does are both calculated as means to an end (the *same* end, we might note); and as such, he is doing what is rationally required in each case. Therefore, contrary to the previous argument, there is nothing inconsistent in the ethical egoist's view. He cannot be refuted by the claim that he contradicts himself.

Is there, then, no way to refute the ethical egoist? If by "refute" we mean show that he has made some *logical* error, the answer is that there is not. However, there is something more that can be said. The egoist challenge to our ordinary moral convictions amounts to a demand for an explanation of why we should adopt certain policies of action, namely, policies in which the good of others is given importance. We can give an answer to this demand, albeit an indirect one. The reason one ought not to do actions that would hurt other people is other people would be hurt. The reason one ought to do actions that would benefit other people is other people would be benefited. This may at first seem like a piece of philosophical sleight-of-hand, but it is not. The point is that the welfare of human beings is something that most of us value *for its own sake*, and not merely for the sake of something else. Therefore, when *further* reasons are demanded for valuing the welfare of human beings, we cannot point to anything further to satisfy this demand. It is not that we have no reason for pursuing these policies, but that our reason *is* that these policies are for the good of human beings.

So if we are asked, "Why shouldn't I set fire to this department store?" one answer would be, "Because if you do, people may be burned to death." This is a complete, sufficient reason which does not require qualification or supplementation of any sort. If someone seriously wants to know why this action shouldn't be done, that's the reason. If we are pressed further and asked the sceptical question, "But why shouldn't I do actions that will harm others?" we may not know what to say—but this is because the questioner has included in his question the very answer we would like to give: "Why shouldn't you do actions that will harm others? Because, doing those actions would harm others."

The egoist, no doubt, will not be happy with this. He will protest that *we* may accept this as a reason, but *he* does not. And here the argument stops: there are limits to what can be accomplished by argument, and if the egoist really doesn't care about other people—if he honestly doesn't care whether they are helped or hurt by his actions—then we have reached those limits. If we want to persuade him to act decently toward his fellow humans, we will have to make our appeal to such other attitudes as he does possess, by threats, bribes, or other cajolery. That is all that we can do.

Though some may find this situation distressing (we would like to be able to show that the egoist is just *wrong*), it holds no embarrassment for common morality. What we have come up against is simply a fundamental requirement of rational action, namely, that the existence of reasons for action always depends on the prior existence of certain attitudes in the agent. For example, the fact that a certain course of action would make the agent a lot of money is a reason for doing it only if the agent wants to make money; the fact that practicing at chess makes one a better player is a reason for practicing only if one wants to be a better player; and so on. Similarly, the fact that a certain action would help the agent is a reason for doing the action only if the agent cares about his own welfare, and the fact that an action would help others is a reason for doing it only if the agent cares about others. In this respect ethical egoism and what we might call ethical altruism are in exactly the same fix: both require that the agent *care* about himself, or about other people, before they can get started.

So a nonegoist will accept "It would harm another person" as a reason not to do an action simply because he cares about what happens to that other person. When the egoist says that he does *not* accept that as a reason, he is saying something quite extraordinary. He is saying that he has no affection for friends or family, that he never feels pity or compassion, that he is the sort of person who can look on scenes of human misery with complete indifference, so long as he is not the one suffering. Genuine egoists, people who really don't care at all about anyone other than themselves, are rare. It is important to keep this in mind when thinking about ethical egoism; it is easy to forget just how fundamental to human psychological makeup the feeling of sympathy is. Indeed, a man without any sympathy at all would scarcely be recognizable as a man; and that is what makes ethical egoism such a disturbing doctrine in the first place.

4. There are, of course, many different ways in which the sceptic might challenge the assumptions underlying our moral practice. In this essay I have discussed only two of them, the two put forward by Glaucon in the passage that I cited from Plato's *Republic*. It is important that the assumptions underlying our moral practice should not be confused with particular judgments made within that practice. To defend one is not to defend the other. We may assume—quite properly, if my analysis has been correct—that the virtue of beneficence does, and indeed should, occupy an important place in "the moral institution of life"; and yet we may make constant and miserable errors when it comes to judging when and in what ways this virtue is to be exercised. Even worse, we may often be able to make accurate moral judgments, and know what we ought to do, but not do it. For these ills, philosophy alone is not the cure.

Notes

1. *The Republic of Plato*, translated by F. M. Cornford (Oxford, 1941), p. 45.
2. Or, as it is sometimes said, "It gives him a clear conscience," or "He couldn't sleep at night if he had done otherwise," or "He would have been ashamed of himself for not doing it," and so on.
3. Frank C. Sharp, *Ethics* (New York, 1928), pp. 74–75. Quoted from the Springfield (IL) *Monitor* in the *Outlook*, vol. 56, p. 1059.
4. *The Works of Joseph Butler*, edited by W. E. Gladstone (Oxford, 1896), vol. II, p. 26. It should be noted that most of the points I am making against psychological egoism were first made by Joseph Butler. Butler made all the important points; all that is left for us is to remember them.
5. The capacity for altruistic behavior is not unique to human beings. Some interesting experiments with rhesus monkeys have shown that these animals will refrain from operating a device for securing food if this causes other animals to suffer pain. See Jules H. Masserman, Stanley Wechkin, and William Terris, "'Altruistic' Behavior in Rhesus Monkeys," *American Journal of Psychiatry*, vol. 121 (1964), pp. 584–85.
6. I take this to be the view of Ayn Rand, insofar as I understand her confused doctrine.
7. Cf. Thomas Hobbes, *Leviathan* (London, 1651), chap. 17.
8. See, for example, Brian Medlin, "Ultimate Principles and Ethical Egoism," *Australasian Journal of Philosophy*, vol. 35 (1957), pp. 111–18; and D. H. Monro, *Empiricism and Ethics* (Cambridge, 1967), chap. 16.

Study Questions

1. Explain the distinction between psychological egoism and ethical egoism.
2. In the story about Abraham Lincoln, was his action motivated by selfishness?
3. Is a concern for one's own welfare incompatible with a concern for the welfare of others?
4. Is it self-defeating for an ethical egoist to urge everyone to act egoistically?

CHAPTER 10

Happiness and Immorality

Steven M. Cahn and Jeffrie G. Murphy

An additional challenge to morality comes from those who believe that sometimes a person may achieve happiness by acting immorally. Is the happiness supposedly attained in this way illusory, or does it provide a reason to disregard moral considerations? The issue is discussed here by Steven M. Cahn and Jeffrie G. Murphy, Regents Professor of Law, Philosophy, and Religious Studies at Arizona State University.

A. The Happy Immoralist

Steven M. Cahn

"Happiness," according to Philippa Foot, "is a most intractable concept." She commits herself, however, to the claim that "great happiness, unlike euphoria or even great pleasure, must come from something related to what is deep in human nature, and fundamental in human life, such as affection for children and friends, the desire to work, and love of freedom and truth."[1] I am not persuaded by this characterization of happiness and offer the following counterexample.

Consider Fred, a fictitious person, but an amalgamation of several people I have known. Fred's life has been devoted to achieving three aims: fame, wealth, and a reputation for probity. He has no interest whatever in friends or truth. Indeed, he is treacherous and thoroughly dishonest. Nevertheless, he has attained his three goals and is, in fact, a rich celebrity renowned for his supposed integrity. His acquiring a good name while acting unscrupulously is a tribute to his audacity, cunning, and luck. Now he rests self-satisfied, basking in renown,

Parts A and B are from *Journal of Social Philosophy*, Vol. 35. Copyright © 2004. Reprinted by permission of Blackwell Publishing Ltd. Parts C and D are reprinted by permission of the author.

delighting in luxuries, and relishing praise for his reputed commitment to the highest moral standards.

That he enjoys great pleasure, even euphoria, is undeniable. But, according to Mrs. Foot, he is not happy. I would say, rather, that *we* are not happy with *him*. We do not wish to see shallowness and hypocrisy rewarded. Indeed, while numerous works of literature describe good persons who are doomed to failure, few works tell of evil persons who ultimately flourish. (An exception to the rule is Natasha in Chekhov's *The Three Sisters*, a play that causes most audiences anguish.)

We can define "happiness" so as to falsify the claim that Fred is happy. This philosophical sleight-of-hand, though, accomplishes little, for Fred is wholly contented, suffering no worries or anxieties. Indeed, he is smug, as he revels in his exalted position.

Happiness may be, as Mrs. Foot says, an "intractable concept." Yet surely Fred is happy. Perhaps later in life he won't be. Or perhaps he will. He may come to the end of his days as happy as he is now. I presume his case provides a reason why God is supposed to have created hell, for if Fred suffers no punishment in the next world, he may escape punishment altogether. And believing in that prospect is yet another reason he is happy.

B. The Unhappy Immoralist

Jeffrie G. Murphy

> All that you've just noted merely confirms my belief . . . that if we are to talk philosophy to any purpose, language must be re-made from the ground up.
>
> —*Doctor Glas*, Hjalmar Söderberg

When presenting his version of the ancient and well-known challenge that the Sophists long ago posed to Socrates, Professor Cahn seems to be assuming at the outset—and asking us to grant—that the man he describes *is* happy. But such an assumption begs the whole question at issue here.

In both *Republic* and *Gorgias*, Plato has Socrates argue that the immoral man—even a tyrant with great power—may of course be happy as the ignorant world understands happiness but will not be happy as this concept will be truly understood by the wise philosopher.

Professor Cahn dismisses this as verbal "sleight-of-hand," but I think that such dismissal is hasty. Plato is trying to advance our philosophical understanding by making a conceptual or linguistic claim—no doubt a revisionary one—and surely not all such claims are merely useless verbal tricks. As I read Plato, he (like Philippa Foot) is suggesting that full human happiness is to be understood as the satisfaction one takes in having a personality wherein all elements required for a fully realized human life are harmoniously integrated. The immoralist lacks some of these attributes—integrity, moral emotions, and the capacity for true friendships, for example. Given what he lacks, it can be granted that he may indeed be happy in some limited way—e.g., enjoying a great deal of pleasure—while insisting that he cannot be happy in the full sense.

As a matter of common language, of course, many people do not use the word "happiness" in this rich sense but tend to mean by it something like "has a whole lot of fun." Because of this, the Greek word *eudaimonia*, which in the past was generally translated as "happiness," is now often rendered as "flourishing" to avoid confusion. But some are not so quick to give up the older and deeper usage.

> [Realizing how little the clergyman cared about his wife's health or even his own] I began to think that Markel and his Cyrenäics are right: people care nothing for happiness, they look only for pleasure. They seek pleasure even flat in the face of their own happiness. (*Doctor Glas* again)

Some of the spirit of Plato and Socrates is to be found in Kierkegaard's *Purity of Heart is to Will One Thing*—where he seeks to expose the conflicts and deficiencies present in the "double-minded" person who does not organize his life around the moral good, a person whom Kierkegaard regards as self-deceived if he thinks of himself as truly happy. Kierkegaard argues for this with a blending of conceptual and psychological claims—claims about the nature of those desires he calls "temporal." The person who wills only in pursuit of temporal rather than eternal (i.e., ethico-religious) desires will, he maintains, ultimately fall into boredom and despair since the objects of these desires are vulnerable to the vicissitudes of fate and fortune and carry only temporary satisfaction. The apparent happiness of the person in bondage to temporal desires will be momentary and will mask what is in fact that person's desperate attempt to generate and satisfy new desires as the old ones become boring or their objects pass away. Kierkegaard, in *Either/ Or*, calls this boredom avoidance strategy "the rotation of crops." The person who lives solely for temporal values will, according to Kierkegaard, remain in his deficient state unless he experiences and listens to the moral emotions of regret and remorse—those "emissaries from eternity" that call us to our full humanity.

Is Professor Cahn's "happy immoralist" captured by Kierkegaard's diagnosis? I think that he is. He does, after all, "relish praise," "bask in renown," and smugly "revel in his exalted position." This suggests that, like the tyrant discussed by Plato, he is attached to temporal values that are *vulnerable*—e.g., dependent on the responses of others. Since these are ultimately out of his control, must he not consciously feel or repress *fear*—a fear that may not be compatible with happiness? Professor Cahn admits that there may be a future time when his immoralist becomes unhappy, and I am inclined to think that the immoralist's conscious or repressed realization of this possibility would at the very least pose a serious obstacle to his being fully happy now. And is happiness simply a matter of *now* anyway? Perhaps, as Aristotle sometimes suggests, happiness is better understood as an attribute, not of a present moment of one's life, but of a whole life— the wisdom in the ancient Greek saying that we should call no man happy until he is dead. Finally, if there is any truth in the idea that love and friendship are among the constituents of the happiest of human lives, must not the immoralist's nature—his inability to make and honor binding commitments—forever foreclose these goods to him?

There is no doubt that Plato's and Kierkegaard's understanding of happiness does not capture everyone's understanding of the concept, and thus it must be admitted that some conceptual or linguistic revision is going on here—just as Socrates was engaged in such revision when he made the revolutionary suggestion (*Apology*) that a good person cannot be harmed because harm (*kakon*), when properly understood, will be understood as loss of moral integrity and not as personal pain or disgrace. And if this was "sleight-of-hand," it strikes me that our concept of morality—indeed our civilization—was enriched by it. Professor Cahn's attempt to undermine the Platonic happiness tradition with his story of "the happy immoralist" thus strikes me as no more successful than an attempt to refute Socrates's claim about a good man's insulation from harm by finding a good man and hitting him in the head with a baseball bat. Doctor Glas's friend certainly overstated the case when he said that philosophy requires that language be remade from the ground up, but it is true, I think, that conceptual or linguistic revision can sometimes enlarge and deepen our moral understanding—perhaps bringing to consciousness something that was latent all along.

To sum up: When I think of the man described by Professor Cahn, I find that I *pity* him—pity him because, with Plato, I think that he is punished simply by being the kind of person that he is. But why would I pity him if I thought that he was truly happy?

C. A Challenge to Morality

Steven M. Cahn

Why have so many philosophers, past and present, been loath to admit even the possibility of a happy immoralist? I believe they rightly regard the concept as a threat to morality. For the greater the divergence between morality and happiness, the greater the loss of motivation to choose the moral path.

Most of us, fortunately, have moral compunctions. But when our moral values and our happiness conflict, what are we to do? Those who doubt that such a situation can ever arise should consider the following example inspired by the plot of Woody Allen's thought-provoking movie *Crimes and Misdemeanors*.

Suppose a happily married, highly respected physician makes the mistake of embarking on an affair with an unmarried airline stewardess. When he tries to break off this relationship, she threatens to expose his adultery, thus wrecking his marriage and career.

All he has worked for his entire life is at risk. He knows that if the affair is revealed, his wife will divorce him, his children will reject him, and the members of his community will no longer support his medical practice. Instead of being the object of people's admiration, he will be viewed with scorn. In short, his life will be shattered.

As the stewardess is about to take the steps that will destroy him, he confides in his brother, who has connections to the criminal underworld. The brother offers to help him by arranging for the stewardess to be murdered without any danger that the crime will be traced to either the physician or his brother.

Should the physician consent to the killing? Doing so is clearly immoral, but, if all goes as planned, he will avoid calamity.

Assume that the physician agrees to the murder and that when it is carried out and the police investigate, they attribute it to a drifter who eventually dies of alcoholism, and the case is closed. The physician's life goes on without further complications from the matter, and years later he is honored at a testimonial dinner where, accompanied by his loving wife and adoring children, he accepts the effusive gratitude of the community for his lifetime of service. He is a happy man, taking pride in both the affection of his family and the admiration of his patients and friends.

Even those who might take issue with my claim that the physician is happy would agree that he is happier than he would have been had his life been destroyed. So his immorality enhanced his happiness. But then the feared question arises: What persuasive reasons, if any, can be offered to demonstrate that in securing his own happiness, the physician acted unwisely? Here is a serious challenge to morality, of a sort we may face quite frequently in our lives, although usually the stakes are less momentous. How we decide tells us not only about morality and happiness but also about the sort of persons we choose to be.

D. A Further Challenge

Steven M. Cahn

For those who find farfetched the case of the adulterous physician, I offer the following fictional but realistic story from the world of academia.

• • •

TWO LIVES

Joan earned a doctoral degree from a first-rate university and sought appointment to a tenure-track position in which she could teach and pursue her research. Unfortunately, she received no offers and reluctantly was about to accept nonacademic employment when an unexpected call came inviting her for an interview at a highly attractive school. During her visit she was told by the Dean that the job was hers, subject to one condition: she was expected to teach a particular course each year in which numerous varsity athletes would enroll, and she would be required to award them all passing grades even if their work was in every respect unsatisfactory. Only the Dean would know of this special arrangement.

Joan rejected the position on moral grounds and continued trying to obtain a suitable opportunity in academic life. Never again, however, was she offered a faculty position, and she was forced to pursue a career path that gave her little satisfaction. Her potential as a teacher went unfulfilled, and her planned research was left undone. Throughout her life she remained embittered.

Kate also earned a doctoral degree from a first-rate university and sought appointment to a tenure-track position in which she could teach and pursue her research. She, too, received no offers and reluctantly was about to accept nonacademic employment when an unexpected call came inviting her for an interview at the same school Joan had visited. The Dean made Kate the same offer that had been made to Joan. After weighing the options, Kate accepted the appointment, even though she recognized that doing so would require her to act unethically.

Kate went on to a highly successful academic career, became a popular teacher and renowned researcher, moved to one of the nation's most prestigious universities, and enjoyed all the perquisites attendant to her membership on that school's renowned faculty. When on rare occasions she recalled the conditions of her initial appointment, she viewed the actions she had taken as an unfortunate but necessary step on her path to a wonderful life.

• • •

Joan acted morally but lived unhappily ever after, while Kate acted immorally but lived happily ever after. So I leave you with this dilemma: Which of the two was the wiser?

Note

1. Philippa Foot, "Moral Relativism," in *Moral Dilemmas and Other Topics in Moral Philosophy* (Oxford: Clarendon, 2002), p. 35.

Study Questions

1. Do you believe Fred can be happy?
2. How might Jeffrie G. Murphy try to convince Fred that he is not happy?
3. Can the adulterous physician ever be truly happy?
4. If you desired an academic position and were offered one under the conditions proposed by the Dean, would you accept?

CHAPTER 11

The Nature of Ethical Disagreement

Charles L. Stevenson

A basic challenge to morality contends that, unlike scientific claims, moral claims cannot be tested and, therefore, ethical disputes are pointless. An influential reply is provided in the next selection, written by Charles L. Stevenson (1908–1979), who was Professor of Philosophy at the University of Michigan. Stevenson believed that ethical disagreements often involve factual disputes, which are open to possible resolution by the methods of science. Once we agree on the relevant facts, our ethical disagreement may also be resolved. But which facts, if any, are in question? We can tell only by analyzing the reasons that support our moral judgments.

1

When people disagree about the value of something—one saying that it is good or right and another that it is bad or wrong—by what methods of argument or inquiry can their disagreement be resolved? Can it be resolved by the methods of science, or does it require methods of some other kind, or is it open to no rational solution at all?

The question must be clarified before it can be answered. And the word that is particularly in need of clarification, as we shall see, is the word "disagreement."

Let us begin by noting that "disagreement" has two broad senses: In the first sense it refers to what I shall call "disagreements in belief." This occurs when Mr. A believes p, when Mr. B believes not-p, or something incompatible with p, and when neither is content to let the

---

belief of the other remain unchallenged. Thus doctors may disagree in belief about the causes of an illness; and friends may disagree in belief about the exact date on which they last met.

In the second sense the word refers to what I shall call "disagreement in attitude." This occurs when Mr. A has a favorable attitude to something, when Mr. B has an unfavorable or less favorable attitude to it, and when neither is content to let the other's attitude remain unchanged. The term "attitude" . . . designates any psychological disposition of being *for* or *against* something. Hence love and hate are relatively specific kinds of attitudes, as are approval and disapproval, and so on.

This second sense can be illustrated in this way: Two men are planning to have dinner together. One wants to eat at a restaurant that the other doesn't like. Temporarily, then, the men cannot "agree" on where to dine. Their argument may be trivial, and perhaps only half serious; but in any case it represents a disagreement *in attitude*. The men have divergent preferences and each is trying to redirect the preference of the other—though normally, of course, each is willing to revise his own preference in the light of what the other may say.

Further examples are readily found. Mrs. Smith wishes to cultivate only the four hundred; Mr. Smith is loyal to his old poker-playing friends. They accordingly disagree, in attitude, about whom to invite to their party. The progressive mayor wants modern school buildings and large parks; the older citizens are against these "newfangled" ways; so they disagree on civic policy. These cases differ from the one about the restaurant only in that the clash of attitudes is more serious and may lead to more vigorous argument.

The difference between the two senses of "disagreement" is essentially this: the first involves an opposition of beliefs, both of which cannot be true, and the second involves an opposition of attitudes, both of which cannot be satisfied.

Let us apply this distinction to a case that will sharpen it. Mr. A believes that most voters will favor a proposed tax and Mr. B disagrees with him. The disagreement concerns attitudes—those of the voters—but note that A and B are *not* disagreeing in attitude. Their disagreement is *in belief about* attitudes. It is simply a special kind of disagreement in belief, differing from disagreement in belief about head colds only with regard to subject matter. It implies not an opposition of the actual attitudes of the speakers but only of their beliefs about certain attitudes. Disagreement *in* attitude, on the other hand, implies that the very attitudes of the speakers are opposed. A and

B may have opposed beliefs about attitudes without having opposed attitudes, just as they may have opposed beliefs about head colds without having opposed head colds. Hence we must not, from the fact that an argument is concerned with attitudes, infer that it necessarily involves disagreement *in* attitude.

2

We may now turn more directly to disagreement about values, with particular reference to normative ethics. When people argue about what is good, do they disagree in belief, or do they disagree in attitude? . . . It must be readily granted that ethical arguments usually involve disagreement in belief; but they *also* involve disagreement in attitude. And the conspicuous role of disagreement in attitude is what we usually take, whether we realize it or not, as the distinguishing feature of ethical arguments. For example:

Suppose that the representative of a union urges that the wage level in a given company ought to be higher—that it is only right that the workers receive more pay. The company representative urges in reply that the workers ought to receive no more than they get. Such an argument clearly represents a disagreement in attitude. The union is *for* higher wages; the company is *against* them, and neither is content to let the other's attitude remain unchanged. *In addition* to this disagreement in attitude, of course, the argument may represent no little disagreement in belief. Perhaps the parties disagree about how much the cost of living has risen and how much the workers are suffering under the present wage scale. Or perhaps they disagree about the company's earnings and the extent to which the company could raise wages and still operate at a profit. Like any typical ethical argument, then, this argument involves both disagreement in attitude and disagreement in belief.

It is easy to see, however, that the disagreement in attitude plays a unifying and predominating role in the argument. This is so in two ways:

In the first place, disagreement in attitude determines what beliefs are *relevant* to the argument. Suppose that the company affirms that the wage scale of fifty years ago was far lower than it is now. The union will immediately urge that this contention, even though true, is irrelevant. And it is irrelevant simply because information about the wage level of fifty years ago, maintained under totally different circumstances, is not likely to affect the present attitudes of either party. To be relevant, any belief that is introduced into the argument must be one that is likely to lead one side or the other to have a different attitude, and so reconcile disagreement in attitude. Attitudes are often functions of beliefs. We often change our attitudes to something when we change our beliefs about it; just as a child ceases to *want* to touch a live coal when he comes to *believe* that it will burn him. Thus in the present argument any beliefs that are at all likely to alter attitudes, such as those about the increasing cost of living or the financial state of the company, will be considered by both sides to be relevant to the argument. Agreement in belief on these matters may lead to agreement in attitude toward the wage scale. But beliefs that are likely to alter the attitudes of neither side will be declared irrelevant. They will have no bearing on the disagreement in attitude, with which both parties are primarily concerned.

In the second place, ethical argument usually terminates when disagreement in attitude terminates, even though a certain amount of disagreement in belief remains. Suppose, for instance, that the company and the union continue to disagree in belief about the increasing cost of living, but that the company, even so, ends by favoring the higher wage scale. The union will then be content to end the argument and will cease to press its point about living costs. It may bring up that point again, in some future argument of the same sort, or in urging the righteousness of its victory to the newspaper columnists; but for the moment the fact that the company has agreed in attitude is sufficient to terminate the argument. On the other hand: suppose that both parties agreed on all beliefs that were introduced into the argument, but even so continued to disagree in attitude. In that case neither party would feel that their dispute had been successfully terminated. They might look for other beliefs that could be introduced into the argument. They might use words to play on each other's emotion. They might agree (in attitude) to submit the case to arbitration, both feeling that a decision, even if strongly adverse to one party or the other, would be preferable to a continued impasse. Or, perhaps, they might abandon hope of settling their dispute by any peaceable means.

In many other cases, of course, men discuss ethical topics without having the strong, uncompromising attitudes that the present example has illustrated. They are often as much concerned with redirecting their own attitudes, in the light of greater knowledge, as with redirecting the attitudes of others. And the attitudes involved are often altruistic rather than selfish. Yet the above example will serve, so long as that is understood, to suggest the nature of ethical disagreement. Both disagreement in attitude and disagreement in belief are involved, but the former predominates in that (1) it determines what sort of disagreement in belief is relevantly disputed in a given ethical argument, and (2) it determines by its continued presence or its resolution whether or not the argument has been settled. We may see further how intimately the two sorts of disagreement are related: since attitudes are often functions of beliefs, an agreement in belief may lead people, as a matter of psychological fact, to agree in attitude.

3

Having discussed disagreement, we may turn to the broad question that was first mentioned, namely, By what methods of argument or inquiry may disagreement about matters of value be resolved?

It will be obvious that to whatever extent an argument involves disagreement in belief, it is open to the usual methods of the sciences. If these methods are the *only* rational methods for supporting beliefs—as I believe to be so, but cannot now take time to discuss—then scientific methods are the only rational methods for resolving the disagreement in *belief* that arguments about values may include.

But if science is granted an undisputed sway in reconciling beliefs, it does not thereby acquire, without qualification, an undisputed sway in reconciling attitudes. We have seen that arguments about values include disagreement in attitude, no less than disagreement in belief, and that in certain ways the disagreement in attitude predominates. By what methods shall the latter sort of disagreement be resolved?

The methods of science are still available for that purpose, but only in an indirect way. Initially, these methods have only to do with establishing agreement in belief. If they serve further to establish agreement in attitude, that will be due simply to the psychological fact that altered beliefs may cause altered attitudes. Hence scientific methods are conclusive in ending arguments about values only to the extent that their success in obtaining agreement in belief will in turn lead to agreement in attitude.

In other words, the extent to which scientific methods can bring about agreement on values depends on the extent to which a commonly accepted body of scientific beliefs would cause us to have a commonly accepted set of attitudes.

How much is the development of science likely to achieve, then, with regard to values? To what extent *would* common beliefs lead to common attitudes? It is, perhaps, a pardonable enthusiasm to *hope* that science will do everything—to hope that in some rosy future, when all men know the consequences of their acts, they will all have common aspirations and live peaceably in complete moral accord. But if we speak not from our enthusiastic hopes but from our present knowledge, the answer must be far less exciting. We usually *do not know*, at the beginning of any argument about values, whether an agreement in belief, scientifically established, will lead to an agreement in attitude or not. It is logically possible, at least, that two men should continue to disagree in attitude even though they had all their beliefs in common, and even though neither had made any logical or inductive error, or omitted any relevant evidence. Differences in temperament, or in early training, or in social status, might make the men retain different attitudes even though both were possessed of the complete scientific truth. Whether this logical possibility is an empirical likelihood I shall not presume to say; but it is unquestionably a possibility that must not be left out of account.

To say that science can always settle arguments about value, we have seen, is to make this assumption: Agreement in attitude will always be consequent upon complete agreement in belief, and science can always bring about the latter. Taken as purely heuristic, this assumption has its usefulness. It leads people to discover the discrepancies in their beliefs and to prolong enlightening argument that *may* lead, as a matter of fact, from commonly accepted beliefs to commonly accepted attitudes. It leads people to reconcile their attitudes in a rational, permanent way, rather than by rhapsody or exhortation. But the assumption is *nothing more*, for present knowledge, than a heuristic maxim. It is wholly without any proper foundation of probability. I conclude, therefore, that scientific methods cannot be guaranteed the definite role in the so-called normative sciences that they may have in the natural sciences. Apart from a heuristic assumption to the contrary, it is possible that the growth of scientific knowledge may leave many disputes about values permanently unsolved. Should these disputes persist, there are nonrational methods for dealing with them, of course, such as impassioned, moving oratory. But the purely intellectual methods of science, and indeed, *all* methods of reasoning, may be insufficient to settle disputes about values even though they may greatly help to do so.

Study Questions

1. How do disagreements in belief differ from disagreements in attitude?
2. Can science ever help resolve a moral disagreement?
3. Are disagreements in belief about attitudes the same as disagreements in attitude?
4. Do disagreements in attitude predominate in a moral disagreement?

PART II

Moral Theories

CHAPTER 12

The Categorical Imperative

Immanuel Kant

Having considered various challenges to morality, we turn next to some of the most important moral theories, competing explanations of why certain actions are right and others are wrong. One of the most influential of all ethical systems is that developed by the German philosopher Immanuel Kant (1724–1804), a dominant figure in the history of modern philosophy. Because his views are not easy to grasp, I shall offer a brief overview of them.

Kant argues that the moral worth of an action is to be judged not by its consequences but by the nature of the maxim or principle that motivated the action. Thus right actions are not necessarily those with favorable consequences but those performed in accordance with correct maxims. But which maxims are correct? According to Kant, the only correct ones are those that can serve as universal laws because they are applicable without exception to every person at any time. In other words, you should act only on a maxim that can be universalized without contradiction.

To see what Kant has in mind, consider a specific example he uses to illustrate his view. Suppose you need to borrow money, but it will be lent to you only if you promise to pay it back. You realize, however, that you will not be able to honor the debt. Is it permissible for you to promise to repay the money, knowing you will not keep the promise? Kant argues that doing so is not permissible because if it were a universal law that promises could be made with no intention of keeping them, then the practice of promising would be destroyed.

Kant refers to his supreme moral principle as the "categorical imperative"—categorical because it does not depend on anyone's particular desires, and an imperative because it is a command of reason. Kant also claims that the categorical imperative can be reformulated

From Immanuel Kant, *Groundwork for the Metaphysics of Morals,* translated by Arnulf Zweig. Copyright © 2002. Reprinted by permission of Oxford University Press.

as follows: So act that you treat humanity, whether in your own person or in any other person, always at the same time as an end, never merely as a means. Using this version, Kant argues that a deceitful promise is immoral because a person making such a promise is using another person only as a means, not treating that individual as an end, a rational being worthy of respect.

It is impossible to imagine anything at all in the world, or even beyond it, that can be called good without qualification—except a *good will*. Intelligence, wit, judgement, and the other mental talents, whatever we may call them, or courage, decisiveness, and perseverance, are, as qualities of *temperament*, certainly good and desirable in many respects; but they can also be extremely bad and harmful when the will which makes use of these *gifts of nature* and whose specific quality we refer to as *character*, is not good. It is exactly the same with *gifts of fortune*. Power, wealth, honour, even health and that total well-being and contentment with one's condition which we call "happiness," can make a person bold but consequently often reckless as well, unless a good will is present to correct their influence on the mind, thus adjusting the whole principle of one's action to render it conformable to universal ends. It goes without saying that the sight of a creature enjoying uninterrupted prosperity, but never feeling the slightest pull of a pure and good will, cannot excite approval in a rational and impartial spectator. Consequently, a good will seems to constitute the indispensable condition even of our worthiness to be happy.

Some qualities, even though they are helpful to this good will and can make its task very much easier, nevertheless have no intrinsic unconditional worth. Rather, they presuppose a good will which puts limits on the esteem in which they are rightly held and forbids us to regard them as absolutely good. Moderation in emotions and passions, self-control, and sober reflection are not only good in many respects: they may even seem to constitute part of the inner worth of a person. Yet they are far from being properly described as good without qualification (however unconditionally they were prized by the ancients). For without the principles of a good will those qualities may become exceedingly bad; the passionless composure of a villain makes him not merely more dangerous but also directly more detestable in our eyes than we would have taken him to be without it.

A good will is not good because of its effects or accomplishments, and not because of its adequacy to achieve any proposed end: it is good only by virtue of its willing—that is, it is good in itself. Considered in itself it is to be treasured as incomparably higher than anything it could ever bring about merely in order to satisfy some inclination or, if you like, the sum total of all inclinations. Even if it were to happen that, because of some particularly unfortunate face or the miserly bequest of a step-motherly nature, this will were completely powerless to carry out its aims; if with even its utmost effort it still accomplished nothing, so that only good will itself remained (not, of course, as a mere wish, but as the summoning of every means in our power), even then it would still, like a jewel, glisten in its own right, as something that has its full worth in itself. . . .

We must thus develop the concept of a will estimable in itself and good apart from any further aim. This concept is already present in the natural, healthy mind, which requires not so much instruction as merely clarification. It is this concept that always holds the highest place in estimating the total worth of our actions and it constitutes the condition of all the rest. Let us then take up the concept of *duty*, which includes that of a good will, the latter however being here under certain subjective limitations and obstacles. These, so far from hiding a good will or disguising it, rather bring it out by contrast and make it shine forth more brightly. . . .

It is a duty to help others where one can, and besides this many souls are so compassionately disposed that, without any further motive of vanity or self-interest, they find an inner pleasure in spreading joy around them, taking delight in the contentment of others, so far as they have brought it about. Yet I maintain that, however dutiful and kind an action of this sort may be, it still has no genuinely moral worth. It is on a level with other inclinations—for example, the inclination to pursue honour, which if fortunate enough to aim at something generally useful and consistent with duty, something consequently honourable, deserves praise and encouragement but not esteem. For its maxim lacks the moral merit of such actions done not out of inclination but out of *duty*. Suppose then that the mind of this humanitarian were overclouded by sorrows of his own which extinguished all compassion for the fate of others, but that he still had the power to assist others in distress; suppose though that their adversity no longer stirred him, because he is preoccupied with his own; and now imagine that, though no longer moved by any inclination, he nevertheless tears himself out of this deadly apathy and does the action without any inclination, solely out of duty. Then for the first time his action has its genuine moral worth. Furthermore, if nature had put little sympathy into this or that person's heart; if he, though an honest man, were cold in temperament and indifferent to the sufferings of others—perhaps because he has the special gifts of patience and fortitude in his own sufferings and he assumes or even demands the same of others; if such a man (who would in truth not be the worst product of nature) were not exactly fashioned by nature to be a humanitarian, would he not still find in himself a source from which he might give himself a worth far higher than that of a good-natured temperament? Assuredly he would. It is precisely in this that the worth of character begins to show—a moral worth, and incomparably the highest—namely, that he does good, not out of inclination, but out of duty. . . .

The moral worth of an action done out of duty has its moral worth, not *in the objective* to be reached by that action, but in the maxim in accordance with which the action is decided upon; it depends, therefore, not on actualizing the object of the action, but solely on the *principle of volition* in accordance with which the action was done, without any regard for objects of the faculty of desire. It is clear from our previous discussion that the objectives we may have in acting, and also our actions' effects considered as ends and as what motivates our volition, can give to actions no unconditional or moral worth. Where then can this worth be found if not in the willing of the action's hoped for effect? It can be found nowhere but *in the principle of the will*, irrespective of the ends that can be brought about by such action. . . .

Duty is the necessity of an act done out of respect for the law. While I can certainly have an *inclination* for an object that results from my proposed action, I can never *respect* it, precisely because it is nothing but an effect of a will and not its activity. Similarly I cannot respect any inclination whatsoever, whether it be my own inclination or that of another. At most I can approve of that towards which I feel an inclination, and occasionally I can like the object of somebody else's inclination myself—that is, see it as conducive to my own advantage. But the only thing that could be an object of respect (and thus a commandment) for me is something that is conjoined with my will purely as a ground and never as a consequence, something that does not serve my inclination but overpowers it or at least excludes it entirely from my decision-making—consequently, nothing but the law itself. Now if an action done out of duty is supposed to exclude totally the influence of inclination, and, along with inclination, every object of volition, then nothing remains that could determine the will except objectively *the law* and subjectively *pure respect* for this practical law. What is left therefore is the maxim, to obey this sort of law even when doing so is prejudicial to all my inclinations.

Thus the moral worth of an action depends neither on the result expected from that action nor on any principle of action that has to borrow its motive from this expected result. For all these results (such as one's own pleasurable condition or even the promotion of the happiness of others) could have been brought about by other causes as well. It would not require the will of a rational being to produce them, but it is only in such a will that the highest and unconditional good can be found. That pre-eminent good which we call "moral" consists therefore in nothing but *the idea of the law* in itself, which certainly *is present only in a rational being*—so far as that idea, and not an expected result, is the determining ground of the will. And this pre-eminent good is already present in the person who acts in accordance with this idea; we need not await the result of the action in order to find it. . . .

Everything in nature works in accordance with laws. Only a rational being has the power to act in accordance with the idea of laws—that is, in accordance with principles—and thus has a will. . . .

The idea of an objective principle, in so far as it constrains a will, is called a commandment (of reason), and the formulation of this commandment is called an Imperative. . . .

All imperatives command either hypothetically or categorically. Hypothetical imperatives declare a possible action to be practically necessary as a means to the attainment of something else that one wants (or that one may want). A categorical imperative would be one that represented an action as itself objectively necessary, without regard to any further end.

Since every practical law presents a possible action as good and therefore as necessary for a subject whose actions are determined by reason, all imperatives are therefore formulae for determining an action which is necessary according to the principle of a will in some way good. If the action would be good only as a means to something else, the imperative is hypothetical; if the action is thought of as good in itself and therefore as necessary for a will which of itself conforms to reason as its principle, then the imperative is categorical. . . .

There is, however, *one* end that we may presuppose as actual in all rational beings (so far as they are dependent beings to whom imperatives apply); and thus there is one aim which they not only *might* have, but which we can assume with certainty that they all *do* have by a necessity of nature and that aim is *perfect happiness*. The hypothetical imperative which affirms the practical necessity of an action as a means to the promotion of perfect happiness is an assertoric imperative. We must not characterize it as necessary merely for some uncertain, merely possible purpose, but as necessary for a purpose that we can presuppose a priori and with certainty to be present in everyone because it belongs to the essence of human beings. Now we can call skill in the choice of the means to one's own greatest well-being "prudence" in the narrowest sense of the word. So the imperative concerning the choice of means to one's own happiness—that is, the precept of prudence—still remains hypothetical; the action is commanded not absolutely but only as a means to a further end.

Finally, there is one imperative which commands a certain line of conduct directly, without assuming or being conditional on any further goal to be reached by that conduct. This imperative is categorical. It is concerned not with the material of the action and its anticipated result, but with its form and with the principle from which the action itself results. And what is essentially good in the action consists in the [agent's] disposition, whatever the result may be. This imperative may be called the imperative of morality. . . .

The question now arises "How are all these imperatives possible?" This question does not ask how an action commanded by the imperative can be performed, but merely how we can understand the constraining of the will, which imperatives express in setting us a task. How an imperative of skill is possible requires no special discussion. Whoever wills the end also wills (so far as reason has decisive influence on his actions) the means which are indispensably necessary and in his power. . . .

By contrast, "How is the imperative of morality possible?" is beyond all doubt the one question in need of solution. For the moral imperative is in no way hypothetical, and consequently the objective necessity, which it affirms, cannot be supported by any presupposition, as was the case with hypothetical imperatives. But we must never forget that it is impossible to settle by any example, i.e., empirically, whether there is any imperative of this kind at all; we should rather worry that all imperatives that seem to be categorical may yet be hypothetical in some hidden way. For example, when it is said, "You must abstain from making deceitful promises," one assumes that the necessity for this abstention is not mere advice so as to avoid some further evil—as though the meaning of what was said was, You ought not to make a deceitful promise lest, when it comes to light, you destroy your credit. On the contrary, an action of this kind would have to be considered as bad in itself, and the imperative of the prohibition would be therefore categorical. Even so, no example can show with certainty that the will would be determined here solely by the law without any further motivation, although it may appear to be so; for it is always possible that fear of disgrace, perhaps also hidden dread of other risks, may unconsciously influence the will. Who can prove by experience the non-existence of a cause? For experience shows only that we do not perceive it. In such a case, however, the so-called moral imperative, which as such appears to be categorical and unconditional, would in fact be only a pragmatic prescription calling attention to our own advantage and merely instructing us to take this into account. . . .

If I think of a *hypothetical* imperative as such, I do not know beforehand what it will contain—not until I am given its condition. But if I think of a *categorical imperative,* I know right away what it contains. For since this imperative contains, besides the law, only the necessity that the maxim conform to this law, while the law, as we have seen, contains no condition limiting it, there is nothing left over to which the maxim of action should conform except the universality of a law as such; and it is only this conformity that the imperative asserts to be necessary.

There is therefore only one categorical imperative and it is this: "Act only on that maxim by which you can at the same time will that it should become a universal law." . . .

We shall now enumerate some duties. . . .

1. A man feels sick of life as the result of a mounting series of misfortunes that has reduced him to hopelessness, but he still possesses enough of his reason to ask himself whether it would not be contrary to his duty to himself to take his own life. Now he tests whether the maxim of his action could really become a universal law of nature. His maxim, however, is: "I make it my principle out of self-love to shorten my life if its continuance threatens more evil than it promises advantage." The only further question is whether this principle of self-love can become a universal law of nature. But one sees at once that a nature whose law was that the very same feeling meant to promote life should actually destroy life would contradict itself, and hence would not endure as nature. The maxim therefore could not possibly be a general law of nature and thus it wholly contradicts the supreme principle of all duty.

2. Another finds himself driven by need to borrow money. He knows very well that he will not be able to pay it back, but he sees too that nobody will lend him anything unless he firmly promises to pay it back within a fixed time. He wants to make such a promise, but he still has enough conscience to ask himself, "Isn't it impermissible and contrary to duty to get out of one's difficulties this way?" Suppose, however, that he did decide to do it. The maxim of his action would run thus: "When I believe myself short of money, I will borrow money and promise to pay it back, even though I know that this will never be done." Now this principle of self-love or personal advantage is perhaps quite compatible with my own entire future welfare; only there remains the question "Is it right?" I therefore transform the unfair demand of self-love into a universal law and frame my question thus: "How would things stand if my maxim became a universal law?" I then see immediately that this maxim can never qualify as a self-consistent universal law of nature, but must necessarily contradict itself. For the universality of a law that permits anyone who believes himself to be in need to make any promise he pleases with the intention of not keeping it would make promising, and the very purpose one has in promising, itself impossible. For no one would believe he was being promised anything, but would laugh at any such utterance as hollow pretense.

3. A third finds in himself a talent that, with a certain amount of cultivation, could make him a useful man for all sorts of purposes. But he sees himself in comfortable circumstances, and he prefers to give himself up to pleasure rather than to bother about increasing and improving his fortunate natural aptitudes. Yet he asks himself further "Does my maxim of neglecting my natural gifts, besides agreeing with my taste for amusement, agree also with what is called duty?" He then sees that a nature could indeed endure under such a universal law, even if (like the South Sea Islanders) every man should let his talents rust and should be bent on devoting his life solely to idleness, amusement, procreation—in a word, to enjoyment. Only he cannot possibly *will* that this should become a universal law of nature or should be implanted in us as such a law by a natural instinct. For as a rational being he necessarily wills that all his powers should be developed, since they are after all useful to him and given to him for all sorts of possible purposes.

4. A fourth man, who is himself flourishing but sees others who have to struggle with great hardships (and whom he could easily help) thinks to himself: "What do I care? Let every one be as happy

as Heaven intends or as he can make himself; I won't deprive him of anything; I won't even envy him; but I don't feel like contributing anything to his well-being or to helping him in his distress!" Now admittedly if such an attitude were a universal law of nature, the human race could survive perfectly well and doubtless even better than when everybody chatters about sympathy and good will, and even makes an effort, now and then, to practise them, but, when one can get away with it, swindles, traffics in human rights, or violates them in other ways. But although it is possible that a universal law of nature in accord with this maxim could exist, it is impossible to *will* that such a principle should hold everywhere as a law of nature. For a will that intended this would be in conflict with itself, since many situations might arise in which the man needs love and sympathy from others, and in which, by such a law of nature generated by his own will, he would rob himself of all hope of the help he wants.

These are some of the many actual duties—or at least of what we take to be actual—whose derivation from the single principle cited above is perspicuous. We must be able to will that a maxim of our action should become a universal law—this is the authoritative model for moral judging of action generally. Some actions are so constituted that we cannot even *conceive* without contradiction that their maxim be a universal law of nature, let alone that we could *will* that it *ought* to become one. In the case of other actions, we do not find this inner impossibility, but it is still impossible to *will* that their maxim should be raised to the universality of a law of nature, because such a will would contradict itself. . . .

If we now look at ourselves whenever we transgress a duty, we find that we in fact do not intend that our maxim should become a universal law. For this is impossible for us. What we really intend is rather that its opposite should remain a law generally; we only take the liberty of making an *exception* to it, for ourselves or (of course just this once) to satisfy our inclination. Consequently if we weighed it all up from one and the same perspective—that of reason—we should find a contradiction in our own will, the contradiction that a certain principle should be objectively necessary as a universal law and yet subjectively should not hold universally but should admit of exceptions. . . .

Suppose, however, there were something *whose existence in itself* had an absolute worth, something that, as an end *in itself,* could be a ground of definite laws. Then in it and in it alone, would the ground of a possible categorical imperative, that is, of a practical law, reside.

Now, I say, a human being, and in general every rational being, *does exist* as an end in himself, *not merely as a means* to be used by this or that will as it pleases. In all his actions, whether they are directed to himself or to other rational beings, a human being must always be viewed *at the same time as an end.* . . . Beings whose existence depends not on our will but on nature still have only a relative value as means and are therefore called *things,* if they lack reason. Rational beings, on the other hand, are called *persons* because, their nature already marks them out as ends in themselves—that is, as something which ought not to be used *merely* as a means— and consequently imposes restrictions on all choice making (and is an object of respect). Persons, therefore, are not merely subjective ends whose existence as an effect of our actions has a value *for us.* They are *objective ends*—that is, things whose existence is in itself an end, and indeed an end such that no other end can be substituted for it, no end to which they should serve *merely* as a means. For if this were not so, there would be nothing at all having *absolute value* anywhere. But if all value were conditional, and thus contingent, then no supreme principle could be found for reason at all.

If then there is to be a supreme practical principle and a categorical imperative for the human will, it must be such that it forms an objective principle of the will from the idea of something which is necessarily an end for everyone because *it is an end in itself,* a principle that can therefore serve as a universal practical law. The ground of this principle is: *Rational nature exists as an end in itself.* This is the way in which a human being necessarily conceives his own existence, and it is therefore a *subjective* principle of human actions. But it is also the way in which every other rational being conceives his existence, on the same rational ground which holds also for me; hence it is at the same time an *objective* principle from which, since it is a supreme practical ground, it must be possible to derive all laws of the will. The practical imperative will therefore be the following: *Act in such a way that you treat humanity, whether in your own person or in any other person, always at the same time as an end, never merely as a means.* We will now see whether this can be carried out in practice.

Let us keep to our previous examples.

First, . . . the man who contemplates suicide will ask himself whether his action could be compatible with the Idea of humanity as *an end in itself.* If he damages himself in order to escape from a painful situation, he is making use of a person *merely as a means* to maintain a tolerable state of affairs till the end of his life. But a human being is not a thing—not something to be used *merely* as a means: he must always in all his actions be regarded as an end in himself. Hence I cannot dispose of a human being in my own person, by maiming, corrupting, or killing him. (I must here forego a more precise definition of this principle that would forestall any misunderstanding—for example, as to having limbs amputated to save myself or exposing my life to danger in order to preserve it, and so on—this discussion belongs to ethics proper.)

Secondly, . . . the man who has in mind making a false promise to others will see at once that he is intending to make use of another person *merely as a means* to an end which that person does not share. For the person whom I seek to use for my own purposes by such a promise cannot possibly agree with my way of treating him, and so cannot himself share the end of the action. This incompatibility with the principle of duty to others can be seen more distinctly when we bring in examples of attacks on the freedom and property of others. For then it is manifest that a violator of the rights of human beings intends to use the person of others merely as a means without taking into consideration that, as rational beings, they must always at the same time be valued as ends—that is, treated only as beings who must themselves be able to share in the end of the very same action.

Thirdly, . . . it is not enough that an action not conflict with humanity in our own person as an end in itself: it must also *harmonize with this end.* Now there are in humanity capacities for greater perfection that form part of nature's purpose for humanity in our own person. To neglect these can perhaps be compatible with the *survival* of humanity as an end in itself, but not with the *promotion* of that end.

Fourthly, . . . the natural end that all human beings seek is their own perfect happiness. Now the human race might indeed exist if everybody contributed nothing to the happiness of others but at the same time refrained from deliberately impairing it. This harmonizing with humanity *as an end in itself* would, however, be merely negative and not positive, unless everyone also endeavours, as far as he can, to further the ends of others. For the ends of any person who is an end in himself must, if this idea is to have its full effect in me, be also, as far as possible, *my* ends.

Study Questions

1. According to Kant, what is the only thing in the world that is good without limitation?
2. What does Kant mean by acting from duty?
3. How does Kant differentiate between a hypothetical and a categorical imperative?
4. By what argument does Kant seek to prove that the first formulation of the categorical imperative demonstrates the immorality of your making a promise you don't intend to keep?

CHAPTER 13

A Simplified Account of Kant's Ethics

Onora O'Neill

Onora O'Neill is Principal of Newnham College, Cambridge University. In the next selection she explains Kant's second formulation of his categorical imperative, the requirement that each person be treated as an end and never merely as a means.

Kant's moral theory has acquired the reputation of being forbiddingly difficult to understand and, once understood, excessively demanding in its requirements. I don't believe that this reputation has been wholly earned, and I am going to try to undermine it. . . .

The main method by which I propose to avoid some of the difficulties of Kant's moral theory is by explaining only one part of the theory. This does not seem to me to be an irresponsible approach in this case. One of the things that makes Kant's moral theory hard to understand is that he gives a number of different versions of the principle that he calls the Supreme Principle of Morality, and these different versions don't look at all like one another. . . .

Kant calls his Supreme Principle the *Categorical Imperative*; its various versions also have sonorous names. . . . The one on which I shall concentrate is known as the *Formula of the End in Itself.* . . .

From Tom Regan, *Matters of Life and Death: New Introductory Essays in Moral Philosophy*, 3rd edition. Copyright © 1993 by McGraw-Hill. Reprinted by permission of The McGraw-Hill Companies.

The Formula of the End in Itself

Kant states the Formula of the End in Itself as follows:

> Act in such a way that you always treat humanity, whether in your own person or in the person of any other, never simply as a means but always at the same time as an end.

To understand this we need to know what it is to treat a person as a means or as an end. According to Kant, each of our acts reflects one or more *maxims*. The maxim of the act is the principle on which one sees oneself as acting. A maxim expresses a person's policy, or if he or she has no settled policy, the principle underlying the particular intention or decision on which he or she acts. Thus, a person who decides, "This year I'll give 10 percent of my income to famine relief," has as a maxim the principle of tithing his or her income for famine relief. In practice, the difference between intentions and maxims is of little importance, for given any intention, we can formulate the corresponding maxim by deleting references to particular times, places, and persons. In what follows I shall take the terms "maxim" and "intention" as equivalent.

Whenever we act intentionally, we have at least one maxim and can, if we reflect, state what it is. (There is of course room for self-deception here—"I'm only keeping the wolf from the door," we may claim as we wolf down enough to keep ourselves overweight, or, more to the point, enough to feed someone else who hasn't enough food.)

When we want to work out whether an act we propose to do is right or wrong, according to Kant, we should look at our maxims and not at how much misery or happiness the act is likely to produce, and whether it does better at increasing happiness than other available acts. We just have to check that the act we have in mind will not use anyone as a mere means, and, if possible, that it will treat other persons as ends in themselves.

Using Persons as Mere Means

To use someone as a *mere means* is to involve them in a scheme of action *to which they could not in principle consent*. Kant does not say that there is anything wrong about using someone as a means. Evidently we have to do so in any cooperative scheme of action. If I cash a check I use the teller as a means, without whom I could not lay my hands on the cash; the teller in turn uses me as a means to earn his or her living. But in this case, each party consents to her or his part in the transaction. Kant would say that though they use one another as means, they do not use one another as *mere* means. Each person assumes that the other has maxims of his or her own and is not just a thing or a prop to be manipulated.

But there are other situations where one person uses another in a way to which the other could not in principle consent. For example, one person may make a promise to another with every intention of breaking it. If the promise is accepted, then the person to whom it was given must be ignorant of what the promisor's intention (maxim) really is. If one knew that the promisor did not intend to do what he or she was promising, one would, after all, not accept or rely on the promise. It would be as though there had been no promise made. Successful false promising depends on deceiving the person to whom the promise is made about what one's real maxim is. And since the person who is deceived doesn't know that real maxim, he or she can't in principle consent to his or her part in the proposed scheme of action. The person who is deceived is, as it were, a prop or a tool—a mere means—in the false promisor's scheme. A person who promises falsely treats the acceptor of the promise as a prop or a thing and not as a person. In Kant's view, it is this that makes false promising wrong.

One standard way of using others as mere means is by deceiving them. By getting someone involved in a business scheme or a criminal activity on false pretenses, or by giving a misleading account of what one is about, or by making a false promise or a fraudulent contract, one involves another in something to which he or she in principle cannot consent, since the scheme requires that he or she doesn't know what is going on. Another standard way of using others as mere means is by coercing them. If a rich or powerful person threatens a debtor with bankruptcy unless he or she joins in some scheme, then the creditor's intention is to coerce; and the debtor, if coerced, cannot consent to his or her part in the creditor's scheme. To make the example more specific: If a moneylender in an Indian village threatens not to renew a vital loan unless he is given the debtor's land, then he uses the debtor as a mere means. He coerces the debtor, who cannot truly consent to this "offer he can't refuse." (Of course the outward form of such transactions may look like ordinary commercial dealings, but we know very well that some offers and demands couched in that form are coercive.)

In Kant's view, acts that are done on maxims that require deception or coercion of others, and so cannot have the consent of those others (for consent precludes both deception and coercion), are wrong. When we act on such maxims, we treat others as mere means, as things rather than as ends in themselves. If we act on such maxims, our acts are not only wrong but unjust: such acts wrong the particular others who are deceived or coerced.

Study Questions

1. According to Kant, is using someone as a means always wrong?
2. What does Kant mean by the maxim of an action?
3. Why is it wrong to deceive others?
4. Can you imagine circumstances in which breaking a promise would not be wrong?

CHAPTER 14

Utilitarianism

John Stuart Mill

John Stuart Mill (1806–1873) was the leading English philosopher of the nineteenth century. Whereas Kant's ethical system concentrates exclusively on the reason for an action and does not take account of its results, Mill's system focuses only on consequences. Mill defends utilitarianism, the view that the supreme principle of morality is to act so as to produce as much happiness as possible, each person counting equally. By "happiness" Mill means pleasure and the absence of pain. He grants, however, that some pleasures are more worthwhile than others. "It is . . . better to be Socrates dissatisfied than a fool satisfied." His evidence for this claim is that anyone who knew the lives of both would choose the former rather than the latter.

Utilitarianism provides a means of dealing with the quandary of conflicting obligations. For instance, suppose you promised to meet someone for lunch but on the way encounter a child in need of immediate aid. What should you do? Utilitarianism solves the problem by telling you to give priority to helping the child because that course of action will produce more happiness. Shouldn't we keep our promises? Mill says that usually we should because the practice of keeping one's promises produces important social benefits. An exception should be made, however, on those occasions when more happiness will be produced by not keeping a promise.

What Utilitarianism Is

. . . The creed which accepts as the foundation of morals "utility" or the "greatest happiness principle" holds that actions are right in proportion as they tend to promote happiness; wrong as they tend to produce the reverse of happiness. By happiness is intended pleasure

From John Stuart Mill, *Utilitarianism* (1863).

and the absence of pain; by unhappiness, pain and the privation of pleasure. To give a clear view of the moral standard set up by the theory, much more requires to be said; in particular, what things it includes in the ideas of pain and pleasure, and to what extent this is left an open question. But these supplementary explanations do not affect the theory of life on which this theory of morality is grounded—namely, that pleasure and freedom from pain are the only things desirable as ends; and that all desirable things (which are as numerous in the utilitarian as in any other scheme) are desirable either for pleasure inherent in themselves or as means to the promotion of pleasure and the prevention of pain.

Now such a theory of life excites in many minds, and among them in some of the most estimable in feeling and purpose, inveterate dislike. To suppose that life has (as they express it) no higher end than pleasure—no better and nobler object of desire and pursuit—they designate as utterly mean and groveling, as a doctrine worthy only of swine. . . .

But there is no known . . . theory of life which does not assign to the pleasures of the intellect, of the feelings and imagination, and of the moral sentiments a much higher value as pleasures than to those of mere sensation. It must be admitted, however, that utilitarian writers in general have placed the superiority of mental over bodily pleasures chiefly in the greater permanency, safety, uncostliness, etc., of the former—that is, in their circumstantial advantages rather than in their intrinsic nature. And on all these points utilitarians have fully proved their case; but they might have taken the other and, as it may be called, higher ground with entire consistency. It is quite compatible with the principle of utility to recognize the fact that some kinds of pleasure are more desirable and more valuable than others. It would be absurd that, while in estimating all other things quality is considered as well as quantity, the estimation of pleasure should be supposed to depend on quantity alone.

If I am asked what I mean by difference in quality in pleasures, or what makes one pleasure more valuable than another, merely as a pleasure, except its being greater in amount, there is but one possible answer. Of two pleasures, if there be one to which all or almost all who have experience of both give a decided preference, irrespective of any feeling of moral obligation to prefer it, that is the more desirable pleasure. If one of the two is, by those who are competently acquainted with both, placed so far above the other that they prefer it, even though knowing it to be attended with a greater amount of discontent, and would not resign it for any quantity of the other plea-sure which their nature is capable of, we are justified in ascribing to the preferred enjoyment a superiority in quality so far outweighing quantity as to render it, in comparison, of small account.

Now it is an unquestionable fact that those who are equally acquainted with and equally capable of appreciating and enjoying both do give a most marked preference to the manner of existence which employs their higher faculties. Few human creatures would consent to be changed into any of the lower animals for a promise of the fullest allowance of a beast's pleasures; no intelligent human being would consent to be a fool, no instructed person would be an ignoramus, no person of feeling and conscience would be selfish and base, even though they should be persuaded that the fool, the dunce, or the rascal is better satisfied with his lot than they are with theirs. They would not resign what they possess more than he for the most complete satisfaction of all the desires which they have in common with him. If they ever fancy they would, it is only in cases of unhap-piness so extreme that to escape from it they would exchange their lot for almost any other, however undesirable in their own eyes. A being of higher faculties requires more to make him happy, is capa-ble probably of more acute suffering, and certainly accessible to it at more points, than one of an inferior type; but in spite of these liabili-ties, he can never really wish to sink into what he feels to be a lower grade of existence. . . .

It is better to be a human being dissatisfied than a pig satisfied; better to be Socrates dissatisfied than a fool satisfied. And if the fool, or the pig, are of a different opinion, it is because they only know their own side of the question. The other party to the comparison knows both sides.

It may be objected that many who are capable of the higher plea-sures occasionally, under the influence of temptation, postpone them to the lower. But this is quite compatible with a full appreciation of the intrinsic superiority of the higher. Men often, from infirmity of character, make their election for the nearer good, though they know it to be the less valuable; and this no less when the choice is between two bodily pleasures than when it is between bodily and mental. They pursue sensual indulgences to the injury of health, though perfectly aware that health is the greater good. It may be further objected that many who begin with youthful enthusiasm for everything noble, as they advance in years, sink into indolence and selfishness. But I do not believe that those who undergo this very common change voluntarily

choose the lower description of pleasures in preference to the higher.
I believe that, before they devote themselves exclusively to the one,
they have already become incapable of the other. Capacity for the
nobler feelings is in most natures a very tender plant, easily killed, not
only by hostile influences, but by mere want of sustenance; and in
the majority of young persons it speedily dies away if the occupations
to which their position in life has devoted them, and the society into
which it has thrown them, are not favorable to keeping that higher
capacity in exercise. Men lose their high aspirations as they lose their
intellectual tastes, because they have not time or opportunity for
indulging them; and they addict themselves to inferior pleasures, not
because they deliberately prefer them, but because they are either
the only ones to which they have access or the only ones which they
are any longer capable of enjoying. It may be questioned whether
anyone who has remained equally susceptible to both classes of pleasures ever knowingly and calmly preferred the lower, though many,
in all ages, have broken down in an ineffectual attempt to combine
both.

From this verdict of the only competent judges, I apprehend there
can be no appeal. On a question which is the best worth having of
two pleasures, or which of the two modes of existence is the most
grateful to the feelings, apart from its moral attributes and from its
consequences, the judgment of these who are qualified by knowledge
of both, or, if they differ, that of the majority among them, must be
admitted as final. And there needs to be the less hesitation to accept
this judgment respecting the quality of pleasures, since there is no
other tribunal to be referred to even on the question of quantity.
What means are there of determining which is the acutest of two
pains, or the intensest of two pleasurable sensations, except the general suffrage of those who are familiar with both? . . .

I must again repeat what the assailants of utilitarianism seldom
have the justice to acknowledge, that the happiness which forms
the utilitarian standard of what is right in conduct is not the agent's
own happiness but that of all concerned. As between his own happiness and that of others, utilitarianism requires him to be as strictly
impartial as a disinterested and benevolent spectator. In the golden
rule of Jesus of Nazareth, we read the complete spirit of the ethics of
utility. "To do as you would be done by," and "to love your neighbor
as your self," constitute the ideal perfection of utilitarian morality.
As the means of making the nearest approach to this ideal, utility
would enjoin, first, that laws and social arrangements should place

the happiness or (as, speaking practically, it may be called) the interest of every individual as nearly as possible in harmony with the interest of the whole; and, secondly, that education and opinion, which have so vast a power over human character, should so use that power as to establish in the mind of every individual an indissoluble association between his own happiness and the good of the whole, especially between his own happiness and the practice of such modes of conduct, negative and positive, as regard for the universal happiness prescribes; so that not only he may be unable to conceive the possibility of happiness to himself, consistently with conduct opposed to the general good, but also that a direct impulse to promote the general good may be in every individual one of the habitual motives of action, and the sentiments connected therewith may fill a large and prominent place in every human being's sentient existence. If the impugners of the utilitarian morality represented it to their own minds in this its true character, I know not what recommendation possessed by any other morality they could possibly affirm to be wanting to it; what more beautiful or more exalted developments of human nature any other ethical system can be supposed to foster; or what springs of action, not accessible to the utilitarian, such systems rely on for giving effect to their mandates.

The objectors to utilitarianism cannot always be charged with representing it in a discreditable light. On the contrary, those among them who entertain anything like a just idea of its disinterested character sometimes find fault with its standard as being too high for humanity. They say it is exacting too much to require that people shall always act from the inducement of promoting the general interest of society. But this is to mistake the very meaning of a standard of morals and confound the rule of action with the motive of it. It is the business of ethics to tell us what are our duties, or by what test we may know them; but no system of ethics requires that the sole motive of all we do shall be a feeling of duty; on the contrary, ninety-nine hundredths of all our actions are done from other motives, and rightly so done if the rule of duty does not condemn them. It is the more unjust to utilitarianism that this particular misapprehension should be made a ground of objection to it, inasmuch as utilitarian moralists have gone beyond almost all others in affirming that the motive has nothing to do with the morality of the action, though much with the worth of the agent. He who saves a fellow creature from drowning does what is morally right, whether his motive be duty or the hope of being paid for his trouble; he who betrays the friend that trusts him is guilty of a crime, even if his object be to serve another friend to whom he is under greater obligations. But to speak only of actions done from the motive of duty, and in direct obedience to principle: it is a misapprehension of the utilitarian mode of thought to conceive it as implying that people should fix their minds upon so wide a generality as the world, or society at large. The greatest majority of good actions are intended not for the benefit of the world, but for that of individuals, of which the good of the world is made up; and the thoughts of the most virtuous man need not on these occasions travel beyond the particular persons concerned, except so far as is necessary to assure himself that in benefiting them he is not violating the rights, that is, the legitimate and authorized expectations, of anyone else. The multiplication of happiness is, according to the utilitarian ethics, the object of virtue: the occasions on which any person (except one in a thousand) has it in his power to do this on an extended scale—in other words, to be a public benefactor—are but exceptional; and on these occasions alone is he called on to consider public utility; in every other case, private utility, the interest or happiness of some few persons, is all he has to attend to. Those alone the influence of whose actions extends to society in general need concern themselves habitually about so large an object. In the case of abstinences indeed—of things which people forbear to do from moral considerations, though the consequences in the particular case might be beneficial—it would be unworthy of an intelligent agent not to be consciously aware that the action is of a class which, if practiced generally, would be generally injurious, and that this is the ground of the obligation to abstain from it. The amount of regard for the public interest implied in this recognition is no greater than is demanded by every system of morals, for they all enjoin to abstain from whatever is manifestly pernicious to society. . . .

Again, utility is often summarily stigmatized as an immoral doctrine by giving it the name of "expediency," and taking advantage of the popular use of that term to contrast it with principle. But the expedient, in the sense in which it is opposed to the right, generally means that which is expedient for the particular interest of the agent himself, as when a minister sacrifices the interests of his country to keep himself in place. When it means anything better than this, it means that which is expedient for some immediate object, some temporary purpose, but which violates a rule whose observance is expedient in a much higher degree. The expedient, in this sense, instead of being the same thing with the useful, is a branch of the hurtful.

Thus it would often be expedient, for the purpose of getting over some momentary embarrassment, or attaining some object immediately useful to ourselves or others, to tell a lie. But inasmuch as the cultivation in ourselves of a sensitive feeling on the subject of veracity is one of the most useful, and the enfeeblement of that feeling one of the most hurtful, things to which our conduct can be instrumental; and inasmuch as any, even unintentional, deviation from truth does that much toward weakening the trustworthiness of human assertion, which is not only the principal support of all present social well-being, but the insufficiency of which does more than any one thing that can be named to keep back civilization, virtue, everything on which human happiness on the largest scale depends—we feel that the violation, for a present advantage, of a rule of such transcendent expediency is not expedient, and that he who, for the sake of convenience to himself or to some other individual, does what depends on him to deprive mankind of the good, and inflict upon them the evil, involved in the greater or less reliance which they can place in each other's words, acts the part of one of their worst enemies. Yet that even this rule, sacred as it is, admits of possible exceptions is acknowledged by all moralists, the chief of which is when the withholding of some fact (as of information from a malefactor, or of bad news from a person dangerously ill) would save an individual (especially an individual other than oneself) from great and unmerited evil, and when the withholding can only be effected by denial. But in order that the exception may not extend itself beyond the need, and may have the least possible effect in weakening reliance on veracity, it ought to be recognized and, if possible, its limits defined; and, if the principle of utility is good for anything, it must be good for weighing these conflicting utilities against one another and marking out the region within which one or the other preponderates.

Again, defenders of utility often find themselves called upon to reply to such objections as this—that there is not time, previous to action, for calculating and weighing the effects of any line of conduct on the general happiness. This is exactly as if anyone were to say that it is impossible to guide our conduct by Christianity because there is not time, on every occasion on which anything has to be done, to read through the Old and New Testaments. The answer to the objection is that there has been ample time, namely, the whole past duration of the human species. During all that time mankind have been learning by experience the tendencies of actions, on which experience all the prudence as well as all the morality of life are dependent.

People talk as if the commencement of this course of experience had hitherto been put off, and as if, at the moment when some man feels tempted to meddle with the property or life of another, he had to begin considering for the first time whether murder and theft are injurious to human happiness. Even then I do not think that he would find the question very puzzling; but, at all events, the matter is now done to his hand. It is truly a whimsical supposition that, if mankind were agreed in considering utility to be the test of morality, they would remain without any agreement as to what *is* useful, and would take no measures for having their notions on the subject taught to the young and enforced by law and opinion. There is no difficulty in proving any ethical standard whatever to work ill if we suppose universal idiocy to be conjoined with it; but on any hypothesis short of that, mankind must by this time have acquired positive beliefs as to the effects of some actions on their happiness; and the beliefs which have thus come down are the rules of morality for the multitude, and for the philosopher until he has succeeded in finding better. That philosophers might easily do this, even now, on many subjects; that the received code of ethics is by no means of divine right; and that mankind have still much to learn as to the effects of actions on the general happiness, I admit or rather earnestly maintain. The corollaries from the principle of utility, like the precepts of every practical art, admit of indefinite improvement, and, in a progressive state of the human mind, their improvement is perpetually going on. But to consider the rules of morality as improvable is one thing; to pass over the intermediate generalization entirely and endeavor to test each individual action directly by the first principle is another. It is a strange notion that the acknowledgment of a first principle is inconsistent with the admission of secondary ones. To inform a traveler respecting the place of his ultimate destination is not to forbid the use of landmarks and direction-posts on the way. The proposition that happiness is the end and aim of morality does not mean that no road ought to be laid down to that goal, or that persons going thither should not be advised to take one direction rather than another. Men really ought to leave off talking a kind of nonsense on this subject, which they would neither talk nor listen to on other matters of practical concernment. Nobody argues that the art of navigation is not founded on astronomy because sailors cannot wait to calculate the Nautical Almanac. Being rational creatures, they go to sea with it ready calculated; and all rational creatures go out upon the sea of life with their minds made up on the common questions of right and wrong, as well as on many of the far more difficult questions of wise and foolish. And this, as long as foresight is a human quality, it is to be presumed they will continue to do. Whatever we adopt as the fundamental principle of morality, we require subordinate principles to apply it by; the impossibility of doing without them, being common to all systems, can afford no argument against any one in particular; but gravely to argue as if no such secondary principles could be had, and as if mankind had remained till now, and always must remain, without drawing any general conclusions from the experience of human life is as high a pitch, I think, as absurdity has ever reached in philosophical controversy. . . .

Of What Sort of Proof the Principle of Utility Is Susceptible

. . . Questions about ends are, in other words, questions about what things are desirable. The utilitarian doctrine is that happiness is desirable and the only thing desirable as an end, all other things being only desirable as means to that end. What ought to be required of the doctrine, what conditions is it requisite that the doctrine should fulfill—to make good its claim to be believed?

The only proof capable of being given that an object is visible is that people actually see it. The only proof that a sound is audible is that people hear it; and so of the other sources of our experience. In like manner, I apprehend, the sole evidence it is possible to produce that anything is desirable is that people do actually desire it. If the end which the utilitarian doctrine proposes to itself were not, in theory and in practice, acknowledged to be an end, nothing could ever convince any person that it was so. No reason can be given why the general happiness is desirable, except that each person, so far as he believes it to be attainable, desires his own happiness. This, however, being a fact, we have not only all the proof which the case admits of, but all which it is possible to require, that happiness is a good, that each person's happiness is a good to that person, and the general happiness, therefore, a good to the aggregate of all persons. Happiness has made out its title as *one* of the ends of conduct and, consequently, one of the criteria of morality.

But it has not, by this alone, proved itself to be the sole criterion. To do that it would seem, by the same rule, necessary to show not only that people desire happiness but that they never desire anything else. Now it is palpable that they do desire things which, in common language, are decidedly distinguished from happiness. They desire, for example, virtue and the absence of vice no less really than pleasure and the absence of pain. The desire of virtue is not as universal, but it is as authentic a fact as the desire of happiness. And hence the opponents of the utilitarian standard deem that they have a right to infer that there are other ends of human action besides happiness, and that happiness is not the standard of approbation and disapprobation.

But does the utilitarian doctrine deny that people desire virtue, or maintain that virtue is not a thing to be desired? The very reverse. It maintains not only that virtue is to be desired, but that it is to be desired disinterestedly, for itself. Whatever may be the opinion of utilitarian moralists as to the original conditions by which virtue is made virtue, however they may believe (as they do) that actions and dispositions are only virtuous because they promote another end than virtue, yet this being granted, and it having been decided, from considerations of this description, what *is* virtuous, they not only place virtue at the very head of the things which are good as means to the ultimate end, but they also recognize as a psychological fact the possibility of its being, to the individual, a good in itself, without looking to any end beyond it; and hold that the mind is not in a right state, not in a state conformable to utility, not in the state most conducive to the general happiness, unless it does love virtue in this manner—as a thing desirable in itself, even although, in the individual instance, it should not produce those other desirable consequences which it tends to produce, and on account of which it is held to be virtue. This opinion is not, in the smallest degree, a departure from the happiness principle. The ingredients of happiness are very various, and each of them is desirable in itself, and not merely when considered as swelling an aggregate. The principle of utility does not mean that any given pleasure, as music, for instance, or any given exemption from pain, as for example health, is to be looked upon as means to a collective something termed happiness, and to be desired on that account. They are desired and desirable in and for themselves; besides being means, they are a part of the end. Virtue, according to the utilitarian doctrine, is not naturally and originally part of the end, but it is capable of becoming so; and in those who live it disinterestedly it has become so, and is desired and cherished, not as a means to happiness, but to a part of their happiness.

To illustrate this further, we may remember that virtue is not the only thing originally a means, and which if it were not a means to

anything else would be and remain indifferent, but which by association with what it is a means to comes to be desired for itself, and
that too with the utmost intensity. What, for example, shall we say of
the love of money? There is nothing originally more desirable about
money than about any heap of glittering pebbles. Its worth is solely
that of the things which it will buy; the desires for other things than
itself, which it is a means of gratifying. Yet the love of money is not
one of the strongest moving forces of human life, but money is, in
many cases, desired in and for itself; the desire to possess it is often
stronger than the desire to use it, and goes on increasing when all
the desires which point to ends beyond it, to be compassed by it, are
falling off. It may, then, be said truly that money is desired not for
the sake of an end, but as part of the end. From being a means to
happiness, it has come to be itself a principal ingredient of the individual's conception of happiness. The same may be said of the majority of the great objects of human life: power, for example, or fame,
except that to each of these there is a certain amount of immediate
pleasure annexed, which has at least the semblance of being naturally inherent in them—a thing which cannot be said of money. Still,
however, the strongest natural attraction, both of power and of fame,
is the immense aid they give to the attainment of our other wishes;
and it is the strong association thus generated between them and all
our objects of desire which gives to the direct desire of them the
intensity it often assumes, so as in some characters to surpass in
strength all other desires. In these cases the means have become
a part of the end, and a more important part of it than any of the
things which they are means to. What was once desired as an instru-
ment for the attainment of happiness has come to be desired for its
own sake. In being desired for its own sake it is, however, desired
as *part* of happiness. The person is made, or thinks he would be
made, happy by its mere possession and is made unhappy by failure
to obtain it. The desire of it is not a different thing from the desire
of happiness any more than the love of music or the desire of health.
They are included in happiness. They are some of the elements
of which the desire of happiness is made up. Happiness is not an
abstract idea but a concrete whole; and these are some of its parts.
And the utilitarian standard sanctions and approves their being so.
Life would be a poor thing, very ill provided with sources of happiness, if there were not this provision of nature by which things originally indifferent, but conducive to, or otherwise associated with, the
satisfaction of our primitive desires, become in themselves sources

of pleasure more valuable than the primitive pleasures, both in permanency, in the space of human existence that they are capable of covering, and even in intensity.

Virtue, according to the utilitarian conception, is a good of this description. There was no original desire of it, or motive to it, save its conduciveness to pleasure, and especially to protection from pain. But through the association thus formed it may be felt a good in itself, and desired as such with as great intensity as any other good; and with this difference between it and the love of money, of power, or of fame—that all of these may, and often do, render the individual noxious to the other members of the society to which he belongs, whereas there is nothing which makes him so much a blessing to them as the cultivation of the disinterested love of virtue. And consequently, the utilitarian standard, while it tolerates and approves those other acquired desires, up to the point beyond which they would be more injurious to the general happiness than promotive of it, enjoins and requires the cultivation of the love of virtue up to the greatest strength possible, as being above all things important to the general happiness.

It results from the preceding considerations that there is in reality nothing desired except happiness. Whatever is desired otherwise than as a means to some end beyond itself, and ultimately to happiness, is desired as itself a part of happiness, and is not desired for itself until it has become so. Those who desire virtue for its own sake desire it either because the consciousness of it is a pleasure, or because the consciousness of being without it is a pain, or for both reasons united, as in truth the pleasure and pain seldom exist separately, but almost always together—the same person feeling pleasure in the degree of virtue attained, and pain in not having attained more. If one of these gave him no pleasure, and the other no pain, he would not love or desire virtue, or would desire it only for the other benefits which it might produce to himself or to persons whom he cared for.

We have now, then, an answer to the question, of what sort of proof the principle of utility is susceptible.

Study Questions

1. According to Mill, is the agent's own happiness the standard of right conduct?
2. Are some types of pleasure more worthwhile than others?
3. Why does Mill believe lying is wrong?
4. Does Mill believe the principle of utilitarianism can be proved?

CHAPTER 15

Strengths and Weaknesses of Utilitarianism

Louis P. Pojman

Utilitarianism has been subject to a variety of criticisms. Louis P. Pojman (1935–2005), who was Professor of Philosophy at the United States Military Academy, explains the grounds on which utilitarianism has been attacked and the possible responses available to its defenders.

There are two classical types of utilitarianism: act utilitarianism and rule utilitarianism. In applying the principle of utility, act utilitarians . . . say that ideally we ought to apply the principle to all of the alternatives open to us at any given moment. We may define act utilitarianism in this way:

> **act utilitarianism:** An act is right if and only if it results in as much good as any available alternative.

Of course, we cannot do the necessary calculations to determine which act is the correct one in each case, for often we must act spontaneously and quickly. So rules of thumb (for example, "In general don't lie," and "Generally keep your promises") are of practical importance. However, the right act is still that alternative that results in the most utility.

The obvious criticism of act utility is that it seems to fly in the face of fundamental intuitions about minimally correct behavior. Consider Richard Brandt's criticism of act utilitarianism:

> It implies that if you have employed a boy to mow your lawn and he has finished the job and asks for his pay, you should pay him what

you promised only if you cannot find a better use for your money. It implies that when you bring home your monthly paycheck you should use it to support your family and yourself only if it cannot be used more effectively to supply the needs of others. It implies that if your father is ill and he has no prospect of good in his life, and maintaining him is a drain on the energy and enjoyments of others, then, if you can end his life without provoking any public scandal or setting a bad example, it is your positive duty to take matters into your own hands and bring his life to a close.[1]

Rule utilitarians like Brandt attempt to offer a more credible version of the theory. They state that an act is right if it conforms to a valid rule within a system of rules that, if followed, will result in the best possible state of affairs (or the least bad state of affairs, if it is a question of all the alternatives being bad). We may define rule utilitarianism this way:

> **rule utilitarianism**: An act is right if and only if it is required by a rule that is itself a member of a set of rules whose acceptance would lead to greater utility for society than any available alternative.

Human beings are rule-following creatures. We learn by adhering to the rules of a given subject, whether it is speaking a language, driving a car, dancing, writing an essay, rock climbing, or cooking. We want to have a set of action-guiding rules to live by. The act-utilitarian rule, to do the act that maximizes utility, is too general for most purposes. Often we don't have time to deliberate whether lying will produce more utility than truth telling, so we need a more specific rule prescribing truthfulness, which passes the test of rational scrutiny. Rule utilitarianism asserts that the best chance of maximizing utility is by following the *set of rules* most likely to give us our desired results. . . .

An often-debated question in ethics is whether rule utilitarianism is a consistent version of utilitarianism. . . . [F]or example, we could imagine a situation in which breaking the general rule "Never lie" in order to spare someone's feelings would create more utility . . . than keeping the rule would. It would seem that we could always improve on any version of rule utilitarianism by breaking the set of rules whenever we judge that by so doing we could produce even more utility than by following the set. . . .

Whatever the answers . . . utilitarianism does have two very positive features. It also has several problems. The first attraction or strength is that it is a single principle, an absolute system with a potential answer for every situation. Do what will promote the most utility! It's good to have a simple, action-guiding principle that is applicable to every occasion—even if it may be difficult to apply (life's not simple). Its second strength is that utilitarianism seems to get to the substance of morality. It is not merely a formal system (that is, a system that sets forth broad guidelines for choosing principles but offers no principles; such a guideline would be "Do whatever you can universalize") but rather has a material core: Promote human (and possibly animal) flourishing and ameliorate suffering. The first virtue gives us a clear decision procedure in arriving at our answer about what to do. The second virtue appeals to our sense that morality is made for humans (and other animals?) and that morality is not so much about rules as about helping people and alleviating the suffering in the world. . . .

Opponents raise several . . . objections against utilitarianism. We discuss five of them: (1) the no-rest objection, (2) the absurd-implications objection, (3) the integrity objection, (4) the justice objection, and (5) the publicity objection. . . .

Problem 1: The No-Rest Objection: According to utilitarianism, one should always do that act that promises to promote the most utility. However, there is usually an infinite set of possible acts to choose from, and even if I can be excused from considering all of them, I can be fairly sure that there is often a preferable act that I could be doing. For example, when I am about to go to the movies with a friend, I should ask myself if helping the homeless in my community wouldn't promote more utility. When I am about to go to sleep, I should ask myself whether I could at that moment be doing something to help save the ozone layer. And why not simply give all my assets (beyond what is absolutely necessary to keep me alive) to the poor in order to promote utility? Following utilitarianism, I should get little or no rest, and, certainly, I have no right to enjoy life when, by sacrificing, I can make others happier. Similar to this point is Peter Singer's contention that middle-class people have a duty to contribute to poor people (especially in undeveloped countries) more than one-third of their income and all of us have a duty to contribute every penny above $30,000 that we possess until we are only marginally better off than the worst-off people on Earth. But, the objection goes, this makes morality too demanding, creates a disincentive to work, and fails to account for differential obligation. So utilitarianism must be a false doctrine.

Response: The utilitarian responds . . . by insisting that a rule prescribing rest and entertainment is actually the kind of rule that would have a place in a utility-maximizing set of rules. The agent should aim at maximizing his or her own happiness as well as other people's happiness. For the same reason, it is best not to worry much about the needs of those not in our primary circle. Although we should be concerned about the needs of future and distant (especially poor) people, it actually would promote disutility for the average person to become preoccupied with these concerns. Peter Singer represents a radical act-utilitarian position, which fails to give adequate attention to the rules that promote human flourishing, such as the right to own property, educate one's children, and improve one's quality of life, all of which probably costs more than $30,000 per year in many parts of North America. But, the utilitarian would remind us, we can surely do a lot more for suffering humanity than we now are doing—especially if we join together and act cooperatively. And we can simplify our lives, cutting back on conspicuous consumption, while improving our overall quality.

Problem 2: The Absurd-Implications Objection: W. D. Ross has argued that utilitarianism is to be rejected because it is counterintuitive. If we accept it, we would have to accept an absurd implication. Consider two acts, A and B, that will both result in 100 hedons (units of pleasure of utility). The only difference is that A involves telling a lie and B involves telling the truth. The utilitarian must maintain that the two acts are of equal value. But this seems implausible; truth seems to be an intrinsically good thing. . . .

Response: . . . [U]tilitarians can agree that there is something counterintuitive in the calculus of equating an act of lying with one of honesty; but, they argue, we must be ready to change our culture-induced moral biases. What is so important about truth telling or so bad about lying? If it turned out that lying really promoted human welfare, we'd have to accept it. But that's not likely. Our happiness is tied up with a need for reliable information (truth) on how to achieve our ends. So truthfulness will be a member of rule utility's set. But when lying will clearly promote utility without undermining the general adherence to the rule, we simply ought to lie. Don't we already accept lying to a gangster or telling white lies to spare people's feelings? . . .

Problem 3: The Integrity Objection: Bernard Williams argues that utilitarianism violates personal integrity by commanding that we violate our most central and deeply held principles. He illustrates this with the following example:

> Jim finds himself in the central square of a small South American town. Tied up against the wall [is] a row of twenty Indians, most terrified, a few defiant, in front of them several armed men in uniform. A heavy man in a sweat-stained khaki shirt turns out to be the captain in charge and, after a good deal of questioning of Jim which establishes that he got there by accident while on a botanical expedition, explains that the Indians are a random group of inhabitants who, after recent acts of protest against the government, are just about to be killed to remind other possible protesters of the advantages of not protesting. However, since Jim is an honored visitor from another land, the captain is happy to offer him a guest's privilege of killing one of the Indians himself. If Jim accepts, then as a special mark of the occasion, the other Indians will be let off. Of course, if Jim refuses, then there is no special occasion, and Pedro here will do what he was about to do when Jim arrived, and kill them all. Jim, with some desperate recollection of schoolboy fiction, wonders whether if he got hold of a gun, he could hold the captain, Pedro and the rest of the soldiers to threat, but it is quite clear from the set-up that nothing of that kind is going to work: any attempt of that sort of thing will mean that all the Indians will be killed, and himself. The men against the wall, the other villagers, understand the situation, and are obviously begging him to accept. What should he do?[2]

Williams asks rhetorically,

> How can a man, as a utilitarian agent, come to regard as one satisfaction among others, and a dispensable one, a project or attitude round which he has built his life, just because someone else's projects have so structured the causal scene that *that* is how the utilitarian sum comes out?

Williams's conclusion is that utilitarianism leads to personal alienation and so is deeply flawed.

Response: . . . [T]he utilitarian can argue that (1) some alienation may be necessary for the moral life but (2) the utilitarian (even the act utilitarian) can take this into account in devising strategies of action. That is, integrity is not an absolute that must be adhered to at all costs. Even when it is required that we sacrifice our lives or limit our freedom for others, we may have to limit or sacrifice something of what Williams calls our integrity. We may have to do the "lesser of evils" in many cases. If the utilitarian doctrine of negative responsibility is correct, we need to realize that we are responsible for the evil that we knowingly allow, as well as for the evil we commit.

But . . . a utilitarian may realize that there are important social benefits in having people who are squeamish about committing acts of violence, even those that preliminary utility calculations seem to prescribe. It may be that becoming certain kinds of people (endorsed by utilitarianism) may rule out being able to commit certain kinds of horrors—like Jim's killing of an innocent Indian. That is, utilitarianism recognizes the utility of good character and conscience, which may militate against certain apparently utility-maximizing acts.

Problem 4: The Justice Objection: Suppose a rape and murder is committed in a racially volatile community. As the sheriff of the town, you have spent a lifetime working for racial harmony. Now, just when your goal is being realized, this incident occurs. The crime is thought to be racially motivated, and a riot is about to break out that will very likely result in the death of several people and create long-lasting racial antagonism. You see that you could frame a derelict for the crime so that a trial will find him guilty and he will be executed. There is every reason to believe that a speedy trial and execution will head off the riot and save community harmony. Only you (and the real criminal, who will keep quiet about it) will know that an innocent man has been tried and executed. What is the morally right thing to do? The utilitarian seems committed to framing the derelict, but many would find this appalling.

Or consider [that you] are a utilitarian physician who has five patients under your care. One needs a heart transplant, two need one lung each, one needs a liver, and the last one needs a kidney. Now into your office comes a healthy bachelor needing an immunization. You judge that he would make a perfect sacrifice for your five patients. Via a utility calculus, you determine that, without doubt, you could do the most good by injecting the healthy man with a fatal drug and then using his organs to save your five patients.

This cavalier view of justice offends us. The very fact that utilitarians even countenance such actions—that they would misuse the legal system or the medical system to carry out their schemes—seems frightening. . . .

Response: . . . The utilitarian counters that justice is not an absolute—mercy and benevolence and the good of the whole society sometimes should override it; but, the sophisticated utilitarian insists, it makes good utilitarian sense to have a principle of justice that we generally adhere to. It may not be clear what the sheriff should do in the racially torn community. . . . If we could be certain that it would not set a precedent of sacrificing innocent people, it may be right to sacrifice one person for the good of the whole. Wouldn't we all agree, the utilitarian continues, that it would be right to sacrifice one innocent person to prevent a great evil?

Virtually all standard moral systems have a rule against torturing innocent people. But suppose a maniac . . . has a lethal gas that will spread throughout the globe and wipe out all life within a few weeks. His psychiatrist knows the lunatic well and assures us that there is one way to stop him—torture his 10-year-old daughter and televise it. Suppose, for the sake of the argument, there is no way to simulate the torture. Would you not consider torturing the child in this situation?

Is it not right to sacrifice one innocent person to stop a war or to save the human race from destruction? We seem to proceed on this assumption in wartime, in every bombing raid. . . . We seem to be following this rule in our decision to drive automobiles and trucks even though we are fairly certain the practice will result in the death of thousands of innocent people each year.

On the other hand, the sophisticated utilitarian may argue that, in the case of the sheriff framing the innocent derelict, justice should not be overridden by current utility concerns, for human rights themselves are outcomes of utility consideration and should not lightly be violated. That is, because we tend subconsciously to favor our own interests and biases, we institute the principle of rights to protect ourselves and others from capricious and biased acts that would in the long run have great disutility. So we must not undermine institutional rights too easily—we should not kill the bachelor in order to provide a heart, two lungs, a liver, and one kidney to the five other patients—at least not at the present time, given people's expectations of what will happen to them when they enter hospitals. But neither should we worship rights! They are to be taken seriously but not given ultimate authority. The utilitarian cannot foreclose the possibility of sacrificing innocent people for the greater good of humanity. If slavery could be humane and yield great overall utility, utilitarians would accept it. . . .

Problem 5: The Publicity Objection: It is usually thought that all must know moral principles so that all may freely obey the principles.

But utilitarians usually hesitate to recommend that everyone act as a utilitarian, especially an act utilitarian, for it takes a great deal of deliberation to work out the likely consequences of alternative courses of action. . . . So utilitarianism seems to contradict our notion of publicity.

Response: . . . [U]tilitarians have two responses. First, they can counter that the objection only works against act utilitarianism. Rule utilitarianism can allow for greater publicity, for it is not the individual act that is important but the set of rules that is likely to bring about the most good. But then the act utilitarian may respond that this objection only shows a bias toward publicity (or even democracy). It may well be that publicity is only a rule of thumb to be overridden whenever there is good reason to believe that we can obtain more utility by not publicizing act-utilitarian ideas. Since we need to coordinate our actions with other people, moral rules must be publicly announced, typically through legal statutes. I may profit from cutting across the grass in order to save a few minutes in getting to class, but I also value a beautiful green lawn. We need public rules to ensure the healthy state of the lawn. So we agree on a rule to prohibit walking on the grass—even when it may have a utility function. There are many activities that individually may bring about individual utility advancement or even communal good, which if done regularly, would be disastrous, such as cutting down trees in order to build houses or to make newspaper or paper for books like this one, valuable as it is. We thus regulate the lumber industry so that every tree cut down is replaced with a new one and large forests are kept inviolate. So moral rules must be publicly advertised, often made into laws and enforced.

There is one further criticism of rule utilitarianism, which should be mentioned. Sometimes students accuse this version as being relativistic, since it seems to endorse different rules in different societies. Society A may uphold polygamy, whereas our society defends monogamy. A desert society upholds the rule "Don't waste water," but in a community where water is plentiful no such rule exists. However, this is not really conventional relativism, since the rule is not made valid by the community's choosing it but by the actual situation. In the first case, the situation is an imbalance in the ratio of women to men; in the second case, the situation is environmental factors, concerning the availability of water. . . .

The worry is that utilitarianism becomes so plastic as to be guilty of becoming a justification for our intuitions. Asked why we support justice . . . it seems too easy to respond, "Well, this principle will likely contribute to the greater utility in the long run." The utilitarian may sometimes become self-serving in such rationalizations. Nevertheless, there may be truth in such a defense.

Notes

1. Richard Brandt, "Towards a Credible Form of Utilitarianism," in *Morality and the Language of Conduct*, ed. H. Castaneda and G. Naknikian (Detroit: Wayne State University Press, 1963), pp. 109–110.
2. Bernard Williams, "A Critique of Utilitarianism," in *Utilitarianism: For and Against*, ed. J. C. C. Smart and Bernard Williams (Cambridge, UK: Cambridge University Press, 1973), p. 98ff.

Study Questions

1. Explain the difference between act utilitarianism and rule utilitarianism.
2. What is the justice objection to utilitarianism?
3. What is the integrity objection to utilitarianism?
4. Does utilitarianism imply that under certain circumstances a physician may be morally justified in killing one patient to save the lives of five others?

CHAPTER 16

The Nature of Virtue

Aristotle

Aristotle (384–322 B.C.E.), a student of Plato, had an enormous impact on the development of Western thought. He grounds morality in human nature, viewing the good as the fulfillment of the human potential to live well. To live well is to live in accordance with virtue. But how does one acquire virtue? Aristotle's answer is that we acquire it by habit; one becomes good by doing good. Repeated acts of justice and self-control result in a just, self-controlled person who not only performs just and self-controlled actions but does so from a fixed character. The virtuous act is a mean between two extremes, which are vices; for example, courage is the mean between rashness and cowardice.

Every art and every inquiry, and similarly every action and pursuit, is thought to aim at some good; and for this reason the good has rightly been declared to be that at which all things aim. . . .

If, then, there is some end of the things we do, which we desire for its own sake (everything else being desired for the sake of this), . . . clearly this must be . . . the chief good. . . .

Now such a thing happiness, above all else, is held to be; for this we choose always for itself and never for the sake of something else. . . .

Presumably, however, to say that happiness is the chief good seems a platitude, and a clearer account of what it is is still desired. This might perhaps be given, if we could first ascertain the function of man. For just as for a flute player, a sculptor, or any artist, and, in general, for all things that have a function or activity, the good and the "well" is thought to reside in the function, so would it seem to be for

From Aristotle, *Nicomachean Ethics*, revised edition, edited and translated by David Ross. Copyright © 1998. Reprinted by permission of Oxford University Press.

man, if he has a function. Have the carpenter, then, and the tanner certain functions or activities, and has man none? Is he born without a function? Or as eye, hand, foot, and in general each of the parts evidently has a function, may one lay it down that man similarly has a function apart from all these? What then can this be? Life seems to belong even to plants, but we are seeking what is peculiar to man. Let us exclude, therefore, the life of nutrition and growth. Next there would be a life of perception, but *it* also seems to be shared even by the horse, the ox, and every animal. There remains, then, an active life of the element that has a rational principle. . . . Now if the function of man is an activity of soul which follows or implies a rational principle, and if . . . any action is well performed when it is performed in accordance with the appropriate excellence . . . human good turns out to be activity of soul exhibiting excellence. . . .

But we must add "in a complete life." For one swallow does not make a summer, nor does one day; and so too one day, or a short time, does not make a man blessed and happy. . . .

Virtue, then, being of two kinds, intellectual and moral, intellectual virtue in the main owes both its birth and its growth to teaching (for which reason it requires experience and time), while moral virtue comes about as a result of habit. . . . From this it is also plain that none of the moral virtues arises in us by nature; for nothing that exists by nature can form a habit contrary to its nature. For instance, the stone which by nature moves downwards cannot be habituated to move upwards, not even if one tries to train it by throwing it up ten thousand times; nor can fire be habituated to move downwards, nor can anything else that by nature behaves in one way be trained to behave in another. Neither by nature, then, nor contrary to nature do the virtues arise in us; rather we are adapted by nature to receive them, and are made perfect by habit.

Again, of all the things that come to us by nature we first acquire the potentiality and later exhibit the activity (this is plain in the case of the senses; for it was not by often seeing or often hearing that we got these senses, but on the contrary we had them before we used them, and did not come to have them by using them); but the virtues we get by first exercising them, as also happens in the case of the arts as well. For the things we have to learn before we can do them, we learn by doing them, e.g., men become builders by building and lyre players by playing the lyre; so too we become just by doing just acts, temperate by doing temperate acts, brave by doing brave acts. . . .

It makes no small difference, then, whether we form habits of one kind or of another from our very youth; it makes a very great difference, or rather *all* the difference.

Since, then, the present inquiry does not aim at theoretical knowledge like the others (for we are inquiring not in order to know what virtue is, but in order to become good, since otherwise our inquiry would have been of no use), we must examine the nature of actions, namely, how we ought to do them; for these determine also the nature of the states of character that are produced, as we have said. . . .

First, then, let us consider this, that it is the nature of such things to be destroyed by defect and excess, as we see in the case of strength and of health (for to gain light on things imperceptible we must use the evidence of sensible things); exercise either excessive or defective destroys the strength, and similarly drink or food which is above or below a certain amount destroys the health, while that which is proportionate both produces and increases and preserves it. So too is it, then, in the case of temperance and courage and the other virtues. For the man who flies from and fears everything and does not stand his ground against anything becomes a coward, and the man who fears nothing at all but goes to meet every danger becomes rash; and similarly the man who indulges in every pleasure and abstains from none becomes self-indulgent, while the man who shuns every pleasure, as boors do, becomes in a way insensible; temperance and courage, then, are destroyed by excess and defect, and preserved by the mean.

But not only are the sources and causes of their origination and growth the same as those of their destruction, but also the sphere of their actualization will be the same; for this is also true of the things which are more evident to sense, e.g., of strength; it is produced by taking much food and undergoing much exertion, and it is the strong man that will be most able to do these things. So too is it with the virtues; by abstaining from pleasures we become temperate, and it is when we have become so that we are most able to abstain from them; and similarly too in the case of courage; for by being habituated to despise things that are fearful and to stand our ground against them we become brave, and it is when we have become so that we shall be most able to stand our ground against them. . . .

The question might be asked what we mean by saying that we must become just by doing just acts, and temperate by doing temperate acts; for if men do just and temperate acts, they are already just and temperate, exactly as if they do what is in accordance with the laws of grammar and of music, they are grammarians and musicians.

Or is this not true even of the arts? It is possible to do something that is in accordance with the laws of grammar, either by chance or under the guidance of another. A man will be a grammarian, then, only when he has both said something grammatical and said it grammatically; and this means doing it in accordance with the grammatical knowledge in himself.

Again, the case of the arts and that of the virtues are not similar; for the products of the arts have their goodness in themselves, so that it is enough that they should have a certain character, but if the acts that are in accordance with the virtues have themselves a certain character it does not follow that they are done justly or temperately. The agent also must be in a certain condition when he does them; in the first place he must have knowledge, secondly he must choose the acts, and choose them for their own sakes, and thirdly his action must proceed from a firm and unchangeable character. These are not reckoned in as conditions of the possession of the arts, except the bare knowledge, but as a condition of the possession of the virtues knowledge has little or no weight, while the other conditions count not for a little but for everything, i.e., the very conditions which result from often doing just and temperate acts.

Actions, then, are called just and temperate when they are such as the just or the temperate man would do; but it is not the man who does these that is just and temperate, but the man who also does them *as* just and temperate men do them. It is well said, then, that it is by doing just acts that the just man is produced, and by doing temperate acts the temperate man; without doing these no one would have even a prospect of becoming good.

But most people do not do these, but take refuge in theory and think they are being philosophers and will become good in this way, behaving somewhat like patients who listen attentively to their doctors, but do none of the things they are ordered to do. As the latter will not be made well in body by such a course of treatment, the former will not be made well in soul by such a course of philosophy. . . .

[E]very virtue or excellence both brings into good condition the thing of which it is the excellence and makes the work of that thing be done well; e.g., the excellence of the eye makes both the eye and its work good; for it is by the excellence of the eye that we see well. Similarly the excellence of the horse makes a horse both good in itself and good at running and at carrying its rider and at awaiting the attack of the enemy. Therefore, if this is true in every case, the virtue of man also will be the state of character which makes a man good and which makes him do his own work well.

How this is to happen we have stated already, but it will be made plain also by the following consideration of the specific nature of virtue. In everything that is continuous and divisible it is possible to take more, less, or an equal amount, and that either in terms of the thing itself or relatively to us; and the equal is an intermediate between excess and defect. By the intermediate in the object I mean that which is equidistant from each of the extremes, which is one and the same for all men; by the intermediate relatively to us that which is neither too much nor too little—and this is not one, nor the same for all. For instance, if ten is many and two is few, six is the intermediate, taken in terms of the object; for it exceeds and is exceeded by an equal amount; this is intermediate according to arithmetical proportion. But the intermediate relatively to us is not to be taken so; if ten pounds are too much for a particular person to eat and two too little, it does not follow that the trainer will order six pounds; for this also is perhaps too much for the person who is to take it, or too little— too little for Milo, too much for the beginner in athletic exercises. The same is true of running and wrestling. Thus a master of any art avoids excess and defect, but seeks the intermediate and chooses this—the intermediate not in the object but relatively to us.

If it is thus, then, that every art does its work well—by looking to the intermediate and judging its works by this standard (so that we often say of good works of art that it is not possible either to take away or to add anything, implying that excess and defect destroy the goodness of works of art, while the mean preserves it; and good artists, as we say, look to this in their work), and if, further, virtue is more exact and better than any art, as nature also is, then virtue must have the quality of aiming at the intermediate. I mean moral virtue; for it is this that is concerned with passions and actions, and in these there is excess, defect, and the intermediate. For instance, both fear and confidence and appetite and anger and pity and in general pleasure and pain may be felt both too much and too little, and in both cases not well; but to feel them at the right times, with reference to the right objects, towards the right people, with the right motive, and in the right way, is what is both intermediate and best, and this is characteristic of virtue. Similarly with regard to actions also there is excess, defect, and the intermediate. Now virtue is concerned with passions and actions, in which excess is a form of failure, and so is defect, while the intermediate is praised and is a form of success; and being praised and being successful are both characteristics of virtue. Therefore virtue is a kind of mean, since, as we have seen, it aims at what is intermediate. . . .

But not every action nor every passion admits of a mean; for some have names that already imply badness, e.g., spite, shamelessness, envy, and in the case of actions adultery, theft, murder; for all of these and suchlike things imply by their names that they are themselves bad, and not the excesses or deficiencies of them. It is not possible, then, ever to be right with regard to them; one must always be wrong. Nor does goodness or badness with regard to such things depend on committing adultery with the right woman, at the right time, and in the right way, but simply to do any of them is to go wrong. . . .

The moral virtue is a mean, then, and in what sense it is so, and that it is a mean between two vices, the one involving excess, the other deficiency, and that it is such because its character is to aim at what is intermediate in passions and in actions, has been sufficiently stated. Hence also it is no easy task to be good. For in everything it is no easy task to find the middle, e.g., to find the middle of a circle is not for everyone but for him who knows; so, too, anyone can get angry—that is easy—or give or spend money; but to do this to the right person, to the right extent, at the right time, with the right motive, and in the right way, *that* is not for everyone, nor is it easy; wherefore goodness is both rare and laudable and noble. . . .

But we must consider the things towards which we ourselves also are easily carried away; for some of us tend to one thing, some to another; and this will be recognizable from the pleasure and the pain we feel. We must drag ourselves away to the contrary extreme; for we shall get into the intermediate state by drawing well away from error. . . .

So much, then, is plain, that the intermediate state is in all things to be praised, but that we must incline sometimes towards the excess, sometimes towards the deficiency; for so shall we most easily hit the mean and what is right.

Study Questions

1. According to Aristotle, what is the function of a human being?
2. How does moral virtue differ from intellectual virtue?
3. How is moral virtue acquired?
4. What is Aristotle's doctrine of the mean?

CHAPTER 17

Virtue Ethics

Bernard Mayo

Bernard Mayo (1920–2000) held the Chair of Moral Philosophy at the
University of St. Andrews in Scotland. In the next selection he explains
the difference between an ethical theory, like Aristotle's, that focuses
on the development of a person's character and an ethical theory, like
Kant's or Mill's, that concentrates on the formulation of rules for right
action.

If we wish to inquire about Aristotle's moral views, it is no use looking for a set of principles. Of course we can find *some* principles to
which he must have subscribed—for instance, that one ought not
to commit adultery. But what we find much more prominently is a set
of character traits, a list of certain types of person—the courageous
. . . [person] . . . , the boaster, the lavish spender, and so on. The basic
moral question, for Aristotle, is not, What shall I do? but, What shall
I be? . . .

When we speak of a moral quality such as courage, and say that a
certain action was courageous, we are not merely saying something
about the action. We are referring, not so much to what is done, as
to the kind of person by whom we take it to have been done. We con-
nect, by means of imputed motives and intentions, with the character of the agent as courageous. This explains, incidentally, why both
Kantians and Utilitarians encounter, in their different ways, such difficulties in dealing with motives, which their principles, on the face
of it, have no room for. A Utilitarian, for example, can only praise a
courageous action in some such way as this: the action is of a sort such

From Bernard Mayo, *Ethics and the Moral Life*. Copyright © 1958. Reprinted by permission
of Palgrave Macmillan Ltd.

as a person of courage is likely to perform, and courage is a quality of character the cultivation of which is likely to increase rather than diminish the sum total of human happiness. But Aristotelians have no need of such circumlocution. For them a courageous action just is one which proceeds from and manifests a certain type of character, and is praised because such a character trait is good, or better than others, or is a virtue. An evaluative criterion is sufficient: there is no need to look for an imperative criterion as well, or rather instead, according to which it is not the character which is good, but the cultivation of the character which is right. . . .

No doubt the fundamental moral question is just "What ought I to do?" And according to the philosophy of moral principles, the answer (which must be an imperative "Do this") must be derived from a conjunction of premises consisting (in the simplest case) firstly of a rule, or universal imperative, enjoining (or forbidding) all actions of a certain type in situations of a certain type, and, secondly, a statement to the effect that this is a situation of that type, falling under the rule. In practice the emphasis may be on supplying only one of these premises, the other being assumed or taken for granted: one may answer the question "What ought I do?" either by quoting a rule which I am to adopt, or by showing that my case is legislated for by a rule which I do adopt. . . .

Now, according to the philosophy of moral character, there is another way of answering the fundamental question "What ought I to do?" Instead of quoting a rule, we quote a quality of character, a virtue: we say "Be brave," or "Be patient" or "Be lenient." . . . And now the question "What ought I to do?" turns into the question "What ought I to be?" . . . And here the ethics of character gains a practical simplicity which offsets the greater logical simplicity of the ethics of principles. We do not have to give a list of characteristics or virtues, as we might list a set of principles. We can give a unity to our answer.

Of course we can in theory give a unity to our principles: this is implied by speaking of a *set* of principles. But if such a set is to be a system and not merely aggregate, the unity we are looking for is a logical one, namely, the possibility that some principles are deductible from others, and ultimately from one. But the attempt to construct a deductive moral system is notoriously difficult, and in any case illfounded. Why should we expect that all rules of conduct should be ultimately reducible to a few?

But when we are asked "What shall I be?" we can readily give a unity to our answer, though not a logical unity. It is the unity of character.

A person's character is not merely a list of dispositions; it has the organic unity of something that is more than the sum of its parts. And we can say, in answer to our morally perplexed questioner, not only "Be this" and "Be that," but also "Be like So-and-So"—where So-and-So is either an ideal type of character, or else an actual person taken as representative of the ideal, as exemplar. . . . Examples of . . . the exemplar are Socrates, Christ, [the] Buddha, St. Francis, the heroes of epic writers and of novelists. Indeed the idea of the Hero, as well as the idea of the Saint, are very much the expression of this attitude to morality. Heroes and saints are not merely people who did things. They are people whom we are expected, and expect ourselves, to imitate. And imitating them means not merely doing what they did; it means being like them. Their status is not in the least like that of legislators whose laws we admire; for the character of a legislator is irrelevant to our judgment about his legislation. The heroes and saints did not merely give us principles to live by (though some of them did that as well): they gave us examples to follow.

Study Questions

1. When you make a moral judgment, which question should you ask yourself: "What should I do?" or "What sort of person should I be?"
2. Should moral decisions always be based on rules?
3. How is a person's character revealed?
4. Do exemplars play a significant role in our moral reasoning?

CHAPTER 18

The Ethics of Care

Virginia Held

Virginia Held is Professor Emerita of Philosophy at Hunter College and the Graduate Center of the City University of New York. In the following selection she develops what she terms "the ethics of care," which some philosophers have viewed as one form of virtue ethics. She emphasizes, however, that while the two are in some ways similar, virtue ethics focuses on the character of individuals, whereas the ethics of care is concerned especially with fostering connectedness among people.

I

The ethics of care is only a few decades old. Some theorists do not like the term "care" to designate this approach to moral issues and have tried substituting "the ethic of love," or "relational ethics," but the discourse keeps returning to "care" as the so far more satisfactory of the terms considered, though dissatisfactions with it remain. The concept of care has the advantage of not losing sight of the work involved in caring for people and of not lending itself to the interpretation of morality as ideal but impractical to which advocates of the ethics of care often object. . . ,

I think one can discern among various versions of the ethics of care a number of major features.

First, the central focus of the ethics of care is on the compelling moral salience of attending to and meeting the needs of the particular others for whom we take responsibility. Caring for one's child, for instance, may well and defensibly be at the forefront of a person's

---

moral concerns. The ethics of care recognizes that human beings are dependent for many years of their lives, that the moral claims of those dependent on us for the care they need is pressing, and that there are highly important moral aspects in developing the relations of caring that enable human beings to live and progress. All persons need care for at least their early years. Prospects for human progress and flourishing hinge fundamentally on the care that those needing it receive, and the ethics of care stresses the moral force of the responsibility to respond to the needs of the dependent. Many persons will become ill and dependent for some periods of their later lives, including in frail old age, and some who are permanently disabled will need care the whole of their lives. Moralities built on the image of the independent, autonomous, rational individual largely overlook the reality of human dependence and the morality for which it calls. The ethics of care attends to this central concern of human life and delineates the moral values involved. . . .

Second, in the epistemological process of trying to understand what morality would recommend and what it would be morally best for us to do and to be, the ethics of care values emotion rather than rejects it. Not all emotion is valued, of course, but in contrast with the dominant rationalist approaches, such emotions as sympathy, empathy, sensitivity, and responsiveness are seen as the kind of moral emotions that need to be cultivated not only to help in the implementation of the dictates of reason but to better ascertain what morality recommends. Even anger may be a component of the moral indignation that should be felt when people are treated unjustly or inhumanely, and it may contribute to (rather than interfere with) an appropriate interpretation of the moral wrong. This is not to say that raw emotion can be a guide to morality; feelings need to be reflected on and educated. But from the care perspective, moral inquiries that rely entirely on reason and rationalistic deductions or calculations are seen as deficient.

The emotions that are typically considered and rejected in rationalistic moral theories are the egoistic feelings that undermine universal moral norms, the favoritism that interferes with impartiality, and the aggressive and vengeful impulses for which morality is to provide restraints. The ethics of care, in contrast, typically appreciates the emotions and relational capabilities that enable morally concerned persons in actual interpersonal contexts to understand what would be best. Since even the helpful emotions can often become misguided or worse—as when excessive empathy with others leads to a wrongful degree of self-denial or when benevolent concern crosses over into controlling domination—we need an *ethics* of care, not just care itself. The various aspects and expressions of care and caring relations need to be subjected to moral scrutiny and *evaluated*, not just observed and described.

Third, the ethics of care rejects the view of the dominant moral theories that the more abstract the reasoning about a moral problem the better because the more likely to avoid bias and arbitrariness, the more nearly to achieve impartiality. The ethics of care respects rather than removes itself from the claims of particular others with whom we share actual relationships. It calls into question the universalistic and abstract rules of the dominant theories. When the latter consider such actual relations as between a parent and child, if they say anything about them at all, they may see them as permitted and cultivating them a preference that a person may have. Or they may recognize a universal obligation for all parents to care for their children. But they do not permit actual relations ever to take priority over the requirements of impartiality. . . .

The ethics of care may seek to limit the applicability of universal rules to certain domains where they are more appropriate, like the domain of law, and resist their extension to other domains. Such rules may simply be inappropriate in, for instance, the contexts of family and friendship, yet relations in these domains should certainly be *evaluated*, not merely described, hence morality should not be limited to abstract rules. We should be able to give moral guidance concerning actual relations that are trusting, considerate, and caring and concerning those that are not.

Dominant moral theories tend to interpret moral problems as if they were conflicts between egoistic individual interests on the one hand, and universal moral principles on the other. The extremes of "selfish individual" and "humanity" are recognized, but what lies between these is often overlooked. The ethics of care, in contrast, focuses especially on the area between these extremes. Those who conscientiously care for others are not seeking primarily to further their own *individual* interests; their interests are intertwined with the persons they care for. Neither are they acting for the sake of *all others* or *humanity in general*; they seek instead to preserve or promote an actual human relation between themselves and *particular others*. Persons in caring relations are acting for self-and-other together. Their characteristic stance is neither egoistic nor altruistic; these are the options in a conflictual situation, but the well-being of a caring relation involves the cooperative well-being of those in the relation and the well-being of the relation itself. . . .

II

What *is* care? What do we mean by the term "care"? Can we define it in anything like a precise way? There is not yet anything close to agreement among those writing on care on what exactly we should take the meaning of this term to be, but there have been many suggestions, tacit and occasionally explicit.

For over two decades, the concept of care as it figures in the ethics of care has been assumed, explored, elaborated, and employed in the development of theory. But definitions have often been imprecise, or trying to arrive at them has simply been postponed (as in my own case), in the growing discourse. Perhaps this is entirely appropriate for new explorations, but the time may have come to seek greater clarity. Some of those writing on care have attempted to be precise, with mixed results, whereas others have proceeded with the tacit understanding that of course to a considerable extent we know what we are talking about when we speak of taking care of a child or providing care for the ill. But care has many forms, and as the ethics of care evolves, so should our understanding of what care is.

The last words I spoke to my older brother after a brief visit and with special feeling were: "take care." He had not been taking good care of himself, and I hoped he would do better; not many days later he died, of problems quite possibly unrelated to those to which I had been referring. "Take care" was not an expression he and I grew up with. I acquired it over the years in my life in New York City. It may be illuminating to begin thinking about the meaning of "care" with an examination of this expression.

We often say "take care" as routinely as "goodbye" or some abbreviation and with as little emotion. But even then it does convey some sense of connectedness. More often, when said with some feeling, it means something like "take care of yourself because I care about you." Sometimes we say it, especially to children or to someone embarking on a trip or an endeavor, meaning "I care what happens to you, so please don't do anything dangerous or foolish." Or, if we know the danger is inevitable and inescapable, it may be more like a wish that the elements will let the person take care so the worst can be evaded. And sometimes we mean it as a plea: Be careful not to harm yourself or others because our connection will make us feel with and for you. We may be harmed ourselves or partly responsible, or if you do something you will regret we will share that regret.

One way or another, this expression (like many others) illustrates human relatedness and the daily reaffirmations of connection. It is the relatedness of human beings, built and rebuilt, that the ethics of care is being developed to try to understand, evaluate, and guide. The expression has more to do with the feelings and awareness of the persons expressing and the persons receiving such expressions than with the actual tasks and work of "taking care" of a person who is dependent on us, or in need of care, but such attitudes and shared awareness seem at least one important component of care.

A seemingly easy distinction to make is between care as the activity of taking care of someone and the mere "caring about" of how we feel about certain issues. Actually "caring for" a small child or a person who is ill is quite different from merely "caring for" something (or not) in the sense of liking it or not, as in "I don't care for that kind of music." But these distinctions may not be as clear as they appear, since when we take care of a child, for instance, we usually also care about him or her, and although we could take care of a child we do not like, the caring will usually be better care if we care for the child in both senses. If we really do care about world hunger, we will probably be doing something about it, such as at least giving money to alleviate it or to change the conditions that bring it about, and thus establishing some connection between ourselves and the hungry we say we care about. And if we really do care about global climate change and the harm it will bring to future generations, we imagine a connection between ourselves and those future people who will judge our irresponsibility, and we change our consumption practices or political activities to decrease the likely harm. . . .

My own view, then, is that care is both a practice and a value. As a practice, it shows us how to respond to needs and why we should. It builds trust and mutual concern and connectedness between persons. It is not a series of individual actions, but a practice that develops, along with its appropriate attitudes. It has attributes and standards that can be described, but more important that can be recommended and that should be continually improved as adequate care comes closer to being good care. Practices of care should express the caring relations that bring persons together, and they should do so in ways that are progressively more morally satisfactory. Caring practices should gradually transform children and others into human beings who are increasingly morally admirable. . . .

In addition to being a practice, care is also a value. Caring persons and caring attitudes should be valued, and we can organize many evaluations of how persons are interrelated around a constellation of moral considerations associated with care or its absence. For instance, we can ask of a relation whether it is trusting and mutually considerate or hostile and vindictive. We can ask if persons are attentive and responsive to each other's needs or indifferent and self-absorbed. Care is not the same as benevolence, in my view, since it is more the characterization of a social relation than the description of an individual disposition, and social relations are not reducible to individual states. Caring relations ought to be cultivated, between persons in their personal lives and between the members of caring societies. Such relations are often reciprocal over time if not at given times. The values of caring are especially exemplified in caring relations, rather than in persons as individuals.

Study Questions

1. According to Held, what is "the ethics of care"?
2. What does Held mean by her claim that care is both a practice and a value?
3. Is the ethics of care a form of virtue ethics?
4. Does analyzing a moral problem from the perspective of the ethics of care sometimes yield a different result than that obtained by using either a Kantian or utilitarian standard?

CHAPTER 19

The Social Contract

Thomas Hobbes

Thomas Hobbes (1588–1679) was an English philosopher who played a crucial role in the history of social thought. He developed a moral and political theory that views justice and other ethical ideals as resting on an implied agreement among individuals to relinquish the right to do whatever they please, thus achieving security for all.

Of the Natural Condition of Mankind as Concerning Their Felicity, and Misery

Nature hath made men so equal, in the faculties of body, and mind; as that though there be found one man sometimes manifestly stronger in body, or of quicker mind than another; yet when all is reckoned together, the difference between man, and man, is not so considerable, as that one man can thereupon claim to himself any benefit, to which another may not pretend, as well as he. For as to the strength of body, the weakest has strength enough to kill the strongest, either by secret machination, or by confederacy with others, that are in the same danger as himself.

And as to the faculties of the mind, (setting aside the arts grounded upon words, and especially that skill of proceeding upon general, and infallible rules, called science; which very few have, and but in few things; as being not a native faculty, born with us; nor attained, (as prudence,) while we look after someone else,) I find yet a greater equality amongst men, than that of strength. For prudence, is but experience; which equal time, equally bestows on all men, in those

From Thomas Hobbes, *Leviathan* (1651).

things they equally apply themselves unto. That which may perhaps make such equality incredible, is but a vain conceit of one's own wisdom, which almost all men think they have in a greater degree, than the vulgar; that is, than all men but themselves, and a few others, whom by fame, or for concurring with themselves, they approve. For such is the nature of men, that howsoever they may acknowledge many others to be more witty, or more eloquent, or more learned; yet they will hardly believe there be many so wise as themselves: For they see their own wit at hand, and other men's at a distance. But this proveth rather that men are in that point equal, than unequal. For there is not ordinarily a greater sign of the equal distribution of any thing, than that every man is contented with his share.

From this equality of ability, ariseth equality of hope in the attaining of our ends. And therefore if any two men desire the same thing, which nevertheless they cannot both enjoy, they become enemies; and in the way to their end, (which is principally their own conservation, and sometimes their delectation only,) endeavour to destroy, or subdue one another. And from hence it comes to pass, that where an invader hath no more to fear, than another man's single power; if one plant, sow, build, or possess a convenient seat, others may probably be expected to come prepared with forces united, to dispossess, and deprive him, not only of the fruit of his labour, but also of his life, or liberty. And the invader again is in the like danger of another.

And from this diffidence of one another, there is no way for any man to secure himself, so reasonable, as anticipation; that is, by force, or wiles, to master the persons of all men he can, so long, till he see no other power great enough to endanger him: and this is no more than his own conservation requireth, and is generally allowed. Also because there be some, that taking pleasure in contemplating their own power in the acts of conquest, which they pursue farther than their security requires; if others, that otherwise would be glad to be at ease within modest bounds, should not by invasion increase their power, they would not be able, long time, by standing only on their defence, to subsist. And by consequence, such augmentation of dominion over men, being necessary to a man's conservation, it ought to be allowed him.

Again, men have no pleasure, (but on the contrary a great deal of grief) in keeping company, where there is no power able to over-awe them all. For every man looketh that his companion should value him, at the same rate he sets upon himself: and upon all signs of contempt, or undervaluing, naturally endeavours, as far as he dares (which amongst them that have no common power to keep them in quiet, is far enough to make them destroy each other,) to extort a greater value from his contemners, by damage; and from others, by the example.

So that in the nature of man, we find three principal causes of quarrel. First, competition; secondly, diffidence; thirdly, glory.

The first, maketh man invade for gain; the second, for safety; and the third, for reputation. The first use violence, to make themselves masters of other men's persons, wives, children, and cattle; the second, to defend them; the third for trifles, as a word, a smile, a different opinion, and any other sign of undervalue, either direct in their persons, or by reflection in their kindred, their friends, their nation, their profession, or their name.

Hereby it is manifest, that during the time men live without a common power to keep them all in awe, they are in that condition which is called war; and such a war, as is of every man, against every man. For WAR, consisteth not in battle only, or the act of fighting; but in a tract of time, wherein the will to contend by battle is sufficiently known: and therefore the notion of *time*, is to be considered in the nature of war; as it is in the nature of weather. For as the nature of foul weather, lieth not in a shower or two of rain; but in an inclination thereto of many days together: so the nature of war, consisteth not in actual fighting; but in the known disposition thereto, during all the time there is no assurance to the contrary. All other time is PEACE.

Whatsoever therefore is consequent to a time of war, where every man is enemy to every man; the same is consequent to the time, wherein men live without other security, than what their own strength, and their own invention shall furnish them withal. In such condition, there is no place for industry; because the fruit thereof is uncertain: and consequently no culture of the earth; no navigation, nor use of the commodities that may be imported by sea; no commodious building; no instruments of moving, and removing such things as require much force; no knowledge of the face of the earth; no account of time; no arts; no letters; no society; and which is worst of all, continual fear, and danger of violent death; and the life of man, solitary, poor, nasty, brutish, and short.

It may seem strange to some man, that has not well weighed these things; that nature should thus dissociate, and render men apt to invade, and destroy one another: and he may therefore, not trusting to this inference, made from the passions, desire perhaps to have the same confirmed by experience. Let him therefore consider with himself, when taking a journey, he arms himself, and seeks to go well accompanied; when going to sleep, he locks his doors; when even in his house he locks his chests; and this when he knows there be laws, and public officers, armed, to revenge all injuries shall be done him; what opinion he has of his fellow subjects, when he rides armed; of his fellow citizens, when he locks his doors; and of his children, and servants, when he locks his chests. Does he not there as much accuse mankind by his actions, as I do by my words? But neither of us accuse man's nature in it. The desires, and other passions of man, are in themselves no sin. No more are the actions, that proceed from those passions, till they know a law that forbids them: which till laws be made they cannot know: nor can any law be made, till they have agreed upon the person that shall make it.

It may peradventure be thought, there was never such a time, nor condition of war as this; and I believe it was never generally so, over all the world: but there are many places, where they live so now. For the savage people in many places of *America*, except the government of small families, the concord whereof dependeth on natural lust, have no government at all: and live at this day in that brutish manner, as I said before. Howsoever, it may be perceived what manner of life there would be, where there were no common power to fear; by the manner of life, which men that have formerly lived under a peacefull government, use to degenerate into, in a civil war.

But though there had never been any time, wherein particular men were in a condition of war one against another; yet in all times, kings, and persons of sovereign authority, because of their independency, are in continual jealousies, and in the state and posture of gladiators; having their weapons pointing, and their eyes fixed on one another; that is, their forts, garrisons, and guns upon the frontiers of their kingdoms; and continual spies upon their neighbours; which is a posture of war. But because they uphold thereby; the industry of their subjects; there does not follow from it, that misery, which accompanies the liberty of particular men.

To this war of every man against every man, this also is consequent; that nothing can be unjust. The notions of right and wrong, justice and injustice have there no place. Where there is no common power, there is no law: where no law, no injustice. Force, and fraud, are in war the two cardinal virtues. Justice, and injustice are none of the faculties neither of the body, nor mind. If they were, they might be in a man that were alone in the world, as well as his senses, and passions. They are qualities, that relate to men in society, not in solitude. It is consequent also to the same condition, that there be no propriety, no dominion, no *mine* and *thine* distinct; but only that to be every man's, that he can get; and for so long, as he can keep it. And thus much for the ill condition which many by mere nature is actually placed in; though with a possibility to come out of it, consisting partly in the passions, partly in his reason.

The passions that incline men to peace, are fear of death; desire of such things as are necessary to commodious living; and a hope by their industry to obtain them. And reason suggesteth convenient articles of peace, upon which men may be drawn to agreement. These articles, are they, which otherwise are called the Laws of Nature: whereof I shall speak more particularly, in the two following chapters.

Of the First and Second Natural Laws, and of Contracts

The RIGHT OF NATURE, which writers commonly call *jus naturale*, is the liberty each man hath, to use his own power, as he will himself, for the preservation of his own nature; that is to say, of his own life; and consequently, of doing any thing, which in his own judgment, and reason, he shall conceive to be the aptest means thereunto.

By LIBERTY, is understood, according to the proper signification of the word, the absence of external impediments: which impediments, may oft take away part of a man's power to do what he would; but cannot hinder him from using the power left him, according as his judgment, and reason shall dictate to him.

A LAW OF NATURE, (*lex naturalis,*) is a precept, or general rule, found out by reason, by which a man is forbidden to do that, which is destructive of his life, or taketh away the means of preserving the same; and to omit that, by which he thinketh it may be best preserved. For though they that speak of this subject, use to confound *jus*, and *lex*, *right* and *law*; yet they ought to be distinguished; because RIGHT, consisteth in liberty to do, or to forbear; whereas LAW, determineth, and bindeth to one of them: so that law, and right, differ as much, as obligation, and liberty, which in one and the same matter are inconsistent.

And because the condition of man, (as hath been declared in the precedent chapter) is a condition of war of every one against every one; in which case every one is governed by his own reason; and there is nothing he can make use of, that may not be a help unto him, in preserving his life against his enemies, it followeth, that in such a condition, every man has a right to every thing: even to one another's body. And therefore, as long as this natural right of every man to every thing endureth, there can be no security to any man, (how strong or wise soever he be,) of living out the time, which nature ordinarily alloweth men to live. And consequently it is a precept, or general rule of reason, *that every man, ought to endeavour peace, as far as he has hope of obtaining it; and when he cannot obtain it, that he may seek, and use, all helps, and advantages of war.* The first branch of which rule, containeth the first, and fundamental law of nature; which is, *to seek peace, and follow it.* The second, the sum of the right of nature; which is, *by all means we can, to defend ourselves.*

From this fundamental law of nature, by which men are commanded to endeavor peace, is derived this second law; *that a man be willing, when others are so too, as farforth, as for peace, and defence of himself he shall think it necessary, to lay down this right to all things; and be contented with so much liberty against other men, as he would allow other men against himself.* For as long as every man holdeth this right, of doing any thing he liketh; so long are all men in the condition of war. But if other men will not lay down their right, as well as he; then there is no reason for any one, to divest himself of his: for that were to expose himself to prey, (which no man is bound to) rather than to dispose himself to peace. This is that law of the Gospel, *whatsoever you require that others should do for you, that do ye to them.* . . .

Of Other Laws of Nature

From that law of nature, by which we are obliged to transfer to another, such rights, as being retained, hinder the peace of mankind, there followeth a third; which is this, *that men perform their covenants made*: without which, covenants are in vain, and but empty words; and the right of all men to all things remaining, we are still in the condition of war.

And in this law of nature, consisteth the fountain and original of JUSTICE. For where no covenant hath preceded, there hath no right been transferred, and every man has right to every thing; and consequently, no action can be unjust. But when a covenant is made, then to break it is *unjust*; and the definition of INJUSTICE, is no other than *the not performance of covenant.* And whatsoever is not unjust, is *just.*

But because covenants of mutual trust, where there is fear of not performance on either part, (as hath been said in the former chapter,) are invalid; though the original of justice be the making of covenants; yet injustice actually there can be none, till the cause of such fear be taken away; which while men are in the natural condition of war, cannot be done. Therefore before the names of just, and unjust can have place, there must be some coercive power, to compel men equally to the performance of their covenants, by the terror of some punishment, greater than the benefit they expect by the breach of their convenant; and to make good that propriety, which by mutual contract men acquire, in recompense of the universal right they abandon: and such power there is none before the erection of a commonwealth. And this is also to be gathered out of the ordinary definition of justice in the Schools: for they say, that *justice is the constant will of giving to every man his own.* And therefore where there is no *own*, that is, no propriety, there is no injustice; and where there is no coercive power erected, that is, where there is no commonwealth, there is no propriety; all men having right to all things: therefore where there is no commonwealth, there nothing is unjust. So that the nature of justice, consisteth in keeping of valid covenants: but the validity of covenants begins not but with the constitution of a civil power, sufficient to compel men to keep them: and then it is also that propriety begins. . . .

The fool hath said in his heart, there is no such thing as justice; and sometimes also with his tongue; seriously alleging, that every man's conservation, and contentment, being committed to his own care, there could be no reason, why every man might not do what he thought conduced thereunto: and therefore also to make, or not make: keep, or not keep covenants, was not against reason, when it conduced to one's benefit. He does not therein deny, that there be covenants; and that they are sometimes broken, sometimes kept; and that such breach of them may be called injustice, and the observance of them justice: but he questioneth, whether injustice, taking away the fear of God, (for the same fool hath said in his heart there is no God,) may not sometimes stand with that reason, which dictateth to every man his own good; and particularly then, when it conduceth to such a benefit, as shall put a man in a condition, to neglect not only the dispraise, and reviling, but also the power of other men. . . . This specious reasoning is nevertheless false.

For the question is not of promises mutual, where there is no security of performance on either side; as when there is no civil power erected over the parties promising; for such promises are no covenants: but either where one of the parties has performed already; or where there is a power to make him perform; there is the question whether it be against reason, that is, against the benefit of the other to perform, or not. And I say it is not against reason. For the manifestation whereof, we are to consider; first, that when a man doth a thing, which notwithstanding any thing can be foreseen, and reckoned on, tendeth to his own destruction, howsoever some accident which he could not expect, arriving may turn it to his benefit; yet such events do not make it reasonably or wisely done. Secondly, that in a condition of war, wherein every man to every man, for want of a common power to keep them all in awe, is an enemy, there is no man can hope by his own strength, or wit, to defend himself from destruction, without the help of confederates; where every one expects the same defence by the confederation, that any one else does: and therefore he which declares he thinks it reason to deceive those that help him, can in reason expect no other means of safety, than what can be had from his own single power. He therefore that breaketh his covenant, and consequently declareth that he thinks he may with reason do so, cannot be received into any society, that unite themselves for peace and defence, but by the error of them that receive him; nor when he is received, be retained in it, without seeing the danger of their error; which errors a man cannot reasonably reckon upon as the means of his security: and therefore if he be left, or cast out of society, he perisheth; and if he live in society, it is by the errors of other men, which he could not foresee, nor reckon upon; and consequently against the reason of his preservation; and so, as all men that contribute not to his destruction, forbear him only out of ignorance of what is good for themselves.

Study Questions

1. Without government to enforce laws, would life be, as Hobbes says, "nasty, brutish, and short"?
2. What does Hobbes mean by "the right of nature"?
3. What does he mean by a "law of nature"?
4. Why are we obliged to keep our agreements?

CHAPTER 20

A Theory of Justice

John Rawls

John Rawls (1921–2002) was Professor of Philosophy at Harvard University. He views justice as a social arrangement that ensures that the interests of some are not sacrificed to the arbitrary advantages held by others. Like Hobbes, Rawls defends his view by appealing to an implied agreement among individuals to engage in social cooperation in accord with certain principles. Hobbes and Rawls, however, derive their principles by different chains of reasoning and reach different conclusions.

The Main Idea of the Theory of Justice

. . . [T]he principles of justice . . . are the principles that free and rational persons concerned to further their own interests would accept in an initial position of equality. . . .

[T]he original position of equality corresponds to the state of nature in the traditional theory of the social contract. This original position is not, of course, thought of as an actual historical state of affairs, much less as a primitive condition of culture. It is understood as a purely hypothetical situation. . . . Among the essential features of this situation is that no one knows his place in society, his class position or social status, nor does any one know his fortune in the distribution of natural assets and abilities, his intelligence, strength, and the like. I shall even assume that the parties do not know their conceptions of the good or their special psychological propensities. The principles of justice are chosen behind a veil of ignorance. This ensures that no one is advantaged or disadvantaged in the choice of principles by the outcome of natural chance or the contingency of social circumstances. Since all are similarly situated and no one is able to design principles to favor his particular condition, the principles of justice are the result of a fair agreement or bargain. For given the circumstances of the original position, the symmetry of everyone's relations to each other, this initial situation is fair between individuals as moral persons, that is, as rational beings with their own ends and capable, I shall assume, of a sense of justice. The original position is, one might say, the appropriate initial status quo, and thus the fundamental agreements reached in it are fair. This explains the propriety of the name "justice as fairness": it conveys the idea that the principles of justice are agreed to in an initial situation that is fair. . . .

I shall maintain . . . that the persons in the initial situation would choose two . . . principles: the first requires equality in the assignment of basic rights and duties, while the second holds that social and economic inequalities, for example inequalities of wealth and authority, are just only if they result in compensating benefits for everyone, and in particular for the least advantaged members of society. These principles rule out justifying institutions on the grounds that the hardships of some are offset by a greater good in the aggregate. It may be expedient but it is not just that some should have less in order that others may prosper. But there is no injustice in the greater benefits earned by a few provided that the situation of persons not so fortunate is thereby improved. The intuitive idea is that since everyone's well-being depends upon a scheme of cooperation without which no one could have a satisfactory life, the division of advantages should be such as to draw forth the willing cooperation of everyone taking part in it, including those less well situated. The two principles mentioned seem to be a fair basis on which those better endowed, or more fortunate in their social position, neither of which we can be said to deserve, could expect the willing cooperation of others when some workable scheme is a necessary condition of the welfare of all. Once we decide to look for a conception of justice that prevents the use of the accidents of natural endowment and the contingencies of social circumstance as counters in a quest of political and economic advantage, we are led to these principles. They express the result of leaving aside those aspects of the social world that seem arbitrary from a moral point of view. . . .

The Original Position and Justification

. . . One should not be misled . . . by the somewhat unusual conditions which characterize the original position. The idea here is simply to make vivid to ourselves the restrictions that it seems reasonable to impose on arguments for principles of justice, and therefore on these principles themselves. Thus it seems reasonable and generally acceptable that no one should be advantaged or disadvantaged by natural fortune or social circumstances in the choice of principles. It also seems widely agreed that it should be impossible to tailor principles to the circumstances of one's own case. We should insure further that particular inclinations and aspirations, and persons' conceptions of their good, do not affect the principles adopted. The aim is to rule out those principles that it would be rational to propose for acceptance, however little the chance of success, only if one knew certain things that are irrelevant from the standpoint of justice. For example, if a man knew that he was wealthy, he might find it rational to advance the principle that various taxes for welfare measures be counted unjust; if he knew that he was poor, he would most likely propose the contrary principle. To represent the desired restrictions one imagines a situation in which everyone is deprived of this sort of information. One excludes the knowledge of those contingencies which sets men at odds and allows them to be guided by their prejudices. In this manner the veil of ignorance is arrived at in a natural way. This concept should cause no difficulty if we keep in mind the constraints on arguments that it is meant to express. At any time we can enter the original position, so to speak, simply by following a certain procedure, namely, by arguing for principles of justice in accordance with these restrictions.

It seems reasonable to suppose that the parties in the original position are equal. That is, all have the same rights in the procedure for choosing principles; each can make proposals, submit reasons for their acceptance, and so on. Obviously the purpose of these conditions is to represent equality between human beings as moral persons, as creatures having a conception of their good and capable of a sense of justice. The basis of equality is taken to be similarity in these two respects. Systems of ends are not ranked in value; and each man is presumed to have the requisite ability to understand and to act upon whatever principles are adopted. Together with the veil of ignorance, these conditions define the principles of justice as those which rational persons concerned to advance their interests would

consent to as equals when none are known to be advantaged or disadvantaged by social and natural contingencies. . . .

Two Principles of Justice

I shall now state in a provisional form the two principles of justice
that I believe would be chosen in the original position. . . .

The first statement of the two principles reads as follows.

First: each person is to have an equal right to the most extensive
scheme of equal basic liberties compatible with a similar scheme of
liberties for others.

Second: social and economic inequalities are to be arranged so
that they are both (a) reasonably expected to be to everyone's advantage, and (b) attached to positions and offices open to all. . . .

These principles primarily apply . . . to the basic structure of society and govern the assignment of rights and duties and regulate the
distribution of social and economic advantages. . . . [I]t is essential
to observe that the basic liberties are given by a list of such liberties.
Important among these are political liberty (the right to vote and to
hold public office) and freedom of speech and assembly; liberty of
conscience and freedom of thought; freedom of the person, which
includes freedom from psychological oppression and physical assault
and dismemberment (integrity of the person); the right to hold personal property and freedom from arbitrary arrest and seizure as
defined by the concept of the rule of law. These liberties are to be
equal by the first principle.

The second principle applies . . . to the distribution of income
and wealth and to the design of organizations that make use of differences in authority and responsibility. While the distributions of
wealth and income need not be equal, it must be to everyone's advantage, and at the same time, positions of authority and responsibility
must be accessible to all. One applies the second principle by holding
positions open, and then, subject to this constraint, arranges social
and economic inequalities so that everyone benefits.

These principles are to be arranged in a serial order with the first
principle prior to the second. This ordering means that infringe-
ments of the basic equal liberties protected by the first principle cannot be justified, or compensated for, by greater social and economic
advantages. . . .

[I]n regard to the second principle, the distribution of wealth
and income, and positions of authority and responsibility, are

to be consistent with both the basic liberties and equality of opportunity. . . .

[T]hese principles are a special case of a more general conception of justice that can be expressed as follows.

> All social values—liberty and opportunity, income and wealth, and the social bases of self-respect—are to be distributed equally unless an unequal distribution of any, or all, of these values is to everyone's advantage.

Injustice, then, is simply inequalities that are not to the benefit of all. . . .

The Veil of Ignorance

. . . The notion of the veil of ignorance raises several difficulties. Some may object that the exclusion of nearly all particular information makes it difficult to grasp what is meant by the original position. Thus it may be helpful to observe that one or more persons can at any time enter this position, or perhaps better, simulate the deliberations of this hypothetical situation, simply by reasoning in accordance with the appropriate restrictions. . . .

It may be protested that the condition of the veil of ignorance is irrational. Surely, some may object, principles should be chosen in the light of all the knowledge available. There are various replies to this contention. . . . To begin with, it is clear that since the differences among the parties are unknown to them, and everyone is equally rational and similarly situated, each is convinced by the same arguments. Therefore, we can view the agreement in the original position from the standpoint of one person selected at random. If anyone after due reflection prefers a conception of justice to another, then they all do, and a unanimous agreement can be reached. We can, to make the circumstances more vivid, imagine that the parties are required to communicate with each other through a referee as intermediary, and that he is to announce which alternatives have been suggested and the reasons offered in their support. He forbids the attempt to form coalitions, and he informs the parties when they have come to an understanding. But such a referee is actually superfluous, assuming that the deliberations of the parties must be similar.

Thus there follows the very important consequence that the parties have no basis for bargaining in the usual sense. No one knows his situation in society nor his natural assets, and therefore no one is in a position to tailor principles to his advantage. We might imagine that one of the contractees threatens to hold out unless the others agree to principles favorable to him. But how does he know which principles are especially in his interests? The same holds for the formation of coalitions: if a group were to decide to band together to the disadvantage of the others, they would not know how to favor themselves in the choice of principles. Even if they could get everyone to agree to their proposal, they would have no assurance that it was to their advantage, since they cannot identify themselves either by name or description. . . .

The restrictions on particular information in the original position are, then, of fundamental importance. Without them we would not be able to work out any definite theory of justice at all. We would have to be content with a vague formula stating that justice is what would be agreed to without being able to say much, if anything, about the substance of the agreement itself . . . The veil of ignorance makes possible a unanimous choice of a particular conception of justice. Without these limitations on knowledge the bargaining problem of the original position would be hopelessly complicated.

Study Questions

1. What is "the original position"?
2. What is "the veil of ignorance"?
3. According to Rawls, what are the two principles of justice?
4. Do you agree with Rawls that these two principles would be chosen in the original position?

PART III

Moral Problems

A. Abortion

CHAPTER 21

A Defense of Abortion

Judith Jarvis Thomson

In recent decades philosophers have examined a variety of practical issues involving ethical concerns.

In particular, the morality of abortion has been the focus of much attention. In this selection Judith Jarvis Thomson, Professor Emerita of Philosophy at the Massachusetts Institute of Technology, argues that even if the human fetus is a person, abortion is often morally permissible.

Most opposition to abortion relies on the premise that the fetus is a human being, a person, from the moment of conception. The premise is argued for, but, as I think, not well. Take, for example, the most common argument. We are asked to notice that the development of a human being from conception through birth into childhood is continuous; then it is said that to draw a line, to choose a point in this development and say "before this point the thing is not a person, after this point it is a person" is to make an arbitrary choice, a choice for which in the nature of things no good reason can be given. It is concluded that the fetus is, or anyway that we had better say it is, a person from the moment of conception. But this conclusion does not follow. Similar things might be said about the development of an acorn into an oak tree, and it does not follow that acorns are oak trees, or that we had better say they are. Arguments of this form are somtimes called "slippery slope arguments"—the phrase is perhaps self-explanatory—and it is dismaying that opponents of abortion rely on them so heavily and uncritically.

From *Philosophy & Public Affairs*, Vol. 1. Copyright © 1971. Reprinted by permission of Blackwell Publishing Ltd.

I am inclined to agree, however, that the prospects for "drawing a line" in the development of the fetus look dim. I am inclined to think also that we shall probably have to agree that the fetus has already become a human person well before birth. Indeed, it comes as a surprise when one first learns how early in its life it begins to acquire human characteristics. By the tenth week, for example, it already has a face, arms and legs, fingers and toes; it has internal organs, and brain activity is detectable.[1] On the other hand, I think that the premise is false, that the fetus is not a person from the moment of conception. A newly fertilized ovum, a newly implanted clump of cells, is no more a person than an acorn is an oak tree. But I shall not discuss any of this. For it seems to me to be of great interest to ask what happens if, for the sake of argument, we allow the premise. How, precisely, are we supposed to get from there to the conclusion that abortion is morally impermissible? Opponents of abortion commonly spend most of their time establishing that the fetus is a person, and hardly any time explaining the step from there to the impermissibility of abortion. Perhaps they think the step too simple and obvious to require much comment. Or perhaps instead they are simply being economical in argument. Many of those who defend abortion rely on the premise that the fetus is not a person, but only a bit of tissue that will become a person at birth; and why pay out more arguments than you have to? Whatever the explanation, I suggest that the step they take is neither easy nor obvious, that it calls for closer examination than it is commonly given, and that when we do give it this closer examination we shall feel inclined to reject it.

I propose, then, that we grant that the fetus is a person from the moment of conception. How does the argument go from here? Something like this, I take it. Every person has a right to life. So the fetus has a right to life. No doubt the mother has a right to decide what shall happen in and to her body; everyone would grant that. But surely a person's right to life is stronger and more stringent than the mother's right to decide what happens in and to her body, and so outweighs it. So the fetus may not be killed; an abortion may not be performed.

It sounds plausible. But now let me ask you to imagine this. You wake up in the morning and find yourself back to back in bed with an unconscious violinist. A famous unconscious violinist. He has been found to have a fatal kidney ailment, and the Society of Music Lovers has canvassed all the available medical records and found that you alone have the right blood type to help. They have therefore kidnapped you, and last night the violinist's circulatory system was plugged into yours, so that your kidneys can be used to extract poisons from his blood as well as your own. The director of the hospital now tells you, "Look, we're sorry the Society of Music Lovers did this to you—we would never have permitted it if we had known. But still, they did it, and the violinist now is plugged into you. To unplug you would be to kill him. But never mind, it's only for nine months. By then he will have recovered from his ailment, and can safely be unplugged from you." Is it morally incumbent on you to accede to this situation? No doubt it would be very nice of you if you did, a great kindness. But do you *have* to accede to it? What if it were not nine months, but nine years? Or longer still? What if the director of the hospital says, "Tough luck, I agree, but you've now got to stay in bed, with the violinist plugged into you, for the rest of your life. Because remember this. All persons have a right to life, and violinists are persons. Granted you have a right to decide what happens in and to your body, but a person's right to life outweighs your right to decide what happens in and to your body. So you cannot ever be unplugged from him." I imagine you would regard this as outrageous, which suggests that something really is wrong with that plausible-sounding argument I mentioned a moment ago.

In this case, of course, you were kidnapped; you didn't volunteer for the operation that plugged the violinist into your kidneys. Can those who oppose abortion on the ground I mentioned make an exception for a pregnancy due to rape? Certainly. They can say that persons have a right to life only if they didn't come into existence because of rape; or they can say that all persons have a right to life, but that some have less of a right to life than others, in particular, that those who came into existence because of rape have less. But these statements have a rather unpleasant sound. Surely the question of whether you have a right to life at all, or how much of it you have, shouldn't turn on the question of whether or not you are the product of a rape. And in fact the people who oppose abortion on the ground I mentioned do not make this distinction, and hence do not make an exception in case of rape.

Nor do they make an exception for a case in which the mother has to spend the nine months of her pregnancy in bed. They would agree that would be a great pity, and hard on the mother; but all the same, all persons have a right to life, the fetus is a person, and so on. I suspect, in fact, that they would not make an exception for a case in which, miraculously enough, the pregnancy went on for nine years, or even the rest of the mother's life.

Some won't even make an exception for a case in which continuation of the pregnancy is likely to shorten the mother's life; they regard abortion as impermissible even to save the mother's life. Such cases are nowadays very rare, and many opponents of abortion do not accept this extreme view. All the same, it is a good place to begin: a number of points of interest come out in respect to it.

1. Let us call the view that abortion is impermissible even to save the mother's life "the extreme view." I want to suggest first that it does not issue from the argument I mentioned earlier without the addition of some fairly powerful premises. Suppose a woman has become pregnant, and now learns that she has a cardiac condition such that she will die if she carries the baby to term. What may be done for her? The fetus, being a person, has a right to life, but as the mother is a person too, so has she a right to life. Presumably they have an equal right to life. How is it supposed to come out that an abortion may not be performed? If mother and child have an equal right to life, shouldn't we perhaps flip a coin? Or should we add to the mother's right to life her right to decide what happens in and to her body, which everybody seems to be ready to grant—the sum of her rights now outweighing the fetus' right to life?

The most familiar argument here is the following: We are told that performing the abortion would be directly killing[2] the child, whereas doing nothing would not be killing the mother, but only letting her die. Moreover, in killing the child, one would be killing an innocent person, for the child has committed no crime, and is not aiming at his mother's death. And then there are a variety of ways in which this might be continued. (1) But as directly killing an innocent person is always and absolutely impermissible, an abortion may not be performed. Or, (2) as directly killing an innocent person is murder, and murder is always and absolutely impermissible, an abortion may not be performed.[3] Or, (3) as one's duty to refrain from directly killing an innocent person is more stringent than one's duty to keep a person from dying, an abortion may not be performed. Or, (4) if one's only options are directly killing an innocent person or letting a person die, one must prefer letting the person die, and thus an abortion may not be performed.[4]

Some people seem to have thought that these are not further premises which must be added if the conclusion is to be reached, but that they follow from the very fact that an innocent person has a right to life.[5] But this seems to me to be a mistake, and perhaps the simplest way to show this is to bring out that while we must certainly grant that innocent persons have a right to life, the theses in (1) through (4) are all false. Take (2), for example. If directly killing an innocent person is murder, and thus is impermissible, then the mother's directly killing the innocent person inside her is murder, and thus is impermissible. But it cannot seriously be thought to be murder if the mother performs an abortion on herself to save her life. It cannot seriously be said that she *must* refrain, that she *must* sit passively by and wait for her death. Let us look again at the case of you and the violinist. There you are, in bed with the violinist, and the director of the hospital says to you, "It's all most distressing, and I deeply sympathize, but you see this is putting an additional strain on your kidneys, and you'll be dead within the month. But you *have* to stay where you are all the same. Because unplugging you would be directly killing an innocent violinist, and that's murder, and that's impermissible." If anything in the world is true, it is that you do not commit murder, you do not do what is impermissible, if you reach around to your back and unplug yourself from that violinist to save your life.

The main focus of attention in writings on abortion has been on what a third party may or may not do in answer to a request from a woman for an abortion. This is in a way understandable. Things being as they are, there isn't much a woman can safely do to abort herself. So the question asked is what a third party may do, and what the mother may do, if it is mentioned at all, is deduced, almost as an afterthought, from what it is concluded that third parties may do. But it seems to me that to treat the matter in this way is to refuse to grant to the mother that very status of person which is so firmly insisted on for the fetus. For we cannot simply read off what a person may do from what a third party may do. Suppose you find yourself trapped in a tiny house with a growing child. I mean a very tiny house, and a rapidly growing child—you are already up against the wall of the house and in a few minutes you'll be crushed to death. The child on the other hand won't be crushed to death; if nothing is done to stop him from growing he'll be hurt, but in the end he'll simply burst open the house and walk out a free man. Now I could well understand it if a bystander were to say, "There's nothing we can do for you. We cannot choose between your life and his, we cannot be the ones to decide who is to live, we cannot intervene." But it cannot be concluded that you too can do nothing, that you cannot attack it to save your life. However innocent the child may be, you do not have to wait passively while it crushes you to death. Perhaps a pregnant woman is vaguely felt to have the status of house, to which we don't allow the right of self-defense. But if the woman houses the child, it should be remembered that she is a person who houses it.

I should perhaps stop to say explicitly that I am not claiming that people have a right to do anything whatever to save their lives. I think, rather, that there are drastic limits to the right of self-defense. If someone threatens you with death unless you torture someone else to death, I think you have not the right, even to save your life, to do so. But the case under consideration here is very different. In our case there are only two people involved, one whose life is threatened, and one who threatens it. Both are innocent: the one who is threatened is not threatened because of any fault, the one who threatens does not threaten because of any fault. For this reason we may feel that we bystanders cannot intervene. But the person threatened can.

In sum, a woman surely can defend her life against the threat to it posed by the unborn child, even if doing so involves its death. And this shows not merely that the theses in (1) through (4) are false; it shows also that the extreme view of abortion is false, and so we need not canvass any other possible ways of arriving at it from the argument I mentioned at the outset.

2. The extreme view could of course be weakened to say that while abortion is permissible to save the mother's life, it may not be performed by a third party, but only by the mother herself. But this cannot be right either. For what we have to keep in mind is that the mother and the unborn child are not like two tenants in a small house which has, by an unfortunate mistake, been rented to both: the mother *owns* the house. The fact that she does adds to the offensiveness of deducing that the mother can do nothing from the supposition that third parties can do nothing. But it does more than this: it casts a bright light on the supposition that third parties can do nothing. Certainly it lets us see that a third party who says "I cannot choose between you" is fooling himself if he thinks this is impartiality. If Jones has found and fastened on a certain coat, which he needs to keep him from freezing, but which Smith also needs to keep him from freezing, then it is not impartiality that says "I cannot choose between you" when Smith owns the coat. Women have said again and again, "This body is *my* body!" and they have reason to feel angry, reason to feel that it has been like shouting into the wind. Smith, after all, is hardly likely to bless us if we say to him, "Of course it's your coat, anybody would grant that it is. But no one may choose between you and Jones who is to have it."

We should really ask what it is that says "no one may choose" in the face of the fact that the body that houses the child is the mother's body. It may be simply a failure to appreciate this fact. But it may be something more interesting, namely, the sense that one has a right to refuse to lay hands on people, even where it would be just and fair to do so, even where justice seems to require that somebody do so. Thus justice might call for somebody to get Smith's coat back from Jones, and yet you have a right to refuse to be the one to lay hands on Jones, a right to refuse to do physical violence to him. This, I think, must be granted. But then what should be said is not "no one may choose," but only "*I* cannot choose," and indeed not even this, but "*I* will not *act*," leaving it open that somebody else can or should, and in particular that anyone in a position of authority, with the job of securing people's rights, both can and should. So this is no difficulty. I have not been arguing that any given third party must accede to the mother's request that he perform an abortion to save her life, but only that he may.

I suppose that in some views of human life the mother's body is only on loan to her, the loan not being one which gives her any prior claim to it. One who held this view might well think it impartiality to say "I cannot choose." But I shall simply ignore this possibility. My own view is that if a human being has any just, prior claim to anything at all, he has a just, prior claim to his own body. And perhaps this needn't be argued for here anyway, since, as I mentioned, the arguments against abortion we are looking at do grant that the woman has a right to decide what happens in and to her body.

But although they do grant it, I have tried to show that they do not take seriously what is done in granting it. I suggest the same thing will reappear even more clearly when we turn away from cases in which the mother's life is at stake, and attend, as I propose we now do, to the vastly more common cases in which a woman wants an abortion for some less weighty reason than preserving her own life.

3. Where the mother's life is not at stake, the argument I mentioned at the outset seems to have a much stronger pull. "Everyone has a right to life, so the unborn person has a right to life." And isn't the child's right to life weightier than anything other than the mother's own right to life, which she might put forward as ground for an abortion?

This argument treats the right to life as if it were unproblematic. It is not, and this seems to me to be precisely the source of the mistake.

For we should now, at long last, ask what it comes to, to have a right to life. In some views having a right to life includes having a right to be given at least the bare minimum one needs for continued life. But suppose that what in fact *is* the bare minimum a man needs for continued life is something he has no right at all to be given. If I am sick unto death, and the only thing that will save my life is the touch of Henry Fonda's cool hand on my fevered brow, then all the same, I have no right to be given the touch of Henry Fonda's cool hand on my fevered brow. It would be frightfully nice of him to fly in from the West Coast to provide it. It would be less nice, though no doubt well meant, if my friends flew out to the West Coast and carried Henry Fonda back with them. But I have no right at all against anybody that he should do this for me. Or again, to return to the story I told earlier, the fact that for continued life that violinist needs the continued use of your kidneys does not establish that he has a right to be given the continued use of your kidneys. He certainly has no right against you that *you* should give him continued use of your kidneys. For nobody has any right to use our kidneys unless you give him such a right; and nobody has the right against you that you shall give him this right—if you do allow him to go on using your kidneys, this is a kindness on your part, and not something he can claim from you as his due. Nor has he any right against anybody else that *they* should give him continued use of your kidneys. Certainly he had no right against the Society of Music Lovers that they should plug him into you in the first place. And if you now start to unplug yourself, having learned that you will otherwise have to spend nine years in bed with him, there is nobody in the world who must try to prevent you, in order to see to it that he is given something he has a right to be given.

Some people are rather stricter about the right to life. In their view, it does not include the right to be given anything, but amounts to, and only to, the right not to be killed by anybody. But here a related difficulty arises. If everybody is to refrain from killing that violinist, then everybody must refrain from doing a great many different sorts of things. Everybody must refrain from slitting his throat, everybody must refrain from shooting him—and everybody must refrain from unplugging you from him. But does he have a right against everybody that they shall refrain from unplugging you from him? To refrain from doing this is to allow him to continue to use your kidneys. It could be argued that he has a right against us that *we* should allow him to continue to use your kidneys. That is, while he had no right against us that we should give him the use of your kidneys, it might be argued that he anyway has a right against us that we shall not now intervene and deprive him of the use of your kidneys. I shall come back to third-party interventions later. But certainly the violinist has no right against you that *you* shall allow him to continue to use your kidneys. As I said, if you do allow him to continue to use them, it is a kindness on your part, and not something you owe him.

The difficulty I point to here is not peculiar to the right to life. It reappears in connection with all the other natural rights; and it is something which an adequate account of rights must deal with. For present purposes it is enough just to draw attention to it. But I would stress that I am not arguing that people do not have a right to life—quite to the contrary, it seems to me that the primary control we must place on the acceptability of an account of rights is that it should turn out in that account to be a truth that all persons have a right to life. I am arguing only that having a right to life does not guarantee having either a right to be given the use of or a right to be allowed continued use of another person's body—even if one needs it for life itself. So the right to life will not serve the opponents of abortion in the very simple and clear way in which they seem to have thought it would.

4. There is another way to bring out the difficulty. In the most ordinary sort of case, to deprive someone of what he has a right to is to treat him unjustly. Suppose a boy and his small brother are jointly given a box of chocolates for Christmas. If the older boy takes the box and refuses to give his brother any of the chocolates, he is unjust to him, for the brother has been given a right to half of them. But suppose that, having learned that otherwise it means nine years in bed with that violinist, you unplug yourself from him. You surely are not being unjust to him, for you gave him no right to use your kidneys, and no one else can have given him any such right. But we have to notice that in unplugging yourself, you are killing him; and violinists, like everybody else, have a right to life, and thus in the view we were considering just now, the right not to be killed. So here you do what he supposedly has a right you shall not do, but you do not act unjustly to him in doing it.

The emendation which may be made at this point is this: the right to life consists not in the right not to be killed, but rather in the right not to be killed unjustly. This runs a risk of circularity, but never mind: it would enable us to square the fact that the violinist has a right to life with the fact that you do not act unjustly toward him in unplugging yourself, thereby killing him. For if you do not kill him unjustly, you do not violate his right to life, and so it is no wonder you do him no injustice.

But if this emendation is accepted, the gap in the argument against abortion stares us plainly in the face: it is by no means enough to show that the fetus is a person, and to remind us that all persons have a right to life—we need to be shown also that killing the fetus violates its right to life, i.e., that abortion is unjust killing. And is it?

I suppose we may take it as a datum that in a case of pregnancy due to rape the mother has not given the unborn person a right to the use of her body for food and shelter. Indeed, in what pregnancy could it be supposed that the mother has given the unborn person such a right? It is not as if there were unborn persons drifting about the world, to whom a woman who wants a child says, "I invite you in."

But it might be argued that there are other ways one can have acquired a right to the use of another person's body than by having been invited to use it by that person. Suppose a woman voluntarily indulges in intercourse, knowing of the chance it will issue in pregnancy, and then she does become pregnant; is she not in part responsible for the presence, in fact the very existence, of the unborn person inside her? No doubt she did not invite it in. But doesn't her partial responsibility for its being there itself give it a right to the use of her body?[6] If so, then her aborting it would be more like the boy's taking away the chocolates, and less like your unplugging yourself from the violinist—doing so would be depriving it of what it does have a right to, and thus would be doing it an injustice.

And then, too, it might be asked whether or not she can kill it even to save her own life: If she voluntarily called it into existence, how can she now kill it, even in self-defense?

The first thing to be said about this is that it is something new. Opponents of abortion have been so concerned to make out the independence of the fetus, in order to establish that it has a right to life, just as its mother does, that they have tended to overlook the possible support they might gain from making out that the fetus is *dependent* on the mother, in order to establish that she has a special kind of responsibility for it, a responsibility that gives it rights against her which are not possessed by any independent person—such as an ailing violinist who is a stranger to her.

On the other hand, this argument would give the unborn person a right to its mother's body only if her pregnancy resulted from a voluntary act, undertaken in full knowledge of the chance a pregnancy might result from it. It would leave out entirely the unborn person whose existence is due to rape. Pending the availability of some further argument, then, we would be left with the conclusion that unborn persons whose existence is due to rape have no right to the use of their mothers' bodies, and thus that aborting them is not depriving them of anything they have a right to and hence is not unjust killing.

And we should also notice that it is not at all plain that this argument really does go even as far as it purports to. For there are cases and cases, and the details make a difference. If the room is stuffy, and I therefore open a window to air it, and a burglar climbs in, it would be absurd to say, "Ah, now he can stay, she's given him a right to the use of her house—for she is partially responsible for his presence there, having voluntarily done what enabled him to get in, in full knowledge that there are such things as burglars, and that burglars burgle." It would be still more absurd to say this if I had had bars installed outside my windows, precisely to prevent burglars from getting in, and a burglar got in only because of a defect in the bars. It remains equally absurd if we imagine it is not a burglar who climbs in, but an innocent person who blunders or falls in. Again, suppose it were like this: people-seeds drift about in the air like pollen, and if you open your windows, one may drift in and take root in your carpets or upholstery. You don't want children, so you fix up your windows with fine mesh screens, the very best you can buy. As can happen, however, and on very, very rare occasions does happen, one of the screens is defective; and a seed drifts in and takes root. Does the person-plant who now develops have a right to the use of your house? Surely not—despite the fact that you voluntarily opened your windows, you knowingly kept carpets and upholstered furniture, and you knew that screens were sometimes defective. Someone may argue that you are responsible for its rooting, that it does have a right to your house, because after all you *could* have lived out your life with bare floors and furniture, or with sealed windows and doors. But this won't do—for by the same token anyone can avoid a pregnancy due to rape by having a hysterectomy, or anyway by never leaving home without a (reliable!) army.

It seems to me that the argument we are looking at can establish at most that there are *some* cases in which the unborn person has a right to the use of its mother's body, and therefore *some* cases in which abortion is unjust killing. There is room for much discussion and argument as to precisely which, if any. But I think we should sidestep this issue and leave it open, for at any rate the argument certainly does not establish that all abortion is unjust killing.

5. There is room for yet another argument here, however. We surely must all grant that there may be cases in which it would be morally indecent to detach a person from your body at the cost of his life. Suppose you learn that what the violinist needs is not nine years of your life, but only one hour: all you need do to save his life is to spend one hour in that bed with him. Suppose also that letting him use your kidneys for that one hour would not affect your health in the slightest. Admittedly you were kidnapped. Admittedly you did not give anyone permission to plug him into you. Nevertheless it seems to me plain you *ought* to allow him to use your kidneys for that hour—it would be indecent to refuse.

Again, suppose pregnancy lasted only an hour, and constituted no threat to life or health. And suppose that a woman becomes pregnant as a result of rape. Admittedly she did not voluntarily do anything to bring about the existence of a child. Admittedly she did nothing at all which would give the unborn person a right to the use of her body. All the same it might well be said, as in the newly emended violinist story, that she *ought* to allow it to remain for that hour—that it would be indecent of her to refuse.

Now some people are inclined to use the term "right" in such a way that it follows from the fact that you ought to allow a person to use your body for the hour he needs, that he has a right to use your body for the hour he needs, even though he has not been given that right by any person or act. They may say that it follows also that if you refuse, you act unjustly toward him. This use of the term is perhaps so common that it cannot be called wrong; nevertheless it seems to me to be an unfortunate loosening of what we would do better to keep a tight rein on. Suppose that box of chocolates I mentioned earlier had not been given to both boys jointly, but was given only to the older boy. There he sits, stolidly eating his way through the box, his small brother watching enviously. Here we are likely to say, "You ought not to be so mean. You ought to give your brother some of those chocolates." My own view is that it just does not follow from the truth of this that the brother has any right to any of the chocolates. If the boy refuses to give his brother any, he is greedy, stingy, callous—but not unjust. I suppose that the people I have in mind will say it does follow that the brother has a right to some of the chocolates, and thus that the boy does act unjustly if he refuses to give his brother any. But the effect of saying this is to obscure what we should keep distinct, namely, the difference between the boy's refusal in this case and the boy's refusal in the earlier case, in which the box was given to both boys jointly, and in which the small brother thus had what was from any point of view clear title to half.

A further objection to so using the term "right" that from the fact that A ought to do a thing for B, it follows that B has a right against A that A do it for him, is that it is going to make the question of whether or not a man has a right to a thing turn on how easy it is to provide him with it; and this seems not merely unfortunate, but morally unacceptable. Take the case of Henry Fonda again. I said earlier that I had no right to the touch of his cool hand on my fevered brow, even though I needed it to save my life. I said it would be frightfully nice of him to fly in from the West Coast to provide me with it, but that I had no right against him that he should do so. But suppose he isn't on the West Coast. Suppose he has only to walk across the room, place a hand briefly on my brow—and lo, my life is saved. Then surely he ought to do it, it would be indecent to refuse. Is it to be said, "Ah, well, it follows that in this case she has a right to the touch of his hand on her brow, and so it would be an injustice in him to refuse"? So that I have a right to it when it is easy for him to provide it, though no right when it's hard? It's rather a shocking idea that anyone's rights should fade away and disappear as it gets harder and harder to accord them to him.

So my own view is that even though you ought to let the violinist use your kidneys for the one hour he needs, we should not conclude that he has a right to do so—we should say that if you refuse, you are, like the boy who owns all the chocolates and will give none away, self-centered and callous, indecent in fact, but not unjust. And similarly, that even supposing a case in which a woman pregnant due to rape ought to allow the unborn person to use her body for the hour he needs, we should not conclude that he has a right to do so; we should conclude that she is self-centered, callous, indecent, but not unjust, if she refuses. The complaints are no less grave; they are just different. However, there is no need to insist on this point. If anyone does wish to deduce "he has a right" from "you ought," then all the same he must surely grant that there are cases in which it is not morally required of you that you allow that violinist to use your kidneys, and in which he does not have a right to use them, and in which you do not do him an injustice if you refuse. And so also for mother and unborn child. Except in such cases as the unborn person has a right to demand it—and we were leaving open the possibility that there may be such cases—nobody is morally *required* to make large sacrifices, of health, of all other interests and concerns, of all other duties and commitments, for nine years, or even for nine months, in order to keep another person alive.

6. We have in fact to distinguish between two kinds of Samaritan: the Good Samaritan and what we might call the Minimally Decent Samaritan. The story of the Good Samaritan, you will remember, goes like this:

> A certain man went down from Jerusalem to Jericho, and fell among thieves, which stripped him of his raiment, and wounded him, and departed, leaving him half dead.
>
> And by chance there came down a certain priest that way; and when he saw him, he passed by on the other side.
>
> And likewise a Levite, when he was at the place, came and looked on him, and passed by on the other side.
>
> But a certain Samaritan, as he journeyed, came where he was; and when he saw him he had compassion on him.
>
> And went to him, and bound up his wounds, pouring in oil and wine, and set him on his own beast, and brought him to an inn, and took care of him.
>
> And on the morrow, when he departed, he took out two pence, and gave them to the host, and said unto him, "Take care of him; and whatsoever thou spendest more, when I come again, I will repay thee."
>
> —(Luke 10:30–35)

The Good Samaritan went out of his way, at some cost to himself, to help one in need of it. We are not told what the options were, that is, whether or not the priest and the Levite could have helped by doing less than the Good Samaritan did, but assuming they could have, then the fact they did nothing at all shows they were not even Minimally Decent Samaritans, not because they were not Samaritans, but because they were not even minimally decent.

These things are a matter of degree, of course, but there is a difference, and it comes out perhaps most clearly in the story of Kitty Genovese, who, as you will remember, was murdered while thirty-eight people watched or listened, and did nothing at all to help her. A Good Samaritan would have rushed out to give direct assistance against the murderer. Or perhaps we had better allow that it would have been a Splendid Samaritan who did this, on the ground that it would have involved a risk of death for himself. But the thirty-eight not only did not do this, they did not even trouble to pick up a phone to call the police. Minimally Decent Samaritanism would call for doing at least that, and their not having done it was monstrous.

After telling the story of the Good Samaritan, Jesus said, "Go, and do thou likewise." Perhaps he meant that we are morally required to act as the Good Samaritan did. Perhaps he was urging people to do more than is morally required of them. At all events it seems plain that it was not morally required of any of the thirty-eight that he rush out to give direct assistance at the risk of his own life, and that it is not morally required of anyone that he give long stretches of his life—nine years or nine months—to sustaining the life of a person who has no special right (we were leaving open the possibility of this) to demand it.

Indeed, with one rather striking class of exceptions, no one in any country in the world is *legally* required to do anywhere near as much as this for anyone else. The class of exceptions is obvious. My main concern here is not the state of the law in respect to abortion, but it is worth drawing attention to the fact that in no state in this country is any man compelled by law to be even a Minimally Decent Samaritan to any person; there is no law under which charges could be brought against the thirty-eight who stood by while Kitty Genovese died. By contrast, in most states in this country women are compelled by law to be not merely Minimally Decent Samaritans, but Good Samaritans to unborn persons inside them. This doesn't by itself settle anything one way or the other, because it may well be argued that there should be laws in this country—as there are in many European countries—compelling at least Minimally Decent Samaritanism.[7] But it does show that there is a gross injustice in the existing state of the law. And it shows also that the groups currently working against liberalization of abortion laws, in fact working toward having it declared unconstitutional for a state to permit abortion, had better start working for the adoption of Good Samaritan laws generally, or earn the charge that they are acting in bad faith.

I should think, myself, that Minimally Decent Samaritan laws would be one thing, Good Samaritan laws quite another, and in fact highly improper. But we are not here concerned with the law. What we should ask is not whether anybody should be compelled by law to be a Good Samaritan, but whether we must accede to a situation in which somebody is being compelled—by nature, perhaps—to be a Good Samaritan. We have, in other words, to look now at third-party interventions. I have been arguing that no person is morally required to make large sacrifices to sustain the life of another who has no right to demand them, and this even where the sacrifices do not include life itself; we are not morally required to be Good Samaritans or anyway Very Good Samaritans to one another. But what if a man cannot extricate himself from such a situation? What if he appeals to us to extricate him? It seems to me plain that there are cases in which we can, cases in which a Good Samaritan would extricate him. There you are, you were kidnapped, and nine years in bed with that violinist lie ahead of you. You have your own life to lead. You are sorry, but you simply cannot see giving up so much of your life to the sustaining of his. You cannot extricate yourself, and ask us to do so. I should have thought that—in light of his having no right to the use of your body—it was obvious that we do not have to accede to your being forced to give up so much. We can do what you ask. There is no injustice to the violinist in our doing so.

7. Following the lead of the opponents of abortion, I have throughout been speaking of the fetus merely as a person, and what I have been asking is whether or not the argument we began with, which proceeds only from the fetus' being a person, really does establish its conclusion. I have argued that it does not.

But of course there are arguments and arguments, and it may be said that I have simply fastened on the wrong one. It may be said that what is important is not merely the fact that the fetus is a person, but that it is a person for whom the woman has a special kind of responsibility issuing from the fact that she is its mother. And it might be argued that all my analogies are therefore irrelevant—for you do not have that special kind of responsibility for that violinist, Henry Fonda does not have that special kind of responsibility for me. And our attention might be drawn to the fact that men and women both *are* compelled by law to provide support for their children.

I have in effect dealt (briefly) with this argument in section 4 above; but a (still briefer) recapitulation now may be in order. Surely we do not have any such "special responsibility" for a person unless we have assumed it, explicitly or implicitly. If a set of parents do not try to prevent pregnancy, do not obtain an abortion, and then at the time of birth of the child do not put it out for adoption, but rather take it home with them, then they have assumed responsibility for it, they have given it rights, and they cannot *now* withdraw support from it at the cost of its life because they now find it difficult to go on providing for it. But if they have taken all reasonable precautions against having a child, they do not simply by virtue of their biological relationship to the child who comes into existence have a special responsibility for it. They may wish to assume responsibility for it, or they may not wish to. And I am suggesting that if assuming responsibility for it would require large sacrifices, then they may refuse. A Good Samaritan would not refuse—or anyway, a Splendid Samaritan, if the sacrifices that had to be made were enormous. But then so would a Good Samaritan assume responsibility for that violinist; so would Henry Fonda, if he is a Good Samaritan, fly in from the West Coast and assume responsibility for me.

8. My argument will be found unsatisfactory on two counts by many of those who want to regard abortion as morally permissible. First, while I do argue that abortion is not impermissible, I do not argue that it is always permissible. There may well be cases in which carrying the child to term requires only Minimally Decent Samaritanism of the mother, and this is a standard we must not fall below. I am inclined to think it a merit of my account precisely that it does *not* give a general yes or a general no. It allows for and supports our sense that, for example, a sick and desperately frightened fourteen-year-old schoolgirl, pregnant due to rape, may *of course* choose abortion, and that any law which rules this out is an insane law. And it also allows for and supports our sense that in other cases resort to abortion is even positively indecent. It would be indecent in the woman to request an abortion, and indecent in the doctor to perform it, if she is in her seventh month, and wants the abortion just to avoid the nuisance of postponing a trip abroad. The very fact that the arguments I have been drawing attention to treat all cases of abortion, or even all cases of abortion in which the mother's life is not at stake, as morally on a par ought to have made them suspect at the outset.

Secondly, while I am arguing for the permissibility of abortion in some cases, I am not arguing for the right to secure the death of the unborn child. It is easy to confuse these two things in that up to a certain point in the life of the fetus it is not able to survive outside the mother's body; hence removing it from her body guarantees its death. But they are importantly different. I have argued that you are not morally required to spend nine months in bed, sustaining the life of that violinist; but to say this is by no means to say that if, when you unplug yourself, there is a miracle and he survives, you then have a right to turn round and slit his throat. You may detach yourself even if this costs him his life; you have no right to be guaranteed his death, by some other means, if unplugging yourself does not kill him. There are some people who will feel dissatisfied by this feature of my argument. A woman may be utterly devastated by the thought of a child, a bit of herself, put out for adoption and never seen or heard of again. She may therefore want not merely that the child be detached from her, but more, that it die. Some opponents of abortion are inclined to regard this as beneath contempt—thereby showing insensitivity to what is surely a powerful source of despair. All the same, I agree that the desire for the child's death is not one which anybody may gratify, should it turn out to be possible to detach the child alive.

At this place, however, it should be remembered that we have only been pretending throughout that the fetus is a human being from the moment of conception. A very early abortion is surely not the killing of a person, and so is not dealt with by anything I have said here.

Notes

1. Daniel Callahan, *Abortion: Law, Choice and Morality* (New York, 1970), p. 373. This book gives a fascinating survey of the available information on abortion. The Jewish tradition is surveyed in David M. Feldman, *Birth Control in Jewish Law* (New York, 1968), Part 5, the Catholic tradition in John T. Noonan, Jr., "An Almost Absolute Value in History," in *The Morality of Abortion*, ed. John T. Noonan, Jr. (Cambridge, MA, 1970).

2. The term "direct" in the arguments I refer to is a technical one. Roughly, what is meant by "direct killing" is either killing as an end in itself, or killing as a means to some end, for example, the end of saving someone else's life. See note 5, below, for an example of its use.

3. Cf. *Encyclical Letter of Pope Pius XI on Christian Marriage*, St. Paul Editions (Boston, n.d.), p. 32: "however much we may pity the mother whose health and even life is gravely imperiled in the performance of the duty allotted to her by nature, nevertheless what could ever be a sufficient reason for excusing in any way the direct murder of the innocent? This is precisely what we are dealing with here." Noonan (*The Morality of Abortion*, p. 43) reads this as follows: "What cause can ever avail to excuse in any way the direct killing of the innocent? For it is a question of that."

4. The thesis in (4) is in an interesting way weaker than those in (1), (2), and (3): they rule out abortion even in cases in which both mother *and* child will die if the abortion is not performed. By contrast, one who held the view expressed in (4) could consistently say that one needn't prefer letting two persons die to killing one.

5. Cf. the following passage from Pius XII, *Address to the Italian Catholic Society of Midwives*: "The baby in the maternal breast has the right to life immediately from God.—Hence there is no man, no human authority, no science, no medical, eugenic, social, economic or moral 'indication' which

can establish or grant a valid juridical ground for a direct deliberate disposition of an innocent human life, that is a disposition which looks to its destruction either as an end or as a means to another end perhaps in itself not illicit.—The baby, still not born, is a man in the same degree and for the same reason as the mother" (quoted in Noonan, *The Morality of Abortion*, p. 45).

6. The need for a discussion of this argument was brought home to me by members of the Society for Ethical and Legal Philosophy, to whom this paper was originally presented.

7. For a discussion of the difficulties involved, and a survey of the European experience with such laws, see *The Good Samaritan and the Law*, ed. James M. Ratcliffe (New York, 1966).

Study Questions

1. What are the main points Thomson seeks to make by the example of the unconscious violinist?

2. Does the morality of aborting a fetus depend on the conditions surrounding its conception?

3. If abortion is murder, who is the murderer, and what is the appropriate punishment?

4. If the abortion controversy is described as a debate between those who believe in a right to life and those who affirm a woman's right to choose, on which side is Thomson?

CHAPTER 22

On the Moral and Legal Status of Abortion

Mary Anne Warren

Mary Anne Warren (1942–2010) was a professor of philosophy at San Francisco State University. She argued that because women are persons and fetuses are not, women's rights override whatever right to life a fetus may possess.

For our purposes, abortion may be defined as the act a woman performs in deliberately terminating her pregnancy before it comes to term, or in allowing another person to terminate it. Abortion usually entails the death of a fetus.[1] Nevertheless, I will argue that it is morally permissible, and should be neither legally prohibited nor made needlessly difficult to obtain, e.g., by obstructive legal regulations.[2]

Some philosophers have argued that the moral status of abortion cannot be resolved by rational means.[3] If this is so then liberty should prevail; for it is not a proper function of the law to enforce prohibitions upon personal behavior that cannot clearly be shown to be morally objectionable, and seriously so. But the advocates of prohibition believe that their position is objectively correct, and not merely a result of religious beliefs or personal prejudices. They argue that the humanity of the fetus is a matter of scientific fact, and that abortion is therefore the moral equivalent of murder, and must be prohibited in all or most cases. (Some would make an exception when the woman's life is in danger, or when the pregnancy is due to rape or incest; others would prohibit abortion even in these cases.)

In response, advocates of a right to choose abortion point to the terrible consequences of prohibiting it, especially while contraception is still unreliable, and is financially beyond the reach of much of the world's population. Worldwide, hundreds of thousands of women die each year from illegal abortions, and many more suffer from complications that may leave them injured or infertile. Women who are poor, underage, disabled, or otherwise vulnerable, suffer most from the absence of safe and legal abortion. Advocates of choice also argue that to deny a woman access to abortion is to deprive her of the right to control her own body—a right so fundamental that without it other rights are often all but meaningless.

These arguments do not convince abortion opponents. The tragic consequences of prohibition leave them unmoved, because they regard the deliberate killing of fetuses as even more tragic. Nor do appeals to the right to control one's own body impress them, since they deny that this right includes the right to destroy a fetus. We cannot hope to persuade those who equate abortion with murder that they are mistaken, unless we can refute the standard anti-abortion argument: that because fetuses are human beings, they have a right to life equal to that of any other human being. Unfortunately, confusion has prevailed with respect to the two important questions which that argument raises: (1) Is a human fetus really a human being at all stages of prenatal development? and (2) If so, what (if anything) follows about the moral and legal status of abortion?

John Noonan says that "the fundamental question in the long history of abortion is, How do you determine the humanity of a being?"[4] His anti-abortion argument is essentially that of the Roman Catholic Church. In his words:

> it is wrong to kill humans, however poor, weak, defenseless, and lacking in opportunity to develop their potential they may be. It is therefore morally wrong to kill Biafrans. Similarly, it is morally wrong to kill embryos.[5]

Noonan bases his claim that fetuses are human beings from the time of conception upon what he calls the theologians' criterion of humanity: that whoever is conceived of human beings is a human being. But although he argues at length for the appropriateness of this criterion of humanity, he does not question the assumption that if a fetus is a human being then abortion is almost always immoral.[6]

Judith Thomson has questioned this assumption. She argues that, even if we grant the anti-abortionist the claim that a fetus is a human being with the same right to life as any other human being, we can still demonstrate that women are not morally obliged to complete every unwanted pregnancy.[7] Her argument is worth examining, because if it is sound it may enable us to establish the moral permissibility of abortion without having to decide just what makes an entity a human being, or what entitles it to full moral rights. This would represent a considerable gain in the power and simplicity of the pro-choice position.

Even if Thomson's argument does not hold up, her essential insight—that it requires *argument* to show that if fetuses are human beings then abortion is murder—is a valuable one. The assumption that she attacks is invidious, for it requires that in our deliberations about the ethics of abortion we must ignore almost entirely the needs of the pregnant woman and other persons for whom she is responsible. This will not do; determining what moral rights a fetus has is only one step in determining the moral status of abortion. The next step is finding a just solution to conflicts between whatever rights the fetus has, and the rights and responsibilities of the woman who is unwillingly pregnant.

My own inquiry will also have two stages. In Section I, I consider whether abortion can be shown to be morally permissible even on the assumption that a fetus is a human being with a strong right to life. I argue that this cannot be established, except in special cases. Consequently, we cannot avoid facing the question of whether or not a fetus has the same right to life as any human being.

In Section II, I propose an answer to this question, namely, that a fetus is not a member of the moral community—the set of beings with full and equal moral rights. The reason that a fetus is not a member of the moral community is that it is not yet a person, nor is it enough like a person in the morally relevant respects to be regarded the equal of those human beings who are persons. I argue that it is personhood, and not genetic humanity, which is the fundamental basis for membership in the moral community. A fetus, especially in the early stages of its development, satisfies none of the criteria of personhood. Consequently, it makes no sense to grant it moral rights strong enough to override the woman's moral rights to liberty, bodily integrity, and sometimes life itself. Unlike an infant who has already been born, a fetus cannot be granted full and equal moral rights without severely threatening the rights and well-being of women. Nor, as we will see, is a fetus's *potential* personhood a threat to the moral permissibility of abortion, since merely potential persons do not have a moral right to become actual—or none that is strong enough to override the fundamental moral rights of actual persons.

I

Judith Thomson argues that, even if a fetus has a right to life, abortion is often morally permissible. Her argument is based upon an imaginative analogy. She asks you to picture yourself waking up one day, in bed with a famous violinist, who is a stranger to you. Imagine that you have been kidnapped, and your bloodstream connected to that of the violinist, who has an ailment that will kill him unless he is permitted to share your kidneys for nine months. No one else can save him, since you alone have the right type of blood. Consequently, the Society of Music Lovers has arranged for you to be kidnapped and hooked up. If you unhook yourself, he will die. But if you remain in bed with him, then after nine months he will be cured and able to survive without further assistance from you.

Now, Thomson asks, what are your obligations in this situation? To be consistent, the anti-abortionist must say that you are obliged to stay in bed with the violinist: for violinists are human beings, and all human beings have a right to life.[8] But this is outrageous; thus, there must be something very wrong with the same argument when it is applied to abortion. It would be extremely generous of you to agree to stay in bed with the violinist; but it is absurd to suggest that your refusal to do so would be the moral equivalent of murder. The violinist's right to life does not oblige you to do whatever is required to keep him alive; still less does it justify anyone else in forcing you to do so. A law which required you to stay in bed with the violinist would be an unjust law, since unwilling persons ought not to be required to be Extremely Good Samaritans, i.e., to make enormous personal sacrifices for the sake of other individuals toward whom they have no special prior obligation.

Thomson concludes that we can grant the anti-abortionist his claim that a fetus is a human being with a right to life, and still hold that a pregnant woman is morally entitled to refuse to be an Extremely Good Samaritan toward the fetus. For there is a great gap between the claim that a human being has a right to life, and the claim that other human beings are morally obligated to do whatever is necessary to keep him alive. One has no duty to keep another human being alive *at a great personal cost,* unless one has somehow contracted a special obligation toward that individual; and a woman who is pregnant may have done nothing that morally obliges her to make the burdensome personal sacrifices necessary to preserve the life of the fetus.

This argument is plausible, and in the case of pregnancy due to rape it is probably conclusive. Difficulties arise, however, when we attempt to specify the larger range of cases in which abortion can be justified on the basis of this argument. Thomson considers it a virtue of her argument that it does not imply that abortion is *always* morally permissible. It would, she says, be indecent for a woman in her seventh month of pregnancy to have an abortion in order to embark on a trip to Europe. On the other hand, the violinist analogy shows that, "a sick and desperately frightened fourteen-year-old schoolgirl, pregnant due to rape, may *of course* choose abortion, and that any law which rules this out is an insane law."[9] So far, so good; but what are we to say about the woman who becomes pregnant not through rape but because she and her partner did not use available forms of contraception, or because their attempts at contraception failed? What about a woman who becomes pregnant intentionally, but then re-evaluates the wisdom of having a child? In such cases, the violinist analogy is considerably less useful to advocates of the right to choose abortion.

It is perhaps only when a woman's pregnancy is due to rape, or some other form of coercion, that the situation is sufficiently analogous to the violinist case for our moral intuitions to transfer convincingly from the one case to the other. One difference between a pregnancy caused by rape and most unwanted pregnancies is that only in the former case is it perfectly clear that the woman is in no way responsible for her predicament. In the other cases, she *might* have been able to avoid becoming pregnant, e.g., by taking birth control pills (more faithfully), or insisting upon the use of high-quality condoms, or even avoiding heterosexual intercourse altogether throughout her fertile years. In contrast, if you are suddenly kidnapped by strange music lovers and hooked up to a sick violinist, then you are in no way responsible for your situation, which you could not have foreseen or prevented. And responsibility does seem to matter here. If a person behaves in a way which she could have avoided, and which she knows might bring into existence a human being who will depend upon her for survival, then it is not entirely clear that if and when that happens she may rightly refuse to do what she must in order to keep that human being alive.

This argument shows that the violinist analogy provides a persuasive defense of a woman's right to choose abortion only in cases where she is in no way morally responsible for her own pregnancy. In all other cases, the assumption that a fetus has a strong right to life makes it necessary to look carefully at the particular circumstances in order to determine the extent of the woman's responsibility, and hence the extent of her obligation. This outcome is unsatisfactory to advocates of the right to choose abortion, because it suggests that the decision should not be left in the woman's own hands, but should be supervised by other persons, who will inquire into the most intimate aspects of her personal life in order to determine whether or not she is entitled to choose abortion.

A supporter of the violinist analogy might reply that it is absurd to suggest that forgetting her pill one day might be sufficient to morally oblige a woman to complete an unwanted pregnancy. And indeed it is absurd to suggest this. As we will see, a woman's moral right to choose abortion does not depend upon the extent to which she might be thought to be morally responsible for her own pregnancy. But once we allow the assumption that a fetus has a strong right to life, we cannot avoid taking this absurd suggestion seriously. On this assumption, it is a vexing question whether and when abortion is morally justifiable. The violinist analogy can at best show that aborting a pregnancy is a deeply tragic act, though one that is sometimes morally justified.

My conviction is that an abortion is not always this deeply tragic, because a fetus is not yet a person, and therefore does not yet have a strong moral right to life. Although the truth of this conviction may not be self-evident, it does, I believe, follow from some highly plausible claims about the appropriate grounds for ascribing moral rights. It is worth examining these grounds, since this has not been adequately done before.

II

The question we must answer in order to determine the moral status of abortion is, How are we to define the moral community, the set of beings with full and equal moral rights? What sort of entity has the inalienable moral rights to life, liberty, and the pursuit of happiness? Thomas Jefferson attributed these rights to all *men*, and he may have intended to attribute them *only* to men. Perhaps he ought to have attributed them to all human beings. If so, then we arrive, first, at Noonan's problem of defining what makes an entity a human being, and second, at the question which Noonan does not consider: What reason is there for identifying the moral community with the set of all human beings, in whatever way we have chosen to define that term?

On the Definition of "Human"

The term "human being" has two distinct, but not often distinguished, senses. This results in a slide of meaning, which serves to conceal the fallacy in the traditional argument that, since (1) it is wrong to kill innocent human beings, and (2) fetuses are innocent human beings, therefore (3) it is wrong to kill fetuses. For if "human being" is used in the same sense in both (1) and (2), then whichever of the two senses is meant, one of these premises is question-begging. And if it is used in different senses then the conclusion does not follow.

Thus, (1) is a generally accepted moral truth,[10] and one that does not beg the question about abortion, only if "human being" is used to mean something like "a full-fledged member of the moral community, who is also a member of the human species." I will call this the *moral* sense of "human being." It is not to be confused with what I will call the *genetic* sense, i.e., the sense in which any individual entity that belongs to the human species is a human being, regardless of whether or not it is rightly considered to be an equal member of the moral community. Premise (1) avoids begging the question only if the moral sense is intended, while premise (2) avoids it only if what is intended is the genetic sense.

Noonan argues for the classification of fetuses with human beings by pointing, first, to the presence of the human genome in the cell nuclei of the human conceptus from conception onwards; and secondly, to the potential capacity for rational thought.[11] But what he needs to show, in order to support his version of the traditional anti-abortion argument, is that fetuses are human beings in the moral sense—the sense in which all human beings have full and equal moral rights. In the absence of any argument showing that whatever is genetically human is also morally human—and he gives none—nothing more than genetic humanity can be demonstrated by the presence of human chromosomes in the fetus's cell nuclei. And, as we will see, the strictly potential capacity for rational thought can at most show that the fetus may later *become* human in the moral sense.

Defining the Moral Community

Is genetic humanity sufficient for moral humanity? There are good reasons for not defining the moral community in this way. I would suggest that the moral community consists, in the first instance, of all *persons*, rather than all genetically human entities.[12] It is persons who invent moral rights, and who are (sometimes) capable of respecting them. It does not follow from this that only persons can have moral rights. However, persons are wise not to ascribe to entities that clearly are not persons moral rights that cannot in practice be respected without severely undercutting the fundamental moral rights of those who clearly are.

What characteristics entitle an entity to be considered a person? This is not the place to attempt a complete analysis of the concept of personhood; but we do not need such an analysis to explain why a fetus is not a person. All we need is an approximate list of the most basic criteria of personhood. In searching for these criteria, it is useful to look beyond the set of people with whom we are acquainted, all of whom are human. Imagine, then, a space traveler who lands on a new planet, and encounters organisms unlike any she has ever seen or heard of. If she wants to behave morally toward these organisms, she has somehow to determine whether they are people and thus have full moral rights, or whether they are things that she need not feel guilty about treating, for instance, as a source of food.

How should she go about making this determination? If she has some anthropological background, she might look for signs of religion, art, and the manufacturing of tools, weapons, or shelters, since these cultural traits have frequently been used to distinguish our human ancestors from prehuman beings, in what seems to be closer to the moral than the genetic sense of "human being." She would be right to take the presence of such traits as evidence that the extra-terrestrials were persons. It would, however, be anthropocentric of her to take the absence of these traits as proof that they were not, since they could be people who have progressed beyond, or who have never needed, these particular cultural traits.

I suggest that among the characteristics which are central to the concept of personhood are the following:

1. *sentience*—the capacity to have conscious experiences, usually including the capacity to experience pain and pleasure;
2. *emotionality*—the capacity to feel happy, sad, angry, loving, etc.;

3. *reason*—the capacity to solve new and relatively complex problems;
4. *the capacity to communicate*, by whatever means, messages of an indefinite variety of types; that is, not just with an indefinite number of possible contents, but on indefinitely many possible topics;
5. *self-awareness*—having a concept of oneself as an individual and/or as a member of a social group; and finally
6. *moral agency*—the capacity to regulate one's own actions through moral principles or ideals.

It is difficult to produce precise definitions of these traits, let alone to specify universally valid behavioral indications that these traits are present. But let us assume that our explorer knows approximately what these six characteristics mean, and that she is able to observe whether or not the extraterrestrials possess these mental and behavioral capacities. How should she use her findings to decide whether or not they are persons?

An entity need not have *all* of these attributes to be a person. And perhaps none of them is absolutely necessary. For instance, the absence of emotion would not disqualify a being that was person-like in all other ways. Think, for instance, of two of the *Star Trek* characters, Mr. Spock (who is half human and half alien), and Data (who is an android). Both are depicted as lacking the capacity to feel emotion; yet both are sentient, reasoning, communicative, self-aware moral agents, and unquestionably persons. Some people are unemotional; some cannot communicate well; some lack self-awareness; and some are not moral agents. It should not surprise us that many people do not meet all of the criteria of personhood. Criteria for the applicability of complex concepts are often like this: none may be logically necessary, but the more criteria that are satisfied, the more confident we are that the concept is applicable. Conversely, the fewer criteria are satisfied, the less plausible it is to hold that the concept applies. And if none of the relevant criteria are met, then we may be confident that it does not.

Thus, to demonstrate that a fetus is not a person, all I need to claim is that an entity that has *none* of these six characteristics is not a person. Sentience is the most basic mental capacity, and the one that may have the best claim to being a necessary (though not sufficient) condition for personhood. Sentience can establish a claim to moral considerability, since sentient beings can be harmed in ways that matter to them; for instance, they can be caused to feel pain, or deprived of the continuation of a life that is pleasant to them. It is unlikely that an entirely insentient organism could develop the other mental behavioral capacities that are characteristic of persons. Consequently, it is odd to claim that an entity that is not sentient, and that has never been sentient, is nevertheless a person. Persons who have permanently and irreparably lost all capacity for sentience, but who remain biologically alive, arguably still have strong moral rights by virtue of what they have been in the past. But small fetuses, which have not yet begun to have experiences, are not persons yet and do not have the rights that persons do.

The presumption that all persons have full and equal basic moral rights may be part of the very concept of a person. If this is so, then the concept of a person is in part a moral one; once we have admitted that X is a person, we have implicitly committed ourselves to recognizing X's right to be treated as a member of the moral community.[13] The claim that X is a *human being* may also be voiced as an appeal to treat X decently; but this is usually either because "human being" is used in the moral sense, or because of a confusion between genetic and moral humanity.

If (1)–(6) are the primary criteria of personhood, then genetic humanity is neither necessary nor sufficient for personhood. Some genetically human entities are not persons, and there may be persons who belong to other species. A man or woman whose consciousness has been permanently obliterated but who remains biologically alive is a human entity who may no longer be a person; and some unfortunate humans, who have never had any sensory or cognitive capacities at all, may not be people either. Similarly, an early fetus is a human entity which is not yet a person. It is not even minimally sentient, let alone capable of emotion, reason, sophisticated communication, self-awareness, or moral agency.[14] Thus, while it may be greatly valued as a future child, it does not yet have the claim to moral consideration that it may come to have later.

Moral agency matters to moral status, because it is moral agents who invent moral rights, and who can be obliged to respect them. Human beings have become moral agents from social necessity. Most social animals exist well enough, with no evident notion of a moral right. But human beings need moral rights, because we are not only highly social, but also sufficiently clever and self-interested to be capable of undermining our societies through violence and duplicity. For human persons, moral rights are essential for peaceful and mutually beneficial social life. So long as some moral agents are denied basic rights, peaceful existence is difficult, since moral agents justly resent being treated as something less. If animals of some terrestrial species are found to be persons, or if alien persons come from other worlds, or if human beings someday invent machines whose mental and behavioral capacities make them persons, then we will be morally obliged to respect the moral rights of these nonhuman persons—at least to the extent that they are willing and able to respect ours in turn.

Although only those persons who are moral agents can participate directly in the shaping and enforcement of moral rights, they need not and usually do not ascribe moral rights only to themselves and other moral agents. Human beings are social creatures who naturally care for small children, and other members of the social community who are not currently capable of moral agency. Moreover, we are all vulnerable to the temporary or permanent loss of the mental capacities necessary for moral agency. Thus, we have self-interested as well as altruistic reasons for extending basic moral rights to infants and other sentient human beings who have already been born, but who currently lack some of these other mental capacities. These human beings, despite their current disabilities, are persons and members of the moral community.

But in extending moral rights to beings (human or otherwise) that have few or none of the morally significant characteristics of persons, we need to be careful not to burden human moral agents with obligations that they cannot possibly fulfill, except at unacceptably great cost to their own well-being and that of those they care about. Women often cannot complete unwanted pregnancies, except at intolerable mental, physical, and economic cost to themselves and their families. And heterosexual intercourse is too important a part of the social lives of most men and women to be reserved for times when pregnancy is an acceptable outcome. Furthermore, the world cannot afford the continued rapid population growth which is the inevitable consequence of prohibiting abortion, so long as contraception is neither very reliable nor available to everyone. If fetuses were persons, then they would have rights that must be respected, even at great social or personal cost. But given that early fetuses, at least, are unlike persons in the morally relevant respects, it is unreasonable to insist that they be accorded exactly the same moral and legal status.

Fetal Development and the Right to Life

Two questions arise regarding the application of these suggestions to the moral status of the fetus. First, if indeed fetuses are not yet persons, then might they nevertheless have strong moral rights based upon the degree to which they *resemble* persons? Secondly, to what extent, if any, does a fetus's potential to *become* a person imply that we ought to accord to it some of the same moral rights? Each of these questions requires comment.

It is reasonable to suggest that the more like a person something is—the more it appears to meet at least some of the criteria of personhood—the stronger is the case for according it a right to life, and perhaps the stronger its right to life is. That being the case, perhaps the fetus gradually gains a stronger right to life as it develops. We should take seriously the suggestion that, just as "the human individual develops biologically in a continuous fashion,

> the rights of a human person . . . develop in the same way."[15]

A seven-month fetus can apparently feel pain, and can respond to such stimuli as light and sound. Thus, it may have a rudimentary form of consciousness. Nevertheless, it is probably not as conscious, or as capable of emotion, as even a very young infant is; and it has as yet little or no capacity for reason, sophisticated intentional communication, or self-awareness. In these respects, even a late-term fetus is arguably less like a person than are many nonhuman animals. Many animals (e.g., large-brained mammals such as elephants, cetaceans, or apes) are not only sentient, but clearly possessed of a degree of reason, and perhaps even of self-awareness. Thus, on the basis of its resemblance to a person, even a late-term fetus can have no more right to life than do these animals.

Animals may, indeed, plausibly be held to have some moral rights, and perhaps rather strong ones.[16] But it is impossible in practice to accord full and equal moral rights to all animals. When an animal poses a serious threat to the life or well-being of a person, we do not, as a rule, greatly blame the person for killing it; and there are good reasons for this species-based discrimination. Animals, however intelligent in their own domains, are generally not beings with whom we can reason; we cannot persuade mice not to invade our dwellings or consume our food. That is why their rights are necessarily weaker than those of a being who can understand and respect the rights of other beings.

But the probable sentience of late-term fetuses is not the only argument in favor of treating late abortion as a morally more serious matter than early abortion. Many—perhaps most—people are repulsed by the thought of needlessly aborting a late-term fetus. The late-term fetus has features which cause it to arouse in us almost the same powerful protective instinct as does a small infant.

This response needs to be taken seriously. If it were impossible to perform abortions early in pregnancy, then we might have to tolerate the mental and physical trauma that would be occasioned by the routine resort to late abortion. But where early abortion is safe, legal, and readily available to all women, it is not unreasonable to expect most women who wish to end a pregnancy to do so prior to the third trimester. Most women strongly prefer early to late abortion, because it is far less physically painful and emotionally traumatic. Other things being equal, it is better for all concerned that pregnancies that are not to be completed should be ended as early as possible. Few women would consider ending a pregnancy in the seventh month in order to take a trip to Europe. If, however, a woman's own life or health is at stake, or if the fetus has been found to be so severely abnormal as to be unlikely to survive or to have a life worth living, then late abortion may be the morally best choice. For even a late-term fetus is not a person yet, and its rights must yield to those of the woman whenever it is impossible for both to be respected.

Potential Personhood and the Right to Life

We have seen that a presentient fetus does not yet resemble a person in ways which support the claim that it has strong moral rights. But what about its *potential*, the fact that if nurtured and allowed to develop it may eventually become a person? Doesn't that potential give it at least some right to life? The fact that something is a potential person may be a reason for not destroying it; but we need not conclude from this that potential people have a strong right to life. It may be that the feeling that it is better not to destroy a potential person is largely due to the fact that potential people are felt to be an invaluable resource, not to be lightly squandered. If every speck of dust were a potential person, we would be less apt to suppose that all potential persons have a right to become actual.

We do not need to insist that a potential person has no right to life whatever. There may be something immoral, and not just imprudent, about wantonly destroying potential people, when doing so isn't necessary. But even if a potential person does have some right to life, that right could not outweigh the right of a woman to obtain an abortion; for the basic moral rights of an actual person outweigh the rights of a merely potential person, whenever the two conflict. Since this may not be immediately obvious in the case of a human fetus, let us look at another case.

Suppose that our space explorer falls into the hands of an extraterrestrial civilization, whose scientists decide to create a few thousand new human beings by killing her and using some of her cells to create clones. We may imagine that each of these newly created women will have all of the original woman's abilities, skills, knowledge, and so on, and will also have an individual self-concept; in short, that each of them will be a bona fide (though not genetically unique) person. Imagine, further, that our explorer knows all of this, and knows that these people will be treated kindly and fairly. I maintain that in such a situation she would have the right to escape if she could, thus depriving all of the potential people of their potential lives. For her right to life outweighs all of theirs put together, even though they are not genetically human, and have a high probability of becoming people, if only she refrains from acting.

Indeed, I think that our space traveler would have a right to escape even if it were not her life which the aliens planned to take, but only a year of her freedom, or only a day. She would not be obliged to stay, even if she had been captured because of her own lack of caution—or even if she had done so deliberately, knowing the possible consequences. Regardless of why she was captured, she is not obliged to remain in captivity for *any* period of time in order to permit merely potential people to become actual people. By the same token, a woman's rights to liberty and the control of her own body outweigh whatever right a fetus may have merely by virtue of its potential personhood.

The Objection From Infanticide

One objection to my argument is that it appears to justify not only abortion, but also infanticide. A newborn infant is not much more personlike than a nine-month fetus, and thus it might appear that if late-term abortion is sometimes justified then infanticide must also sometimes be justified. Yet most people believe that infanticide is a form of murder, and virtually never justified.

This objection is less telling than it may seem. There are many reasons why infanticide is more difficult to justify than abortion, even though neither fetuses nor newborn infants are clearly persons. In this period of history, the deliberate killing of newborns is virtually never justified. This is in part because newborns are so close to being persons that to kill them requires a very strong moral justification—as does the killing of dolphins, chimpanzees, and other highly person-like creatures. It is certainly wrong to kill such beings for the sake of convenience, or financial profit, or "sport." Only the most vital human needs, such as the need to defend one's own life and physical integrity, can provide a plausible justification for killing such beings.

In the case of an infant, there is no such vital need, since in the contemporary world there are usually other people who are eager to provide a good home for an infant whose own parents are unable or unwilling to care for it. Many people wait years for the opportunity to adopt a child, and some are unable to do so, even though there is every reason to believe that they would be good parents. The needless destruction of a viable infant not only deprives a sentient human being of life, but also deprives other persons of a source of great satisfaction, perhaps severely impoverishing *their* lives.

Even if an infant is unadoptable (e.g., because of some severe physical disability), it is still wrong to kill it. For most of us value the lives of infants, and would greatly prefer to pay taxes to support foster care and state institutions for disabled children, rather than to allow them to be killed or abandoned. So long as most people feel this way, and so long as it is possible to provide care for infants who are unwanted, or who have special needs that their parents cannot meet without assistance, it is wrong to let any infant die who has a chance of living a reasonably good life.

If these arguments show that infanticide is wrong, at least in today's world, then why don't they also show that late-term abortion is always wrong? After all, third-trimester fetuses are almost as personlike as infants, and many people value them and would prefer that they be preserved. As a potential source of pleasure to some family, a fetus is just as valuable as an infant. But there is an important difference between these two cases: once the infant is born, its continued life cannot pose any serious threat to the woman's life or health, since she is free to put it up for adoption or to place it in foster care. While she might, in rare cases, prefer that the child die rather than being raised by others, such a preference would not establish a right on her part.

In contrast, a pregnant woman's right to protect her own life and health outweighs other people's desire that the fetus be preserved— just as, when a person's desire for life or health is threatened by an animal, and when the threat cannot be removed without killing the animal, that person's right to self-defense outweighs the desires of those who would prefer that the animal not be killed. Thus, while the moment of birth may mark no sharp discontinuity in the degree to which an infant resembles a person, it does mark the end of the mother's right to determine its fate. Indeed, if a late abortion can be safely performed without harming the fetus, the mother has in most cases no right to insist upon its death, for the same reason that she has no right to insist that a viable infant be killed or allowed to die.

It remains true that, on my view, neither abortion nor the killing of newborns is obviously a form of murder. Perhaps our legal system is correct in its classification of infanticide as murder, since no other legal category adequately expresses the force of our disapproval of this action. But some moral distinction remains, and it has important consequences. When a society cannot possibly care for all of the children who are born, without endangering the survival of adults and older children, allowing some infants to die may be the best of a bad set of options. Throughout history, most societies—from those that lived by gathering and hunting to the highly civilized Chinese, Japanese, Greeks, and Romans—have permitted infanticide under such unfortunate circumstances, regarding it as a necessary evil. It shows a lack of understanding to condemn these societies as morally benighted for this reason alone, since in the absence of safe and effective means of contraception and abortion, parents must sometimes have had no morally better options.

Conclusion

I have argued that fetuses are neither persons nor members of the moral community. Furthermore, neither a fetus's resemblance to a person, nor its potential for becoming a person, provides an adequate basis for the claim that it has a full and equal right to life. At the same time, there are medical as well as moral reasons for preferring early to late abortion when the pregnancy is unwanted.

Women, unlike fetuses, are undeniably persons and members of the human moral community. If unwanted or medically dangerous pregnancies never occurred, then it might be possible to respect women's basic moral rights, while at the same time extending the same basic rights to fetuses. But in the real world such pregnancies do occur—often despite the woman's best efforts to prevent them. Even if the perfect contraceptive were universally available, the continued occurrence of rape and incest would make access to abortion a vital human need. Because women are persons, and fetuses are not, women's rights to life, liberty, and physical integrity morally override whatever right to life it may be appropriate to ascribe to a fetus. Consequently, laws that deny women the right to obtain abortions, or that make safe early abortions difficult or impossible for some women to obtain, are an unjustified violation of basic moral and constitutional rights.

Notes

1. Strictly speaking, a human conceptus does not become a fetus until the primary organ systems have formed, at about six to eight weeks gestational age. However, for simplicity I shall refer to the conceptus as a fetus at every stage of its prenatal development.
2. The views defended in this article are set forth in greater depth in my book *Moral Status* (New York: Oxford University Press, 2000).
3. For example, Roger Wertheimer argues, in "Understanding the Abortion Argument," *Philosophy and Public Affairs* 1 (Fall 1971), that the moral status of abortion is not a question of fact, but only of how one responds to the fact.
4. John Noonan, "Abortion and the Catholic Church: A Summary History," *Natural Law Forum* 12 (1967): p. 125.
5. John Noonan, "Deciding Who Is Human," *Natural Law Forum* 13 (1968): p. 134.
6. Noonan deviates from the current position of the Roman Catholic Church in that he thinks that abortion is morally permissible when it is the only way of saving the woman's life. See "An Almost Absolute Value in History," in *Contemporary Issues in Bioethics*, ed. Tom L. Beauchamp and LeRoy Walters (Belmont, CA: Wadsworth, 1994), p. 283.
7. Judith Jarvis Thomson, "A Defense of Abortion," *Philosophy and Public Affairs* 1, no. 1 (Fall 1971): pp. 47–66.
8. Ibid., p. 174.
9. Ibid., p. 187.
10. The principle that it is always wrong to kill innocent human beings may be in need of other modifications, e.g., that it may be permissible to kill innocent human beings in order to save a larger number of equally innocent human beings; but we may ignore these complications here.
11. Noonan, "Deciding Who Is Human," p. 135.
12. From here on, I will use "human" to mean "genetically human," since the moral sense of the term seems closely connected to, and perhaps derived from, the assumption that genetic humanity is both necessary and sufficient for membership in the moral community.
13. Alan Gewirth defends a similar claim in *Reason and Morality* (Chicago: University of Chicago Press, 1978).
14. Fetal sentience is impossible prior to the development of neurological connections between the sense organs and the brain, and between the various parts of the brain involved in the processing of conscious experience. This stage of neurological development is currently thought to occur at some point in the late second or early third trimester.

15. Thomas L. Hayes, "A Biological View," *Commonweal* 85 (March 17, 1967): pp. 677–78; cited by Daniel Callahan in *Abortion: Law, Choice, and Morality* (London: Macmillan, 1970).
16. See, for instance, Tom Regan, *The Case for Animal Rights* (Berkeley: University of California Press, 1983).

Study Questions

1. What characteristics entitle an entity to be considered a person?
2. Is infanticide more difficult to justify than abortion?
3. If a fetus is a human being, is abortion ever morally permissible?
4. If a fetus is not a human being, is abortion ever morally wrong?

CHAPTER 23

Why Abortion Is Immoral

Don Marquis

Don Marquis, who is Professor of Philosophy at the University of Kansas, disagrees with the views of Mary Anne Warren presented in the previous selection. He argues that, with rare exceptions, abortion is immoral. Note that he does not base his reasoning on the claim that the fetus is a person but rather on the view that the fetus has a valuable future.

The view that abortion is, with rare exceptions, seriously immoral has received little support in the recent philosophical literature. No doubt most philosophers affiliated with secular institutions of higher education believe that the anti-abortion position is either a symptom of irrational religious dogma or a conclusion generated by seriously confused philosophical argument. The purpose of this essay is to undermine this general belief. This essay sets out an argument that purports to show, as well as any argument in ethics can show, that abortion is, except possibly in rare cases, seriously immoral, that it is in the same moral category as killing an innocent adult human being. . . .

I

A sketch of standard anti-abortion and pro-choice arguments exhibits how those arguments possess certain symmetries that explain why partisans of those positions are so convinced of the correctness of their own positions, why they are not successful in convincing their opponents, and why, to others, this issue seems to be unresolvable.

From Don Marquis, "Why Abortion is Immoral," in *The Journal of Philosophy*, Vol. 86. Copyright © 1989. Reprinted by permission of the author and *The Journal of Philosophy*.

An analysis of the nature of this standoff suggests a strategy for sur-
mounting it.

Consider the way a typical anti-abortionist argues. She will argue
or assert that life is present from the moment of conception or that
fetuses look like babies or that fetuses possess a characteristic such as
a genetic code that is both necessary and sufficient for being human.
Anti-abortionists seem to believe that (1) the truth of all of these
claims is quite obvious, and (2) establishing any of these claims is sufficient to show that abortion is morally akin to murder.

A standard pro-choice strategy exhibits similarities. The pro-
choicer will argue or assert that fetuses are not persons or that
fetuses are not rational agents or that fetuses are not social beings.
Pro-choicers seem to believe that (1) the truth of any of these claims
is quite obvious, and (2) establishing any of these claims is sufficient
to show that an abortion is not a wrongful killing.

In fact, both the pro-choice and the anti-abortion claims do seem
to be true, although the "it looks like a baby" claim is more difficult
to establish the earlier the pregnancy. We seem to have a standoff.
How can it be resolved?

As everyone who has taken a bit of logic knows, if any of these
arguments concerning abortion is a good argument, it requires not
only some claim characterizing fetuses, but also some general moral
principle that ties a characteristic of fetuses to having or not having
the right to life or to some other moral characteristic that will generate the obligation or the lack of obligation not to end the life of
a fetus. Accordingly, the arguments of the anti-abortionist and the
pro-choicer need a bit of filling in to be regarded as adequate.

Note what each partisan will say. The anti-abortionist will claim
that her position is supported by such generally accepted moral principles as "It is always prima facie seriously wrong to take a human
life" or "It is always prima facie seriously wrong to end the life of
a baby." Since these are generally accepted moral principles, her
position is certainly not obviously wrong. The pro-choicer will claim
that her position is supported by such plausible moral principles as
"Being a person is what gives an individual intrinsic moral worth" or
"It is only seriously prima facie wrong to take the life of a member of
the human community." Since these are generally accepted moral
principles, the pro-choice position is certainly not obviously wrong.
Unfortunately, we have again arrived at a standoff.

Now, how might one deal with this standoff? The standard
approach is to try to show how the moral principles of one's opponent

lose their plausibility under analysis. It is easy to see how this is possible. On the one hand, the anti-abortionist will defend a moral principle concerning the wrongness of killing which tends to be broad in scope in order that even fetuses at an early stage of pregnancy will fall under it. The problem with broad principles is that they often embrace too much. In this particular instance, the principle "It is always prima facie wrong to take a human life" seems to entail that it is wrong to end the existence of a living human cancer cell culture, on the grounds that the culture is both living and human. Therefore, it seems that the anti-abortionist's favored principle is too broad.

On the other hand, the pro-choicer wants to find a moral principle concerning the wrongness of killing which tends to be narrow in scope in order that fetuses will *not* fall under it. The problem with narrow principles is that they often do not embrace enough. Hence, the needed principles such as "It is prima facie seriously wrong to kill only persons" or "It is prima facie seriously wrong to kill only rational agents" do not explain why it is wrong to kill infants or young children or the severely retarded or even perhaps the severely mentally ill. Therefore, we seem again to have a standoff. The anti-abortionist charges, not unreasonably, that pro-choice principles concerning killing are too narrow to be acceptable; the pro-choicer charges, not unreasonably, that anti-abortionist principles concerning killing are too broad to be acceptable. . . .

All this suggests that a necessary condition of resolving the abortion controversy is a more theoretical account of the wrongness of killing. After all, if we merely believe, but do not understand, why killing adult human beings such as ourselves is wrong, how could we conceivably show that abortion is either immoral or permissible?

II

In order to develop such an account, we can start from the following unproblematic assumption concerning our own case: it is wrong to kill *us*. Why is it wrong? Some answers can be easily eliminated. It might be said that what makes killing us wrong is that a killing brutalizes the one who kills. But the brutalization consists of being inured to the performance of an act that is hideously immoral; hence, the brutalization does not explain the immorality. It might be said that what makes killing us wrong is the great loss others would experience due to our absence. Although such hubris is understandable, such an explanation does not account for the wrongness of killing hermits, or those whose lives are relatively independent and whose friends find it easy to make new friends.

A more obvious answer is better. What primarily makes killing wrong is neither its effect on the murderer nor its effect on the victim's friends and relatives, but its effect on the victim. The loss of one's life is one of the greatest losses one can suffer. The loss of one's life deprives one of all the experiences, activities, projects, and enjoyments that would otherwise have constituted one's future. Therefore, killing someone is wrong, primarily because the killing inflicts (one of) the greatest possible losses on the victim. To describe this as the loss of life can be misleading, however. The change in my biological state does not by itself make killing me wrong. The effect of the loss of my biological life is the loss to me of all those activities, projects, experiences, and enjoyments which would otherwise have constituted my future personal life. These activities, projects, experiences, and enjoyments are either valuable for their own sakes or are means to something else that is valuable for its own sake. Some parts of my future are not valued by me now, but will come to be valued by me as I grow older and as my values and capacities change. When I am killed, I am deprived both of what I now value which would have been part of my future personal life, but also what I would come to value. Therefore, when I die, I am deprived of all of the value of my future. Inflicting this loss on me is ultimately what makes killing me wrong. This being the case, it would seem that what makes killing *any* adult human being prima facie seriously wrong is the loss of his or her future.[1]

How should this rudimentary theory of the wrongness of killing be evaluated? It cannot be faulted for deriving an "ought" from an "is," for it does not. The analysis assumes that killing me (or you, reader) is prima facie seriously wrong. The point of the analysis is to establish which natural property ultimately explains the wrongness of the killing, given that it is wrong. A natural property will ultimately explain the wrongness of killing, only if (1) the explanation fits with our intuitions about the matter and (2) there is no other natural property that provides the basis for a better explanation of the wrongness of killing. This analysis rests on the intuition that what makes killing a particular human or animal wrong is what it does to that particular human or animal. What makes killing wrong is some natural effect or other of the killing. Some would deny this. For instance, a divine command theorist in ethics would deny it. Surely this denial is, however, one of those features of divine command theory which renders it so implausible.

The claim that what makes killing wrong is the loss of the victim's future is directly supported by two considerations. In the first place, this theory explains why we regard killing as one of the worst of crimes. Killing is especially wrong, because it deprives the victim of more than perhaps any other crime. In the second place, people with AIDS or cancer who know they are dying believe, of course, that dying is a very bad thing for them. They believe that the loss of a future to them that they would otherwise have experienced is what makes their premature death a very bad thing for them. A better theory of the wrongness of killing would require a different natural property associated with killing which better fits with the attitudes of the dying. What could it be?

The view that what makes killing wrong is the loss to the victim of the value of the victim's future gains additional support when some of its implications are examined. In the first place, it is incompatible with the view that it is wrong to kill only beings who are biologically human. It is possible that there exists a different species from another planet whose members have a future like ours. Since having a future like that is what makes killing someone wrong, this theory entails that it would be wrong to kill members of such a species. Hence, this theory is opposed to the claim that only life that is biologically human has great moral worth, a claim which many anti-abortionists have seemed to adopt. This opposition, which this theory has in common with personhood theories, seems to be a merit of the theory.

In the second place, the claim that the loss of one's future is the wrong-making feature of one's being killed entails the possibility that the futures of some actual nonhuman mammals on our own planet are sufficiently like ours that it is seriously wrong to kill them also. Whether some animals do have the same right to life as human beings depends on adding to the account of the wrongness of killing some additional account of just what it is about my future or the futures of other adult human beings which makes it wrong to kill us. No such additional account will be offered in this essay. Undoubtedly, the provision of such an account would be a very difficult matter. Undoubtedly, any such account would be quite controversial. Hence, it surely should not reflect badly on this sketch of an elementary theory of the wrongness of killing that it is indeterminate with respect to some very difficult issues regarding animal rights.

In the third place, the claim that the loss of one's future is the wrong-making feature of one's being killed does not entail, as sanctity of human life theories do, that active euthanasia is wrong. Persons who are severely and incurably ill, who face a future of pain and despair, and who wish to die will not have suffered a loss if they are killed. It is, strictly speaking, the value of a human's future which makes killing wrong in this theory. This being so, killing does not necessarily wrong some persons who are sick and dying. Of course, there may be other reasons for a prohibition of active euthanasia, but that is another matter. Sanctity-of-human-life theories seem to hold that active euthanasia is seriously wrong even in an individual case where there seems to be good reason for it independently of public policy considerations. This consequence is most implausible, and it is a plus for the claim that the loss of a future of value is what makes killing wrong that it does not share this consequence.

In the fourth place, the account of the wrongness of killing defended in this essay does straightforwardly entail that it is prima facie seriously wrong to kill children and infants, for we do presume that they have futures of value. Since we do believe that it is wrong to kill defenseless little babies, it is important that a theory of the wrongness of killing easily account for this. Personhood theories of the wrongness of killing, on the other hand, cannot straightforwardly account for the wrongness of killing infants and young children. Hence, such theories must add special ad hoc accounts of the wrongness of killing the young. The plausibility of such ad hoc theories seems to be a function of how desperately one wants such theories to work. The claim that the primary wrong-making feature of a killing is the loss to the victim of the value of its future accounts for the wrongness of killing young children and infants directly; it makes the wrongness of such acts as obvious as we actually think it is. This is a further merit of this theory. Accordingly, it seems that this value of a future-like-ours theory of the wrongness of killing shares strengths of both sanctity-of-life and personhood accounts while avoiding weaknesses of both. In addition, it meshes with a central institution concerning what makes killing wrong.

The claim that the primary wrong-making feature of a killing is the loss to the victim of the value of its future has obvious consequences for the ethics of abortion. The future of a standard fetus includes a set of experiences, projects, activities, and such which are identical with the futures of adult human beings and are identical with the futures of young children. Since the reason that is sufficient to explain why it is wrong to kill human beings after the time of birth is a reason that also applies to fetuses, it follows that abortion is prima facie seriously morally wrong.

This argument does not rely on the invalid inference that, since it is wrong to kill persons, it is wrong to kill potential persons also. The category that is morally central to this analysis is the category of having a valuable future like ours; it is not the category of personhood. The argument to the conclusion that abortion is prima facie seriously morally wrong proceeded independently of the notion of person or potential person or any equivalent. Someone may wish to start with this analysis in terms of the value of a human future, conclude that abortion is, except perhaps in rare circumstances, seriously morally wrong, infer that fetuses have the right to life, and then call fetuses "persons" as a result of their having the right to life. Clearly, in this case, the category of person is being used to state the *conclusion* of the analysis rather than to generate the *argument* of the analysis. . . .

Of course, this value of a future-like-ours argument, if sound, shows only that abortion is prima facie wrong, not that it is wrong in any and all circumstances. Since the loss of the future to a standard fetus, if killed, is, however, at least as great a loss as the loss of the future to a standard adult human being who is killed, abortion, like ordinary killing, could be justified only by the most compelling reasons. The loss of one's life is almost the greatest misfortune that can happen to one. Presumably abortion could be justified in some circumstances, only if the loss consequent on failing to abort would be at least as great. Accordingly, morally permissible abortions will be rare indeed unless, perhaps, they occur so early in pregnancy that a fetus is not yet definitely an individual. Hence, this argument should be taken as showing that abortion is presumptively very seriously wrong, where the presumption is very strong—as strong as the presumption that killing another adult human being is wrong.

. . .

V

In this essay, it has been argued that the correct ethic of the wrongness of killing can be extended to fetal life and used to show that there is a strong presumption that any abortion is morally impermissible. If the ethic of killing adopted here entails, however, that contraception is also seriously immoral, then there would appear to be a difficulty with the analysis of this assay.

But this analysis does not entail that contraception is wrong. Of course, contraception prevents the actualization of a possible future of value. Hence, it follows from the claim that futures of value should be maximized that contraception is prima facie immoral. This obligation to maximize does not exist, however; furthermore, nothing in the ethics of killing in this paper entails that it does. The ethics of killing in this essay would entail that contraception is wrong only if something were denied a human future of value by contraception. Nothing at all is denied such a future by contraception, however.

Candidates for a subject of harm by contraception fall into four categories: (1) some sperm or other, (2) some ovum or other, (3) a sperm and an ovum separately, and (4) a sperm and an ovum together. Assigning the harm to some sperm is utterly arbitrary, for no reason can be given for making a sperm the subject of harm rather than an ovum. Assigning the harm to some ovum is utterly arbitrary, for no reason can be given for making an ovum the subject of harm rather than a sperm. One might attempt to avoid these problems by insisting that contraception deprives both the sperm and the ovum separately of a valuable future like ours. On this alternative, too many futures are lost. Contraception was supposed to be wrong, because it deprived us of one future of value, not two. One might attempt to avoid this problem by holding that contraception deprives the combination of sperm and ovum of a valuable future like ours. But here the definite article misleads. At the time of contraception, there are hundreds of millions of sperm, one (released) ovum and millions of possible combinations of all of these. There is no actual combination at all. Is the subject of the loss to be a merely possible combination? Which one? This alternative does not yield an actual subject of harm either. Accordingly, the immorality of contraception is not entailed by the loss of a future-like-ours argument simply because there is no nonarbitrarily identifiable subject of the loss in the case of contraception.

VI

The purpose of this essay has been to set out an argument for the serious presumptive wrongness of abortion subject to the assumption that the moral permissibility of abortion stands or falls on the moral status of the fetus. Since a fetus possesses a property, the possession of which in adult human beings is sufficient to make killing an adult human being wrong, abortion is wrong. This way of dealing with the problem of abortion seems superior to other approaches to the ethics of abortion, because it rests on an ethics of killing which is close to self-evident, because the crucial morally relevant property clearly applies to fetuses, and because the argument avoids the usual equivocations of "human life," "human being," or "person." . . . Its soundness is compatible with the moral permissibility of euthanasia and contraception. It deals with our intuitions concerning young children.

Finally, this analysis can be viewed as resolving a standard problem—indeed, *the* standard problem—concerning the ethics of abortion. Clearly, it is wrong to kill adult human beings. Clearly, it is not wrong to end the life of some arbitrarily chosen single human cell. Fetuses seem to be like arbitrarily chosen human cells in some respects and like adult humans in other respects. The problem of the ethics of abortion is the problem of determining the fetal property that settles this moral controversy. The thesis of this essay is that the problem of the ethics of abortion, so understood, is solvable.

Note

1. I have been most influenced on this matter by Jonathan Glover, *Causing Death and Saving Lives* (New York: Penguin, 1977), chap. 3; and Robert Young, "What Is So Wrong with Killing People?" *Philosophy* LIV, 210 (1979), pp. 518–28.

Study Questions

1. Is the loss of one's future as devastating for a fetus as for a child?
2. Does Marquis's argument that abortion is immoral depend on religious considerations?
3. Does Marquis accept the argument that because killing persons is wrong, killing potential persons is also wrong?
4. According to Marquis, in what circumstances is abortion not wrong?

CHAPTER 24

Virtue Theory and Abortion

Rosalind Hursthouse

Rosalind Hursthouse is Professor of Philosophy at the University of Auckland in New Zealand. She demonstrates how virtue theory can be applied to the issue of abortion. The term "deontological" that she uses refers to an ethical theory, such as Kant's, based on fulfilling duties, as opposed to a consequentialist theory, such as utilitarianism, that appeals to achieving good states of affairs.

The sort of ethical theory derived from Aristotle, variously described as virtue ethics, virtue-based ethics, or neo-Aristotelianism, is becoming better known, and is now quite widely recognized as at least a possible rival to deontological and utilitarian theories. . . . I aim to deepen that understanding . . . by illustrating what the theory looks like when it is applied to a particular issue, in this case, abortion. . . .

As everyone knows, the morality of abortion is commonly discussed in relation to just two considerations: first, and predominantly, the status of the fetus and whether or not it is the sort of thing that may or may not be innocuously or justifiably killed; and second, and less predominantly (when, that is, the discussion concerns the *morality* of abortion rather than the question of permissible legislation in a just society), women's rights. If one thinks within this familiar framework, one may well be puzzled about what virtue theory, as such, could contribute. Some people assume the discussion will be conducted solely in terms of what the virtuous agent would or would not do. . . . Others assume that only justice, or at most justice and charity, will be applied to the issue, generating a discussion very similar to Judith Jarvis Thomson's.[1]

Now if this is the way the virtue theorist's discussion of abortion is imagined to be, no wonder people think little of it. It seems obvious in

From *Philosophy & Public Affairs*. 20 (1991), by permission of Blackwell Publishing.

advance that in any such discussion there must be either a great deal of extremely tendentious application of the virtue terms *just, charitable,* and so on or a lot of rhetorical appeal to "this is what only the virtuous agent knows." But these are caricatures; they fail to appreciate the way in which virtue theory quite transforms the discussion of abortion by dismissing the two familiar dominating considerations as, in a way, fundamentally irrelevant. In what way or ways, I hope to make both clear and plausible.

Let us first consider women's rights. Let me emphasize again that we are discussing the *morality* of abortion, not the rights and wrongs of laws prohibiting or permitting it. If we suppose that women do have a moral right to do as they choose with their own bodies, or, more particularly, to terminate their pregnancies, then it may well follow that a *law* forbidding abortion would be unjust. Indeed, even if they have no such right, such a law might be, as things stand at the moment, unjust, or impractical, or inhumane: on this issue I have nothing to say in this article. But, putting all questions about the justice or injustice of laws to one side, and supposing only that women have such a moral right, *nothing* follows from this supposition about the morality of abortion, according to virtue theory, once it is noted (quite generally, not with particular reference to abortion) that in exercising a moral right I can do something cruel, or callous, or selfish, light-minded, self-righteous, stupid, inconsiderate, disloyal, dishonest—that is act viciously.[2] Love and friendship do not survive their parties constantly insisting on their rights, nor do people live well when they think that getting what they have a right to is of pre-eminent importance; they harm others, and they harm themselves. So whether women have a moral right to terminate their pregnancies is irrelevant within virtue theory, for it is irrelevant to the question "In having an abortion in these circumstances, would the agent be acting virtuously or viciously or neither?"

What about the consideration of the status of the fetus—what can virtue theory say about that? One might say that this issue is not in the province of *any* moral theory; it is a metaphysical question, and an extremely difficult one at that. Must virtue theory then wait upon metaphysics to come up with the answer?

At first sight it might seem so. For virtue is said to involve knowledge, and part of this knowledge consists in having the *right* attitude to things. "Right" here does not just mean "morally right" or "proper" or "nice" in the modern sense; it means "accurate, true." One cannot have the right or correct attitude to something if the attitude is based on or involves false beliefs. And this suggests that if the status of the fetus is relevant to the rightness or wrongness of abortion, its status must be known, as a truth, to the fully wise and virtuous person.

But the sort of wisdom that the fully virtuous person has is not supposed to be recondite; it does not call for fancy philosophical sophistication, and it does not depend upon, let alone wait upon, the discoveries of academic philosophers.[3] And this entails the following, rather startling, conclusion: that the status of the fetus—that issue over which so much ink has been spilt—is, according to virtue theory, simply not relevant to the rightness or wrongness of abortion (within, that is, a secular morality).

Or rather, since that is clearly too radical a conclusion, it is in a sense relevant, but only in the sense that the familiar biological facts are relevant. By "the familiar biological facts" I mean the facts that most human societies are and have been familiar with—that, standardly (but not invariably), pregnancy occurs as the result of sexual intercourse, that it lasts about nine months, during which time the fetus grows and develops, that standardly it terminates in the birth of a living baby, and that this is how we all come to be.

It might be thought that this distinction—between the familiar biological facts and the status of the fetus—is a distinction without a difference. But this is not so. To attach relevance to the status of the fetus, in the sense in which virtue theory claims it is not relevant, is to be gripped by the conviction that we must go beyond the familiar biological facts, deriving some sort of conclusion from them, such as that the fetus has rights, or is not a person, or something similar. It is also to believe that this exhausts the relevance of the familiar biological facts, that all they are relevant to is the status of the fetus and whether or not it is the sort of thing that may or may not be killed.

These convictions, I suspect, are rooted in the desire to solve the problem of abortion by getting it to fall under some general rule such as "You ought not to kill anything with the right to life but may kill anything else." But they have resulted in what should surely strike any nonphilosopher as a most bizarre aspect of nearly all the current philosophical literature on abortion, namely, that, far from treating abortion as a unique moral problem, markedly unlike any other, nearly everything written on the status of the fetus and its bearing on the abortion issue would be consistent with the human reproductive facts' (to say nothing of family life) being totally different from what they are. Imagine that you are an alien extraterrestrial anthropologist who does not know that the human race is roughly

50 percent female and 50 percent male, or that our only (natural) form of reproduction involves heterosexual intercourse, viviparous birth, and the female's (and only the female's) being pregnant for nine months, or that females are capable of childbearing from late childhood to late middle age, or that childbearing is painful, dangerous, and emotionally charged—do you think you would pick up these facts from the hundreds of articles written on the status of the fetus? I am quite sure you would not. And that, I think, shows that the current philosophical literature on abortion has got badly out of touch with reality.

Now if we are using virtue theory, our first question is not "What do the familiar biological facts show—what can be derived from them about the status of the fetus?" but "How do these facts figure in the practical reasoning, actions and passions, thoughts and reactions, of the virtuous and the nonvirtuous? What is the mark of having the right attitude to these facts and what manifests having the wrong attitude to them?" This immediately makes essentially relevant not only all the facts about human reproduction I mentioned above, but a whole range of facts about our emotions in relation to them as well. I mean such facts as that human parents, both male and female, tend to care passionately about their offspring, and that family relationships are among the deepest and strongest in our lives—and, significantly, among the longest-lasting.

These facts make it obvious that pregnancy is not just one among many other physical conditions; and hence that anyone who genuinely believes that an abortion is comparable to a haircut or an appendectomy is mistaken.[4] The fact that the premature termination of a pregnancy is, in some sense, the cutting off of a new human life, and thereby, like the procreation of a new human life, connects with all our thoughts about human life and death, parenthood, and family relationships, must make it a serious matter. To disregard this fact about it, to think of abortion as nothing but the killing of something that does not matter, or as nothing but the exercise of some right or rights one has, or as the incidental means to some desirable state of affairs, is to do something callous and light-minded, the sort of thing that no virtuous and wise person would do. It is to have the wrong attitude not only to fetuses, but more generally to human life and death, parenthood, and family relationships.

Although I say that the facts make this obvious, I know that this is one of my tendentious points. In partial support of it I note that even the most dedicated proponents of the view that deliberate abortion is just like an appendectomy or haircut rarely hold the same view of spontaneous abortion, that is, miscarriage. It is not so tendentious of me to claim that to react to people's grief over miscarriage by saying, or even thinking, "What a fuss about nothing!" would be callous and light-minded, whereas to try to laugh someone out of grief over an appendectomy scar or a botched haircut would not be. It is hard to give this point due prominence within act-centered theories, for the inconsistency is an inconsistency in attitude about the seriousness of loss of life, not in beliefs about which acts are right or wrong. Moreover, an act-centered theorist may say, "Well, there is nothing wrong with *thinking* 'What a fuss about nothing!' as long as you do not say it and hurt the person who is grieving. And besides, we cannot be held responsible for our thoughts, only for the intentional actions they give rise to." But the character traits that virtue theory emphasizes are not simply dispositions to intentional actions, but a seamless disposition to certain actions and passions, thoughts and reactions.

To say that the cutting off of a human life is always a matter of some seriousness, at any stage, is not to deny the relevance of gradual fetal development. Notwithstanding the well-worn point that clear boundary lines cannot be drawn, our emotions and attitudes regarding the fetus do change as it develops, and again when it is born, and indeed further as the baby grows. Abortion for shallow reasons in the later stages is much more shocking than abortion for the same reasons in the early stages in a way that matches the fact that deep grief over miscarriage in the later stages is more appropriate than it is over miscarriage in the earlier stages (when, that is, the grief is solely about the loss of *this* child, not about, as might be the case, the loss of one's only hope of having a child or of having one's husband's child). Imagine (or recall) a woman who already has children; she had not intended to have more, but finds herself unexpectedly pregnant. Though contrary to her plans, the pregnancy, once established as a fact, is welcomed—and then she loses the embryo almost immediately. If this were bemoaned as a tragedy, it would, I think, be a misapplication of the concept of what is tragic. But it may still properly be mourned as a loss. The grief is expressed in such terms as "I shall always wonder how she or he would have turned out" or "When I look at the others, I shall think, 'How different their lives would have been if this other one had been part of them.'" It would, I take it, be callous and light-minded to say, or think, "Well, she has already *got* four children; what's the problem?"; it would be neither, nor arrogantly intrusive in the case of a close friend, to try to correct prolonged mourning by saying, "I know it's sad, but it's not a tragedy; rejoice in the ones you have." The application of *tragic* becomes more appropriate as the fetus grows, for the mere fact that one has lived with it for longer, conscious of its existence, makes a difference. To shrug off an early abortion is understandable just because it is very hard to be fully conscious of the fetus's existence in the early stages and hence hard to appreciate that an early abortion is the destruction of life. It is particularly hard for the young and inexperienced to appreciate this, because appreciation of it usually comes only with experience.

I do not mean "with the experience of having an abortion" (though that may be part of it) but, quite generally, "with the experience of life." Many women who have borne children contrast their later pregnancies with their first successful one, saying that in the later ones they were conscious of a new life growing in them from very early on. And, more generally, as one reaches the age at which the next generation is coming up close behind one, the counterfactuals "If I, or she, had had an abortion, Alice, or Bob, would not have been born" acquire a significant application, which casts a new light on the conditionals "If I or Alice have an abortion then some Caroline or Bill will not be born."

The fact that pregnancy is not just one among many physical conditions does not mean that one can never regard it in that light without manifesting a vice. When women are in very poor physical health, or worn out from childbearing, or forced to do very physically demanding jobs, then they cannot be described as self-indulgent, callous, irresponsible, or light-minded if they seek abortions mainly with a view to avoiding pregnancy as the physical condition that it is. To go through with a pregnancy when one is utterly exhausted, or when one's job consists of crawling along tunnels hauling coal, as many women in the nineteenth century were obliged to do, is perhaps heroic, but people who do not achieve heroism are not necessarily vicious. That they can view the pregnancy only as eight months of misery, followed by hours if not days of agony and exhaustion, and abortion only as the blessed escape from this prospect, is entirely understandable and does not manifest any lack of serious respect for human life or a shallow attitude to motherhood. What it does show is that something is terribly amiss in the conditions of their lives, which make it so hard to recognize pregnancy and childbearing as the good that they can be.

In relation to this last point I should draw attention to the way in which virtue theory has a sort of built-in indexicality. Philosophers arguing against anything remotely resembling a belief in the sanctity of life (which the above claims clearly embody) frequently appeal to the existence of other communities in which abortion and infanticide are practiced. We should not automatically assume that it is impossible that some other communities could be morally inferior to our own; maybe some are, or have been, precisely insofar as their members are, typically, callous or light-minded or unjust. But in communities in which life is a great deal tougher for everyone than it is in ours, having the right attitude to human life and death, parenthood, and family relationships might well manifest itself in ways that are unlike ours. When it is essential to survival that most members of the community fend for themselves at a very young age or work during most of their waking hours, selective abortion or infanticide might be practiced either as a form of genuine euthanasia or for the sake of the community and not, I think, be thought callous or light-minded. But this does not make everything all right; as before, it shows that there is something amiss with the conditions of their lives, which are making it impossible for them to live really well.

The foregoing discussion, insofar as it emphasizes the right attitude to human life and death, parallels to a certain extent those standard discussions of abortion that concentrate on it solely as an issue of killing. But it does not, as those discussions do, gloss over the fact, emphasized by those who discuss the morality of abortion in terms of women's rights, that abortion, wildly unlike any other form of killing, is the termination of a pregnancy, which is a condition of a woman's body and results in *her* having a child if it is not aborted. This fact is given due recognition not by appeal to women's rights but by emphasizing the relevance of the familiar biological and psychological facts and their connection with having the right attitude to parenthood and family relationships. But it may well be thought that failing to bring in women's rights still leaves some important aspects of the problem of abortion untouched.

Speaking in terms of women's rights, people sometimes say things like, "Well, it's her life you're talking about too, you know; she's got a right to her own life, her own happiness." And the discussion stops there. But in the context of virtue theory, given that we are particularly concerned with what constitutes a good human life, with what true happiness or *eudaimonia* is, this is no place to stop. We go on to ask, "And is this life of hers a good one? Is she living well?"

If we are to go on to talk about good human lives, in the context of abortion, we have to bring in our thoughts about the value of love and family life, and our proper emotional development through a natural life cycle. The familiar facts support the view that parenthood in general, and motherhood and childbearing in particular, are intrinsically worthwhile, are among the things that can be correctly thought to be partially constitutive of a flourishing human life.[5] If this is right, then a woman who opts for not being a mother (at all, or again, or now) by opting for abortion may thereby be manifesting a flawed grasp of what her life should be, and be about—a grasp that is childish, or grossly materialistic, or short-sighted, or shallow.

I said "*may* thereby"; this *need* not be so. Consider, for instance, a woman who has already had several children and fears that to have another will seriously affect her capacity to be a good mother to the ones she has—she does not show a lack of appreciation of the intrinsic value of being a parent by opting for abortion. Nor does a woman who has been a good mother and is approaching the age at which she may be looking forward to being a good grandmother. Nor does a woman who discovers that her pregnancy may well kill her, and opts for abortion and adoption. Nor, necessarily, does a woman who has decided to lead a life centered around some other worthwhile activity or activities with which motherhood would compete.

People who are childless by choice are sometimes described as "irresponsible," or "selfish," or "refusing to grow up," or "not knowing what life is about." But one can hold that having children is intrinsically worthwhile without endorsing this, for we are, after all, in the happy position of there being more worthwhile things to do than can be fitted into one lifetime. Parenthood, and motherhood in particular, even if granted to be intrinsically worthwhile, undoubtedly take up a lot of one's adult life, leaving no room for some other worthwhile pursuits. But some women who choose abortion rather than have their first child, and some men who encourage their partners to choose abortion, are not avoiding parenthood for the sake of other worthwhile pursuits, but for the worthless one of "having a good time," or for the pursuit of some false vision of the ideals of freedom or self-realization. And some others who say "I am not ready for parenthood yet" are making some sort of mistake about the extent to which one can manipulate the circumstances of one's life so as to make it fulfill some dream that one has. Perhaps one's dream is to have two perfect children, a girl and a boy, within a perfect marriage, in financially secure circumstances, with an interesting job of one's own. But to care too much about that dream, to demand of life that it give it to one and act accordingly, may be both greedy and foolish, and is to run the risk of missing out on happiness entirely. Not only may fate make the dream impossible, or destroy it, but one's own attachment to it may make it impossible. Good marriages, and the most promising children, can be destroyed by just one adult's excessive demand for perfection.

Once again, this is not to deny that girls may quite properly say "I am not ready for motherhood yet," especially in our society, and, far from manifesting irresponsibility or light-mindedness, show an appropriate modesty or humility, or a fearfulness that does not amount to cowardice. However, even when the decision to have an abortion is the right decision—one that does not itself fall under a vice-related term and thereby one that the perfectly virtuous could recommend—it does not follow that there is no sense in which having the abortion is wrong, or guilt inappropriate. For, by virtue of the fact that a human life has been cut short, some evil has probably been brought about,[6] and that circumstances make the decision to bring about some evil the right decision will be a ground for guilt if getting into those circumstances in the first place itself manifested a flaw in character.

What "gets one into those circumstances" in the case of abortion is, except in the case of rape, one's sexual activity and one's choices, or the lack of them, about one's sexual partner and about contraception. The virtuous woman (which here of course does not mean simply "chaste woman" but "woman with the virtues") has such character traits as strength, independence, resoluteness, decisiveness, self-confidence, responsibility, serious-mindedness, and self-determination—and no one, I think, could deny that many women become pregnant in circumstances in which they cannot welcome or cannot face the thought of having *this* child precisely because they lack one or some of these character traits. So even in the cases where the decision to have an abortion is the right one, it can still be the reflection of a moral failing—not because the decision itself is weak or cowardly or irresolute or irresponsible or light-minded, but because lack of the requisite opposite of these failings landed one in the circumstances in the first place. Hence the common universalized claim that guilt and remorse are never appropriate emotions about an abortion is denied. They may be appropriate, and appropriately inculcated, even when the decision was the right one.

Another motivation for bringing women's rights into the discussion may be to attempt to correct the implication, carried by the killing-centered approach, that insofar as abortion is wrong, it is a wrong that only women do, or at least (given the preponderance of male doctors) that only women instigate. I do not myself believe that we can thus escape the fact that nature bears harder on women than it does on men,[7] but virtue theory can certainly correct many of the injustices that the emphasis on women's rights is rightly concerned about. With very little amendment, everything that has been said above applies to boys and men too. Although the abortion decision is, in a natural sense, the woman's decision, proper to her, boys and men are often party to it, for well or ill, and even when they are not, they are bound to have been party to the circumstances that brought it up. No less than girls and women, boys and men can, in their actions, manifest self-centeredness, callousness, and light-mindedness about life and parenthood in relation to abortion. They can be self-centered or courageous about the possibility of disability in their offspring; they need to reflect on their sexual activity and their choices, or the lack of them, about their sexual partner and contraception; they need to grow up and take responsibility for their own actions and life in relation to fatherhood. If it is true, as I maintain, that insofar as motherhood is intrinsically worthwhile, being a mother is an important purpose in women's lives, being a father (rather than a mere generator) is an important purpose in men's lives as well, and it is adolescent of men to turn a blind eye to this and pretend that they have many more important things to do.

Much more might be said, but I shall end the actual discussion of the problem of abortion here, and conclude by highlighting what I take to be its significant features. . . .

The discussion does not proceed simply by our trying to answer the question "Would a perfectly virtuous agent ever have an abortion and, if so, when?"; virtue theory is not limited to considering "Would Socrates have had an abortion if he were a raped, pregnant fifteen-year-old?" nor automatically stumped when we are considering circumstances into which no virtuous agent would have got herself. Instead, much of the discussion proceeds in the virtue- and vice-related terms whose application, in several cases, yields practical conclusions . . . These terms are difficult to apply correctly, and anyone might challenge my application of any one of them. So, for example, I have claimed that some abortions, done for certain reasons, would be callous or light-minded; that others might indicate an appropriate modesty or humility; that others would reflect a greedy and foolish attitude to what one could expect out of life. Any of these examples may be disputed, but what is at issue is, should these difficult terms be there, or should the discussion be couched in terms that all clever adolescents can apply correctly? . . .

Proceeding as it does in the virtue- and vice-related terms, the discussion thereby, inevitably, also contains claims about what is worthwhile, serious and important, good and evil, in our lives. So, for example, I claimed that parenthood is intrinsically worthwhile, and that having a good time was a worthless end (in life, not on individual occasions); that losing a fetus is always a serious matter (albeit not a tragedy in itself in the first trimester) whereas acquiring an appendectomy scar is a trivial one; that (human) death is an evil. Once again, these are difficult matters, and anyone might challenge any one of my claims. But what is at issue is, as before, should those difficult claims be there or can one reach practical conclusions about real moral issues that are in no way determined by premises about such matters? . . .

The discussion also thereby, inevitably, contains claims about what life is like (e.g., my claim that love and friendship do not survive their parties' constantly insisting on their rights; or the claim that to demand perfection of life is to run the risk of missing out on happiness entirely). What is at issue is, should those disputable claims be there, or is our knowledge (or are our false opinions) about what life is like irrelevant to our understanding of real moral issues? . . .

Naturally, my own view is that all these concepts should be there in any discussion of real moral issues and that virtue theory, which uses all of them, is the right theory to apply to them. I do not pretend to have shown this. I realize that proponents of rival theories may say that, now that they have understood how virtue theory uses the range of concepts it draws on, they are more convinced than ever that such concepts should not figure in an adequate normative theory, because they are sectarian, or vague or too particular, or improperly anthropocentric. . . . Or, finding many of the details of the discussion appropriate, they may agree that many, perhaps even all, of the concepts should figure, but argue that virtue theory gives an inaccurate account of the way the concepts fit together (and indeed of the concepts themselves) and that another theory provides a better account; that would be interesting to see.

Notes

1. Judith Jarvis Thomson, "A Defense of Abortion," *Philosophy & Public Affairs* 1, no. 1 (Fall 1971): 47–66. One could indeed regard this article as proto-virtue theory (no doubt to the surprise of the author) if the concepts of callousness and kindness were allowed more weight.

2. One possible qualification: if one ties the concept of justice very closely to rights, then if women do have a moral right to terminate their pregnancies it *may* follow that in doing so they do not act unjustly. (Cf. Thomson, "A Defense of Abortion.") But it is debatable whether even that much follows.

3. This is an assumption of virtue theory, and I do not attempt to defend it here. An adequate discussion of it would require a separate article, since, although most moral philosophers would be chary of claiming that intellectual sophistication is a necessary condition of moral wisdom or virtue, most of us, from Plato onward, tend to write as if this were so. Sorting out which claims about moral knowledge are committed to this kind of elitism and which can, albeit with difficulty, be reconciled with the idea that moral knowledge can be acquired by anyone who really wants it would be a major task.

4. Mary Anne Warren, in "On the Moral and Legal Status of Abortion," *Monist* 57 (1973), sec. 1, says of the opponents of restrictive laws governing abortion that "their conviction (for the most part) is that abortion is not a *morally* serious and extremely unfortunate, even though sometimes justified, act, comparable to killing in self-defense or to letting the violinist die, but rather is closer to being a *morally neutral* act, like cutting one's hair" (italics mine). I would like to think that no one *genuinely* believes this. But certainly in discussion, particularly when arguing against restrictive laws or the suggestion that remorse over abortion might be appropriate, I have found that some people *say* they believe it . . . Those who allow that it is morally serious, and far from morally neutral, have to argue against restrictive laws, or the appropriateness of remorse, on a very different ground from that laid down by the premise "The fetus is just part of the woman's body (and she has a right to determine what happens to her body and should not feel guilt about anything she does to it)."

5. I take this as a premise here, but argue for it in some detail in my *Beginning Lives* (Oxford: Basil Blackwell, 1987). In this connection I also discuss adoption and the sense in which it may be regarded as "second best," and the difficult question of whether the good of parenthood may properly be sought, or indeed bought, by surrogacy.

6. I say "some evil has probably been brought about" on the ground that (human) life is (usually) a good and hence (human) death usually an evil. The exceptions would be (*a*) where death is actually a good or a benefit, because the baby that would come to be if the life were not cut short would be better off dead than alive, and (*b*) where death, though

not a good, is not an evil either, because the life that would be led (e.g., in a state of permanent coma) would not be a good.

7. I discuss this point at greater length in *Beginning Lives*.

Study Questions

1. According to Hursthouse, do women's rights have anything to do with the morality of abortion?
2. According to Hursthouse, is the status of the fetus relevant to the rightness or wrongness of abortion?
3. What connections does Hursthouse draw between good human lives and a decision about abortion?
4. Can a correct moral decision result in some evil?

B. Euthanasia

CHAPTER 25

Active and Passive Euthanasia

James Rachels

The American Medical Association takes the position that while at a patient's request a physician may withhold extraordinary means of prolonging the patient's life, a physician may not take steps, even if requested by the patient, to terminate that life intentionally. Is this distinction viable? In the next selection James Rachels, whose work we read previously, argues that no moral difference between active and passive euthanasia is defensible.

The distinction between active and passive euthanasia is thought to be crucial for medical ethics. The idea is that it is permissible, at least in some cases, to withhold treatment and allow a patient to die, but it is never permissible to take any direct action designed to kill the patient. This doctrine seems to be accepted by most doctors, and it is endorsed in a statement adopted by the House of Delegates of the American Medical Association on 4 December 1973:

> The intentional termination of the life of one human being by another—mercy killing—is contrary to that for which the medical profession stands and is contrary to the policy of the American Medical Association.
>
> The cessation of the employment of extraordinary means to prolong the life of the body when there is irrefutable evidence that biological death is imminent is the decision of the patient and/or his immediate family. The advice and judgement of the physician should be freely available to the patient and/or his immediate family.

From James Rachels, "Active and Passive Euthanasia," in *New England Journal of Medicine*, Vol. 292. Copyright © 1975 by Massachusetts Medical Society. Reprinted by permission. All rights reserved.

However, a strong case can be made against this doctrine. In what follows I will set out some of the relevant arguments, and urge doctors to reconsider their views on this matter.

To begin with a familiar type of situation, a patient who is dying of incurable cancer of the throat is in terrible pain, which can no longer be satisfactorily alleviated. He is certain to die within a few days, even if present treatment is continued, but he does not want to go on living for those days since the pain is unbearable. So he asks the doctor for an end to it, and his family joins in the request.

Suppose the doctor agrees to withhold treatment, as the conventional doctrine says he may. The justification for his doing so is that the patient is in terrible agony, and since he is going to die anyway, it would be wrong to prolong his suffering needlessly. But now notice this. If one simply withholds treatment, it may take the patient longer to die, and so he may suffer more than he would if more direct action were taken and a lethal injection given. This fact provides strong reason for thinking that, once the initial decision not to prolong his agony has been made, active euthanasia is actually preferable to passive euthanasia, rather than the reverse. To say otherwise is to endorse the opinion that leads to more suffering rather than less, and is contrary to the humanitarian impulse that prompts the decision not to prolong his life in the first place.

Part of my point is that the process of being "allowed to die" can be relatively slow and painful, whereas being given a lethal injection is relatively quick and painless. Let me give a different sort of example. In the United States about one in 600 babies is born with Down's syndrome. Most of these babies are otherwise healthy—that is, with only the usual pediatric care, they will proceed to an otherwise normal infancy. Some, however, are born with congenital defects such as intestinal obstructions that require operations if they are to live. Sometimes, the parents and the doctor will decide not to operate, and let the infant die. Anthony Shaw describes what happens then:

> When surgery is denied [the doctor] must try to keep the infant from suffering while natural forces sap the baby's life away. As a surgeon whose natural inclination is to use the scalpel to fight off death, standing by and watching a salvageable baby die is the most emotionally exhausting experience I know. It is easy at a conference, in a theoretical discussion to decide that such infants should be allowed to die. It is altogether different to stand by in the nursery and watch as dehydration and infection wither a tiny being over hours and days. This is

a terrible ordeal for me and the hospital staff—much more so than for the parents who never set foot in the nursery.[1]

I can understand why some people are opposed to all euthanasia, and insist that such infants must be allowed to live. I think I can also understand why other people favour destroying these babies quickly and painlessly. But why should anyone favour letting "dehydration and infection wither a tiny being over hours and days"? The doctrine that says a baby may be allowed to dehydrate and wither, but may not be given an injection that would end its life without suffering, seems so patently cruel as to require no further refutation. The strong language is not intended to offend, but only to put the point in the clearest possible way.

My second argument is that the conventional doctrine leads to decisions concerning life and death made on irrelevant grounds.

Consider again the case of the infants with Down's syndrome who need operations for congenital defects unrelated to the syndrome to live. Sometimes, there is no operation, and the baby dies, but when there is no such defect, the baby lives on. Now, an operation such as that to remove an intestinal obstruction is not prohibitively difficult. The reason why such operations are not performed in these cases is, clearly, that the child has Down's syndrome and the parents and the doctor judge that because of that fact it is better for the child to die.

But notice that this situation is absurd, no matter what view one takes of the lives and potentials of such babies. If the life of such an infant is worth preserving, what does it matter if it needs a simple operation? Or, if one thinks it better that such a baby should not live on, what difference does it make that it happens to have an unobstructed intestinal tract? In either case, the matter of life and death is being decided on irrelevant grounds. It is the Down's syndrome, and not the intestines, that is the issue. The matter should be decided, if at all, on that basis, and not be allowed to depend on the essentially irrelevant question of whether the intestinal tract is blocked.

What makes this situation possible, of course, is the idea that when there is an intestinal blockage, one can "let the baby die," but when there is no such defect there is nothing that can be done, for one must not "kill" it. The fact that this idea leads to such results as deciding life or death on irrelevant grounds is another good reason why the doctrine would be rejected.

One reason why so many people think that there is an important moral difference between active and passive euthanasia is that they think killing someone is morally worse than letting someone die. But is it? Is killing, in itself, worse than letting die? To investigate this issue, two cases may be considered that are exactly alike except that one involves killing whereas the other involves letting someone die. Then, it can be asked whether this difference makes any difference to the moral assessments. It is important that the cases be exactly alike, except for this one difference, since otherwise one cannot be confident that it is this difference and not some other that accounts for any variation in the assessments of the two cases. So, let us consider this pair of cases:

In the first, Smith stands to gain a large inheritance if anything should happen to his six-year-old cousin. One evening while the child is taking his bath, Smith sneaks into the bathroom and drowns the child, and then arranges things so that it will look like an accident.

In the second, Jones also stands to gain if anything should happen to his six-year-old cousin. Like Smith, Jones sneaks in planning to drown the child in his bath. However, just as he enters the bathroom Jones sees the child slip and hit his head, and fall facedown in the water. Jones is delighted; he stands by, ready to push the child's head back under if it is necessary, but it is not necessary. With only a little thrashing about, the child drowns all by himself, "accidentally," as Jones watches and does nothing.

Now Smith killed the child, whereas Jones "merely" let the child die. That is the only difference between them. Did either man behave better, from a moral point of view? If the difference between killing and letting die were in itself a morally important matter, one should say that Jones's behaviour was less reprehensible than Smith's. But does one really want to say that? I think not. In the first place, both men acted from the same motive, personal gain, and both had exactly the same end in view when they acted. It may be inferred from Smith's conduct that he is a bad man, although that judgement may be withdrawn or modified if certain further facts are learned about him—for example, that he is mentally deranged. But would not the very same thing be inferred about Jones from his conduct? And would not the same further considerations also be relevant to any modification of this judgement? Moreover, suppose Jones pleaded, in his own defence, "After all, I didn't do anything except just stand there and watch the child drown. I didn't kill him; I only let him die." Again, if letting die were in itself less bad than killing, this defence should have at least some weight. But it does not. Such a "defence" can only be regarded as a grotesque perversion of moral reasoning. Morally speaking, it is no defence at all.

Now, it may be pointed out, quite properly, that the cases of euthanasia with which doctors are concerned are not like this at all. They do not involve personal gain or the destruction of normal, healthy children. Doctors are concerned only with cases in which the patient's life is of no further use to him, or in which the patient's life has become or will soon become a terrible burden. However, the point is the same in these cases: the bare difference between killing and letting die does not, in itself, make a moral difference. If a doctor lets a patient die, for humane reasons, he is in the same moral position as if he had given the patient a lethal injection for humane reasons. If his decision was wrong—if, for example, the patient's illness was in fact curable—the decision would be equally regrettable no matter which method was used to carry it out. And if the doctor's decision was the right one, the method used is not in itself important.

The AMA policy statement isolates the crucial issue very well; the crucial issue is "the intentional termination of the life of one human being by another." But after identifying this issue, and forbidding "mercy killing," the statement goes on to deny that the cessation of treatment is the intentional termination of a life. This is where the mistake comes in, for what is the cessation of treatment, in these circumstances, if it is not "the intentional termination of the life of one human being by another"? Of course it is exactly that, and if it were not, there would be no point to it.

Many people will find this judgement hard to accept. One reason, I think, is that it is very easy to conflate the question of whether killing is, in itself, worse than letting die, with the very different question of whether most actual cases of killing are more reprehensible than most actual cases of letting die. Most actual cases of killing are clearly terrible (think, for example, of all the murders reported in the newspapers), and one hears of such cases every day. On the other hand, one hardly ever hears of a case of letting die, except for the actions of doctors who are motivated by humanitarian reasons. So one learns to think of killing in a much worse light than of letting die. But this does not mean that there is something about killing that makes it in itself worse than letting die, for it is not the bare difference between killing and letting die that makes the difference in these cases. Rather, the other factors—the murderer's motive of personal gain, for example, contrasted with the doctor's humanitarian motivation—account for different reactions to the different cases.

I have argued that killing is not in itself any worse than letting die; if my contention is right, it follows that active euthanasia is not any worse than passive euthanasia. What arguments can be given on the other side? The most common, I believe, is the following:

> The important difference between active and passive euthanasia is that, in passive euthanasia, the doctor does not do anything to bring about the patient's death. The doctor does nothing, and the patient dies of whatever ills already afflict him. In active euthanasia, however, the doctor does something to bring about the patient's death: he kills him. The doctor who gives the patient with cancer a lethal injection has himself caused his patient's death; whereas if he merely ceases treatment, the cancer is the cause of the death.

A number of points need to be made here. The first is that it is not exactly correct to say that in passive euthanasia the doctor does nothing, for he does do one thing that is very important: he lets the patient die. "Letting someone die" is certainly different, in some respects, from other types of action—mainly in that it is a kind of action that one may perform by way of not performing certain other actions. For example, one may let a patient die by way of not giving medication, just as one may insult someone by way of not shaking his hand. But for any purpose of moral assessment, it is a type of action nonetheless. The decision to let a patient die is subject to moral appraisal in the same way that a decision to kill him would be subject to moral appraisal: it may be assessed as wise or unwise, compassionate or sadistic, right or wrong. If a doctor deliberately let a patient die who was suffering from a routinely curable illness, the doctor would certainly be to blame for what he had done, just as he would be to blame if he had needlessly killed the patient. Charges against him would then be appropriate. If so, it would be no defence at all for him to insist that he didn't "do anything." He would have done something very serious indeed, for he let his patient die.

Fixing the cause of death may be very important from a legal point of view, for it may determine whether criminal charges are brought against the doctor. But I do not think that this notion can be used to show a moral difference between active and passive euthanasia. The reason why it is considered bad to be the cause of someone's death is that death is regarded as a great evil—and so it is. However, if it has been decided that euthanasia—even passive euthanasia—is desirable in a given case, it has also been decided that in this instance death is no greater an evil than the patient's continued existence. And if this is true, the usual reason for not wanting to be the cause of someone's death simply does not apply.

Finally, doctors may think that all of this is only of academic interest—the sort of thing that philosophers may worry about but that has no practical bearing on their own work. After all, doctors must be concerned about the legal consequences of what they do, and active euthanasia is clearly forbidden by the law. But even so, doctors should also be concerned with the fact that the law is forcing upon them a moral doctrine that may be indefensible, and has a considerable effect on their practices. Of course, most doctors are not now in the position of being coerced in this matter, for they do not regard themselves as merely going along with what the law requires. Rather, in statements such as the AMA policy statement that I have quoted, they are endorsing this doctrine as a central point of medical ethics. In that statement, active euthanasia is condemned not merely as illegal but as "contrary to that for which the medical profession stands," whereas passive euthanasia is approved. However, the preceding considerations suggest that there is really no moral difference between the two, considered in themselves (there may be important moral differences in some cases in their *consequences*, but, as I pointed out, these differences may make active euthanasia, and not passive euthanasia, the morally preferable option). So, whereas doctors may have to discriminate between active and passive euthanasia to satisfy the law, they should not do any more than that. In particular, they should not give the distinction any added authority and weight by writing it into official statements of medical ethics.

Note

1. Anthony Shaw, "Doctor, Do We Have a Choice?" *New York Times Magazine*, 30 January 1972, p. 54.

Study Questions

1. According to Rachels, in passive euthanasia does the physician do anything?
2. Once a decision has been made for a terminally ill patient to die, is letting the person die better than killing the person?
3. Is someone who allows another person to drown morally guilty of killing the person?
4. According to Rachels, under what circumstances is active euthanasia morally preferable to passive euthanasia?

CHAPTER 26

The Intentional Termination of Life

Bonnie Steinbock

Bonnie Steinbock, Professor of Philosophy at the University at Albany
(State University of New York), wrote the following essay responding to
the previous article by James Rachels. Who has the better of the argument? That question is for each reader to answer.

According to James Rachels, . . . a common mistake in medical ethics
is the belief that there is a moral difference between active and passive euthanasia. This is a mistake, [he argues], because the rationale
underlying the distinction between active and passive euthanasia is
the idea that there is a significant moral difference between intentionally killing and intentionally letting die. . . .

Whether . . . there is a significant moral difference . . . is not my
concern here. For it is far from clear that this distinction *is* the basis
of the doctrine of the American Medical Association which Rachels
attacks. And if the killing/letting die distinction is not the basis of
the AMA doctrine, then arguments showing that the distinction has
no moral force do not, in themselves, reveal in the doctrine's adherents either "confused thinking" or "a moral point of view unrelated
to the interests of individuals." Indeed, as we examine the AMA doctrine, I think it will become clear that it appeals to and makes use of
a number of overlapping distinctions, which may have moral significance in particular cases, such as the distinction between intending
and foreseeing, or between ordinary and extraordinary care. Let us

---

Bonnie Steinbock, "The Intentional Termination of Life," *Social Science & Medicine*, Vol.
6, No. 1, 1979, pp. 59–64. Reprinted by permission of the journal. The footnotes were
edited.

then turn to the 1973 statement, from the House of Delegates of the American Medical Association, which Rachels cites:

> The intentional termination of the life of one human being by another—mercy killing—is contrary to that for which the medical profession stands and is contrary to the policy of the American Medical Association.
>
> The cessation of the employment of extraordinary means to prolong the life of the body when there is irrefutable evidence that biological death is imminent is the decision of the patient and/or his immediate family. The advice and judgment of the physician should be freely available to the patient and/or his immediate family.

Rachels attacks this statement because he believes that it contains a moral distinction between active and passive euthanasia. . . .

[He takes] the AMA position to prohibit active euthanasia, while allowing, under certain conditions, passive euthanasia.

I intend to show that the AMA statement does not imply support of the active/passive euthanasia distinction. In forbidding the intentional termination of life, the statement rejects both active and passive euthanasia. It does allow for "the cessation of the employment of extraordinary means" to prolong life. The mistake Rachels . . . make[s] is in identifying the cessation of life-prolonging treatment with passive euthanasia, or intentionally letting die. If it were right to equate the two, then the AMA statement would be self-contradictory, for it would begin by condemning, and end by allowing, the intentional termination of life. But if the cessation of life-prolonging treatment is not always or necessarily passive euthanasia, then there is no confusion and no contradiction.

Why does Rachels think that the cessation of life-prolonging treatment is the intentional termination of life? He says:

> The AMA policy statement isolates the crucial issue very well: the crucial issue is "the intentional termination of the life of one human being by another." But after identifying this issue, and forbidding "mercy killing," the statement goes on to deny that the cessation of treatment is the intentional termination of a life. This is where the mistake comes in, for what is the cessation of treatment, in these circumstances, if it is not "the intentional termination of the life of one human being by another"? Of course it is exactly that, and if it were not, there would be no point to it.

However, there *can* be a point (to the cessation of life-prolonging treatment) other than an endeavor to bring about the patient's death, and so the blanket identification of cessation of treatment with the intentional termination of a life is inaccurate. There are at least two situations in which the termination of life-prolonging treatment cannot be identified with the intentional termination of the life of one human being by another.

The first situation concerns the patient's right to refuse treatment. . . . Rachels give[s] the example of a patient dying of an incurable disease, accompanied by unrelievable pain, who wants to end the treatment which cannot cure him but can only prolong his miserable existence. Why, they ask, may a doctor accede to the patient's request to stop treatment, but not provide a patient in a similar situation with a lethal dose? The answer lies in the patient's right to refuse treatment. In general, a competent adult has the right to refuse treatment, even where such treatment is necessary to prolong life. Indeed, the right to refuse treatment has been upheld even when the patient's reason for refusing treatment is generally agreed to be inadequate.[1] This right can be overridden (if, for example, the patient has dependent children) but, in general, no one may legally compel you to undergo treatment to which you have not consented. "Historically, surgical intrusion has always been considered a technical battery upon the person and one to be excused or justified by consent of the patient or justified by necessity created by the circumstances of the moment. . . ."[2]

At this point, an objection might be raised that if one has the right to refuse life-prolonging treatment, then consistency demands that one have the right to decide to end his or her life, and to obtain help in doing so. The idea is that the right to refuse treatment somehow implies a right to voluntary euthanasia, and we need to see why someone might think this. The right to refuse treatment has been considered by legal writers as an example of the right to privacy or, better, the right to bodily self-determination. You have the right to decide what happens to your own body, and the right to refuse treatment is an instance of that right. But if you have the right to determine what happens to your own body, then should you not have the right to choose to end your life, and even a right to get help in doing so?

However, it is important to see that the right to refuse treatment is not the same as, nor does it entail, a right to voluntary euthanasia, even if both can be derived from the right to bodily self-determination. The right to refuse treatment is not itself a "right to die"; that one may choose to exercise this right even at the risk of death, or even *in order to die,* is irrelevant. The purpose of the right to refuse medical treatment is not to give persons a right to decide whether to live or die, but to protect them from the unwanted interferences of others. Perhaps we ought to interpret the right to bodily self-determination more broadly, so as to include a right to die; but this would be a substantial extension of our present understanding of the right to bodily self-determination, and not a consequence of it. If we were to recognize a right to voluntary euthanasia, we would have to agree that people have the right not merely to be left alone but also the right to be killed. I leave to one side that substantive moral issue. My claim is simply that there can be a reason for terminating life-prolonging treatment other than "to bring about the patient's death."

The second case in which termination of treatment cannot be identified with intentional termination of life is where continued treatment has little chance of improving the patient's condition and brings greater discomfort than relief.

The question here is what treatment is appropriate to the particular case. A cancer specialist describes it in this way:

> My general rule is to administer therapy as long as a patient responds well and has the potential for a reasonably good quality of life. But when all feasible therapies have been administered and a patient shows signs of rapid deterioration, the continuation of therapy can cause more discomfort than the cancer. From that time I recommend surgery, radiotherapy, or chemotherapy only as a means of relieving pain. But if a patient's condition should once again stabilize after the withdrawal of active therapy and if it should appear that he could still gain some good time, I would immediately reinstitute active therapy. The decision to cease anticancer treatment is never irrevocable, and often the desire to live will push a patient to try for another remission, or even a few more days of life.[3]

The decision here to cease anticancer treatment cannot be construed as a decision that the patient die, or as the intentional termination of life. It is a decision to provide the most appropriate treatment for that patient at that time. Rachels suggests that the point of the cessation of treatment is the intentional termination of life. But here the point of discontinuing treatment is not to bring about the patient's death but to avoid treatment that will cause more discomfort than the cancer and has little hope of benefiting the patient. Treatment that meets this description is often called "extraordinary."[4] The concept is flexible, and what might be considered "extraordinary" in one situation might be ordinary in another. The use of a respirator to sustain a patient through a severe bout with a respiratory disease would be considered ordinary; its use to sustain the life of a severely brain-damaged person in an irreversible coma would be considered extraordinary.

Contrasted with extraordinary treatment is ordinary treatment, the care a doctor would normally be expected to provide. Failure to provide ordinary care constitutes neglect, and can even be construed as the intentional infliction of harm, where there is a legal obligation to provide care. The importance of the ordinary/extraordinary care distinction lies partly in its connection to the doctor's intention. The withholding of extraordinary care should be seen as a decision not to inflict painful treatment on a patient without reasonable hope of success. The withholding of ordinary care, by contrast, must be seen as neglect. Thus, one doctor says, "We have to draw a distinction between ordinary and extraordinary means. We never withdraw what's needed to make a baby comfortable, we would never withdraw the care a parent would provide. We never kill a baby. . . . But we may decide certain heroic intervention is not worthwhile."[5]

We should keep in mind the ordinary/extraordinary care distinction when considering an example given by . . . Rachels to show the irrationality of the active/passive distinction with regard to infanticide. The example is this: a child is born with [Down] syndrome and also has an intestinal obstruction that requires corrective surgery. If the surgery is not performed, the infant will starve to death, since it cannot take food orally. This may take days or even weeks, as dehydration and infection set in. Commenting on this situation in his article in this book, Rachels says:

> I can understand why some people are opposed to all euthanasia, and insist that such infants must be allowed to live. I think I can also understand why other people favor destroying these babies quickly and painlessly. But why should anyone favor letting "dehydration and infection wither a tiny being over hours and days"? The doctrine that says that a baby may be allowed to dehydrate and wither, but may not be given an injection that would end its life without suffering, seems so patently cruel as to require no further refutation.

Such a doctrine perhaps does not need further refutation; but this is not the AMA doctrine. The AMA statement criticized by Rachels allows only for the cessation of extraordinary means to prolong life when death is imminent. Neither of these conditions is satisfied in this example. Death is not imminent in this situation, any more than it would be if a normal child had an attack of appendicitis. Neither the corrective surgery to remove the intestinal obstruction nor the intravenous feeding required to keep the infant alive until such surgery is performed can be regarded as extraordinary means, for neither is particularly expensive, nor does either place an overwhelming burden on the patient or others. (The continued existence of the child might be thought to place an overwhelming burden on its parents, but that has nothing to do with the characterization of the means to prolong its life as extraordinary. If it had, then *feeding* a severely defective child who required a great deal of care could be regarded as extraordinary.) The chances of success if the operation is undertaken are quite good, though there is always a risk in operating on infants. Though the [Down] syndrome will not be alleviated, the child will proceed to an otherwise normal infancy.

It cannot be argued that the treatment is withheld for the infant's sake, unless one is prepared to argue that all mentally retarded babies are better off dead. This is particularly implausible in the case of [Down] syndrome babies, who generally do not suffer and are capable of giving and receiving love, of learning and playing, to varying degrees.

In a film on this subject entitled, "Who Should Survive?" a doctor defended a decision not to operate, saying that since the parents did not consent to the operation, the doctor's hands were tied. As we have seen, surgical intrusion requires consent, and in the case of infants, consent would normally come from the parents. But, as legal guardians, parents are required to provide medical care for their children, and failure to do so can constitute criminal neglect or even homicide. In general, courts have been understandably reluctant to recognize a parental right to terminate life-prolonging treatment.[6] Although prosecution is unlikely, physicians who comply with invalid instructions from the parents and permit the infant's death could be liable for aiding and abetting, failure to report child neglect, or even homicide. So it is not true that, in this situation, doctors are legally bound to do as the parents wish.

To sum up, I think that Rachels is right to regard the decision not to operate in the [Down] syndrome example as the intentional termination of life. But there is no reason to believe that either the law or the AMA would regard it otherwise. Certainly the decision to withhold treatment is not justified by the AMA statement. That such infants have been allowed to die cannot be denied; but this, I think, is the result of doctors misunderstanding the law and the AMA position.

Withholding treatment in this case is the intentional termination of life because the infant is deliberately allowed to die; that is the point of not operating. But there are other cases in which that is not the point. If the point is to avoid inflicting painful treatment on a patient with little or no reasonable hope of success, this is not the intentional termination of life. The permissibility of such withholding of treatment, then, would have no implications for the permissibility of euthanasia, active or passive.

The decision whether or not to operate, or to institute vigorous treatment, is particularly agonizing in the case of children born with spina bifida, an opening in the base of the spine usually accompanied by hydrocephalus and mental retardation. If left unoperated, these children usually die of meningitis or kidney failure within the first few years of life. Even if they survive, all affected children face a lifetime of illness, operations, and varying degrees of disability. The policy used to be to save as many as possible, but the trend now is toward selective treatment, based on the physician's estimate of the chances of success. If operating is not likely to improve significantly the child's condition, parents and doctors may agree not to operate. This is not the intentional termination of life, for again the purpose is not the termination of the child's life but the avoidance of painful and pointless treatment. Thus, the fact that withholding treatment is justified does not imply that killing the child would be equally justified.

Throughout the discussion, I have claimed that intentionally ceasing life-prolonging treatment is not the intentional termination of life unless the doctor has, as his or her purpose in stopping treatment, the patient's death.

It may be objected that I have incorrectly characterized the conditions for the intentional termination of life. Perhaps it is enough that the doctor intentionally ceases treatment, foreseeing that the patient will die.

In many cases, if one acts intentionally, foreseeing that a particular result will occur, one can be said to have brought about that result intentionally. Indeed, this is the general legal rule. Why, then, am I not willing to call the cessation of life-prolonging treatment, in compliance with the patient's right to refuse treatment, the intentional termination of life? It is not because such an *identification* is necessarily opprobrious; for we could go on to *discuss* whether such cessation of treatment is a *justifiable* intentional termination of life. Even in the law, some cases of homicide are justifiable; e.g., homicide in self-defense.

However, the cessation of life-prolonging treatment, in the cases which I have discussed, is not regarded in law as being justifiable homicide, because it is not homicide at all. Why is this? Is it because the doctor "doesn't do anything," and so cannot be guilty of homicide? Surely not, since, as I have indicated, the law sometimes treats an omission as the cause of death. A better explanation, I think, has to do with the fact that in the context of the patient's right to refuse treatment, a doctor is not at liberty to continue treatment. It seems a necessary ingredient of intentionally letting die that one could have done something to prevent the death. In this situation, of course the doctor can physically prevent the patient's death, but since we do not regard the doctor as *free* to continue treatment, we say that there is "nothing he can do." Therefore he does not intentionally let the patient die.

To discuss this suggestion fully, I would need to present a full-scale theory of intentional action. However, at least I have shown, through the discussion of the above examples, that such a theory will be very complex, and that one of the complexities concerns the agent's reason for acting. The reason why an agent acted (or failed to act) may affect the characterization of what he did intentionally. The mere fact that he did *something* intentionally, foreseeing a certain result, does not necessarily mean that he brought about that *result* intentionally.

In order to show that the cessation of life-prolonging treatment, in the cases I've discussed, is the intentional termination of life, one would either have to show that treatment was stopped in order to bring about the patient's death, or provide a theory of intentional action according to which the reason for ceasing treatment is irrelevant to its characterization as the intentional termination of life. I find this suggestion implausible, but am willing to consider arguments for it. Rachels has provided no such arguments: indeed, he apparently shares my view about the intentional termination of life. For when he claims that the cessation of life-prolonging treatment is the intentional termination of life, his reason for making the claim is that "if it were not, there would be no point to it." Rachels believes that the point of ceasing treatment, "in these cases," is to bring about the patient's death. If that were not the point, he suggests, why would the doctor cease treatment? I have shown, however, that there can be a point to ceasing treatment which is not the death of the patient. In showing this, I have refuted Rachels' reason for identifying the cessation of life-prolonging treatment with the intentional termination of life, and thus his argument against the AMA doctrine.

Here someone might say: Even if the withholding of treatment is not the intentional termination of life, does that make a difference, morally speaking? If life-prolonging treatment may be withheld, for the sake of the child, may not an easy death be provided, for the sake of the child, as well? The unoperated child with spina bifida may take months or even years to die. Distressed by the spectacle of children "lying around, waiting to die," one doctor has written, "It is time that society and medicine stopped perpetuating the fiction that withholding treatment is ethically different from terminating a life. It is time that society began to discuss mechanisms by which we can alleviate the pain and suffering for those individuals whom we cannot help."[7]

I do not deny that there may be cases in which death is in the best interests of the patient. In such cases, a quick and painless death may be the best thing. However, I do not think that, once active or vigorous treatment is stopped, a quick death is always preferable to a lingering one. We must be cautious about attributing to defective children *our* distress at seeing them linger. Waiting for them to die may be tough on parents, doctors, and nurses—it isn't necessarily tough on the child. The decision not to operate need not mean a decision to neglect, and it may be possible to make the remaining months of the child's life comfortable, pleasant, and filled with love. If this alternative is possible, surely it is more decent and humane than killing the child. In such a situation, withholding treatment, foreseeing the child's death, is not ethically equivalent to killing the child, and we cannot move from the permissibility of the former to that of the latter. I am worried that there will be a tendency to do precisely that if active euthanasia is regarded as morally equivalent to the withholding of life-prolonging treatment.

Conclusion

The AMA statement does not make the distinction Rachels . . . wish[es] to attack, that between active and passive euthanasia. Instead, the statement draws a distinction between the intentional termination of life, on the one hand, and the cessation of the employment of extraordinary means to prolong life, on the other. Nothing said by Rachels . . . shows that this distinction is confused. It may be that doctors have misinterpreted the AMA statement, and that this has led, for example, to decisions to allow defective infants to starve slowly to death. I quite agree with Rachels . . . that the decisions to which they allude were cruel and made on irrelevant grounds. Certainly it is worth pointing out that allowing someone to die *can* be the intentional termination of life, and that it can be just as bad as, or worse than, killing someone. However, the withholding of life-prolonging treatment is not necessarily the intentional termination of life, so that if it is permissible to withhold life-prolonging treatment it does not follow that, other things being equal, it is permissible to kill. Furthermore, most of the time, other things are not equal. In many of the cases in which it would be right to cease treatment, I do not think that it would also be right to kill.

Notes

1. For example, *In re Yetter,* 62 Pa. D & C. 2d 619 (C.P., Northampton County Ct. 1974).
2. David W. Meyers, "Legal Aspects of Voluntary Euthanasia," in *Dilemmas of Euthanasia,* ed. John Behnke and Sissela Bok (New York: Anchor Books, 1975), p. 56.
3. Ernest H. Rosenbaum, M.D., *Living With Cancer* (New York: Praeger, 1975), p. 27.
4. See Tristram Engelhardt, Jr.; "Ethical Issues in Aiding the Death of Young Children," in *Beneficent Euthanasia,* ed. Marvin Kohl (Buffalo, N.Y.: Prometheus Books, 1975). . . .
5. B. D. Colen, *Karen Ann Quinlan: Living and Dying in the Age of Eternal Life* (Los Angeles: Nash, 1976), p. 115.
6. See Norman L. Cantor, "Law and the Termination of an Incompetent Patient's Life-Preserving Care," in *Dilemmas of Euthanasia,* pp. 69–105.
7. John Freeman, "Is There a Right to Die—Quickly?", *Journal of Pediatrics,* 80, no. 5 (1972), 904–905.

Study Questions

1. Is killing someone always worse than letting the person die?
2. Is the physician's intention crucial to assessing the morality of the means used to bring about death?
3. Are we ever justified in performing actions with unfortunate consequences in an effort to achieve other purposes?
4. What should a physician do if a paralyzed patient on life support asks to be euthanized?

C. World Hunger

CHAPTER 27

Famine, Affluence, and Morality

Peter Singer

Peter Singer is Ira W. Decamp Professor of Bioethics at the University Center for Human Values at Princeton University. He claims that we are morally obligated to sacrifice many of our present luxuries to prevent others from starving, for if we can prevent something bad without thereby sacrificing anything of comparable moral worth, we ought to do so.

As I write this, in November 1971, people are dying in East Bengal from lack of food, shelter, and medical care. The suffering and death that are occurring there now are not inevitable, not unavoidable in any fatalistic sense of the term. Constant poverty, a cyclone, and a civil war have turned at least nine million people into destitute refugees: nevertheless, it is not beyond the capacity of the richer nations to give enough assistance to reduce any further suffering to very small proportions. The decisions and actions of human beings can prevent this kind of suffering. Unfortunately, human beings have not made the necessary decisions. At the individual level, people have, with very few exceptions, not responded to the situation in any significant way. Generally speaking, people have not given large sums to relief funds; they have not written to their parliamentary representatives demanding increased government assistance; they have not demonstrated in the streets, held symbolic fasts, or done anything else directed toward providing the refugees with the means to satisfy their essential needs. At the government level, no government has given the sort of massive aid that would enable the refugees to survive

From Peter Singer, "Famine, Affluence, and Morality," in *Philosophy & Public Affairs*, Vol. 32. Copyright © 1972. Reprinted by permission of Blackwell Publishing Ltd.

for more than a few days. Britain, for instance, has given rather more than most countries. It has, to date, given £14,750,000. For comparative purposes, Britain's share of the nonrecoverable development costs of the Anglo-French Concorde project is already in excess of £275,000,000, and on present estimates will reach £440,000,000. The implication is that the British government values a supersonic transport more than thirty times as highly as it values the lives of the nine million refugees. Australia is another country which, on a per capita basis, is well up in the "aid to Bengal" table. Australia's aid, however, amounts to less than one-twelfth of the cost of Sydney's new opera house. The total amount given, from all sources, now stands at about £65,000,000. The estimated cost of keeping the refugees alive for one year is £464,000,000. Most of the refugees have now been in the camps for more than six months. The World Bank has said that India needs a minimum of £300,000,000 in assistance from other countries before the end of the year. It seems obvious that assistance on this scale will not be forthcoming. India will be forced to choose between letting the refugees starve or diverting funds from her own development program, which will mean that more of her own people will starve in the future.[1]

These are the essential facts about the present situation in Bengal. So far as it concerns us here, there is nothing unique about this situation except its magnitude. The Bengal emergency is just the latest and most acute of a series of major emergencies in various parts of the world, arising both from natural and from man-made causes. There are also many parts of the world in which people die from malnutrition and lack of food independent of any special emergency. I take Bengal as my example only because it is the present concern, and because the size of the problem has ensured that it has been given adequate publicity. Neither individuals nor governments can claim to be unaware of what is happening there.

What are the moral implications of a situation like this? In what follows, I shall argue that the way people in relatively affluent countries react to a situation like that in Bengal cannot be justified; indeed, the whole way we look at moral issues—our moral conceptual scheme—needs to be altered, and with it, the way of life that has come to be taken for granted in our society.

In arguing for this conclusion I will not, of course, claim to be morally neutral. I shall, however, try to argue for the moral position that I take, so that anyone who accepts certain assumptions, to be made explicit, will, I hope, accept my conclusion.

I begin with the assumption that suffering and death from lack of food, shelter, and medical care are bad. I think most people will agree about this, although one may reach the same view by different routes. I shall not argue for this view. People can hold all sorts of eccentric positions, and perhaps from some of them it would not follow that death by starvation is in itself bad. It is difficult, perhaps impossible, to refute such positions, and so for brevity I will henceforth take this assumption as accepted. Those who disagree need read no further.

My next point is this: if it is in our power to prevent something bad from happening, without thereby sacrificing anything of comparable moral importance, we ought, morally, to do it. By "without sacrificing anything of comparable moral importance" I mean without causing anything else comparably bad to happen, or doing something that is wrong in itself, or failing to promote some moral good, comparable in significance to the bad thing that we can prevent. This principle seems almost as uncontroversial as the last one. It requires us only to prevent what is bad, and not to promote what is good, and it requires this of us only when we can do it without sacrificing anything that is, from the moral point of view, comparably important. I could even, as far as the application of my argument to the Bengal emergency is concerned, qualify the point so as to make it: if it is in our power to prevent something very bad from happening, without thereby sacrificing anything morally significant, we ought, morally, to do it. An application of this principle would be as follows: if I am walking past a shallow pond and see a child drowning in it, I ought to wade in and pull the child out. This will mean getting my clothes muddy, but this is insignificant, while the death of the child would presumably be a very bad thing.

The uncontroversial appearance of the principle just stated is deceptive. If it were acted upon, even in its qualified form, our lives, our society, and our world would be fundamentally changed. For the principle takes, firstly, no account of proximity or distance. It makes no moral difference whether the person I can help is a neighbor's child ten yards from me or a Bengali whose name I shall never know, ten thousand miles away. Secondly, the principle makes no distinction between cases in which I am the only person who could possibly do anything and cases in which I am just one among millions in the same position.

I do not think I need to say much in defense of the refusal to take proximity and distance into account. The fact that a person is physically near to us, so that we have personal contact with him, may make it more likely that we *shall* assist him, but this does not show that we *ought* to help him rather than another who happens to be farther away. If we accept any principle of impartiality, universalizability, equality, or whatever, we cannot discriminate against someone merely because he is far away from us (or we are far away from him). Admittedly, it is possible that we are in a better position to judge what needs to be done to help a person near to us than one far away, and perhaps also to provide the assistance we judge to be necessary. If this were the case, it would be a reason for helping those near to us first. This may once have been a justification for being more concerned with the poor in one's own town than with the famine victims in India. Unfortunately for those who like to keep moral responsibilities limited, instant communication and swift transportation have changed the situation. From the moral point of view, the development of the world into a "global village" has made an important, though still unrecognized, difference to our moral situation. Expert observers and supervisors, sent out by famine relief organizations or permanently stationed in famine-prone areas, can direct our aid to a refugee in Bengal almost as effectively as we could get it to someone in our own block. There would seem, therefore, to be no possible justification for discriminating on geographical grounds.

There may be a greater need to defend the second implication of my principle—that the fact that there are millions of other people in the same position, in respect to the Bengali refugees, as I am, does not make the situation significantly different from a situation in which I am the only person who can prevent something very bad from occurring. Again, of course, I admit that there is a psychological difference between the cases; one feels less guilty about doing nothing if one can point to others, similarly placed, who have also done nothing. Yet this can make no real difference to our moral obligations.[2] Should I consider that I am less obliged to pull the drowning child out of the pond if on looking around I see other people, no farther away than I am, who have also noticed the child but are doing nothing? One has only to ask this question to see the absurdity of the view that numbers lessen obligation. It is a view that is an ideal excuse for inactivity; unfortunately most of the major evils—poverty, overpopulation, pollution—are problems in which everyone is almost equally involved.

The view that numbers do make a difference can be made plausible if stated in this way: if everyone in circumstances like mine gave £5 to the Bengal Relief Fund, there would be enough to provide food, shelter, and medical care for the refugees; there is no reason why I should give more than anyone else in the same circumstances as I am; therefore I have no obligation to give more than £5. Each premise in this argument is true, and the argument looks sound. It may convince us, unless we notice that it is based on a hypothetical premise, although the conclusion is not stated hypothetically. The argument would be sound if the conclusion were: if everyone in circumstances like mine were to give £5, I would have no obligation to give more than £5. If the conclusion were so stated, however, it would be obvious that the argument has no bearing on a situation in which it is not the case that everyone else gives £5. This, of course, is the actual situation. It is more or less certain that not everyone in circumstances like mine will give £5. So there will not be enough to provide the needed food, shelter, and medical care. Therefore by giving more than £5 I will prevent more suffering than I would if I gave just £5.

It might be thought that this argument has an absurd consequence. Since the situation appears to be that very few people are likely to give substantial amounts, it follows that I and everyone else in similar circumstances ought to give as much as possible, that is, at least up to the point at which by giving more one would begin to cause serious suffering for oneself and one's dependents—perhaps even beyond this point to the point of marginal utility, at which by giving more one would cause oneself and one's dependents as much suffering as one would prevent in Bengal. If everyone does this, however, there will be more than can be used for the benefit of the refugees, and some of the sacrifice will have been unnecessary. Thus, if everyone does what he ought to do, the result will not be as good as it would be if everyone did a little less than he ought to do, or if only some do all that they ought to do.

The paradox here arises only if we assume that the actions in question—sending money to the relief funds—are performed more or less simultaneously, and are also unexpected. For if it is to be expected that everyone is going to contribute something, then clearly each is not obliged to give as much as he would have been obliged to had others not been giving too. And if everyone is not acting more or less simultaneously, then those giving later will know how much more is needed, and will have no obligation to give more than is necessary to reach this amount. To say this is not to deny the principle that people in the same circumstances have the same obligations, but to point out that the fact that others have given, or may be expected to give, is a relevant circumstance: those giving after it has become known that many others are giving and those giving before are not in the same circumstances. So the seemingly absurd consequence of the principle I have put forward can occur only if people are in error about the actual circumstances—that is, if they think they are giving when others are not, but in fact they are giving when others are. The result of everyone doing what he really ought to do cannot be worse than the result of everyone doing less than he ought to do, although the result of everyone doing what he reasonably believes he ought to do could be.

If my argument so far has been sound, neither our distance from a preventable evil nor the number of other people who, in respect to that evil, are in the same situation as we are, lessens our obligation to mitigate or prevent that evil. I shall therefore take as established the principle I asserted earlier. As I have already said, I need to assert it only in its qualified form: if it is in our power to prevent something very bad from happening, without thereby sacrificing anything else morally significant, we ought, morally, to do it.

The outcome of this argument is that our traditional moral categories are upset. The traditional direction between duty and charity cannot be drawn, or at least, not in the place we normally draw it. Giving money to the Bengal Relief Fund is regarded as an act of charity in our society. The bodies which collect money are known as "charities." These organizations see themselves in this way—if you send them a check, you will be thanked for your "generosity." Because giving money is regarded as an act of charity, it is not thought that there is anything wrong with not giving. The charitable man may be praised, but the man who is not charitable is not condemned. People do not feel in any way ashamed or guilty about spending money on new clothes or a new car instead of giving it to famine relief. (Indeed, the alternative does not occur to them.) This way of looking at the matter cannot be justified. When we buy new clothes not to keep ourselves warm but to look "well-dressed" we are not providing for any important need. We would not be sacrificing anything significant if we were to continue to wear our old clothes, and give the money to famine relief. By doing so, we would be preventing another person from starving. It follows from what I have said earlier that we ought to give money away, rather than spend it on clothes which we do not need to keep us warm. To do so is not charitable, or generous. Nor is it the kind of act which philosophers and theologians have called "supererogatory"—an act which it would be good to do, but not wrong not to do. On the contrary, we ought to give the money away, and it is wrong not to do so.

I am not maintaining that there are no acts which are charitable, or that there are no acts which it would be good to do but not wrong not to do. It may be possible to redraw the distinction between duty and charity in some other place. All I am arguing here is that the present way of drawing the distinction, which makes it an act of charity for a man living at the level of affluence which most people in the "developed nations" enjoy to give money to save someone else from starvation, cannot be supported. It is beyond the scope of my argument to consider whether the distinction should be redrawn or abolished altogether. There would be many other possible ways of drawing the distinction—for instance, one might decide that it is good to make other people as happy as possible, but not wrong not to do so.

Despite the limited nature of the revision in our moral conceptual scheme which I am proposing, the revision would, given the extent of both affluence and famine in the world today, have radical implications. These implications may lead to further objections, distinct from those I have already considered. I shall discuss two of these.

One objection to the position I have taken might be simply that it is too drastic a revision of our moral scheme. People do not ordinarily judge in the way I have suggested they should. Most people reserve their moral condemnation for those who violate some moral norm, such as the norm against taking another person's property. They do not condemn those who indulge in luxury instead of giving to famine relief. But given that I did not set out to present a morally neutral description of the way people make moral judgments, the way people do in fact judge has nothing to do with the validity of my conclusion. My conclusion follows from the principle which I advanced earlier, and unless that principle is rejected, or the arguments shown to be unsound, I think the conclusion must stand, however strange it appears.

It might, nevertheless, be interesting to consider why our society, and most other societies, do judge differently from the way I have suggested they should. In a well-known article, J. O. Urmson suggests that the imperatives of duty, which tell us what we must do, as distinct from what it would be good to do but not wrong not to do, function so as to prohibit behavior that is intolerable if men are to live together in society.[3] This may explain the origin and continued existence of the present division between acts of duty and acts of charity. Moral attitudes are shaped by the needs of society, and no doubt society needs people who will observe the rules that make social existence tolerable. From the point of view of a particular society, it is essential to prevent violations of norms against killing, stealing, and so on. It is quite inessential, however, to help people outside one's own society.

If this is an explanation of our common distinction between duty and supererogation, however, it is not a justification of it. The moral point of view requires us to look beyond the interests of our own society. Previously, as I have already mentioned, this may hardly have been feasible, but it is quite feasible now. From the moral point of view, the prevention of the starvation of millions of people outside our society must be considered at least as pressing as the upholding of property norms within our society.

It has been argued by some writers, among them Sidgwick and Urmson, that we need to have a basic moral code which is not too far beyond the capacities of the ordinary man, for otherwise there will be a general breakdown of compliance with the moral code. Crudely stated, this argument suggests that if we tell people that they ought to refrain from murder and give everything they do not really need to famine relief, they will do neither, whereas if we tell them that they ought to refrain from murder and that it is good to give to famine relief but not wrong not to do so, they will at least refrain from murder. The issue here is, Where should we draw the line between conduct that is required and conduct that is good although not required, so as to get the best possible result? This would seem to be an empirical question, although a very difficult one. One objection to the Sidgwick-Urmson line of argument is that it takes insufficient account of the effect that moral standards can have on the decisions we make. Given a society in which a wealthy man who gives five percent of his income to famine relief is regarded as most generous, it is not surprising that a proposal that we all ought to give away half our incomes will be thought to be absurdly unrealistic. In a society which held that no man should have more than enough while others have less than they need, such a proposal might seem narrow-minded. What it is possible for a man to do and what he is likely to do are both, I think, very greatly influenced by what people around him are doing and expecting him to do. In any case, the possibility that by spreading the idea that we ought to be doing very much more than we are to relieve famine we shall bring about a general breakdown of moral behavior seems remote. If the stakes are an end to widespread starvation, it is worth the risk. Finally, it should be emphasized that these considerations are relevant only to the issue of what we should require from others, and not to what we ourselves ought to do.

The second objection to my attack on the present distinction between duty and charity is one which has from time to time been made against utilitarianism. It follows from some forms of utilitarian theory that we all ought, morally, to be working full time to increase the balance of happiness over misery. The position I have taken here would not lead to this conclusion in all circumstances, for if there were no bad occurrences that we could prevent without sacrificing something of comparable moral importance, my argument would have no application. Given the present conditions in many parts of the world, however, it does follow from my argument that we ought, morally, to be working full time to relieve great suffering of the sort that occurs as a result of famine or other disasters. Of course, mitigating circumstances can be adduced—for instance, that if we wear ourselves out through overwork, we shall be less effective than we would otherwise have been. Nevertheless, when all considerations of this sort have been taken into account, the conclusion remains: we ought to be preventing as much suffering as we can without sacrificing something else of comparable moral importance. This conclusion is one which we may be reluctant to face. I cannot see, though, why it should be regarded as a criticism of the position for which I have argued, rather than a criticism of our ordinary standards of behavior. Since most people are self-interested to some degree, very few of us are likely to do everything that we ought to do. It would, however, hardly be honest to take this as evidence that it is not the case that we ought to do it.

It may still be thought that my conclusions are so wildly out of line with what everyone else thinks and has always thought that there must be something wrong with the argument somewhere. In order to show that my conclusions, while certainly contrary to contemporary Western moral standards, would not have seemed too extraordinary at other times and in other places, I would like to quote a passage from a writer not normally thought of as a way-out radical, Thomas Aquinas.

> Now, according to the natural order instituted by divine providence, material goods are provided for the satisfaction of human needs. Therefore the division and appropriation of property, which proceeds from human law, must not hinder the satisfaction of man's necessity from such goods. Equally, whatever a man has in superabundance is owed, of natural right, to the poor for their sustenance.

So Ambrosius says, and it is also to be found in the *Decretum Gratiani*: "The bread which you withhold belongs to the hungry; the clothing you shut away, to the naked; and the money you bury in the earth is the redemption and freedom of the penniless."[4]

I now want to consider a number of points, more practical than philosophical, which are relevant to the application of the moral conclusion we have reached. These points challenge not the idea that we ought to be doing all we can to prevent starvation, but the idea that giving away a great deal of money is the best means to this end.

It is sometimes said that overseas aid should be a government responsibility, and that therefore one ought not to give to privately run charities. Giving privately, it is said, allows the government and the noncontributing members of society to escape their responsibilities.

This argument seems to assume that the more people there are who give to privately organized famine relief funds, the less likely it is that the government will take over full responsibility for such aid. This assumption is unsupported, and does not strike me as at all plausible. The opposite view—that if no one gives voluntarily, a government will assume that its citizens are uninterested in famine relief and would not wish to be forced into giving aid—seems more plausible. In any case, unless there were a definite probability that by refusing to give one would be helping to bring about massive government assistance, people who do refuse to make voluntary contributions are refusing to prevent a certain amount of suffering without being able to point to any tangible beneficial consequence of their refusal. So the onus of showing how their refusal will bring about government action is on those who refuse to give.

I do not, of course, want to dispute the contention that governments of affluent nations should be giving many times the amount of genuine, no-strings-attached aid that they are giving now. I agree, too, that giving privately is not enough, and that we ought to be campaigning actively for entirely new standards for both public and private contributions to famine relief. Indeed, I would sympathize with someone who thought that campaigning was more important than giving oneself, although I doubt whether preaching what one does not practice would be very effective. Unfortunately, for many people the idea that "it's the government's responsibility" is a reason for not giving which does not appear to entail any political action either.

Another, more serious reason for not giving to famine relief funds is that until there is effective population control, relieving famine merely postpones starvation. If we save the Bengal refugees now, others, perhaps the children of these refugees, will face starvation in a few years' time. In support of this, one may cite the now well-known facts about the population explosion and the relatively limited scope for expanded production.

This point, like the previous one, is an argument against relieving suffering that is happening now, because of a belief about what might happen in the future; it is unlike the previous point in that very good evidence can be adduced in support of this belief about the future. I will not go into the evidence here. I accept that the earth cannot support indefinitely a population rising at the present rate. This certainly poses a problem for anyone who thinks it important to prevent famine. Again, however, one could accept the argument without drawing the conclusion that it absolves one from any obligation to do anything to prevent famine. The conclusion that should be drawn is that the best means of preventing famine, in the long run, is population control. It would then follow from the position reached earlier that one ought to be doing all one can to promote population control (unless one held that all forms of population control were wrong in themselves, or would have significantly bad consequences). Since there are organizations working specifically for population control, one would then support them rather than more orthodox methods of preventing famine.

A third point raised by the conclusion reached earlier relates to the question of just how much we all ought to be giving away. One possibility, which has already been mentioned, is that we ought to give until we reach the level of marginal utility—that is, the level at which, by giving more, I would cause as much suffering to myself or my dependents as I would relieve by my gift. This would mean, of course, that one would reduce oneself to very nearly the material circumstances of a Bengali refugee. It will be recalled that earlier I put forward both a strong and a moderate version of the principle of preventing bad occurrences. The strong version, which required us to prevent bad things from happening unless in doing so we would be sacrificing something of comparable moral significance, does seem to require reducing ourselves to the level of marginal utility. I should also say that the strong version seems to me to be the correct one. I proposed the more moderate version—that we should prevent bad occurrences unless, to do so, we had to sacrifice something morally significant—only in order to show that even on this surely undeniable principle a great change in our way of life is required. On the more moderate principle, it may not follow that we ought to reduce ourselves to the level of marginal utility, for one might hold that to reduce oneself and one's family to this level is to cause something significantly bad to happen. Whether this is so I shall not discuss, since, as I have said, I can see no good reason for holding the moderate version of the principle rather than the strong version. Even if we accepted the principle only in its moderate form, however, it should be clear that we would have to give away enough to ensure that the consumer society, dependent as it is on people spending on trivia rather than giving to famine relief, would slow down and perhaps disappear entirely. There are several reasons why this would be desirable in itself. The value and necessity of economic growth are now being questioned not only by conservationists, but by economists as well.[5] There is no doubt, too, that the consumer society has had a distorting effect on the goals and purposes of its members. Yet looking at the matter purely from the point of view of overseas aid, there must be a limit to the extent to which we should deliberately slow down our economy; for it might be the case that if we gave away, say, forty percent of our Gross National Product, we would slow down the economy so much that in absolute terms we would be giving less than if we gave twenty-five percent of the much larger GNP that we would have if we limited our contribution to this smaller percentage.

I mention this only as an indication of the sort of factor that one would have to take into account in working out an ideal. Since Western societies generally consider one percent of the GNP an acceptable level of overseas aid, the matter is entirely academic. Nor does it affect the question of how much an individual should give in a society in which very few are giving substantial amounts.

It is sometimes said, though less often now than it used to be, that philosophers have no special role to play in public affairs, since most public issues depend primarily on an assessment of facts. On questions of fact, it is said, philosophers as such have no special expertise, and so it has been possible to engage in philosophy without committing oneself to any position on major public issues. No doubt there are some issues of social policy and foreign policy about which it can truly be said that a really expert assessment of the facts is required before taking sides or acting, but the issue of famine is surely not one of these. The facts about the existence of suffering are beyond dispute. Nor, I think, is it disputed that we can do something about it, either through orthodox methods of famine relief or through population control or both. This is therefore an issue on which philosophers are competent to take a position. The issue is one which faces everyone who has more money than he needs to support himself and his dependents, or who is in a position to take some sort of political action. These categories must include practically every teacher and student of philosophy in the universities of the Western world. If philosophy is to deal with matters that are relevant to both teachers and students, this is an issue that philosophers should discuss.

Discussion, though, is not enough. What is the point of relating philosophy to public (and personal) affairs if we do not take our conclusions seriously? In this instance, taking our conclusion seriously means acting upon it. The philosopher will not find it any easier than anyone else to alter his attitudes and way of life to the extent that, if I am right, is involved in doing everything that we ought to be doing. At the very least, though, one can make a start. The philosopher who does so will have to sacrifice some of the benefits of the consumer society, but he can find compensation in the satisfaction of a way of life in which theory and practice, if not yet in harmony, are at least coming together.

Notes

1. There was also a third possibility: that India would go to war to enable the refugees to return to their lands. Since I wrote this paper, India has taken this way out. The situation is no longer that described above, but this does not affect my argument, as the next paragraph indicates.
2. In view of the special sense philosophers often give to the term, I should say that I use "obligation" simply as the abstract noun derived from "ought," so that "I have an obligation to" means no more, and no less, than "I ought to." This usage is in accordance with the definition of "ought" given by the *Shorter Oxford English Dictionary*: "the general verb to express duty or obligation." I do not think any issue of substance hangs on the way the term is used; sentences in which I use "obligation" could all be rewritten, although somewhat clumsily, as sentences in which a clause containing "ought" replaces the term "obligation."
3. J. O. Urmson, "Saints and Heroes," in *Essays in Moral Philosophy*, ed. Abraham I. Melden (Seattle and London, 1958), p. 214. For a related but significantly different view see also Henry Sidgwick, *The Methods of Ethics*, 7th ed. (London, 1907), pp. 220–21, 492–93.
4. *Summa Theologica*, II–II, Question 66, Article 7, in *Aquinas, Selected Political Writings*, ed. A. P. d'Entreves, trans. J. G. Dawson (Oxford, 1948), p. 171.
5. See, for instance, John Kenneth Galbraith, *The New Industrial State* (Boston, 1967); and E. J. Mishan, *The Costs of Economic Growth* (London, 1967).

Study Questions

1. If you can prevent something bad from happening at a comparatively small cost to yourself, are you obligated to do so?
2. Are you acting immorally by buying a luxury car while others are starving?
3. Are you acting immorally by paying college tuition for your own children while other children have no opportunity for any schooling?
4. Do we have a moral obligation to try to alleviate extreme poverty in our own country before attempting to do so in other countries?

CHAPTER 28

World Hunger and Moral Obligation:
The Case against Singer

John Arthur

John Arthur (1946–2007) was Professor of Philosophy at Binghamton University (State University of New York). He wrote the following selection as a response to the previous article by Peter Singer. Again the question is: Who has the better of the argument? And again the answer is for each reader to decide.

My guess is that everyone who reads these words is wealthy by comparison with the poorest millions of people on our planet. Not only do we have plenty of money for food, clothing, housing, and other necessities, but a fair amount is left over for far less important purchases like . . . fancy clothes, trips, intoxicants, movies, and so on. And what's more we don't usually give a thought to whether or not we ought to spend our money on such luxuries rather than to give it to those who need it more; we just assume it's ours to do with as we please.

Peter Singer, "Famine, Affluence, and Morality," argues that our assumption is wrong, that we should not buy luxuries when others are in severe need. But [is he] correct? . . .

He first argues that two general moral principles are widely accepted, and then that those principles imply an obligation to eliminate starvation.

The first principle is simply that "suffering and death from lack of food, shelter, and medical care are bad." Some may be inclined

---

to think that the mere existence of such an evil in itself places an obligation on others, but that is, of course, the problem which Singer addresses. I take it that he is not begging the question in this obvious way and will argue from the existence of evil to the obligation of others to eliminate it. But how, exactly, does he establish this? The second principle, he thinks, shows the connection, but it is here that controversy arises.

This principle, which I will call the greater moral evil rule, is as follows:

> If it is in our power to prevent something bad from happening, without thereby sacrificing anything of comparable moral importance, we ought, morally, to do it.

In other words, people are entitled to keep their earnings only if there is no way for them to prevent a greater evil by giving them away. Providing others with food, clothing, and housing would generally be of more importance than buying luxuries, so the greater moral evil rule now requires substantial redistribution of wealth.

Certainly there are few, if any, of us who live by that rule, although that hardly shows we are *justified* in our way of life: we often fail to live up to our own standards. Why does Singer think our shared morality requires that we follow the greater moral evil rule? What arguments does he give for it?

He begins with an analogy. Suppose you came across a child drowning in a shallow pond. Certainly we feel it would be wrong not to help. Even if saving the child meant we must dirty our clothes, we would emphasize that those clothes are not of comparable significance to the child's life. The greater moral evil rule thus seems a natural way of capturing why we think it would be wrong not to help.

But the argument for the greater moral evil rule is not limited to Singer's claim that it explains our feelings about the drowning child or that it appears "uncontroversial." Moral equality also enters the picture. Besides the Jeffersonian idea that we share certain rights equally, most of us are also attracted to another type of equality, namely, that like amounts of suffering (or happiness) are of equal significance, no matter who is experiencing them. I cannot reasonably say that, while my pain is no more severe than yours, I am somehow special and it's more important that mine be alleviated. Objectivity requires us to admit the opposite, that no one has a unique status which warrants such special pleading. So equality demands equal consideration of interests as well as respect for certain rights.

But if we fail to give to famine relief and instead purchase a new car when the old one will do, or buy fancy clothes for a friend when his or her old ones are perfectly good, are we not assuming that the relatively minor enjoyment we or our friends may get is as important as another person's life? And that is a form of prejudice; we are acting as if people were not equal in the sense that their interests deserve equal consideration. We are giving special consideration to ourselves or to our group, rather like a racist does. Equal consideration of interests thus leads naturally to the greater moral evil rule.

Rights and Desert

Equality, in the sense of giving equal consideration to equally serious needs, is part of our moral code. And so we are led, quite rightly I think, to the conclusion that we should prevent harm to others if in doing so we do not sacrifice anything of comparable moral importance. But there is also another side to the coin, one which Singer ignore[s]. . . . This can be expressed rather awkwardly by the notion of entitlements. These fall into two broad categories, rights and desert. A few examples will show what I mean.

All of us could help others by giving way or allowing others to use our bodies. While your life may be shortened by the loss of a kidney or less enjoyable if lived with only one eye, those costs are probably not comparable to the loss experienced by a person who will die without any kidney or who is totally blind. We can even imagine persons who will actually be harmed in some way by your not granting sexual favors to them. Perhaps the absence of a sexual partner would cause psychological harm or even rape. Now suppose that you can prevent this evil without sacrificing anything of comparable importance. Obviously such relations may not be pleasant, but according to the greater moral evil rule that is not enough; to be justified in refusing, you must show that the unpleasantness you would experience is of equal importance to the harm you are preventing. Otherwise, the rule says you must consent.

If anything is clear, however, it is that our code does not *require* such heroism; you are entitled to keep your second eye and kidney and not bestow sexual favors on anyone who may be harmed without them. The reason for this is often expressed in terms of rights; it's your body, you have a right to it, and that weighs against whatever duty you have to help. To sacrifice a kidney for a stranger is to do more than is required, it's heroic.

Moral rights are normally divided into two categories. Negative rights are rights of noninterference. The right to life, for example, is a right not to be killed. Property rights, the right to privacy, and the right to exercise religious freedom are also negative, requiring only that people leave others alone and not interfere.

Positive rights, however, are rights of recipience. By not putting their children up for adoption, parents give them various positive rights, including rights to be fed, clothed, and housed. If I agree to share in a business venture, my promise creates a right of recipience, so that when I back out of the deal, I've violated your right.

Negative rights also differ from positive in that the former are natural; the ones you have depend on what you are. If lower animals lack rights to life or liberty it is because there is a relevant difference between them and us. But the positive rights you may have are not natural; they arise because others have promised, agreed, or contracted to give you something.

Normally, then, a duty to help a stranger in need is not the result of a right he has. Such a right would be positive, and since no contract or promise was made, no such right exists. An exception to this would be a lifeguard who contracts to watch out for someone's children. The parent whose child drowns would in this case be doubly wronged. First, the lifeguard should not have cruelly or thoughtlessly ignored the child's interests, and second, he ought not to have violated the rights of the parents that he helped. Here, unlike Singer's case, we can say there are rights at stake. Other bystanders also act wrongly by cruelly ignoring the child, but unlike the lifeguard they do not violate anybody's rights. Moral rights are one factor to be weighed, but we also have other obligations; I am not claiming that rights are all we need to consider. That view, like the greater moral evil rule, trades simplicity for accuracy. In fact, our code expects us to help people in need as well as to respect negative and positive rights. But we are also entitled to invoke our own rights as justification for not giving to distant strangers or when the cost to us is substantial, as when we give up an eye or a kidney. . . .

Desert is a second form of entitlement. Suppose, for example, an industrious farmer manages through hard work to produce a surplus of food for the winter while a lazy neighbor spends his summer fishing. Must our industrious farmer ignore his hard work and give the surplus away because his neighbor or his family will suffer? What again seems clear is that we have more than one factor to weigh. Not only should we compare the consequences of his keeping it with his giving it away; we also should weigh the fact that one farmer deserves the food, he earned it through his hard work. Perhaps his deserving the product of his labor is outweighed by the greater need of his lazy neighbor, or perhaps it isn't, but being outweighed is in any case not the same as weighing nothing!

Desert can be negative, too. The fact that the Nazi war criminal did what he did means he deserves punishment, that we have a reason to send him to jail. Other considerations, for example the fact that nobody will be deterred by his suffering, or that he is old and harmless, may weigh against punishment and so we may let him go; but again that does not mean he doesn't still deserve to be punished.

Our moral code gives weight to both the greater moral evil principle and entitlements. The former emphasizes equality, claiming that from an objective point of view all comparable suffering, whoever its victim, is equally significant. It encourages us to take an impartial look at all the various effects of our actions; it is thus forward-looking. When we consider matters of entitlement, however, our attention is directed to the past. Whether we have rights to money, property, eyes, or whatever, depends on how we came to possess them. If they were acquired by theft rather than from birth or through gift exchange, then the right is suspect. Desert, like rights, is also backward-looking, emphasizing past effort or past transgressions which now warrant reward or punishment.

Our commonly shared morality thus requires that we ignore neither consequences nor entitlements, neither the future results of our action nor relevant events in the past. It encourages people to help others in need, especially when it's a friend or someone we are close to geographically, and when the cost is not significant. But it also gives weight to rights and desert, so that we are not usually obligated to give to strangers. . . .

But unless we are moral relativists, the mere fact that entitlements are an important part of our moral code does not in itself justify such a role. Singer . . . can perhaps best be seen as [a moral reformer] advocating the rejection of rules which provide for distribution according to rights and desert. Certainly the fact that in the past our moral code condemned suicide and racial mixing while condoning slavery should not convince us that a more enlightened moral code, one which we would want to support, would take such positions. Rules which define acceptable behavior are continually changing, and we must allow for the replacement of inferior ones.

Why should we not view entitlements as examples of inferior rules we are better off without? What could justify our practice of evaluating actions by looking backward to rights and desert instead of just to their consequences? One answer is that more fundamental values than rights and desert are at stake, namely, fairness, justice, and respect. Failure to reward those who earn good grades or promotions is wrong because it's *unfair*; ignoring past guilt shows a lack of regard for *justice*; and failure to respect rights to life, privacy, or religious choice suggests a lack of *respect for other persons*.

Some people may be persuaded by those remarks, feeling that entitlements are now on an acceptably firm foundation. But an advocate of equality may well want to question why fairness, justice, and respect for persons should matter. But since it is no more obvious that preventing suffering matters than that fairness, respect, and justice do, we again seem to have reached an impasse. . . .

The lesson to be learned here is a general one: The moral code it is rational for us to support must be practical; it must actually work. This means, among other things, that it must be able to gain the support of almost everyone.

But the code must be practical in other respects as well. . . . [It] is wrong to ignore the possibilities of altruism, but it is also important that a code not assume people are more unselfish than they are. Rules that would work only for angels are not the ones it is rational to support for humans. Second, an ideal code cannot assume we are more objective than we are; we often tend to rationalize when our own interests are at stake, and a rational person will also keep that in mind when choosing a moral code. Finally, it is not rational to support a code which assumes we have perfect knowledge. We are often mistaken about the consequences of what we do, and a workable code must take that into account as well. . . .

It seems to me, then, that a reasonable code would require people to help when there is no substantial cost to themselves, that is, when what they are sacrificing would not mean [a] *significant* reduction in their own or their families' level of happiness. Since most people's savings accounts and nearly everybody's second kidney are not insignificant, entitlements would in those cases outweigh another's need. But if what is at stake is trivial, as dirtying one's clothes would normally be, then an ideal moral code would not allow rights to override the greater evil that can be prevented. Despite our code's unclear and sometimes schizophrenic posture, it seems to me that these judgments are not that different from our current moral attitudes.

We tend to blame people who waste money on trivia when they could help others in need, yet not to expect people to make large sacrifices to distant strangers. An ideal moral code thus might not be a great deal different from our own.

Study Questions

1. How do positive rights differ from negative rights?
2. Does Arthur believe residents of wealthy countries ought to be charitable?
3. How might residents of a poor country respond to Arthur?
4. How might he reply to them?

D. Terrorism

CHAPTER 29

Terrorism

Michael Walzer

Michael Walzer is Professor of Social Science at the Institute for Advanced Study in Princeton, New Jersey. He considers the moral justification for terrorism and finds such activity not permissible.

The word "terrorism" is used most often to describe revolutionary violence. That is a small victory for the champions of order, among whom the uses of terror are by no means unknown. The systematic terrorizing of whole populations is a strategy of both conventional and guerrilla war, and of established governments as well as radical movements. Its purpose is to destroy the morale of a nation or a class, to undercut its solidarity; its method is the random murder of innocent people. Randomness is the crucial feature of terrorist activity. If one wishes fear to spread and intensify over time, it is not desirable to kill specific people identified in some particular way with a regime, a party, or a policy. Death must come by chance to individual Frenchmen, or Germans, to Irish Protestants, or Jews, simply because they are Frenchmen or Germans, Protestants or Jews, or until they feel themselves fatally exposed and demand that their governments negotiate for their safety.

In war, terrorism is a way of avoiding engagement with the enemy army. It represents an extreme form of the strategy of the "indirect approach."[1] It is so indirect that many soldiers have refused to call it war at all. This is a matter as much of professional pride as of moral judgment. Consider the statement of a British admiral in World War II,

---

protesting the terror bombing of German cities: "We are a hopelessly unmilitary nation to imagine that we [can] win the war by bombing German women and children instead of defeating their army and navy."[2] The key word here is unmilitary. The admiral rightly sees terrorism as a civilian strategy. One might say that it represents the continuation of war by political means. Terrorizing ordinary men and women is first of all the work of domestic tyranny, as Aristotle wrote: "The first aim and end [of tyrants] is to break the spirit of their subjects."[3] The British described the "aim and end" of terror bombing in the same way: what they sought was the destruction of civilian morale.

Tyrants taught the method to soldiers, and soldiers to modern revolutionaries. That is a crude history; I offer it only in order to make a more precise historical point: that terrorism in the strict sense, the random murder of innocent people, emerged as a strategy of revolutionary struggle only in the period after World War II, that is, only after it had become a feature of conventional war. In both cases, in war and revolution, a kind of warrior honor stood in the way of this development, especially among professional officers and "professional revolutionaries." The increasing use of terror by far left and ultranationalist movements represents the breakdown of a political code first worked out in the second half of the nineteenth century and roughly analogous to the laws of war worked out at the same time. Adherence to this code did not prevent revolutionary militants from being called terrorists, but in fact the violence they committed bore little resemblance to contemporary terrorism. It was not random murder but assassination, and it involved the drawing of a line that we will have little difficulty recognizing as the political parallel of the line that marks off combatants from noncombatants.

The Russian Populists, the IRA, and the Stern Gang

I can best describe the revolutionary "code of honor" by giving some examples of so-called terrorists who acted or tried to act in accordance with its norms. I have chosen three historical cases. The first will be readily recognizable, for Albert Camus made it the basis of his play *The Just Assassins*.

1. In the early twentieth century, a group of Russian revolutionaries decided to kill a Tsarist official, the Grand Duke Sergei, a man personally involved in the repression of radical activity. They planned

to blow him up in his carriage, and on the appointed day one of their number was in place along the Grand Duke's usual route. As the carriage drew near, the young revolutionary, a bomb hidden under his coat, noticed that his victim was not alone; on his lap he held two small children. The would-be assassin looked, hesitated, then walked quickly away. He would wait for another occasion. Camus has one of his comrades say, accepting this decision, "Even in destruction, there's a right way and a wrong way—and there are limits."[4]

2. During the years 1938–39, the Irish Republican Army waged a bombing campaign in Britain. In the course of this campaign, a republican militant was ordered to carry a pre-set time bomb to a Coventry power station. He traveled by bicycle, the bomb in his basket, took a wrong turn, and got lost in a maze of streets. As the time for the explosion drew near, he panicked, dropped his bike, and ran off. The bomb exploded, killing five passersby. No one in the IRA (as it was then) thought this a victory for the cause; the men immediately involved were horrified. The campaign had been carefully planned, according to a recent historian, so as to avoid the killing of innocent bystanders.[5]

3. In November 1944, Lord Moyne, British Minister of State in the Middle East, was assassinated in Cairo by two members of the Stern Gang, a right-wing Zionist group. The two assassins were caught, minutes later, by an Egyptian policeman. One of them described the capture at his trial: "We were being followed by the constable on his motorcycle. My comrade was behind me. I saw the constable approach him . . . I would have been able to kill the constable easily, but I contented myself with . . . shooting several times into the air. I saw my comrade fall off his bicycle. The constable was almost upon him. Again, I could have eliminated the constable with a single bullet, but I did not. Then I was caught."[6]

What is common to these cases is a moral distinction, drawn by the "terrorists," between people who can and people who cannot be killed. The first category is not composed of men and women bearing arms, immediately threatening by virtue of their military training and commitment. It is composed instead of officials, the political agents of regimes thought to be oppressive. Such people, of course, are protected by the war convention and by positive international law. Characteristically (and not foolishly), lawyers have frowned on assassination, and political officials have been assigned to the class of nonmilitary persons, who are never the legitimate objects of attack.[7] But this assignment only partially represents our common moral judgments. For we judge the assassin by his victim, and when the victim is Hitler-like in character, we are likely to praise the assassin's work, though we still do not call him a soldier. The second category is less problematic: ordinary citizens, not engaged in political harming—that is, in administering or enforcing laws thought to be unjust—are immune from attack whether or not they support those laws. Thus the aristocratic children, the Coventry pedestrians, even the Egyptian policeman (who had nothing to do with British imperialism in Palestine)—these people are like civilians in wartime. They are innocent politically as civilians are innocent militarily. It is precisely these people, however, that contemporary terrorists try to kill.

The war convention and the political code are structurally similar, and the distinction between officials and citizens parallels that between soldiers and civilians (though the two are not the same). What lies behind them both, I think, and lends them plausibility, is the moral difference between aiming and not aiming—or, more accurately, between aiming at particular people because of things they have done or are doing, and aiming at whole groups of people, indiscriminately, because of who they are. The first kind of aiming is appropriate to a limited struggle directed against regimes and policies. The second reaches beyond all limits; it is infinitely threatening to whole peoples, whose individual members are systematically exposed to violent death at any and every moment in the course of their (largely innocuous) lives. A bomb planted on a streetcorner, hidden in a bus station, thrown into a cafe or pub—this is aimless killing, except that the victims are likely to share what they cannot avoid, a collective identity. Since some of these victims must be immune from attack (unless liability follows from original sin), any code that directs and controls the fire of political militants is going to be at least minimally appealing. It is so much of an advance over the willful randomness of terrorist attacks. One might even feel easier about killing officials than about killing soldiers, since the state rarely conscripts its political, as it does its military agents; they have chosen officialdom as a career.

Soldiers and officials are, however, different in another respect. The threatening character of the soldier's activities is a matter of fact; the unjust or oppressive character of the official's activities is a matter of political judgment. For this reason, the political code has never attained the same status as the war convention. Nor can assassins claim any rights, even on the basis of the strictest adherence to its principles. In the eyes of those of us whose judgments of oppression and injustice differ from their own, political assassins are simply murderers, exactly like the killers of ordinary citizens. The case is not the same with soldiers, who are not judged politically at all and who are called murderers only when they kill noncombatants. Political killing imposes risks quite unlike those of combat, risks whose character is best revealed by the fact that there is no such thing as benevolent quarantine for the duration of the political struggle. Thus the young Russian revolutionary, who eventually killed the Grand Duke, was tried and executed for murder, as were the Stern Gang assassins of Lord Moyne. All three were treated exactly like the IRA militants, also captured, who were held responsible for the deaths of ordinary citizens. That treatment seems to me appropriate, even if we share the political judgments of the men involved and defend their resort to violence. On the other hand, even if we do not share their judgments, these men are entitled to a kind of moral respect not due to terrorists, because they set limits to their actions.

The Vietcong Assassination Campaign

The precise limits are hard to define, as in the case of noncombatant immunity. But we can perhaps move toward a definition by looking at a guerrilla war in which officials were attacked on a large scale. Beginning at some point in the late 1950s, the NLF waged a campaign aimed at destroying the governmental structure of the South Vietnamese countryside. Between 1960 and 1965, some 7,500 village and district officials were assassinated by Vietcong militants. An American student of the Vietcong, describing these officials as the "natural leaders" of the Vietnamese society, argues that "by any definition this NLF action . . . amounts to genocide."[8] This assumes that all Vietnam's natural leaders were government officials (but then, who was leading the NLF?) and hence that government officials were literally indispensable to national existence. Since these assumptions are not remotely plausible, it has to be said that "by any definition" the killing of leaders is not the same as the destruction of entire peoples. Terrorism may foreshadow genocide, but assassination does not.

On the other hand, the NLF campaign did press against the limits of the notion of officialdom as I have been using it. The Front tended to include among officials anyone who was paid by the government, even if the work he was doing—as a public health officer, for example—had nothing to do with the particular policies the NLF opposed.[9] And it tended to assimilate into officialdom people like priests and landowners who used their nongovernmental authority in specific ways on behalf of the government. They did not kill anyone, apparently, just because he was a priest or a landowner; the assassination campaign was planned with considerable attention to the details of individual action, and a concerted effort was made "to ensure that there were no unexplained killings."[10] Still, the range of vulnerability was widened in disturbing ways.

One might argue, I suppose, that any official is by definition engaged in the political efforts of the (putatively) unjust regime, just as any soldier, whether he is actually fighting or not, is engaged in the war effort. But the variety of activities sponsored and paid for by the modern state is extraordinary, and it seems intemperate and extravagant to make all such activities into occasions for assassination. Assuming that the regime is in fact oppressive, one should look for agents of oppression and not simply for government agents. As for private persons, they seem to me immune entirely. They are subject, of course, to the conventional forms of social and political pressure (which are conventionally intensified in guerrilla wars) but not to political violence. Here the case is the same with citizens as with civilians: if their support for the government or the war were allowable as a reason for killing them, the line that marks off immune from vulnerable persons would quickly disappear. It is worth stressing that political assassins generally don't want that line to disappear; they have reasons for taking careful aim and avoiding indiscriminate murder. "We were told," a Vietcong guerrilla reported to his American captors, "that in Singapore the rebels on certain days would dynamite every 67th streetcar . . . the next day it might be every 30th, and so on; but that this hardened the hearts of the people against the rebels because so many people died needlessly."[11]

I have avoided noticing until now that most political militants don't regard themselves as assassins at all but rather as executioners. They are engaged, or so they regularly claim, in a revolutionary version of vigilante justice. This suggests another reason for killing only some officials and not others, but it is entirely a self-description. Vigilantes in the usual sense apply conventional conceptions of criminality, though in a rough and ready way. Revolutionaries champion a new conception, about which there is unlikely to be wide agreement. They hold that officials are vulnerable because or insofar as they are actually guilty of "crimes against the people." The more impersonal truth is that they are vulnerable, or more vulnerable than ordinary citizens, simply because their activities are open to such descriptions. The exercise of political power is a dangerous business. Saying this, I do not mean to defend assassination. It is most often a vile politics, as vigilante justice is most often a bad kind of law enforcement; its agents are usually gangsters, and sometimes madmen, in political dress. And yet "just assassinations" are at least possible, and men and women who aim at that kind of killing and renounce every other kind need to be marked off from those who kill at random— not as doers of justice, necessarily, for one can disagree about that, but as revolutionaries with honor. They do not want the revolution, as one of Camus' characters says, "to be loathed by the whole human race."

However the political code is specified, terrorism is the deliberate violation of its norms. For ordinary citizens are killed and no defense is offered—none could be offered—in terms of their individual activities. The names and occupations of the dead are not known in advance; they are killed simply to deliver a message of fear to others like themselves. What is the content of the message? I suppose it could be anything at all; but in practice terrorism, because it is directed against entire peoples or classes, tends to communicate the most extreme and brutal intentions—above all, the tyrannical repression, removal, or mass murder of the population under attack. Hence contemporary terrorist campaigns are most often focused on people whose national existence has been radically devalued: the Protestants of Northern Ireland, the Jews of Israel, and so on. The campaign announces the devaluation. That is why the people under attack are so unlikely to believe that compromise is possible with their enemies. In war, terrorism is associated with the demand for unconditional surrender and, in similar fashion, tends to rule out any sort of compromise settlement.

In its modern manifestations, terror is the totalitarian form of war and politics. It shatters the war convention and the political code. It breaks across moral limits beyond which no further limitation seems possible, for within the categories of civilian and citizen, there isn't any smaller group for which immunity might be claimed (except children; but I don't think children can be called "immune" if their parents are attacked and killed). Terrorists anyway make no such claim;

they kill anybody. Despite this, terrorism has been defended, not only by the terrorists themselves, but also by philosophical apologists writing on their behalf. The political defenses mostly parallel those that are offered whenever soldiers attack civilians. They represent one or another version of the argument from military necessity. It is said, for example, that there is no alternative to terrorist activity if oppressed peoples are to be liberated. And it is said, further, that this has always been so: terrorism is the only means and so it is the ordinary means of destroying oppressive regimes and founding new nations.[12] The cases I have already worked through suggest the falsity of these assertions. Those who make them, I think, have lost their grip on the historical past; they suffer from a malign forgetfulness, erasing all moral distinctions along with the men and women who painfully worked them out.

Notes

1. But Liddell Hart, the foremost strategist of the "indirect approach," has consistently opposed terrorist tactics: see, for example, *Strategy* (2nd rev. ed., New York, 1974), pp. 349–50 (on terror bombing).
2. Rear Admiral L. H. K. Hamilton, quoted in Irving, *Destruction of Convoy PQ 17*, p. 44.
3. *Politics*, trans. Ernest Barker (Oxford, 1948), p. 288 (1314a).
4. *The Just Assassins*, in *Caligula and Three Other Plays*, trans. Stuart Gilbert (New York, 1958), p. 258. The actual historical incident is described in Roland Gaucher, *The Terrorists: From Tsarist Russia to the OAS* (London, 1965), pp. 49, 50 n.
5. J. Bowyer Bell, *The Secret Army: A History of the IRA* (Cambridge, MA, 1974), pp. 161–62.
6. Gerold Frank, *The Deed* (New York, 1963), pp. 248–49.
7. James E. Bond, *The Rules of Riot: Internal Conflict and the Law of War* (Princeton, 1974), pp. 89–90.
8. Douglas Pike, *Viet Cong* (Cambridge, MA, 1968), p. 248.
9. Jeffrey Race, *War Comes to Long An* (Berkeley, 1972), p. 83, which suggests that it was precisely the *best* public health officers, teachers, and so on who were attacked—because they constituted a possible anti-communist leadership.
10. Pike, p. 250.
11. Pike, p. 251.
12. The argument, I suppose, goes back to Machiavelli, though most of his descriptions of the necessary violence of founders and reformers have to do with the killing of particular people, members of the old ruling class: see *The Prince*, ch. VIII, and *Discourses*, I:9, for examples.

Study Questions

1. What is terrorism?
2. In a war should a moral distinction be drawn between people who can legitimately be killed and those who cannot?
3. Is assassination ever morally justifiable?
4. Do soldiers differ from political officials as appropriate targets of attack?

CHAPTER 30

Is Terrorism Distinctively Wrong?

Lionel K. McPherson

Lionel K. McPherson is Associate Professor of Philosophy at Tufts University. He argues that terrorism, like war, can be justifiable despite the harm it does to noncombatants.

Many people, including philosophers, believe that terrorism is necessarily and egregiously wrong. I will call this "the dominant view." The dominant view maintains that terrorism is akin to murder. This forecloses the possibility that terrorism, under any circumstances, could be morally permissible—murder, by definition, is wrongful killing. The unqualified wrongness of terrorism is thus part of this understanding of terrorism.

I will criticize the dominant view. . . .

I will define "terrorism" as the deliberate use of force against ordinary noncombatants, which can be expected to cause wider fear among them, for political ends. . . .

Moral evaluation of terrorism might begin with the question of what makes terrorism wrong. A better opening question, I believe, is whether [the] use of force that leads to casualties among ordinary noncombatants is morally objectionable. The latter question prompts [a] comparison of terrorism and conventional war. Judging by practice and common versions of just war theory, the answer is plainly no. The journalist Chris Hedges reports these facts: "Between 1900 and 1990, 43 million soldiers died in wars. During the same period, 62 million civilians were killed. . . . In the wars of the 1990s, civilian deaths constituted between 75 and 90 percent of all war deaths."[1] Such numbers may seem counterintuitive. More noncombatants than combatants have died in war, by a sizable margin, and the margin has only grown in an era of the most advanced weapons technology. We must conclude that war generally is highly dangerous for noncombatants. I will characterize this as the brute reality of war for noncombatants. This reality cannot be attributed simply to the conduct of war departing from the laws of war.

There is an ambiguity in the data I have cited: they do not clearly support the claim that most noncombatants who died in these wars were killed by military actions, for example, through the use of bombs, artillery, and land mines. Many noncombatant deaths in war have been the result of displacement and the lack of shelter, [the] inability to get food, and the spread of disease. At the same time, modern warfare is marked by a nontrivial number of noncombatant deaths that are the direct result of military actions. The ratio of war to "war-related" noncombatant casualties and the distribution of moral responsibility for these casualties will not be at issue here. I proceed on the assumption that evaluating the ethics of war involves recognizing that war, directly or indirectly, leads to a great many noncombatant casualties. Modern warfare and widespread harm to noncombatants are virtually inextricable. . . .

Immediately doubtful is the popular notion that terrorism is distinctively wrong because of the fear it usually spreads among ordinary noncombatants. Recall that my nonmoral definition of terrorism includes a fear effects clause which descriptively distinguishes terrorism from other forms of political violence. However, this does not morally distinguish terrorism and conventional war. The brute reality of war for noncombatants indicates that in general they have more to fear from conventional war than (nonstate) terrorism, particularly since (nonstate) terrorists rarely have had the capacity to employ violence on a mass scale.[2] Noncombatants in states that are military powers might have more to fear from terrorism than conventional war, since these states are relatively unlikely to be conventionally attacked. But surely this situational advantage that does not extend more broadly to noncombatants cannot ground the claim that terrorism is distinctively wrong.

The laws of war recognize a principle that prohibits disproportionate or excessive use of force, with an emphasis on noncombatants. For example, Article 51 (5) (b) of the 1977 Geneva Protocol I rules out use of force "which may be expected to cause incidental loss of civilian life, injury to civilians, damage to civilian objects, or a combination thereof, which would be excessive in relation to the concrete and direct military advantage anticipated."[3] Standard just war theory considers this the proportionality principle. Proponents of the dominant view might take the proportionality principle to illuminate an essential moral difference between conventional war and terrorism. They might claim that, unlike proper combatants, terrorists do not care about disproportionate harm to noncombatants. But the full impact of this charge is not easily sustained for two reasons.

The first reason is that terrorists could have some concern about disproportionate harm to noncombatants. This point is most salient when proportionality is understood in instrumental terms of whether violence is gratuitous, namely, in exceeding what is minimally necessary to achieve particular military or political goals, despite the availability of an alternative course of action that would be less harmful and no less efficacious. Terrorists may possess a normative if flawed sensibility that disapproves of instrumentally gratuitous violence, for the harm done would serve no strategic purpose. So the plausible charge is that terrorists reject the proportionality principle as conventionally construed (since it implicitly rules out deliberate use of force against noncombatants), not that they lack all concern for disproportionate harm to noncombatants.

The second reason is that the proportionality principle requires rather modest due care for noncombatants. Force may be used against them, provided that the incidental, or collateral, harm to them is not excessive when measured against the expected military gains. According to one legal scholar, "the interpretation by the United States and its allies of their legal obligations concerning the prevention of collateral casualties and the concept of proportionality comprehends prohibiting only two types of attacks: first, those that intentionally target civilians; and second, those that involve negligent behavior in ascertaining the nature of a target or the conduct of the attack itself.[4] Such an interpretation seems accurately to reflect the principle's leniency. Indeed, the U.S. general and military theorist James M. Dubik argues that commanders have a special moral duty "not to waste lives of their soldiers" in balancing the responsibility to ensure that due care is afforded to noncombatants.[5] A commander may give priority to limiting risk of harm to his own combatants, for their sake, at the expense of noncombatants on the other side.

We find, then, that the proportionality principle does not express a commitment to minimizing noncombatant casualties. The principle more modestly would reduce noncombatant casualties in requiring that they be worth military interests. Perhaps my reading appears too narrow. A prominent reason for thinking that terrorism is distinctively wrong is that terrorists, unlike combatants who comply with the laws of war, do not acknowledge the moral significance of bearing burdens in order to reduce noncombatant casualties for the sake of noncombatants themselves. To reply that terrorists might well be motivated to reduce noncombatant casualties on strategic grounds, for example, to avoid eroding sympathy for their political goals, would miss the point. Basic respect for the lives of noncombatants seems evidenced instead by a willingness to bear burdens in order to reduce harm to them. Terrorists, the objection goes, do not have this respect for noncombatant lives, which is a major source of the sense that terrorism is distinctively wrong as compared to conventional war.

There are difficulties with this objection. It suggests that the laws of war are imbued with a certain moral character, namely, fundamental moral concern for noncombatants. These laws, though, are part of the war convention, adopted by states and codified in international law for reasons that seem largely to reflect their shared interests, at least in the long run.[6] We do not have to be political realists to see this. Given that noncombatants are vulnerable enough on all sides and no state generally has much to gain by harming them, states usually are prudent to accept mutually a principle that seeks to reduce noncombatant casualties. States usually are also prudent to comply with the laws of war, since this compliance is a benchmark of moral and political respectability on the world stage. Simply put, states, like terrorists, would seem contingently motivated to accept the proportionality principle on broadly strategic grounds.

Now the objection might go that, even if a realist analysis of the proportionality principle's place in the war convention is correct, this is no barrier to states' recognizing that the principle has independent, nonprudential moral standing. But the same can be true for terrorists. Familiar characterizations of them as "evil" or unconstrained by moral boundaries are an unreliable indication of moral indifference to harming noncombatants. As Virginia Held observes, "Terrorists often believe, whether mistakenly or not, that violence is the only course of action open to them that can advance their political objectives."[7] When terrorism is seen by its agents as a means of last resort, this provides some evidence that they acknowledge the moral significance of bearing burdens out of respect for the lives of noncombatants. Such agents will not have employed terrorism earlier, despite their grievances.

A model case is the African National Congress (ANC) in its struggle against apartheid in South Africa. Nelson Mandela, during the 1964 trial that produced his sentence of life imprisonment, summed up the ANC's position as follows:

> *a.* It was a mass political organization with a political function to fulfill. Its members had joined on the express policy of nonviolence.
>
> *b.* Because of all this, it could not and would not undertake violence. This must be stressed.
>
> *c.* On the other hand, in view of this situation I have described, ANC was prepared to depart from its fifty-year-old policy of nonviolence. . . . There is sabotage, there is guerrilla warfare, there is terrorism, and there is open revolution. We chose to adopt the first method and to exhaust it before taking any other decision.[8]

Mandela was implying that violence, including terrorism, became an option "only when all else had failed, when all channels of peaceful protest had been barred to us," which led the ANC to conclude that "to continue preaching peace and nonviolence at a time when the government met our peaceful demands with force" would be "unrealistic and wrong."[9] By the 1980s, at the height of government repression, the ANC did resort to acts of terrorism before reaffirming its earlier position on controlled violence that does not target civilians.[10] The case of the ANC demonstrates that those who employ terrorism can have and sometimes have had fundamental moral concern for noncombatants. Such moral concern, however, is overriding neither for terrorists nor for proper combatants. . . .

I have argued that terrorism is not distinctively wrong as compared to conventional war in the following respects. Both types of political violence may be waged for just or unjust causes. Both types employ use of force against noncombatants, with conventional war usually causing them many more casualties. War and terrorism hence can be expected to produce fear widely among noncombatants where force is used. . . .

If we believe that war can be justifiable on grounds of just cause and the unavailability of less harmful means, despite the harm it does to noncombatants, we must take seriously whether these same grounds could ever justify terrorism. The failures of the dominant view of terrorism should lead us to adopt either a more critical attitude toward conventional war or a less condemnatory attitude toward terrorism.

Notes

1. Chris Hedges, *What Every Person Should Know about War* (New York: Free Press, 2003), p. 7.
2. I add the qualification "nonstate" since states have employed tactics (e.g., firebombing of cities) and weapons (e.g., chemical, biological, and nuclear) that could count as terrorist.
3. Adam Roberts and Richard Guelff, eds., *Documents on the Laws of War,* 3rd ed. (Oxford: Oxford University Press, 1982), p. 489. Also see, e.g., Michael Walzer, *Just and Unjust Wars* (New York: Basic Books, 1977), pp. 145–46.
4. Judith Gail Gardam, "Proportionality and Force in International Law," *American Journal of International Law* 87 (1993): pp. 391–413, 410. To be clear, Gardam is not endorsing this interpretation. For a critical assessment of standard treatments of proportionality and an alternative approach, see Lionel K. McPherson, "Excessive Force in War: A 'Golden Rule' Test," *Theoretical Inquiries in Law* 7 (2005): pp. 81–95.
5. James M. Dubik, *Philosophy & Public Affairs* 11 (1982): pp. 354–71, 368. Dubik is responding to Walzer's more demanding requirement that combatants must accept greater costs to themselves for the sake of minimizing harm to noncombatants. See Walzer, *Just and Unjust Wars,* p. 155.
6. For criticism of the war convention as a source of moral obligation, see Lionel K. McPherson, "The Limits of the War Convention," *Philosophy and Social Criticism* 31 (2005): pp. 147–63.
7. Virginia Held, "Terrorism and War," *Journal of Ethics* 8 (2004): pp. 59–75, 69.
8. Nelson Mandela, "I Am Prepared to Die," in *Mandela, Tambo, and the African National Congress: The Struggle against Apartheid, 1948–1990: A Documentary Survey,* ed. Sheridan Johns and R. Hunt Davis Jr. (New York: Oxford University Press, 1991), pp. 115–33, 121.
9. Ibid., p. 120.
10. Sheridan Johns and R. Hunt Davis, "Conclusion: Mandela, Tambo, and the ANC in the 1990s," in their *Mandela, Tambo, and the African National Congress,* pp. 309–17, 312.

Study Questions

1. Can modern warfare be waged without harm to noncombatants?
2. Do noncombatants have more to fear from war or from terrorism?
3. Might terrorists acknowledge the moral value of the lives of noncombatants?
4. Can terrorism be used on behalf of a just cause?

E. Torture

CHAPTER 31

Torture

Henry Shue

Henry Shue was Professor of Philosophy at Cornell University and Senior Research Fellow at Merton College of the University of Oxford. He acknowledges imaginable circumstances in which torture would be justified but maintains that these rare cases do not warrant relaxing legal prohibitions against the practice.

> But no one dies in the right place
> Or in the right hour
> And everyone dies sooner than his time
> And before he reaches home.
>
> —Reza Baraheni

Whatever one might have to say about torture, there appear to be moral reasons for not saying it. Obviously I am not persuaded by these reasons, but they deserve some mention. Mostly, they add up to a sort of Pandora's Box objection: if practically everyone is opposed to all torture, why bring it up, start people thinking about it, and risk weakening the inhibitions against what is clearly a terrible business?

Torture is indeed contrary to every relevant international law, including the laws of war. No other practice except slavery is so universally and unanimously condemned in law and human convention. Yet, unlike slavery, which is still most definitely practiced but affects relatively few people, torture is widespread and growing. According to Amnesty International, scores of governments are now using some torture—including governments which are widely viewed as fairly

Henry Shue, "Torture," *Philosophy & Public Affairs*, vol 7. No. 2, 1978. Reprinted by permission of Blackwell Publishing.

civilized—and a number of governments are heavily dependent upon torture for their very survival.[1]

So, to cut discussion of this objection short, Pandora's Box is open. . . .

Assault upon the Defenseless

The laws of war include an elaborate, and for the most part long-established, code for what might be described as the proper conduct of the killing of other people. . . .

. . . [O]ne of its moral bases . . . is that it allows for a "fair fight" by means of protecting the utterly defenseless from assault. . . .

At least part of the peculiar disgust which torture evokes may be derived from its apparent failure to satisfy even this weak constraint of being a "fair fight." The supreme reason, of course, is that torture begins only after the fight is—for the victim—finished. Only losers are tortured. A "fair fight" may even in fact already have occurred and led to the capture of the person who is to be tortured. But now that the torture victim has exhausted all means of defense and is powerless before the victors, a fresh assault begins. The surrender is followed by new attacks upon the defeated by the now unrestrained conquerors. In this respect torture is indeed not analogous to the killing in battle of a healthy and well-armed foe; it is a cruel assault upon the defenseless. In combat the other person one kills is still a threat when killed and is killed in part for the sake of one's own survival. The torturer inflicts pain and damage upon another person who, by virtue of now being within his or her power, is no longer a threat and is entirely at the torturer's mercy. . . .

Torture within Constraints?

But is all torture indeed an assault upon the defenseless? For, it could be argued in support of some torture that in many cases there is something beyond the initial surrender which the torturer wants from the victim and that in such cases the victim could comply and provide the torturer with whatever is wanted. To refuse to comply with the further demand would then be to maintain a second line of defense. The victim would, in a sense, not have surrendered—at least not fully surrendered—but instead only retreated. The victim is not, on this view, utterly helpless in the face of unrestrainable assault as long as he or she holds in reserve an act of compliance which would satisfy the torturer and bring the torture to an end.

It might be proposed, then, that there could be at least one type of morally less unacceptable torture. Obviously the torture victim must remain defenseless in the literal sense, because it cannot be expected that his or her captors would provide means of defense against themselves. But an alternative to a capability for a literal defense is an effective capability for surrender, that is, a form of surrender which will in fact bring an end to attacks. In the case of torture the relevant form of surrender might seem to be a compliance with the wishes of the torturer that provides an escape from further torture.

Accordingly, the constraint on the torture that would, on this view, make it less objectionable would be this: the victim of torture must have available an act of compliance which, if performed, will end the torture. In other words, the purpose of the torture must be known to the victim, the purpose must be the performance of some action within the victim's power to perform, and the victim's performance of the desired action must produce the permanent cessation of the torture. I shall refer to torture that provides for such an act of compliance as torture that satisfies the constraint of possible compliance. As soon becomes clear, it makes a great difference what kind of act is presented as the act of compliance. And a person with an iron will, a great sense of honor, or an overwhelming commitment to a cause may choose not to accept voluntarily cessation of the torture on the terms offered. But the basic point would be merely that there should be some terms understood so that the victim retains one last portion of control over his or her fate. Escape is not defense, but it is a manner of protecting oneself. A practice of torture that allows for escape through compliance might seem immune to the charge of engaging in assault upon the defenseless. Such is the proposal.

One type of contemporary torture, however, is clearly incapable of satisfying the constraint of possible compliance. The extraction of information from the victim, which perhaps—whatever the deepest motivations of torturers may have been—has historically been a dominant explicit purpose of torture is now, in world practice, overshadowed by the goal of the intimidation of people other than the victim.[2] Torture is in many countries used primarily to intimidate potential opponents of the government from actively expressing their opposition in any form considered objectionable by the regime. Prohibited forms of expression range, among various regimes, from participation in terroristic guerrilla movements to the publication of accurate news accounts. The extent of the suffering inflicted upon the victims of the torture is proportioned, not according to the responses of the victim, but according to the expected impact of news of the torture upon other people over whom the torture victim normally has no control. The function of general intimidation of others, or deterrence of dissent, is radically different from the function of extracting specific information under the control of the victim of torture, in respects which are central to the assessment of such torture. This is naturally not to deny that any given instance of torture may serve, to varying degrees, both purposes—and, indeed, other purposes still.

Terroristic torture, as we may call this dominant type, cannot satisfy the constraint of possible compliance, because its purpose (intimidation of persons other than the victim of the torture) cannot be accomplished and may not even be capable of being influenced by the victim of the torture. The victim's suffering—indeed, the victim—is being used entirely as a means to an end over which the victim has no control. Terroristic torture is a pure case—the purest possible case—of the violation of the Kantian principle that no person may be used *only* as a means. The victim is simply a site at which great pain occurs so that others may know about it and be frightened by the prospect. The torturers have no particular reason not to make the suffering as great and as extended as possible. Quite possibly the more terrible the torture, the more intimidating it will be—this is certainly likely to be believed to be so. . . .

The degree of need for assaults upon the defenseless initially appears to be quite different in the case of torture for the purpose of extracting information, which we may call *interrogational torture*. This type of torture needs separate examination because, however condemnable we ought in the end to consider it overall, its purpose of gaining information appears to be consistent with the observation of some constraint on the part of any torturer genuinely pursuing that purpose alone. Interrogational torture does have a built-in end-point: when the information has been obtained, the torture has accomplished its purpose and need not be continued. Thus, satisfaction of the constraint of possible compliance seems to be quite compatible with the explicit end of interrogational torture, which could be terminated upon the victim's compliance in providing the information sought. In a fairly obvious fashion the torturer could consider himself or herself to have completed the assigned task—or probably more hopefully, any superiors who were supervising the process at some emotional distance could consider the task to be finished and put a stop to it. A pure case of interrogational torture, then, appears able to satisfy the constraint of possible compliance, since it offers an escape, in the form of providing the information wanted by the torturers, which affords some protection against further assault.

Two kinds of difficulties arise for the suggestion that even largely interrogational torture could escape the charge that it includes assaults upon the defenseless. It is hardly necessary to point out that very few actual instances of torture are likely to fall entirely within the category of interrogational torture. Torture intended primarily to obtain information is by no means always in practice held to some minimum necessary amount. To the extent that the torturer's motivation is sadistic or otherwise brutal, he or she will be strongly inclined to exceed any rational calculations about what is sufficient for the stated purpose. In view of the strength and nature of a torturer's likely passions—of, for example, hate and self-hate, disgust and self-disgust, horror and fascination, subservience toward superiors and aggression toward victims—no constraint is to be counted upon in practice.

Still, it is of at least theoretical interest to ask whether torturers with a genuine will to do so could conduct interrogational torture in a manner which would satisfy the constraint of possible compliance. In order to tell, it is essential to grasp specifically what compliance would normally involve. Almost all torture is "political" in the sense that it is inflicted by the government in power upon people who are, seem to be, or might be opposed to the government. Some torture is also inflicted by opponents of a government upon people who are, seem to be, or might be supporting the government. Possible victims of torture fall into three broad categories: the ready collaborator, the innocent bystander, and the dedicated enemy.

First, the torturers may happen upon someone who is involved with the other side but is not dedicated to such a degree that cooperation with the torturers would, from the victim's perspective, constitute a betrayal of anything highly valued. For such a person a betrayal of cause and allies might indeed serve as a form of genuine escape.

The second possibility is the capture of someone who is passive toward both sides and essentially uninvolved. If such a bystander should happen to know the relevant information—which is very unlikely—and to be willing to provide it, no torture would be called for. But what if the victim would be perfectly willing to provide the information sought in order to escape the torture but does not have the information? Systems of torture are notoriously incompetent. The usual situation is captured with icy accuracy by the reputed informal motto of the Saigon police, "If they are not guilty, beat them until they are."[3] The victims of torture need an escape not only from beatings for what they know but also from beatings for what they do not know. In short, the victim has no convincing way of demonstrating that he or she cannot comply, even when compliance is impossible. (Compare the reputed dunking test for witches: if the woman sank, she was an ordinary mortal.)

Even a torturer who would be willing to stop after learning all that could be learned, which is nothing at all if the "wrong" person is being tortured, would have difficulty discriminating among pleas. Any keeping of the tacit bargain to stop when compliance has been as complete as possible would likely be undercut by uncertainty about when the fullest possible compliance had occurred. The difficulty of demonstrating that one had collaborated as much as one could might in fact haunt the collaborator as well as the innocent, especially if his or her collaboration had struck the torturers as being of little real value.

Finally, when the torturers succeed in torturing someone genuinely committed to the other side, compliance means, in a word, betrayal; betrayal of one's ideals and one's comrades. The possibility of betrayal cannot be counted as an escape. Undoubtedly some ideals are vicious and some friends are partners in crime—this can be true of either the government, the opposition, or both. Nevertheless, a betrayal is no escape for a dedicated member of either a government or its opposition, who cannot collaborate without denying his or her highest values.[4]

For any genuine escape must be something better than settling for the lesser of two evils. One can always try to minimize one's losses—even in dilemmas from which there is no real escape. But if accepting the lesser of two evils always counted as an escape, there would be no situations from which there was no escape, except perhaps those in which all alternatives happened to be equally evil. On such a loose notion of escape, all conscripts would become volunteers, since they could always desert. And all assaults containing any alternatives would then be acceptable. An alternative which is legitimately to count as an escape must not only be preferable but also itself satisfy some minimum standard of moral acceptability. A denial of one's self does not count.

Therefore, on the whole, the apparent possibility of escape through compliance tends to melt away upon examination. The ready collaborator and the innocent bystander have some hope of an acceptable escape, but only provided that the torturers both (a) are persuaded that the victim has kept his or her part of the bargain by telling all there is to tell and (b) choose to keep their side of the bargain in a situation in which agreements cannot be enforced upon them and they have nothing to lose by continuing the torture if they please. If one is treated as if one is a dedicated enemy, as seems likely to be the standard procedure, the fact that one actually belongs in another category has no effect. On the other hand, the dedicated enemies of the torturers, who presumably tend to know more and consequently are the primary intended targets of the torture, are provided with nothing which can be considered an escape and can only protect themselves, as torture victims always have, by pretending to be collaborators or innocents, and thereby imperiling the members of these two categories.

Morally Permissible Torture?

Still, it must reluctantly be admitted that the avoidance of assaults upon the defenseless is not the only, or even in all cases an overriding, moral consideration. And, therefore, even if terroristic and interrogational torture. each in its own way, is bound to involve attacks upon people unable to defend themselves or to escape, it is still not utterly inconceivable that instances of one or the other type of torture might sometimes, all things considered, be justified. Consequently, we must sketch the elements of an overall assessment of these two types of torture, beginning again with the dominant contemporary form: terroristic.

Anyone who thought an overall justification could be given for an episode of terroristic torture would at the least have to provide a clear statement of necessary conditions, all of which would have to be satisfied before any actions so extraordinarily cruel as terroristic torture could be morally acceptable. If the torture were actually to be justified, the conditions would, of course, have to be met in fact. An attempt to specify the necessary conditions for a morally permissible episode of terroristic torture might include conditions such as the following. A first necessary condition would be that the purpose actually being sought through the torture would need to be not only morally good but supremely important, and examples of such purposes would have to be selected by criteria of moral importance which would themselves need to be justified. Second, terroristic torture would presumably have to be the least harmful means of accomplishing the supremely important goal. Given how very harmful terroristic torture is, this could rarely be the case. And it would be unlikely unless the period of use of the torture in the society was limited in an enforceable manner. Third, it would have to be absolutely clear for what purpose the terroristic torture was being used, what would constitute achievement of that purpose, and thus, when the torture would end. The torture could not become a standard practice of government for an indefinite duration. And so on.

But is there any supremely important end to which terroristic torture could be the least harmful means? Could terroristic torture be employed for a brief interlude and then outlawed? Consider what would be involved in answering the latter question. A government could, it might seem, terrorize until the terror had accomplished its purpose and then suspend the terror. There are few, if any, clear cases of a regime's voluntarily renouncing terror after having created, through terror, a situation in which terror was no longer needed. And there is considerable evidence of the improbability of this sequence. Terroristic torture tends to become, according to Amnesty International, "administrative practice": a routine procedure institutionalized into the method of governing.[5] Some bureaus collect taxes, other bureaus conduct torture. First a suspect is arrested, next he or she is tortured. Torture gains the momentum of an ingrained element of a standard operating procedure.

Several factors appear to point in the direction of permanence. From the perspective of the victims, even where the population does not initially feel exploited, terror is very unsuitable to the generation of loyalty. This would add to the difficulty of any transition away from reliance on terror. Where the population does feel exploited even before the torture begins, the sense of outrage (which is certainly rationally justified toward the choice of victims, as we have seen) could often prove stronger than the fear of suffering. Tragically, any unlikelihood that the terroristic torture would "work" would almost guarantee that it would continue to be used. From the perspective of the torturers, it is rare for any entrenched bureau to choose to eliminate itself rather than to try to prove its essential value and the need for its own expansion. This is especially likely if the members of the operation are either thoroughly cynical or thoroughly sincere in their conviction that they are protecting "national security" or some other value taken to be supremely important. The greater burden of proof rests, I would think, on anyone who believes that controllable terroristic torture is possible.

Rousseau says at one point that pure democracy is a system of government suitable only for angels—ordinary mortals cannot handle it. If Rousseau's assumption is that principles for human beings cannot ignore the limits of the capacity of human beings, he is surely right. . . . As devilish as terroristic torture is, in a sense it too may be a technique only for angels: perhaps only angels could use it within the only constraints which would make it permissible and, then, lay it aside. The partial list of criteria for the acceptable use of terroristic torture sketched above, in combination with strong evidence of the uncontrollability of terroristic torture, would come as close to a reductio ad absurdum as one could hope to produce in political philosophy. Observance of merely the constraints listed would require a degree of self-control and self-restraint, individual and bureaucratic, which might turn out to be saintly. If so, terroristic torture would have been shown to be justifiable only if it could be kept within constraints within which it could almost certainly not be kept.

But if the final objection against terroristic torture turned out to be empirical evidence that it is probably uncontrollable, would not the philosophical arguments themselves turn out to have been irrelevant? Why bother to show that terroristic torture assaults the defenseless, if in the end the case against it is going to rest on an empirical hypothesis about the improbability of keeping such torture within reasonable bounds?

The thesis about assault upon the defenseless matters, even though it is not in itself conclusive, because the uncontrollability thesis could only be probable and would also not be conclusive in itself. It could not be shown to be certain that terroristic torture will become entrenched, will be used for minor purposes, will be used when actually not necessary, and so on. And we sometimes go ahead and allow practices which might get out of hand. The relevance of showing the extent of the assault upon defenseless people is to establish how much is at stake if the practice is allowed and then runs amok. If the evidence for uncontrollability were strong, that fact plus the demonstration of extreme cruelty would constitute a decisive case against terroristic torture. It would, then, never be justified.

Much of what can be said about terroristic torture can also be said about instances involving interrogational torture. This is the case primarily because in practice there are evidently few pure cases of interrogational torture.[6] An instance of torture which is to any significant degree terroristic in purpose ought to be treated as terroristic. But if we keep in mind how far we are departing from most actual practice, we may, as before, consider instances in which the *sole* purpose of torture is to extract certain information and therefore the torturer is willing to stop as soon as he or she is sure that the victim has provided all the information which the victim has.

As argued in the preceding section, interrogational torture would in practice be difficult to make into less of an assault upon the defenseless. The supposed possibility of escape through compliance turns out to depend upon the keeping of a bargain which is entirely unenforceable within the torture situation and upon the making of discriminations among victims that would usually be difficult to make until after they no longer mattered. In fact, since any sensible willing collaborator will cooperate in a hurry, only the committed and the innocent are likely to be severely tortured. More important, in the case of someone being tortured because of profoundly held convictions, the "escape" would normally be a violation of integrity.

As with terroristic torture, any complete argument for permitting instances of interrogational torture would have to include a full specification of all necessary conditions of a permissible instance, such as its serving a supremely important purpose (with criteria of importance), its being the least harmful means to that goal, its having a clearly defined and reachable endpoint, and so on. This would not be a simple matter. Also as in the case of terroristic torture, a considerable danger exists that whatever necessary conditions were specified, any practice of torture once set in motion would gain enough momentum to burst any bonds and become a standard operating procedure. Torture is the ultimate shortcut. If it were ever permitted under any conditions, the temptation to use it increasingly would be very strong.

Nevertheless, it cannot be denied that there are imaginable cases in which the harm that could be prevented by a rare instance of pure interrogational torture would be so enormous as to outweigh the cruelty of the torture itself and, possibly, the enormous potential harm which would result if what was intended to be a rare instance was actually the breaching of the dam which would lead to a torrent of torture. There is a standard philosopher's example which someone always invokes: suppose a fanatic, perfectly willing to die rather than collaborate in the thwarting of his own scheme, has set a hidden nuclear device to explode in the heart of Paris. There is no time to evacuate the innocent people or even the movable art treasures—the only hope of preventing tragedy is to torture the perpetrator, find the device, and deactivate it.

I can see no way to deny the permissibility of torture in a case *just like this.* To allow the destruction of much of a great city and many of its people would be almost as wicked as purposely to destroy it, as the Nazis did to London and Warsaw, and the Allies did to Dresden and Tokyo, during World War II. But there is a saying in jurisprudence that hard cases make bad law, and there might well be one in philosophy that artificial cases make bad ethics. If the example is made sufficiently extraordinary, the conclusion that the torture is permissible is secure. But one cannot easily draw conclusions for ordinary cases from extraordinary ones, and as the situations described become more likely, the conclusion that the torture is permissible becomes more debatable.

Notice how unlike the circumstances of an actual choice about torture the philosopher's example is. The proposed victim of our torture is not someone we suspect of planting the device: he *is* the perpetrator. He is not some pitiful psychotic making one last play for attention: he *did* plant the device. The wiring is not backwards, the mechanism is not jammed: the device *will* destroy the city if not deactivated.

Much more important from the perspective of whether general conclusions applicable to ordinary cases can be drawn are the background conditions that tend to be assumed. The torture will not be conducted in the basement of a small-town jail in the provinces by local thugs popping pills; the prime minister and chief justice are being kept informed; and a priest and a doctor are present. The victim will not be raped or forced to eat excrement and will not collapse with a heart attack or become deranged before talking; while avoiding irreparable damage, the antiseptic pain will carefully be increased only up to the point at which the necessary information is divulged, and the doctor will then immediately administer an antibiotic and a tranquilizer. The torture is purely interrogational.[7]

Most important, such incidents do not continue to happen. There are not so many people with grievances against this government that the torture is becoming necessary more often, and in the smaller cities, and for slightly lesser threats, and with a little less care, and so on. Any judgment that torture could be sanctioned in an isolated case without seriously weakening existing inhibitions against the more general use of torture rests on empirical hypotheses about the psychology and politics of torture. There *is* considerable evidence of all torture's metastatic tendency. If there is also evidence that interrogational torture can sometimes be used with the surgical precision which imagined justifiable cases always assume, such rare uses would have to be considered.

Does the possibility that torture might be justifiable in some of the rarefied situations which can be imagined provide any reason to consider relaxing the legal prohibitions against it? Absolutely not. The distance between the situations which must be concocted in order to have a plausible case of morally permissible torture and the situations which actually occur is, if anything, further reason why the existing prohibitions against torture should remain and should be strengthened by making torture an international crime. An act of torture ought to remain illegal so that anyone who sincerely believes such an act to be the least available evil is placed in the position of needing to justify his or her act morally in order to defend himself or herself legally. The torturer should be in roughly the same position as someone who commits civil disobedience. Anyone who thinks an act of torture is justified should have no alternative but to convince a group of peers in a public trial that all necessary conditions for a morally permissible act were indeed satisfied. If it is reasonable to put someone through torture, it is reasonable to put someone else through a careful explanation of why. If the situation approximates those in the imaginary examples in which torture seems possible to justify, a judge can surely be expected to suspend the sentence. Meanwhile, there is little need to be concerned about possible injustice to justified torturers and great need to find means to restrain totally unjustified torture.

Notes

1. See Amnesty International, *Report on Torture* (New York: Farrar, Straus and Giroux, 1975), pp. 21–33.
2. See Amnesty International, 69.
3. Amnesty International, 166.
4. Defenders of privilege customarily portray themselves as defenders of civilization against the vilest barbarians. Self-deception sometimes further smooths the way to treating whoever are the current enemies as beneath contempt and certainly unworthy of equal respect as human beings. Consequently, I am reluctant to concede, even as a limiting case, that there are probably rare individuals so wicked as to lack integrity or

anyway to lack any integrity worthy of respect. But, what sort of integrity could one have violated by torturing Hitler?

Any very slight qualification here must not, however, be taken as a flinging wide open of the doors. To be beyond the pale in the relevant respect must involve far more than simply serving values which the torturers find abhorrent. Otherwise, license has been granted simply to torture whoever are one's greatest enemies—the only victims very many torturers would want in any case. Unfortunately, I cannot see a way to delimit those who are genuinely beyond the pale which does not beg for abuse.

5. I am assuming the unrestrained character of terroristic torture as it is actually practiced. Besides the general study by Amnesty International cited above and below, Amnesty International regularly issues studies of individual countries. Of particular interest, perhaps, is *Report on Allegations of Torture in Brazil*, 3d ed. (London: Amnesty International Publications, 1976). The Committee on International Relations of the United States House of Representatives published from 1975 to 1977 extensive hearings on torture in dozens of countries. And other nongovernmental organizations, such as the International Commission of Jurists and the International League for Human Rights, have published careful accounts of the nature of the torture practiced in various particular countries. I believe that the category of terroristic torture used in this article is an accurate reflection of a very high proportion of the actual cases of contemporary torture. It would be tedious to document this here, but see, for example, Amnesty International, pp. 21, 26, 103, 199.

Nevertheless, it can be granted that terroristic torture is not necessarily unrestrained. It is conceivable for torture to fail to be constrained by the responses of its victim but to be subject to other constraints: to use brutality of only a certain degree, to conduct torture of unlimited (or limited) brutality but for only a limited time, to select victims who "deserve" it, etc. I have not discussed such a category of "constrained terroristic torture" because I believe it to be empty—for very good psychological and political reasons. On the methodological question here, see the concluding paragraphs of this article.

6. Amnesty International, pp. 24–25, 114–242.

7. For a realistic account of the effects of torture, see *Evidence of Torture: Studies by the Amnesty International Danish Medical Group* (London: Amnesty International Publications, 1977). Note in particular: "Undoubtedly the worst sequelae of torture were psychological and neurological" (p. 12). For suggestions about medical ethics for physicians attending persons being tortured, see "Declaration of Tokyo: Guidelines for Medical Doctors Concerning Torture," in United Nations, General Assembly, Note by the Secretary-General, *Torture and other Cruel, Inhuman or Degrading Treatment or Punishment in relation to Detention and Imprisonment* (UN Document A/31/234, 6 October 1976, 31st Session), Annex II.

Study Questions

1. How does Shue distinguish between "terroristic torture" and "interrogational torture"?
2. According to Shue, might torture ever be justifiable?
3. Does Shue believe that torture should be illegal?
4. Might moral considerations ever require illegal actions?

CHAPTER 32

Ticking Bombs, Torture, and the Analogy with Self-Defense

Daniel J. Hill

Daniel J. Hill is Lecturer in Philosophy at the University of Liverpool. He argues that interrogational torture is never morally justified.

1. Introduction

One reads in the press that the agents of many countries, and, indeed, many private individuals, engage in torture to coerce others into performing certain actions, frequently the divulging of information ("interrogational torture"). Sometimes this is undertaken for a good end, such as the saving of lives by the disarming of a ticking time-bomb, or the rescue of a kidnap victim. It will be argued in this paper that such torture and, more generally, interrogational coercion are never morally permissible. This will be a specific application of a general moral principle that will be proposed:

> (P) It is never permissible intentionally to inflict severe pain or severe harm on someone unwilling, unless the pain/harm is intended (i) for their benefit, or (ii) as a punishment, or (iii) as part of the pursuit of a legitimate war, or (iv) to prevent the individual from causing severe pain or severe harm to innocents.[1]

Daniel J. Hill, "Ticking Bombs, Torture, and the Analogy with Self-Defense," *American Philosophical Quarterly*, vol. 44, no. 1. Copyright © 2007 by the journal and published with its permission.

Disagreement with this absolute rejection of interrogational torture could come from several directions. Act utilitarians would assert that it is fairly easy to imagine circumstances in which the ends would justify the means of torture: if it were known that many would be killed or suffer extreme pain as a result of a bomb's exploding it would surely be for the greatest happiness of the greatest number that one inflict some not-too-extreme pain on a single individual with the knowledge of the whereabouts of the bomb—provided, of course, that one knew there to be no danger of setting a precedent that would lead to abuses that would outweigh the happiness of the lives saved and pain averted. The key word here is "imagine"; many of those that assert that it is possible to *imagine* circumstances in which torture would be justified also assert that *in real life* such circumstances will never obtain.[2] It should further be noted that many suggest that our intuitions concerning imaginary cases are not reliable.[3] This point will not be argued against here, however (even though the argument of this paper depends heavily on intuitions), since those opposed to the thesis of this paper—i.e., those that argue that interrogational torture *is* sometimes permissible—defend their position on the basis of intuition, so this is not a disputed point in this context.

On the other hand, some deontologists may object that principle (P) does not, despite its intended purpose, rule out interrogational torture, for interrogational torture is indeed intended to "prevent the individual from causing severe pain or severe harm to innocents." More generally, some deontologists argue that it is permissible to inflict severe pain or severe harm in self-defense or in defense of another, and that cases of interrogational torture are analogous to these in the relevant moral respects.[4] The bulk of this paper will be devoted to resisting these objections and arguments, and, therefore, to arguing that (P) does indeed absolutely prohibit interrogational torture. Because of the close connection between the objection to (P) and the analogy from self-defense this paper will often simply say "in self-defense" rather than "to prevent the individual from causing severe pain or severe harm to innocents"; nevertheless it is the longer formulation that represents the precise position of this paper. This paper will deal only with cases of severe pain/harm, and will also use "torture" interchangeably with "inflict severe pain or severe harm," because the admitted differences in meaning between these two are not in view in this paper. The paper will also ignore, as not relevant to the project in hand, the differences in meaning between "torture" and "coerce."

2. The Intention to Cause Pain

Let us consider a couple of examples that might be cited to support the analogy between self-defense and interrogational torture.

> Defense Case: A police officer spots a known terrorist about to detonate a bomb, which, if it goes off, will illicitly inflict serious harm and serious pain on many innocents.[5] The officer fires a Taser at the terrorist, intending to cause no serious lasting harm but so much pain that the terrorist will be paralyzed and unable to detonate the bomb.[6]

Most deontologists (and consequentialists) would agree here that it is morally permissible for the police officer to Taser the terrorist in self-defense or defense of others. So far so good, but let us now consider the supposedly analogous case from the world of interrogation.

> Interrogation Case: A known terrorist is in the captivity of the security services of a certain country. He is known to have planted somewhere a ticking bomb, which, if it goes off, will illicitly inflict serious harm and serious pain on many innocents. The security services know that he knows where the bomb is, but he is refusing to divulge its whereabouts. In order to get him to talk they give him electric shocks, intending to cause no serious lasting harm but so much pain that he will say where the bomb is.[7]

The contention of this paper will be that the analogy between Defense and Interrogation is superficial. In fact, it will be contended that there is a fundamental difference between the two. There is a way, admittedly, in which they are similar: each case is a case of intent that pain/harm will be caused—in Defense the terrorist is trying there and then to cause severe pain and severe harm, and in Interrogation the terrorist is deliberately not cooperating in order that the earlier causal chain that he set in motion may reach the terminus he desires. There is also, however, a way in which they are different: Interrogation is not a case of aggression, unlike Defense. In Defense the terrorist is *doing* something—he is attempting to inflict severe pain or severe harm—and force is being used to prevent him from causing a tragedy to happen. In Interrogation, by contrast, the terrorist is powerless, in the custody of the security services, and is not *doing* anything—he has *already* set in motion a causal chain threatening a tragedy, and force is being used to cause him to perform the positive action of causing a tragedy not to happen.[8] It will be argued that this distinction is of crucial moral significance.

It is tempting to say that the reason why it is not permissible in Interrogation to inflict pain on the terrorist to get him to talk is that in this case one would be treating him as a mere means. This may well be correct, but this paper will not pursue that line as it is not wholly clear whether cases of self-defense count as treating aggressors as mere means. There will now be adumbrated a case to illustrate this point and to refute another possible objection.

The next possible objection to be considered states that the difference between Defense and Interrogation is merely that in Defense the terrorist is not being caused to perform any action, whereas in Interrogation he is. To show that this is too simple, an example of a *permissible* case in which one *does cause* the terrorist to perform an action will now be presented. This case is a slight variation on Defense above:

> Reflex Case: A police officer spots a known terrorist about to detonate a bomb, which, if it goes off, will illicitly inflict serious harm and serious pain on many innocents. The officer sprays the terrorist with a pepper spray, intending to cause no serious lasting harm but so much pain in his eyes that he will instinctively start rubbing his eyes in an effort to relieve the pain, and so won't be able to press the detonator.

Is it permissible to cause the terrorist this pain in order to cause him to rub his eyes and thereby not be able to detonate the bomb? Intuitively, it is, even though here the terrorist is being prevented from detonating the bomb by being caused to perform an action, unlike in Defense in which the terrorist had been prevented from performing an action (the action of detonation) without being caused to *do* anything.

Is the terrorist being used as a mere means in Reflex? This is not clear, and so this paper will not press the line that this is why it is impermissible to inflict pain in Defense.

3. Causing a Conscious Action

It might yet be pressed, however, that Reflex was not analogous to Interrogation, because the action was a mere reflex action rather than a consciously chosen one. Once more this does not seem a sound objection. For one thing, it might well be that when in great pain some individuals would "break" and instinctively shout out the answers to questions without consciously choosing to do so. But in any case Reflex can itself be adapted, as is demonstrated by the following case:

> Holding Case: A police officer spots a known terrorist about to detonate a bomb, which, if it goes off, will illicitly inflict serious harm and serious pain on many innocents. The detonator button needs to be held down for ten seconds for the bomb to go off. The only way

the terrorist can be prevented from holding down the detonator button for ten seconds is if he is caused such pain that he will choose to
take his finger off the detonator button in order to get the pain to
stop. The officer shoots the terrorist in the foot, intending to cause no
serious lasting harm but so much pain that he will make a conscious
decision to stop priming the bomb and turn his attention to nursing
his foot.[9]

Intuitively, in Holding the police officer is justified in inflicting pain
on the terrorist in order to cause him to choose not to detonate the
bomb by choosing to take his finger off the detonation button.

Compare this with the following case:

> Withholding Case: A police officer spots a known terrorist about to
> detonate a bomb, which, if it goes off, will illicitly inflict serious harm
> and serious pain on many innocents. The detonator button needs to
> be in the down position for ten seconds for the bomb to go off. The
> device works in such a way, however, that once pressed the button will
> remain depressed unless pulled up by someone with the terrorist's fin-
> gerprint. The only way the detonator button can be prevented from
> remaining depressed for ten seconds is if the terrorist is caused such
> pain that he will choose to pull the detonator button up in order to
> get the pain to stop. The officer shoots the terrorist in the foot, telling
> the terrorist that he can expect more pain in the other foot unless he
> pulls up the detonator button.[10]

Withholding and Holding are superficially very similar, but there
is one crucial difference: in Holding the terrorist is prevented from
performing an action (holding the button down) and in Withholding
the terrorist is not preventing from doing anything—instead he is
(just) caused to perform an action, the action of pulling the button
up.[11] It would seem that this makes a moral difference. Intuitively, it
is not permissible to inflict pain in Withholding in order to compel
the terrorist to pull the button up, but intuitively it *is* permissible (as
previously stated) for pain to be inflicted in Holding in order that
the terrorist might be prevented from pushing the button down.

4. A Possible Reply: Loss of Human Rights

It might be replied that it is permissible for pain to be inflicted on
the terrorist in Withholding and similar cases because the terrorist
is guilty of attempting a terrorist atrocity and, as a result of this, has
lost his right not to have pain inflicted on him, just as those guilty of
crimes lose their right to freedom for a certain time.[12] This means,
so the objection goes, that it is morally permissible for pain to be

inflicted on him in order that he might be compelled to pull up the detonator button.

It is curious that, while most of those that advance this argument believe that the removal of freedom is a standard punishment for the guilty, relatively few of them believe that the infliction of pain is a standard punishment for the guilty. Yet the removal of freedom is inflicted as a punishment precisely because (at least on a deontological understanding) it is judged that the guilty party has lost the right to freedom; why then do not the proponents of the objection suggest the infliction of pain as a routine punishment? Furthermore, even the proponents of this objection would still think it morally unacceptable if terrorists were tortured for fun, or if the torturers continued to torture even after the terrorists had aborted the ticking bomb. Of course, it could be replied that the terrorists have lost the right against the infliction of less than a certain amount of pain, such as the amount of pain that they themselves were prepared to inflict. This, however, is in marked contrast to the "I'll do whatever it takes to break you" attitude that is usually associated with the torture of terrorist suspects. It also does not accommodate the intuition accepted by proponents of the objection that it is morally obligatory to try to prevent the torture from passing the minimum level necessary to get the terrorist to abort the tragedy. Finally, the supposition that all terrorists lose their right not to have pain inflicted on them has the counter-intuitive consequence of legitimizing the infliction of pain in the following example:

> Fellow Case: A terrorist from a large terrorist organization has just been captured. The terrorist has planted a ticking bomb somewhere, and it is imperative that its whereabouts be discovered. The terrorist refuses to talk, however. Also in custody is one of his fellow terrorists, from the same terrorist organization, who was captured some time ago, and does not know the whereabouts of the ticking bomb, nor was he involved in this particular attack. The psychologist suggests that the quickest way to get the information out of the newly captured terrorist would be to torture his fellow terrorist in front of him. He says that since both are terrorists, both have lost their right not to have pain inflicted on them.

Surely the psychiatrist would be wrong to suggest the torturing of the fellow, uninvolved, terrorist to get the newly captured one to talk, despite the fact that the fellow terrorist is himself guilty of serious terrorist offences. This seems to show that committing a terrorist outrage does not remove one's right not to be tortured, i.e., to have serious pain or serious harm inflicted on one without one's consent when it is not for one's benefit.

5. Another Possible Reply: Still Causing the Atrocity

It might be responded that the terrorist in Interrogation and Withholding and similar cases *is* still performing an evil action, viz., the causation of the terrorist atrocity, and that, therefore, the torturer *is* preventing the terrorist from performing an action, and so there is, after all, a similarity with Defense and Holding and similar cases. Miller (2006) puts it thus:

> [T]he terrorist is in the process of completing his (jointly undertaken) action of murdering thousands of innocent people. He has already undertaken his individual actions of, say, transporting and arming the nuclear device; he has performed these individual actions (in the context of other individual actions performed by the other members of the terrorist cell) in order to realise the end (shared by the other members of the cell) of murdering thousands of Londoners. In refusing to disclose the location of the device the terrorist is preventing the police from preventing him from completing his (joint) action of murdering thousands of innocent people.

Sussman (2005, p. 16) also defends this line:

> Consider again the captured terrorist who we know to have planted a powerful bomb in some crowded civilian area. Although the terrorist is in our power, he refuses to reveal the bomb's location, hoping to strike one last blow against us by allowing a train of events that he has set in motion to come to its intended conclusion. In one sense, the terrorist is indeed defenseless. We can do anything we like to him, and there is nothing he can do to resist or shield himself against us. But such helplessness means neither that the terrorist has ceased to engage in hostilities against us, nor that he is no longer an active military threat. His placing of the bomb was the beginning of an attack on us; his silence, although not any kind of further overt act, is nevertheless voluntary behavior undertaken for the sake of bringing that act to completion. His continued silence thus might well be considered a part of his attack, understood as a temporally extended action.

This raises the big metaphysical question of when one completes an action, (a) when its effects come about, or (b) when one finishes the *basic* actions (i.e., the bodily movements[13]) that ultimately lead to the effects. Intuitively, only (b) is tenable, as if (a) were correct one would continue performing lots of actions long after one's death. Admittedly, (b) does have the counter-intuitive consequence that a killer kills the victim before the victim dies, but this is less counter-intuitive than the view that one might kill someone after one's death.[14] It follows from (b) that facts about, one's actions are "soft facts,"[15] i.e., facts that obtain at least partly in virtue of later events, so, for example, A's killing B on Monday obtains partly in virtue of B's dying on the following Wednesday, as well as partly in virtue of A's leaving slow-acting poison in B's glass on Monday, and B's drinking the poison on Tuesday. It follows, further, that the torturer in Interrogation and Withholding etc. is not preventing the terrorist from performing an action of terror but preventing him from *having performed* an action of terror, and this difference between such cases as Interrogation and Withholding on the one hand, and Defense and Holding on the other hand, seems to make the difference between the licensing of the intentional infliction of severe pain or severe harm in Defense and Holding, but not in Interrogation and Withholding.

6. Another Possible Reply: Prevention of Non-Cooperation

It might be responded that the terrorist that refuses to abort the bomb or refuses to divulge its whereabouts still uncontroversially intends to perform a different morally evil action, viz., refusing to co-operate with the authorities, and that it is morally permissible to inflict severe pain or severe harm on him to prevent him from fulfilling this intention. The first part of this is quite correct, but not every morally evil action licenses the infliction of severe pain, even in self-defense, as should be made clear by the following example:

> Non-cooperation Case: Suppose the terrorist has been killed but his wife has been detained alive. She didn't know that her husband was a terrorist, but she does know where he's been spending a lot of time lately. She won't, however, say where until a lawyer skilled in the law of her native land and religion arrives to witness her statement. There is no time to wait for this lawyer, however, but the psychologist suggests that if she were tortured she'd divulge the information in a couple of minutes.

Surely it is not morally permissible to torture the terrorist's innocent wife in Non-cooperation. A historically important case of innocent motives behind non-cooperation is that of the "seal of confession": if a terrorist confesses to a Roman Catholic priest the priest is not allowed to reveal the location of the ticking bomb to the authorities. And we might imagine that even those that are not Roman Catholic priests could promise not to reveal what someone was about to tell them and regard themselves, rightly or wrongly, as absolutely bound by their promise. It would surely be unacceptable to torture them to get the information out of them.[16] This would seem to show that the infliction of pain in Withholding and the like cannot be defended on the grounds that it is designed to prevent the terrorist committing the evil of non-cooperation.

Finally, it may be argued that, although the terrorist in cases of torture such as Withholding and the like doesn't have the intention to perform an action evil enough to justify the infliction of pain to prevent him from performing this action, he does have another intention, which *is* evil enough to warrant torture: he intends that the planned atrocity should happen after all, and this is why he refuses to co-operate. But clearly the fact that he has this intention does not license him to be tortured; there are many terrorist sympathizers throughout the world that have this evil intention, and yet it would be wrong to inflict pain on them unless it were to prevent them from performing an evil action themselves. It may be objected that the terrorist and the sympathizers do not have the *intention* that the atrocity occur; they merely have the *desire* that it occur. It is unclear that this is correct, but if it is permissible to speak of the terrorist's having the intention surely it is also permissible to speak of the sympathizers' having it, at least if they intend to aid and abet it in a certain minor way such as by funding it or praying for its success. It is implausible to maintain that funding a terrorist atrocity is an offence that licenses torture; surely it is even less plausible to maintain that praying for the success of a terrorist atrocity is an offence that licenses torture.

7. Positive and Negative Duties

What is the basis of this moral difference between preventing someone from performing an action that will cause a tragedy and causing someone to cause a tragedy not to occur? It is an instance of the distinction between our duties to perform certain acts of causation on the one hand, our "positive" duties, and our duties not to perform certain different acts of causation on the other hand, our "negative" duties. Although both the distinction itself and its moral significance have been much attacked in the literature, they do seem to have intuitive support:[17]

> Drowning Case: Suppose *A*'s father and spouse have been deliberately pushed by *B* into a lake and are drowning: *A* can rescue one,

but only one, of them. *A* chooses to swim past his father to save his spouse.

Intuitively, in Drowning, *A* has not caused the death of his father; that was caused by *B*. And intuitively there is a moral difference between *A*'s choosing to refrain from saving his father in order to save his spouse on the one hand, and the deliberate pushing in by *B* of *A*'s father on the other hand. Even if *A*'s action of refraining from saving his father is morally bad, it surely isn't as morally bad as that of *B*. Finally, intuitively there is a distinction between the negative duty not deliberately to push the unwilling non-swimmer into a lake—a duty flouted by *B*—and the positive duty to save one's father from drowning if one can—a duty not satisfied by *A*, who could have saved his father, but saved his spouse instead.

It seems permissible, then, in some circumstances to inflict pain to force people to comply with their negative duties, but it does not seem permissible to inflict pain in order to force people to comply with their positive duties, even extremely important positive duties, such as the duly to avert an atrocity that the people in question have set in motion. In this sense negative duties are more important than positive duties, and the infliction of pain to force someone to comply with a positive duty would *itself* be a breach of a negative duty. On the other hand, failure to inflict pain to enforce a positive duty would not itself be a breach of a positive duty, though failure to inflict pain to enforce a negative duty in certain circumstances *would* be a breach of a positive duty: if a police officer refuses to shoot a terrorist in the foot when that is the only way to prevent him from detonating a devastating bomb then he or she is in breach of his or her duty to defend innocent citizens. On the other hand, as has been argued, the officer's duty to defend innocent citizens does not extend to a duty to shoot a captured terrorist in the foot to force him to divulge the whereabouts of a ticking bomb, as this would be a breach of a negative duty.

One can see that it is not the case that positive duties should be enforced by the infliction of pain by considering the following case:

> Expert Case: A ticking bomb has been located, and the only person that can defuse it is a retired bomb-disposal expert. He, however, doesn't want to come to defuse the bomb because he doesn't want to leave the bedside of his dying wife.

It would clearly be wrong on the deontological scheme to torture the bomb-disposal expert in Expert to get him to defuse the bomb, even if he has a duty to help. Moreover, intuitively it would still be wrong to torture him even if he was "on duty" and not retired, but was being insubordinate.

8. Conclusion

It appears that what underlies the cases that have been discussed in this paper is the principle mentioned earlier:

> (P) It is never permissible intentionally to inflict severe pain or severe harm on someone unwilling, unless the pain/harm is intended (i) for their benefit, or (ii) as a punishment, or (iii) as part of the pursuit of a legitimate war, or (iv) to prevent the individual from causing severe pain or severe harm to innocents.

(P) implies that it is impermissible to act in standard torture cases (such as Interrogation). It does not imply that it is impermissible to act in standard cases of self-defense and defense of others (such as Defense). This is as it should be, for it is intuitively permissible to inflict severe pain or severe harm in Defense and similar cases to prevent the aggressor from causing severe pain or severe harm to innocents, but intuitively impermissible to inflict severe pain or severe harm in cases such as Interrogation and standard torture cases.

In this paper it has been argued that there is no inconsistency in giving different moral opinions on the different cases: Defense and similar cases on the one hand, and Interrogation and similar cases on the other hand. An attempt has been made to identify the relevant difference in these cases: the fact that in Defense and similar cases pain is being inflicted in order to enforce a negative duty, i.e., to prevent the individual from causing severe pain or severe harm to innocents, whereas in Interrogation and similar cases it is not. It has been conceded that it is not true that it is never permissible to inflict severe pain or severe harm with the intention of causing the aggressor to perform an action—some cases of the infliction of pain in self-defense are counter-examples. A suggestion has been made that it was permissible for a police officer to inflict pain to cause a terrorist to choose to perform the action of nursing his foot (thereby preventing him from holding down the detonator button) in Holding. But it was maintained that this was permissible only as a means to the intended end of enforcing a negative duty, i.e., preventing that same person from causing severe pain or severe harm to innocents. It follows that the common practice of torture cannot successfully be justified on grounds of a supposed similarity to self-defense, for, in the common practice, as opposed to cases of self-defense, pain is not being inflicted in order to enforce a negative duty, but rather to enforce a positive one.

Notes

1. Note that "innocents" here has a technical meaning, intended to exclude material or formal aggressors. It is not intended in a kind of theological sense to exclude all that have ever done wrong. Of course, it is not being suggested that if one of the conditions mentioned (the pain or harm is intended for the individual's benefit, as a punishment, as part of the pursuit of a legitimate war, or to prevent the individual from causing severe pain or harm to innocents) is present that automatically makes the action permissible. Rather, it is being asserted that if none of the conditions mentioned is present that automatically makes the action impermissible.

2. Cf. Davis 2005, p. 174 and Shue 1978, pp. 141–142.

3. Cf. Davis 2005, p. 172.

4. Cf. Kershnar 2005, pp. 228–234.

5. The innocents may or may not include the police officer. Since the police officer is charged by the state with the defense of others, this makes no difference.

6. A Taser is a kind of gun that fires projectiles that administer an electric shock.

7. Note that the political elements of terrorism are not essential to the examples. The examples could be reworked to feature kidnappers instead of terrorists.

8. This point will be defended later.

9. This case is analogous to the case of the fat man sitting on an innocent discussed in Sussman 2005 (pp. 16–17).

10. This case was suggested by Dr. James Heather. Dr. Heather intended this example as a *reductio ad absurdum* of the view of this paper, however. The reader may judge for him- or herself whether he was right.

11. Of course, in causing him to pull the button up, one is thereby preventing him from performing incompatible actions, but this is not to the point, as these preventions are not part of the plan to stop the terrorist outrage.

12. Cf. Kershnar 2005, pp. 228–234.

13. The terms "basic action" and "non-basic action" are due to Danto 1963. Davidson 1971 identifies these with bodily movements.

14. An anonymous referee proposed the following objection in defense of the view that one can perform actions after one's death: "Now, if Stonewall Jackson, the general, ceased to exist when he died, how is it possible to remember his exploits? Surely, they were done by a being

of whom it is still possible to predicate them truthfully or untruthfully (unlike the present King of France)." Against this, surely it is possible to remember the general's exploits and the general himself, and to make true statements about them, because they once existed. Memory is a present mental state whose object is in the past. One cannot remember things that never happened, but one can remember things that no longer obtain. (Indeed, it's even possible to see things that no longer exist, as when one looks up at the night sky and sees a far-off star that has exploded since it sent out its light.) But the fact that one can now remember the general as he was then doesn't imply that the general is *now* doing something. The view here defended is, of course, philosophically controversial: it supposes that the past in some sense exists. The view also supposes that the future in some sense exists: it is possible for *A* to kill *B* today even if *B* doesn't die till tomorrow. It would take too long to defend these views in detail here; suffice it to say that an argument that torture is permissible that rests on the philosophical view that the future or past does not exist looks self-defeating: *ex hypothesi* the terrorist's setting of the ticking bomb is in the past and the bomb's detonation is in the (potential) future.

15. For a detailed definition and discussion of "hard facts" and "soft facts" see Hill 2005, p. 95. The terms seem to have been introduced into the literature by Pike 1966.

16. There have been prosecutions in the past of Roman Catholic priests for not revealing information told to them under the seal of confession. The most famous concerned that early act of terrorism, the gunpowder plot; see http://www.newadvent.org/cathen/13649b.htm, accessed on 7 June 2006.

17. The distinction seems first to have been brought to prominence in contemporary moral philosophy by Foot 1967. It is criticized in, e.g., Glover 1977 (p. 97).

References

Danto, Arthur. 1963. "What We Can Do," *Journal of Philosophy*, vol. 60. pp. 434–445.

Davidson, Donald. 1971. "Agency," in *Agent, Action, and Reason*, ed. R. Binkley, R. Bronaugh, and A. Marras. Toronto: University of Toronto Press.

Davis, Michael. 2005. "The Moral Justification of Torture and Other Cruel, Inhuman, or Degrading Treatment," *International Journal of Applied Philosophy*, vol. 19, no. 2, pp. 161–178; http://www.pdcnet.org/pdf/ijap 192–Davis.pdf. accessed on 19 June 2007.

Foot, Philippa. 1967. "The Problem of Abortion and the Doctrine of Double Effect," *Oxford Review*, vol. 5, pp. 5–15.

Glover, Jonathan. 1977. *Causing Death and Saving Lives*. London: Penguin.

Hill, Daniel J. 2005. *Divinity and Maximal Greatness*. London: Routledge.

Kershnar. Stephen. 2005. "For Interrogational Torture," *International Journal of Applied Philosophy*, vol. 19, no. 2, pp. 223–241: http://www.pdcnet.org/pdf/ijapl92-Kershnar.pdf. accessed on 16 June 2007.

Miller, Seumas. 2006. "Torture," in *The Stanford Encyclopedia of Philosophy* (Spring 2006 Edition), ed. Edward N. Zalta; http ://plato. stanford.edu/archives/spr2006/entries/torture/, accessed on 15 July 2006.

Pike, Nelson. 1966. "Of God and Freedom: A Rejoinder," *The Philosophical Review*, vol. 74, pp. 27–46.

Shue, Henry. 1978. "Torture," *Philosophy & Public Affairs*, vol. 7, pp. 124–143.

Sussman, David. 2005. "What's Wrong with Torture?" *Philosophy & Public Affairs*, vol. 33, no. 1, pp. 1–33.

Study Questions

1. Do you agree with Hill that utilitarians would find it easy to imagine circumstances in which the ends would justify the means of torture?

2. Would those who subscribe to Kant's moral outlook also find it easy to imagine circumstances in which the ends would justify the means of torture?

3. What arguments does Hill offer to differentiate the Defense Case from the Interrogation Case?

4. How do Hill's conclusions regarding the morality of torture depend on a distinction between positive and negative duties?

F. Capital Punishment

CHAPTER 33

The Morality of Capital Punishment

Walter Berns

Leaving aside both the legal issues involved in deciding whether capital punishment is constitutional and the empirical issues regarding its effectiveness as a deterrent and the fairness with which it is applied, is it by its nature a violation of human dignity? Walter Berns, University Professor Emeritus at Georgetown University, argues that the death penalty is a fitting expression of our care for victims of horrendous crimes and our anger at those who have perpetrated brutal injustice. Indeed, by punishing criminals appropriately, we are holding them responsible for their actions and paying them the respect is due them as human beings.

"Many sorrows shall be to the wicked: but he that trusteth in the Lord, mercy shall compass him about. Be glad in the Lord, and rejoice, ye righteous: and shout for joy, all ye that are upright in heart!"[1] What is said in Psalms about the Lord must also be said about the law, and as belief in divine reward and punishment declines, it must be said more emphatically about the law: we must trust in the law, and those who do will be rewarded. The law must respond to the deeds of the wicked, and the righteous must have confidence that the law will respond, and do so in an appropriate manner. It must punish the wicked because the righteous or law-abiding citizens make this demand of it. They are angered by the sight or presence of crime, and anger is not merely a selfish passion.

Roosevelt Grier, the former New York Giants defensive lineman, and the other friends of Robert Kennedy see him shot down before their eyes. They are shocked, then grief stricken, then angry; but

---

California law cannot permit them to discharge that anger on its cause, Kennedy's assassin; they must be restrained, and the appropriate way of restraining them is to assure them that it, the law, will respond to this crime. The law must assuage that anger by satisfying it, but not . . . simply to prevent them from taking the law into their own hands.

Consider another example. A few years ago, a seven-year-old boy was brutally murdered on the lower East Side of Manhattan. The next day, in a nearby neighborhood, a twenty-eight-year-old woman was stabbed to death in the doorway to her apartment. When the police caught the man suspected of doing it, they had a hard time protecting him from an angry crowd of local residents. A week later a thirty-one-year-old man was stabbed to death by a burglar in his apartment (one of the increasing number of felony murders), this before the eyes of his wife. The *Times* account continues as follows:

> On the lower East Side, most residents seemed to agree with the police that the next time a murder suspect is identified, Tuesday's mob scene is very likely to be repeated. There is a widespread feeling that the police, the courts, the entire criminal justice system simply acts out a sort of charade, and that it is up to the community to demand that justice is done. "When the police find him, they'll just say he's a sick man and send him to a hospital for two years," said . . . a Delancey Street shopkeeper. "Then he'll be right back on the street. The only thing to do is to kill this man right away, quickly and quietly."[2]

The law must not allow that to happen, and not merely because the criminal may indeed be sick; it must provide the forms of justice in order to fulfill its educative function.

Robert Kennedy's friends were angry; that East Side mob was angry; and it is not only right that they be angry (for murder is a terrible crime), but punishment depends on it and punishment is a way of promoting justice. . . .

[A] just society is one where everyone gets what he deserves, and the wicked deserve to be punished—they deserve "many sorrows," as the Psalmist says—and the righteous deserve to be joyous. Punishment serves both these ends: it makes the criminal unhappy and it makes the law-abiding person happy. It rewards the law-abiding by satisfying the anger he feels at the sight of crime. It rewards, and by rewarding teaches, law-abidingness. . . .

[T]o the extent that men cease to be loving and hating men, they also become indifferent to what we know as crime. . . . Anger is the passion that recognizes and cares about justice. . . .

Anger is expressed or manifested on those occasions when some-one has acted in a manner that is thought to be unjust, and one of its bases is the opinion that men are responsible, and should be held responsible, for what they do. Thus, anger is accompanied not only by the pain caused by him who is the object of anger, but by the pleasure arising from the expectation of exacting revenge on someone who is thought to deserve it.[3] We can become angry with an inanimate object (the door we run into and then kick in return) only by fool-ishly attributing responsibility to it, and we cannot do that for long, which is why we do not think of returning later to revenge ourselves on the door. For the same reason, we cannot be more than momen-tarily angry with an animate creature other than man; only a fool or worse would dream of taking revenge on a dog. And, finally, we tend to pity rather than to be angry with men who—because they are insane, for example—are not responsible for their acts. Anger, then, is a very human passion not only because only a human being can be angry, but also because it acknowledges the humanity of its objects: it holds them accountable for what they do. It is an expression of that element of the soul that is connected with the view that there is responsibility in the world; and in holding particular men respon-sible, it pays them that respect which is due them as men. Anger rec-ognizes that only men have the capacity to be moral beings and, in so doing, acknowledges the dignity of human beings. Anger is somehow connected with justice, and it is this that modern penology has not understood; it tends, on the whole, to regard anger as merely a self-ish passion.

It can, of course, be that; and if someone does not become angry with an insult or an injury suffered unjustly, we tend to think he does not think much of himself. But it need not be selfish, not in the sense of being provoked only by an injury suffered by oneself. There were many angry men in America when President Kennedy was killed; one of them—Jack Ruby—even took it upon himself to exact the punish-ment that, if indeed deserved, ought to have been exacted by the law. There were perhaps even angrier men when Martin Luther King was killed, for King, more than anyone else at the time, embodied a people's quest for justice; the anger—more, the "black rage"—expressed on that occasion was simply a manifestation of the great change that had occurred among black men in America, a change wrought in large part by King and his associates in the civil rights movement: the servility and fear of the past had been replaced by pride and anger, and the treatment that had formerly been accepted as a matter of course or as if it were deserved was now seen for what it was, unjust and unacceptable. King preached love but the movement he led depended on anger as well as love, and that anger was not despicable, being neither selfish nor unjustified. On the contrary, it was a reflection of what was called solidarity and may more accurately be called a profound caring for others, black for other blacks, white for blacks, and, in the world King was trying to build, American for other Americans. If men are not saddened when someone else suffers, or angry when someone else suffers unjustly, the implication is that they do not care for anyone other than themselves or that they lack some quality that befits a man. When we criticize them for this, we acknowledge that they ought to care for others. If men are not angry when a neighbor suffers at the hands of a criminal, the implication is that their moral faculties have been corrupted, that they are not good citizens.

Criminals are properly the objects of anger, and the perpetrators of terrible crimes—for example, Lee Harvey Oswald and James Earl Ray—are properly the objects of great anger. They have done more than inflict an injury on an isolated individual; they have violated the foundations of trust and friendship, the necessary elements of a moral community, the only community worth living in. A moral community, unlike a hive of bees or a hill of ants, is one whose members are expected freely to obey the laws and, unlike a tyranny, are trusted to obey the laws. The criminal has violated that trust, and in so doing has injured not merely his immediate victim but the community as such. He has called into question the very possibility of that community by suggesting that men cannot be trusted freely to respect the property, the person, and the dignity of those with whom they are associated. If, then, men are not angry when someone else is robbed, raped, or murdered, the implication is that there is no moral community because those men do not care for anyone other than themselves. Anger is an expression of that caring, and society needs men who care for each other, who share their pleasures and their pains, and do so for the sake of the others.[4] It is the passion that can cause us to act for reasons having nothing to do with selfish or mean calculation; indeed, when educated, it can become a generous passion, the passion that protects the community or country by demanding punishment for its enemies. It is the stuff from which heroes are made. . . .

Capital punishment . . . serves to remind us of the majesty of the moral order that is embodied in our law and of the terrible consequences of its breach. The law must not be understood to be merely statute that we enact or repeal at our will and obey or disobey at our convenience, especially not the criminal law. Wherever law is regarded as merely statutory, men will soon enough disobey it, and they will learn how to do so without any inconvenience to themselves. The criminal law must possess a dignity far beyond that possessed by mere statutory enactment or utilitarian and self-interested calculations; the most powerful means we have to give it that dignity is to authorize it to impose the ultimate penalty. The criminal law must be made awful, by which I mean, awe-inspiring, or commanding "profound respect or reverential fear." It must remind us of the moral order by which alone we can live as *human* beings, and in our day the only punishment that can do this is capital punishment.

Notes

1. Ps. 32:10–11.
2. *New York Times*, 26 August 1973, sec. 4, p. 6.
3. Aristotle, *Rhetoric* 1378b1–5.
4. Ibid., 1381a4–6.

Study Questions

1. Is anger ever an appropriate emotion?
2. Is capital punishment a harsher penalty than life in prison without possibility of parole?
3. What message, if any, does inflicting capital punishment send to the community?
4. Is capital punishment sometimes required in order to achieve justice?

CHAPTER 34

The Death Penalty as a Symbolic Issue

Stephen Nathanson

Stephen Nathanson, Professor of Philosophy at Northeastern University, argues against the position of Walter Berns and maintains that the death penalty is inconsistent with respect for the value of human life and, therefore, ought to be renounced. Whereas Berns believes that capital punishment acknowledges the dignity of human beings, Nathanson views the death penalty as a violation of such dignity, for by taking the life of a criminal, we convey the idea that the criminal, although human, is no longer of any worth.

[T]he question whether we ought to punish by death is a question with great symbolic meaning. For people on both sides, whether we impose or refrain from imposing the death penalty seems to say something about our values, about the kind of people we are, about the nature of our society. The death penalty debate is in part a field on which we champion some of our most central social and ethical ideals. We think that retaining or abolishing the death penalty conveys an important message, and we want it to be the right message. . . .

The Morality of Anger

The symbolic importance of the death penalty is strongly emphasized by Walter Berns in his defense of the death penalty. In discussing the symbolism of punishing by death, Berns stresses the moral significance of anger. He writes:

> If . . . men are not angry when someone else is robbed, raped,
> or murdered, the implication is that there is no moral community
> because those men do not care for anyone other than themselves.
> Anger is an expression of that caring, and society needs men who
> care for each other. . . . [Anger] is the passion that can cause us to
> act for reasons having nothing to do with selfish or mean calculation;
> indeed, when educated, it can become a generous passion, the passion
> that protects the community or country by demanding punishment
> for its enemies.

Berns wants to vindicate anger because he regards it as an expression of concern for others, and he fears that society is being undermined by a lack of other-directed concerns. . . . Anger shows that we are not simply self-interested individuals joined together in a marriage of convenience. Instead, we are a community of people who share common concerns and recognize common values.

Berns is certainly correct that anger may reveal important virtues in people, especially if a failure to be angry arises either from callousness or indifference. Nonetheless, whatever virtues are displayed by anger, everyone would agree that the actions that flow from anger must be controlled. The expression of anger needs to be limited by moral constraints. . . .

A person whose family has been killed in an automobile accident caused by the carelessness of another driver may be angry enough to kill the driver. The anger shows the depth of the person's caring for other human beings, but it does not provide a justification for killing the driver. Virtually everyone would agree that execution for carelessness is too severe a response. While some negative response to destructive and harmful actions is appropriate, it does not follow that anything done in the name of righteous anger is morally right.

I know of no one who denies that anger and outrage are the appropriate responses to the murder of innocent human beings. Nor do I know of anyone who argues that murderers should not be punished at all. The question is whether punishing by death is morally required. That we may feel angry enough to kill someone does not imply that doing so would be morally legitimate.

So, one can sympathize and agree with much of Berns's message, but that message does nothing to support the appropriateness of using death as a punishment. To favor severe but lesser punishments is in no way to express indifference or callousness toward the deaths of murder victims. The anger and grief that we feel about these deaths do not give us a license to kill. . . .

Affirming the Moral Order

Berns . . . believes that if people regard laws as conveniences for improving life, then they will not take them seriously enough. They will feel free to disobey the law when obedience is inconvenient. Part of the appeal of the death penalty for Berns is that it suggests that the law possesses a transcendent value. "Capital punishment," he writes,

> serves to remind us of the majesty of the moral order that is embodied in our law and of the terrible consequences of its breach. The law must not be understood to be merely statute that we enact or repeal at our will and obey or disobey at our convenience, especially not the criminal law. . . . The criminal law must be made awful, by which I mean, awe-inspiring. . . . It must remind us of the moral order by which alone we can live as *human* beings, and in our day the only punishment that can do this is capital punishment.

For Berns, permitting the state to punish by death is a means of affirming the moral order and its embodiment in the law.

Berns is correct about one point here. The law must support the moral order in the sense that it must provide appropriate punishments for particular crimes. Morality is subverted when terrible crimes go unpunished or are punished very leniently, since these responses would suggest that the crimes are not really serious. . . .

Berns wants to see the moral order reaffirmed, but he equates this order with the legal system. He does not want us to view the law "merely [as] statute that we enact or repeal at our will." Yet, that is precisely what the law is. While the moral order does not shift with the votes of a legislature, the legal order does. All too frequently, the legal order itself runs quite counter to what morality would require. Berns does the cause of morality no service by offering a blanket sanctification of the law.

Surely Berns is correct in his view that the nature and content of the law is a serious matter, but it is doubtful that we need to kill people in order to convey that message. Moreover, by revering the law when it does not deserve reverence, we help to perpetuate injustice. A critical and sober view of the law may do more to affirm the moral order than an attitude of awe or exaggerated respect. The critic who sees the flaws of the legal system and wants to limit its powers may be as committed to the moral order as Berns and may indeed have a better way to make the legal system conform to the moral order. . . .

The Symbolism of Abolishing the Death Penalty

What is the symbolic message that we would convey by deciding to renounce the death penalty and to abolish its use?

I think that there are two primary messages. The first is the most frequently emphasized and is usually expressed in terms of the sanctity of human life, although I think we could better express it in terms of respect for human dignity. One way we express our respect for the dignity of human beings is by abstaining from depriving them of their lives, even if they have done terrible deeds. In defense of human well-being, we may punish people for their crimes, but we ought not to deprive them of everything, which is what the death penalty does.

If we take the life of a criminal, we convey the idea that by his deeds he has made himself worthless and totally without human value. I do not believe that we are in a position to affirm that of anyone. We may hate such a person and feel the deepest anger against him, but when he no longer poses a threat to anyone, we ought not to take his life.

But, one might ask, hasn't the murderer forfeited whatever rights he might have had to our respect? Hasn't he, by his deeds, given up any rights that he had to decent treatment? Aren't we morally free to kill him if we wish?

These questions express important doubts about the obligation to accord any respect to those who have acted so deplorably, but I do not think that they prove that any such forfeiture has occurred. Certainly, when people murder or commit other crimes, they do forfeit some of the rights that are possessed by the law-abiding. They lose a certain right to be left alone. It becomes permissible to bring them to trial and, if they are convicted, to impose an appropriate— even a dreadful—punishment on them.

Nonetheless, they do not forfeit all their rights. It does not follow from the vileness of their actions that we can do anything whatsoever to them. This is part of the moral meaning of the constitutional ban on cruel and unusual punishments. No matter how terrible a person's deeds, we may not punish him in a cruel and unusual way. We may not torture him, for example. His right not to be tortured has not been forfeited. Why do these limits hold? Because this person remains a human being, and we think that there is something in him that we must continue to respect in spite of his terrible acts.

One way of seeing why those who murder still deserve some consideration and respect is by reflecting again on the idea of what it is to *deserve* something. In most contexts, we think that what people deserve depends on what they have done, intended, or tried to do. It depends on features that are qualities of individuals. The best person for the job deserves to be hired. The person who worked especially hard deserves our gratitude. We can call the concept that applies in these cases *personal* desert.

There is another kind of desert, however, that belongs to people by virtue of their humanity itself and does not depend on their individual efforts or achievements. I will call this impersonal kind of desert *human* desert. We appeal to this concept when we think that everyone deserves a certain level of treatment no matter what their individual qualities are. When the signers of the Declaration of Independence affirmed that people had inalienable rights to "life, liberty, and the pursuit of happiness," they were appealing to such an idea. These rights do not have to be earned by people. They are possessed "naturally," and everyone is bound to respect them.

According to the view that I am defending, people do not lose all of their rights when they commit terrible crimes. They still deserve some level of decent treatment simply because they remain living, functioning human beings. This level of moral desert need not be earned, and it cannot be forfeited. This view may sound controversial, but in fact everyone who believes that cruel and unusual punishment should be forbidden implicitly agrees with it. That is, they agree that even after someone has committed a terrible crime, we do not have the right to do anything whatsoever to him.

What I am suggesting is that by renouncing the use of death as a punishment, we express and reaffirm our belief in the inalienable, unforfeitable core of human dignity.

Why is this a worthwhile message to convey? It is worth conveying because this belief is both important and precarious. Throughout history, people have found innumerable reasons to degrade the humanity of one another. They have found qualities in others that they hated or feared, and even when they were not threatened by these people, they have sought to harm them, deprive them of their liberty, or take their lives from them. They have often felt that they had good reasons to do these things, and they have invoked divine commands, racial purity, and state security to support their deeds.

These actions and attitudes are not relics of the past. They remain an awful feature of the contemporary world. By renouncing the death penalty, we show our determination to accord at least minimal respect even to those whom we believe to be personally vile or morally vicious. This is, perhaps, why we speak of the sanctity of human life rather than its value or worth. That which is sacred remains, in some sense, untouchable, and its value is not dependent on its worth or usefulness to us. Kant expressed this ideal of respect in the famous second version of the Categorical Imperative; "So act as to treat humanity, whether in thine own person or in that of any other, in every case as an end withal, never as a means only."

The Problem of Moral Monsters

One may feel attracted to this ideal and yet resist it by calling to mind people like Hitler or Stalin or their various henchmen, who were responsible for the deaths of millions of innocent people. Aren't such people beyond the pale? Haven't they forfeited *all* claims to even minimal decency so that it would be appropriate to execute them as punishment for their deeds? Doesn't the existence of such people show that the death penalty is legitimate?

These troubling questions raise important issues, and death penalty opponents might meet them in diverse ways. For myself, I am willing to say that even in these cases, so long as these people no longer pose an active threat to others, it would be best not to execute them. Moreover, though their deeds were terrible beyond words, I think it best that we not renounce our respect for their humanity. . . .

Not all opponents of the death penalty would agree with the views I have expressed about figures like Hitler and Stalin, and . . . it would be possible for an opponent of the death penalty . . . to concede that Hitler and Stalin might have gone so far that they no longer merited any consideration as human beings. One could even acknowledge that they should be executed.

All of this is consistent with opposition to the death penalty. Why? Because these cases are extraordinary and atypical. The death penalty controversy is concerned with the use of death as a punishment for murders that occur within society. It is advocated as a part of our ordinary criminal justice system. One could favor executing Hitler because of his extraordinary acts and still think that executions should play no regular role in the achievement of domestic order within a society.

From the perspective of this reply, the whole issue of moral monsters is a distraction that confuses the issue. If death penalty supporters were proposing executions only for extraordinary political criminals like Hitler and Stalin, these examples would be to the point. Since they are proposing executions for people whose deeds do not begin to approach the evil of these famous persons, death penalty supporters must make a different sort of case for their view. The specter of Hitler and Stalin does not help their case at all.

The Morality of Restraint

I have argued that the first symbolic meaning conveyed by a renunciation of the death penalty is that human dignity must be respected in every person. To execute a person for murder is to treat that person as if he were nothing but a murderer and to deprive him of everything that he has. Therefore, if we want to convey the appropriate message about human dignity, we will renounce the death penalty. . . .

[T]he second important message conveyed by the renunciation of punishing by death . . . [is that when] we restrain ourselves and do not take the lives of those who kill, we communicate the importance of minimizing killing and other acts of violence. We reinforce the idea that violence is morally legitimate only as a defensive measure and should be curbed whenever possible.

We can see the point of this message by contrasting it with Walter Berns's emphasis on the morality of anger. Without discounting all that Berns says, it seems to me that the death penalty supports the morality of anger in an unacceptable way. It suggests that if someone's acts have provoked you to be very angry, then you may legitimately act violently against that person. The morality of restraint, on the other hand, requires that one control one's anger and allows one to attack another person only defensively. Anger by itself provides no justification for violence.

When the state has a murderer in its power and could execute him but does not, this conveys the idea that even though this person has done wrong and even though we may be angry, outraged, and indignant with him, we will nonetheless control ourselves in a way that he did not. We will not kill him, even though we could do so and even though we are angry and indignant. We will exercise restraint, sanctioning killing only when it serves a protective function.

Why should we do this? Partly out of a respect for human dignity. But also because we want the state to set an example of proper behavior. We do not want to encourage people to resort to violence to settle conflicts when there are other ways available. We want to avoid the cycle of violence that can come from retaliation and counter-retaliation. Violence is a contagion that arouses hatred and anger, and if unchecked, it simply leads to still more violence. The state can convey the message that the contagion must be stopped, and the most effective principle for stopping it is the idea that only defensive violence is justifiable. Since the death penalty is not an instance of defensive violence, it ought to be renounced.

We show our respect for life best by restraining ourselves and allowing murderers to live, rather than by following a policy of a life for a life. Respect for life and restraint of violence are aspects of the same ideal. The renunciation of the death penalty would symbolize our support of that ideal.

Study Questions

1. Are you persuaded by Nathanson's reply to Berns?
2. Do moral monsters deserve the death penalty?
3. Do we have persuasive reasons to treat moral monsters differently from others who commit murder?
4. Do we show respect for life by not taking the lives of those who commit murder?

G. Animal Rights

CHAPTER 35

The Case for Animal Rights

Tom Regan

Tom Regan, whose work we read previously, here develops the case
for animal rights. He calls for the abolition of animal agriculture,
commercial and sport hunting, and the use of animals in scientific
research.

I regard myself as an advocate of animal rights—as a part of the animal
rights movement. That movement, as I conceive it, is committed to a
number of goals, including,

- the total abolition of the use of animals in science;
- the total dissolution of commercial animal agriculture;
- the total elimination of commercial and sport hunting and
  trapping.

There are, I know, people who profess to believe in animal rights
but do not avow these goals. Factory farming, they say, is wrong—it
violates animals' rights—but traditional animal agriculture is all
right. Toxicity tests of cosmetics on animals violates their rights, but
important medical research—cancer research, for example—does
not. The clubbing of baby seals is abhorrent, but not the harvesting
of adult seals. I used to think I understood this reasoning. Not anymore. You don't change unjust institutions by tidying them up.

What's wrong—fundamentally wrong—with the way animals are
treated isn't the details that vary from case to case. It's the whole
system. The forlornness of the veal calf is pathetic, heart wrenching;
the pulsing pain of the chimp with electrodes planted deep in her

From Peter Singer, ed., *In Defense of Animals*. Copyright © 1985. Reprinted by permission of
Blackwell Publishing Ltd.

brain is repulsive; the slow, tortuous death of the racoon caught in the leg-hold trap is agonizing. But what is wrong isn't the pain, isn't the suffering, isn't the deprivation. These compound what's wrong. Sometimes—often—they make it much, much worse. But they are not the fundamental wrong.

The fundamental wrong is the system that allows us to view animals as *our resources*, here for *us*—to be eaten, or surgically manipulated, or exploited for sport or money. Once we accept this view of animals— as our resources—the rest is as predictable as it is regrettable. Why worry about their loneliness, their pain, their death? Since animals exist for us, to benefit us in one way or another, what harms them really doesn't matter—or matters only if it starts to bother us, makes us feel a trifle uneasy when we eat our veal escalope, for example. So, yes, let us get veal calves out of solitary confinement, give them more space, a little straw, a few companions. But let us keep our veal escalope.

But a little straw, more space and a few companions won't eliminate—won't even touch—the basic wrong that attaches to our viewing and treating these animals as our resources. A veal calf killed to be eaten after living in close confinement is viewed and treated in this way: but so, too, is another who is raised (as they say) "more humanely." To right the wrong of our treatment of farm animals requires more than making rearing methods "more humane"; it requires the total dissolution of commercial animal agriculture.

How we do this, whether we do it or, as in the case of animals in science, whether and how we abolish their use—these are to a large extent political questions. People must change their beliefs before they change their habits. Enough people, especially those elected to public office, must believe in change—must want it—before we will have laws that protect the rights of animals. This process of change is very complicated, very demanding, very exhausting, calling for the efforts of many hands in education, publicity, political organization and activity, down to the licking of envelopes and stamps. As a trained and practising philosopher, the sort of contribution I can make is limited but, I like to think, important. The currency of philosophy is ideas—their meaning and rational foundation—not the nuts and bolts of the legislative process, say, or the mechanics of community organization. That's what I have been exploring over the past ten years or so in my essays and talks and, most recently, in my book, *The Case for Animal Rights*. I believe the major conclusions I reach in the book are true because they are supported by the weight of the best arguments. I believe the idea of animal rights has reason, not just emotion, on its side.

In the space I have at my disposal here I can only sketch, in the barest outline, some of the main features of the book. Its main themes—and we should not be surprised by this—involve asking and answering deep, foundational moral questions about what morality is, how it should be understood, and what is the best moral theory, all considered. I hope I can convey something of the shape I think this theory takes. The attempt to do this will be (to use a word a friendly critic once used to describe my work) cerebral, perhaps too cerebral. But this is misleading. My feelings about how animals are sometimes treated run just as deep and just as strong as those of my more volatile compatriots. Philosophers do—to use the jargon of the day—have a right side to their brains. If it's the left side we contribute (or mainly should), that's because what talents we have reside there.

How to proceed? We begin by asking how the moral status of animals has been understood by thinkers who deny that animals have rights. Then we test the mettle of their ideas by seeing how well they stand up under the heat of fair criticism. If we start our thinking in this way, we soon find that some people believe that we have no duties directly to animals, that we owe nothing to them, that we can do nothing that wrongs them. Rather, we can do wrong acts that involve animals, and so we have duties regarding them, though none to them. Such views may be called indirect duty views. By way of illustration: suppose your neighbour kicks your dog. Then your neighbour has done something wrong. But not to your dog. The wrong that has been done is a wrong to you. After all, it is wrong to upset people, and your neighbour's kicking your dog upsets you. So you are the one who is wronged, not your dog. Or again: by kicking your dog your neighbour damages another person's property. And since it is wrong to damage another person's property, your neighbour has done something wrong—to you, of course, not to your dog. Your neighbour no more wrongs your dog than your car would be wronged if the windshield were smashed. Your neighbour's duties involving your dog are indirect duties to you. More generally, all of our duties regarding animals are indirect duties to one another—to humanity.

How could someone try to justify such a view? Someone might say that your dog doesn't feel anything and so isn't hurt by your neighbour's kick, doesn't care about pain since none is felt, is as unaware of anything as is your windshield. Someone might say this, but no rational person will, since, among other considerations, such a view will commit anyone who holds it to the position that no human being feels pain either—that human beings also don't care about what happens to them. A second possibility is that though both humans and your dog are hurt when kicked, it is only human pain that matters. But, again, no rational person can believe this. Pain is pain wherever it occurs. If your neighbour's causing you pain is wrong because of the pain that is caused, we cannot rationally ignore or dismiss the moral relevance of the pain that your dog feels.

Philosophers who hold indirect duty views—and many still do—have come to understand that they must avoid the two defects just noted: that is, both the view that animals don't feel anything as well as the idea that only human pain can be morally relevant. Among such thinkers the sort of view now favoured is one or other form of what is called *contractarianism*.

Here, very crudely, is the root idea: morality consists of a set of rules that individuals voluntarily agree to abide by, as we do when we sign a contract (hence the name contractarianism). Those who understand and accept the terms of the contract are covered directly; they have rights created and recognized by, and protected in, the contract. And these contractors can also have protection spelled out for others who, though they lack the ability to understand morality and so cannot sign the contract themselves, are loved or cherished by those who can. Thus young children, for example, are unable to sign contracts and lack rights. But they are protected by the contract nonetheless because of the sentimental interests of others, most notably their parents. So we have, then, duties involving these children, duties regarding them, but no duties to them. Our duties in their case are indirect duties to other human beings, usually their parents.

As for animals, since they cannot understand contracts, they obviously cannot sign; and since they cannot sign, they have no rights. Like children, however, some animals are the objects of the sentimental interest of others. You, for example, love your dog or cat. So those animals that enough people care about (companion animals, whales, baby seals, the American bald eagle), though they lack rights themselves, will be protected because of the sentimental interests of people. I have, then, according to contractariansim, no duty directly to your dog or any other animal, not even the duty not to cause them pain or suffering; my duty not to hurt them is a duty I have to those people who care about what happens to them. As for other animals, where no or little sentimental interest is present—in the case of farm animals, for example, or laboratory rats—what duties we have grow weaker and weaker, perhaps to vanishing point. The pain and death they endure, though real, are not wrong if no one cares about them.

When it comes to the moral status of animals, contractarianism could be a hard view to refute if it were an adequate theoretical approach to the moral status of human beings. It is not adequate in this latter respect, however, which makes the question of its adequacy in the former case, regarding animals, utterly moot. For consider: morality, according to the (crude) contractarian position before us, consists of rules that people agree to abide by. What people? Well, enough to make a difference—enough, that is, *collectively* to have the power to enforce the rules that are drawn up in the contract. That is very well and good for the signatories but not so good for anyone who is not asked to sign. And there is nothing in contractarianism of the sort we are discussing that guarantees or requires that every-one will have a chance to participate equally in framing the rules of morality. The result is that this approach to ethics could sanction the most blatant forms of social, economic, moral, and political injustice, ranging from a repressive caste system to systematic racial or sexual discrimination. Might, according to this theory, does make right. Let those who are the victims of injustice suffer as they will. It matters not so long as no one else—no contractor, or too few of them—cares about it. Such a theory takes one's moral breath away . . . as if, for example, there would be nothing wrong with apartheid in South Africa if few white South Africans were upset by it. A theory with so little to recommend it at the level of the ethics of our treatment of our fellow humans cannot have anything more to recommend it when it comes to the ethics of how we treat our fellow animals.

The version of contractarianism just examined is, as I have noted, a crude variety, and in fairness to those of a contractarian persuasion it must be noted that much more refined, subtle, and ingenious varieties are possible. For example, John Rawls, in his *A Theory of Justice*, sets forth a version of contractarianism that forces contrac-tors to ignore the accidental features of being a human being—for example, whether one is white or black, male or female, a genius or of modest intellect. Only by ignoring such features, Rawls believes, can we ensure that the principles of justice that contractors would agree upon are not based on bias or prejudice. Despite the improve-ment a view such as Rawls's represents over the cruder forms of contractarianism, it remains deficient: it systematically denies that we have direct duties to those human beings who do not have a sense of justice—young children, for instance, and many mentally retarded humans. And yet it seems reasonably certain that, were we to torture a young child or a retarded elder, we would be doing something that wronged him or her, not something that would be wrong if (and only if) other humans with a sense of justice were upset. And since this is true in the case of these humans, we cannot rationally deny the same in the case of animals.

Indirect duty views, then, including the best among them, fail to command our rational assent. Whatever ethical theory we should accept rationally, therefore, it must at least recognize that we have some duties directly to animals, just as we have some duties directly to each other. The next two theories I'll sketch attempt to meet this requirement.

The first I call the cruelty-kindness view. Simply stated, this says that we have a direct duty to be kind to animals and a direct duty not to be cruel to them. Despite the familiar, reassuring ring of these ideas, I do not believe that this view offers an adequate theory. To make this clearer, consider kindness. A kind person acts from a certain kind of motive—compassion or concern, for example. And that is a virtue. But there is no guarantee that a kind act is a right act. If I am a generous racist, for example, I will be inclined to act kindly towards members of my own race, favouring their interests above those of others. My kindness would be real and, so far as it goes, good. But I trust it is too obvious to require argument that my kind acts may not be above moral reproach—may, in fact, be positively wrong because rooted in injustice. So kindness, notwithstanding its status as a virtue to be encouraged, simply will not carry the weight of a theory of right action.

Cruelty fares no better. People or their acts are cruel if they display either a lack of sympathy for or, worse, the presence of enjoyment in another's suffering. Cruelty in all its guises is a bad thing, a tragic human failing. But just as a person's being motivated by kindness does not guarantee that he or she does what is right, so the absence of cruelty does not ensure that he or she avoids doing what is wrong. Many people who perform abortions, for example, are not cruel, sadistic people. But that fact alone does not settle the terribly difficult question of the morality of abortion. The case is no different when we examine the ethics of our treatment of animals. So, yes, let us be for kindness and against cruelty. But let us not suppose that being for the one and against the other answers questions about moral right and wrong.

Some people think that the theory we are looking for is utilitarianism. A utilitarian accepts two moral principles. The first is that of equality: everyone's interests count, and similar interests must be counted as having similar weight or importance. White or black, American or Iranian, human or animal—everyone's pain or frustration matter, and matter just as much as the equivalent pain or frustration of anyone else. The second principle a utilitarian accepts is that of utility: do the act that will bring about the best balance between satisfaction and frustration for everyone affected by the outcome.

As a utilitarian, then, here is how I am to approach the task of deciding what I morally ought to do: I must ask who will be affected if I choose to do one thing rather than another, how much each individual will be affected, and where the best results are most likely to lie—which option, in other words, is most likely to bring about the best results, the best balance between satisfaction and frustration. That option, whatever it may be, is the one I ought to choose. That is where my moral duty lies.

The great appeal of utilitarianism rests with its uncompromising *egalitarianism*: everyone's interests count and count as much as the like interests of everyone else. The kind of odious discrimination that some forms of contractarianism can justify—discrimination based on race or sex, for example—seems disallowed in principle by utilitarianism, as is speciesism, systematic discrimination based on species membership.

The equality we find in utilitarianism, however, is not the sort an advocate of animal or human rights should have in mind. Utilitarianism has no room for the equal moral rights of different individuals because it has no room for their equal inherent value or worth. What has value for the utilitarian is the satisfaction of an individual's interests, not the individual whose interests they are. A universe in which you satisfy your desire for water, food, and warmth is, other things being equal, better than a universe in which these desires are frustrated. And the same is true in the case of an animal with similar desires. But neither you nor the animal have any value in your own right. Only your feelings do.

Here is an analogy to help make the philosophical point clearer: a cup contains different liquids, sometimes sweet, sometimes bitter, sometimes a mix of the two. What has value are the liquids: the sweeter the better, the bitterer the worse. The cup, the container, has no value. It is what goes into it, not what they go into, that has value.

For the utilitarian you and I are like the cup; we have no value as individuals and thus no equal value. What has value is what goes into us, what we serve as receptacles for; our feelings of satisfaction have positive value, our feelings of frustration negative value.

Serious problems arise for utilitarianism when we remind ourselves that it enjoins us to bring about the best consequences. What does this mean? It doesn't mean the best consequences for me alone, or for my family or friends, or any other person taken individually. No, what we must do is, roughly, as follows: we must add up (somehow!) the separate satisfactions and frustrations of everyone likely to be affected by our choice, the satisfactions in one column, the frustrations in the other. We must total each column for each of the options before us. That is what it means to say the theory is aggregative. And then we must choose that option which is most likely to bring about the best balance of totalled satisfactions over totalled frustrations. Whatever act would lead to this outcome is the one we ought morally to perform—it is where our moral duty lies. And that act quite clearly might not be the same one that would bring about the best results for me personally, or for my family or friends, or for a lab animal. The best aggregated consequences for everyone concerned are not necessarily the best for each individual.

That utilitarianism is an aggregative theory—different individuals' satisfactions or frustrations are added, or summed, or totalled— is the key objection to this theory. My Aunt Bea is old, inactive, a cranky, sour person, though not physically ill. She prefers to go on living. She is also rather rich. I could make a fortune if I could get my hands on her money, money she intends to give me in any event, after she dies, but which she refuses to give me now. In order to avoid a huge tax bite, I plan to donate a handsome sum of my profits to a local children's hospital. Many, many children will benefit from my generosity, and much joy will be brought to their parents, relatives, and friends. If I don't get the money rather soon, all these ambitions will come to naught. The once-in-a-lifetime opportunity to make a real killing will be gone. Why, then, not kill my Aunt Bea? Oh, of course I *might* get caught. But I'm no fool and, besides, her doctor can be counted on to cooperate (he has an eye for the same investment and I happen to know a good deal about his shady past). The deed can be done . . . professionally, shall we say. There is *very* little chance of getting caught. And as for my conscience being guilt-ridden, I am a resourceful sort of fellow and will take more than sufficient comfort—as I lie on the beach at Acapulco—in contemplating the joy and health I have brought to so many others.

Suppose Aunt Bea is killed and the rest of the story comes out as told. Would I have done anything wrong? Anything immoral? One would have thought that I had. Not according to utilitarianism. Since what I have done has brought about the best balance between totalled satisfaction and frustration for all those affected by the outcome, my action is not wrong. Indeed, in killing Aunt Bea the physician and I did what duty required.

This same kind of argument can be repeated in all sorts of cases, illustrating, time after time, how the utilitarian's position leads to results that impartial people find morally callous. It *is* wrong to kill my Aunt Bea in the name of bringing about the best results for others. A good end does not justify an evil means. Any adequate moral theory will have to explain why this is so. Utilitarianism fails in this respect and so cannot be the theory we seek.

What to do? Where to begin anew? The place to begin, I think, is with the utilitarian's view of the value of the individual—or, rather, lack of value. In its place, suppose we consider that you and I, for example, do have value as individuals—what we'll call *inherent value.* To say we have such value is to say that we are something more than, something different from, mere receptacles. Moreover, to ensure that we do not pave the way for such injustices as slavery or sexual discrimination, we must believe that all who have inherent value have it equally, regardless of their sex, race, religion, birthplace, and so on. Similarly to be discarded as irrelevant are one's talents or skills, intelligence and wealth, personality or pathology, whether one is loved and admired or despised and loathed. The genius and the retarded child, the prince and the pauper, the brain surgeon and the fruit vendor, Mother Teresa and the most unscrupulous used-car salesman—all have inherent value, all possess it equally, and all have an equal right to be treated with respect, to be treated in ways that do not reduce them to the status of things, as if they existed as resources for others. My value as an individual is independent of my usefulness to you. Yours is not dependent on your usefulness to me. For either of us to treat the other in ways that fail to show respect for the other's independent value is to act immorally, to violate the individual's rights.

Some of the rational virtues of this view—what I call the rights view—should be evident. Unlike (crude) contractarianism, for example, the rights view *in principle* denies the moral tolerability of any and all forms of racial, sexual, or social discrimination; and unlike utilitarianism, this view *in principle* denies that we can justify good results by using evil means that violate an individual's rights—denies, for example, that it could be moral to kill my Aunt Bea to harvest beneficial consequences for others. That would be to sanction the disrespectful treatment of the individual in the name of the social good, something the rights view will not—categorically will not—ever allow.

The rights view, I believe, is rationally the most satisfactory moral theory. It surpasses all other theories in the degree to which it illuminates and explains the foundation of our duties to one another—the domain of human morality. On this score it has the best reasons, the best arguments, on its side. Of course, if it were possible to show that only human beings are included within its scope, then a person like myself, who believes in animal rights, would be obliged to look elsewhere.

But attempts to limit its scope to humans only can be shown to be rationally defective. Animals, it is true, lack many of the abilities humans possess. They can't read, do higher mathematics, build a bookcase, or make *baba ghanoush*. Neither can many human beings, however, and yet we don't (and shouldn't) say that they (these humans) therefore have less inherent value, less of a right to be treated with respect, than do others. It is the *similarities* between those human beings who most clearly, most noncontroversially have such value (the people reading this, for example), not our differences, that matter most. And the really crucial, the basic similarity is simply this: we are each of us the experiencing subject of a life, a conscious creature having an individual welfare that has importance to us whatever our usefulness to others. We want and prefer things, believe and feel things, recall and expect things. And all these dimensions of our life, including our pleasure and pain, our enjoyment and suffering, our satisfaction and frustration, our continued existence or our untimely death—all make a difference to the quality of our life as lived, as experienced, by us as individuals. As the same is true of those animals that concern us (the ones that are eaten and trapped, for example), they too must be viewed as the experiencing subjects of a life, with inherent value of their own.

Some there are who resist the idea that animals have inherent value. "Only humans have such value," they profess. How might this narrow view be defended? Shall we say that only humans have the requisite intelligence, or autonomy, or reason? But there are many, many humans who fail to meet these standards and yet are reasonably viewed as having value above and beyond their useful-ness to others. Shall we claim that only humans belong to the right species, the species *Homo sapiens*? But this is blatant speciesism. Will it be said, then, that all—and only—humans have immortal souls? Then our opponents have their work cut out for them. I am myself not ill-disposed to the proposition that there are immortal souls. Personally, I profoundly hope I have one. But I would not want to rest my position on a controversial ethical issue on the even more controversial question about who or what has an immortal soul. That is to dig one's hole deeper, not to climb out. Rationally, it is better to resolve moral issues without making more controversial assumptions than are needed. The question of who has inherent value is such a question, one that is resolved more rationally without the introduc-tion of the idea of immortal souls than by its use.

Well, perhaps some will say that animals have some inherent value, only less than we have. Once again, however, attempts to defend this view can be shown to lack rational justification. What could be the basis of our having more inherent value than animals? Their lack of reason, or autonomy, or intellect? Only if we are willing to make the same judgement in the case of humans who are similarly deficient. But it is not true that such humans—the retarded child, for example, or the mentally deranged—have less inherent value than you or I. Neither, then, can we rationally sustain the view that animals like them in being the experiencing subjects of a life have less inherent value. *All* who have inherent value have it *equally*, whether they be human animals or not.

Inherent value, then, belongs equally to those who are the expe-riencing subjects of a life. Whether it belongs to others—to rocks and rivers, trees and glaciers, for example—we do not know and may never know. But neither do we need to know, if we are to make the case for animal rights. We do not need to know, for example, how many people are eligible to vote in the next presidential election before we can know whether I am. Similarly, we do not need to know how many individuals have inherent value before we can know that some do. When it comes to the case for animal rights, then, what we need to know is whether the animals that, in our culture, are rou-tinely eaten, hunted, and used in our laboratories, for example, are like us in being subjects of a life. And we do know this. We do know that many—literally, billions and billions—of these animals are the subjects of a life in the sense explained and so have inherent value if we do. And since, in order to arrive at the best theory of our duties to one another, we must recognize our equal inherent value as individuals, reason—not sentiment, not emotion—reason compels us to recognize the equal inherent value of these animals and, with this, their equal right to be treated with respect.

That, *very* roughly, is the shape and feel of the case for animal rights. Most of the details of the supporting argument are missing. They are to be found in the book to which I alluded earlier. Here, the details go begging, and I must, in closing, limit myself to four final points.

The first is how the theory that underlies the case for animal rights shows that the animal rights movement is a part of, not antagonistic to, the human rights movement. The theory that rationally grounds the rights of animals also grounds the rights of humans. Thus those involved in the animal rights movement are partners in the struggle to secure respect for human rights—the rights of women, for example, or minorities, or workers. The animal rights movement is cut from the same moral cloth as these.

Second, having set out the broad outlines of the rights view, I can now say why its implications for farming and science, among other fields, are both clear and uncompromising. In the case of the use of animals in science, the rights view is categorically abolitionist. Lab animals are not our tasters; we are not their kings. Because these animals are treated routinely, systematically as if their value were reducible to their usefulness to others, they are routinely, systematically treated with a lack of respect, and thus are their rights routinely, systematically violated. This is just as true when they are used in trivial, duplicative, unnecessary, or unwise research as it is when they are used in studies that hold out real promise of human benefits. We can't justify harming or killing a human being (my Aunt Bea, for example) just for these sorts of reason. Neither can we do so even in the case of so lowly a creature as a laboratory rat. It is not just refinement or reduction that is called for, not just larger, cleaner cages, not just more generous use of anaesthetic or the elimination of multiple surgery, not just tidying up the system. It is complete replacement. The best we can do when it comes to using animals in science is not to use them. That is where our duty lies, according to the rights view.

As for commercial animal agriculture, the rights view takes a similar abolitionist position. The fundamental moral wrong here is not that animals are kept in stressful close confinement or in isolation, or that their pain and suffering, their needs and preferences are ignored or discounted. All these *are* wrong, or course, but they are not the fundamental wrong. They are symptoms and effects of the deeper systematic wrong that allows these animals to be viewed and treated as lacking independent value, as resources for us—as, indeed, a renewable resource. Giving farm animals more space, more natural environments, more companions does not right the fundamental wrong, any more than giving lab animals more anaesthesia or bigger, cleaner cages would right the fundamental wrong in their case. Nothing less than the total dissolution of commercial animal agriculture will do this, just as, for similar reasons I won't develop at length here, morality requires nothing less than the total elimination of hunting and trapping for commercial and sporting ends. The rights view's implications, then, as I have said, are clear and uncompromising.

My last two points are about philosophy, my profession. It is, most obviously, no substitute for political action. The words I have written here and in other places by themselves don't change a thing. It is what we do with the thoughts that the words express—our acts, our deeds—that changes things. All that philosophy can do, and all I have attempted, is to offer a vision of what our deeds should aim at. And the why. But not the how.

Finally, I am reminded of my thoughtful critic, the one I mentioned earlier, who chastised me for being too cerebral. Well, cerebral I have been: indirect duty views, utilitarianism, contractarianism—hardly the stuff deep passions are made of. I am also reminded, however, of the image another friend once set before me—the image of the ballerina as expressive of disciplined passion. Long hours of sweat and toil, of loneliness and practice, of doubt and fatigue: those are the discipline of her craft. But the passion is there too, the fierce drive to excel, to speak through her body, to do it right, to pierce our minds. That is the image of philosophy I would leave with you, not "too cerebral" but *disciplined passion.* Of the discipline enough has been seen. As for the passion: there are times, and these not infrequent, when tears come to my eyes when I see, or read, or hear of the wretched plight of animals in the hands of humans. Their pain, their suffering, their loneliness, their innocence, their death. Anger. Rage. Pity. Sorrow. Disgust. The whole creation groans under the weight of the evil we humans visit upon these mute, powerless creatures. It *is* our hearts, not just our heads, that call for an end to it all, that demand of us that we overcome, for them, the habits and forces behind their systematic oppression. All great movements, it is written, go through three stages: ridicule, discussion, adoption. It is the realization of this third stage, adoption, that requires both our passion and our discipline, our hearts and our heads. The fate of animals is in our hands. God grant we are equal to the task.

Study Questions

1. What does Regan mean by "inherent value"?
2. Why does he believe that limiting inherent value to human beings is a mistake?
3. Does a lion that eats a zebra violate the zebra's right to life?
4. Under what circumstances, if any, are zoos morally acceptable?

CHAPTER 36

Why Animals Have No Rights

Carl Cohen

Carl Cohen is Professor of Philosophy at the University of Michigan. Arguing against the view defended in the previous selection by Tom Regan, Cohen maintains that animals have no rights but should nevertheless be treated humanely.

A right, properly understood, is a claim, or potential claim, that one party may exercise against another. The target against whom such a claim may be registered can be a single person, a group, a community, or (perhaps) all humankind. The content of rights claims also varies greatly: repayment of loans, nondiscrimination by employers, noninterference by the state, and so on. To comprehend any genuine right fully, therefore, we must know *who* holds the right, *against whom* it is held, and *to what* it is a right.

Alternative sources of rights add complexity. Some rights are grounded in constitution and law (e.g., the right of an accused to trial by jury); some rights are moral but give no legal claims (e.g., my right to your keeping the promise you gave me); and some rights (e.g., against theft or assault) are rooted both in morals and in law.

The differing targets, contents, and sources of rights, and their inevitable conflict, together weave a tangled web. Notwithstanding all such complications, this much is clear about rights in general: they are in every case claims, or potential claims, within a community of moral agents. Rights arise, and can be intelligibly defended, only among beings who actually do, or can, make moral claims against one another. Whatever else rights may be, therefore, they are necessarily human; their possessors are persons, human beings. . . .

Humans confront choices that are purely moral; humans—but certainly not dogs or mice—lay down moral laws, for others and for themselves. Human beings are self-legislative, morally *autonomous.*

Animals (that is, nonhuman animals, the ordinary sense of that word) lack this capacity for free moral judgment. They are not beings of a kind capable of exercising or responding to moral claims. Animals therefore have no rights, and they can have none. This is the core of the argument about the alleged rights of animals. The holders of rights must have the capacity to comprehend rules of duty, governing all including themselves. In applying such rules, the holders of rights must recognize possible conflicts between what is in their own interest and what is just. Only in a community of beings capable of self-restricting moral judgments can the concept of a right be correctly invoked.

Humans have such moral capacities. They are in this sense self-legislative, are members of communities governed by moral rules, and do possess rights. Animals do not have such moral capacities. They are not morally self-legislative, cannot possibly be members of a truly moral community, and therefore cannot possess rights. In conducting research on animal subjects, therefore, we do not violate their rights, because they have none to violate.

To animate life, even in its simplest forms, we give a certain natural reverence. But the possession of rights presupposes a moral status not attained by the vast majority of living things. We must not infer, therefore, that a live being has, simply in being alive, a "right" to its life. The assertion that all animals, only because they are alive and have interests, also possess the "right to life"[10] is an abuse of that phrase, and wholly without warrant.

It does not follow from this, however, that we are morally free to do anything we please to animals. Certainly not. In our dealings with animals, as in our dealings with other human beings, we have obligations that do not arise from claims against us based on rights. Rights entail obligations, but many of the things one ought to do are in no way tied to another's entitlement. Rights and obligations are not reciprocals of one another, and it is a serious mistake to suppose that they are.

Illustrations are helpful. Obligations may arise from internal commitments made: physicians have obligations to their patients not grounded merely in their patients' rights. Teachers have such obligations to their students, shepherds to their dogs, and cowboys to their horses. Obligations may arise from differences of status: adults owe special care when playing with young children, and children owe special care when playing with young pets. Obligations may arise from special relationships: the payment of my son's college tuition is something to which he may have no right, although it may be my obligation to bear the burden if I reasonably can; my dog has no right to daily exercise and veterinary care, but I do have the obligation to provide these things for her. Obligations may arise from particular acts or circumstances: one may be obliged to another for a special kindness done, or obliged to put an animal out of its misery in view of its condition—although neither the human benefactor nor the dying animal may have had a claim of right.

Plainly, the grounds of our obligations to humans and to animals are manifold and cannot be formulated simply. Some hold that there is a general obligation to do no gratuitous harm to sentient creatures (the principle of nonmaleficence); some hold that there is a general obligation to do good to sentient creatures when that is reasonably within one's power (the principle of beneficence). In our dealings with animals, few will deny that we are at least obliged to act humanely—that is, to treat them with the decency and concern that we owe, as sensitive human beings, to other sentient creatures. To treat animals humanely, however, is not to treat them as humans or as the holders of rights.

A common objection, which deserves a response, may be paraphrased as follows:

> If having rights requires being able to make moral claims, to grasp and apply moral laws, then many humans—the brain-damaged, the comatose, the senile—who plainly lack those capacities must be without rights. But that is absurd. This proves [the critic concludes] that rights do not depend on the presence of moral capacities.

This objection fails; it mistakenly treats an essential feature of humanity as though it were a screen for sorting humans. The capacity for moral judgment that distinguishes humans from animals is not a test to be administered to human beings one by one. Persons who are unable, because of some disability, to perform the full moral functions natural to human beings are certainly not for that reason ejected from the moral community. The issue is one of kind. Humans are of such a kind that they may be the subject of experiments only with their voluntary consent. The choices they make freely must be respected. Animals are of such a kind that it is impossible for them, in principle, to give or withhold voluntary consent or to make a moral choice. What humans retain when disabled, animals have never had.

A second objection, also often made, may be paraphrased as follows:

> Capacities will not succeed in distinguishing humans from the other animals. Animals also reason; animals also communicate with one another; animals also care passionately for their young; animals also exhibit desires and preferences. Features of moral relevance—rationality, interdependence, and love—are not exhibited uniquely by human beings. Therefore [this critic concludes], there can be no solid moral distinction between humans and other animals.

This criticism misses the central point. It is not the ability to communicate or to reason, or dependence on one another, or care for the young, or the exhibition of preference, or any such behavior that marks the critical divide. Analogies between human families and those of monkeys, or between human communities and those of wolves, and the like, are entirely beside the point. Patterns of conduct are not at issue. Animals do indeed exhibit remarkable behavior at times. Conditioning, fear, instinct, and intelligence all contribute to species survival. Membership in a community of moral agents nevertheless remains impossible for them. Actors subject to moral judgment must be capable of grasping the generality of an ethical premise in a practical syllogism. Humans act immorally often enough, but only they—never wolves or monkeys—can discern, by applying some moral rule to the facts of a case, that a given act ought or ought not to be performed. The moral restraints imposed by humans on themselves are thus highly abstract and are often in conflict with the self-interest of the agent. Communal behavior among animals, even when most intelligent and most endearing, does not approach autonomous morality in this fundamental sense.

Genuinely moral acts have an internal as well as an external dimension. Thus, in law, an act can be criminal only when the guilty deed, the *actus reus*, is done with a guilty mind, mens rea. No animal can ever commit a crime; bringing animals to criminal trial is the mark of primitive ignorance. The claims of moral right are similarly inapplicable to them. Does a lion have a right to eat a baby zebra? Does a baby zebra have a right not to be eaten? Such questions, mistakenly invoking the concept of right where it does not belong, do not make good sense.

Study Questions

1. What are rights?
2. Do all human beings have rights?
3. If some nonhuman animals display mental skills beyond the capacity of human beings, might those nonhuman animals have rights?
4. If a lion was about to attack a zebra and a human being could save the life of the zebra, can you imagine circumstances in which such an intervention would be morally justified?

CHAPTER 37

Speaking of Animal Rights

Mary Anne Warren

Staking out a position between those of Tom Regan and Carl Cohen, Mary Anne Warren, whose work we read previously, maintains that animals do have rights but not identical in strength to those of persons.

Tom Regan has produced what is perhaps the definitive defense of the view that the basic moral rights of at least some non-human animals are in no way inferior to our own. In *The Case for Animal Rights,* he argues that all normal mammals over a year of age have the same basic moral rights.[1] Non-human mammals have essentially the same right not to be harmed or killed as we do. I shall call this "the strong animal rights position," although it is weaker than the claims made by some animal liberationists in that it ascribes rights to only some sentient animals.[2]

I will argue that Regan's case for the strong animal rights position is unpersuasive and that this position entails consequences which a reasonable person cannot accept. I do not deny that some non-human animals have moral rights; indeed, I would extend the scope of the rights claim to include all sentient animals, that is, all those capable of having experiences, including experiences of pleasure or satisfaction and pain, suffering, or frustration.[3] However, I do not think that the moral rights of most nonhuman animals are identical in strength to those of persons.[4] The rights of most non-human animals may be overridden in circumstances which would not justify overriding the rights of persons. There are, for instance, compelling realities which sometimes require that we kill animals for reasons

---

Mary Anne Warren, "Difficulties with the Strong Rights Position," from *Between the Species* 2, No. 4 (Fall 1987). Reprinted by permission.

which could not justify the killing of persons. I will call this view "the weak animal rights" position, even though it ascribes rights to a wider range of animals than does the strong animal rights position.

I will begin by summarizing Regan's case for the strong animal rights position and noting two problems with it. Next, I will explore some consequences of the strong animal rights position which I think are unacceptable. Finally, I will outline the case for the weak animal rights position.

Regan's Case

Regan's argument moves through three stages. First, he argues that normal, mature mammals are not only sentient but have other mental capacities as well. These include the capacities for emotion, memory, belief, desire, the use of general concepts, intentional action, a sense of the future, and some degree of self-awareness. Creatures with such capacities are said to be subjects-of-a-life. They are not only alive in the biological sense but have a psychological identity over time and an existence which can go better or worse for them. Thus, they can be harmed or benefited. These are plausible claims, and well defended. One of the strongest parts of the book is the rebuttal of philosophers, such as R. G. Frey, who object to the application of such mentalistic terms to creatures that do not use a human-style language.[5] The second and third stages of the argument are more problematic.

In the second stage, Regan argues that subjects-of-a-life have inherent value. His concept of inherent value grows out of his opposition to utilitarianism. Utilitarian moral theory, he says, treats individuals as "mere receptacles" for morally significant value, in that harm to one individual may be justified by the production of a greater net benefit to other individuals. In opposition to this, he holds that subjects-of-a-life have a value independent of both the value they may place upon their lives or experiences and the value others may place upon them.

Inherent value, Regan argues, does not come in degrees. To hold that some individuals have more inherent value than others is to adopt a "perfectionist" theory, i.e., one which assigns different moral worth to individuals according to how well they are thought to exemplify some virtue(s), such as intelligence or moral autonomy. Perfectionist theories have been used, at least since the time of Aristotle, to rationalize such injustices as slavery and male domination, as well as the unrestrained exploitation of animals. Regan argues that if we reject these injustices, then we must also reject perfectionism and conclude that all subjects-of-a-life have equal inherent value. Moral agents have no more inherent value than moral patients, i.e., subjects-of-a-life who are not morally responsible for their actions.

In the third phase of the argument, Regan uses the thesis of equal inherent value to derive strong moral rights for all subjects-of-a-life. This thesis underlies the Respect Principle, which forbids us to treat beings who have inherent value as mere receptacles, i.e., mere means to the production of the greatest overall good. This principle, in turn, underlies the Harm Principle, which says that we have a direct prima facie duty not to harm beings who have inherent value. Together, these principles give rise to moral rights. Rights are defined as valid claims, claims to certain goods and against certain beings, i.e., moral agents. Moral rights generate duties not only to refrain from inflicting harm upon beings with inherent value but also to come to their aid when they are threatened by other moral agents. Rights are not absolute but may be overridden in certain circumstances. Just what these circumstances are we will consider later. But first, let's look at some difficulties in the theory as thus far presented.

The Mystery of Inherent Value

Inherent value is a key concept in Regan's theory. It is the bridge between the plausible claim that all normal, mature mammals—human or otherwise—are subjects-of-a-life and the more debatable claim that they all have basic moral rights of the same strength. But it is a highly obscure concept, and its obscurity makes it ill-suited to play this crucial role.

Inherent value is defined almost entirely in negative terms. It is not dependent upon the value which either the inherently valuable individual or anyone else may place upon that individual's life or experiences. It is not (necessarily) a function of sentience or any other mental capacity, because, Regan says, some entities which are not sentient (e.g., trees, rivers, or rocks) may, nevertheless, have inherent value. . . . It cannot attach to anything other than an individual; species, ecosystems, and the like cannot have inherent value.

These are some of the things which inherent value is not. But what is it? Unfortunately, we are not told. Inherent value appears as a mysterious non-natural property which we must take on faith. Regan says that it is a *postulate* that subjects-of-a-life have inherent value, a postulate justified by the fact that it avoids certain absurdities which he thinks follow from a purely utilitarian theory. . . . But why is the postulate that *subjects-of-a-life* have inherent value? If the inherent value of a being is completely independent of the value that it or anyone else places upon its experiences, then why does the fact that it has certain sorts of experiences constitute evidence that it has inherent value? If the reason is that subjects-of-a-life have an existence which can go better or worse for them, then why isn't the appropriate conclusion that all sentient beings have inherent value, since they would all seem to meet that condition? Sentient but mentally unsophisticated beings may have a less extensive range of possible satisfactions and frustrations, but why should it follow that they have—or may have—no inherent value at all?

In the absence of a positive account of inherent value, it is also difficult to grasp the connection between being inherently valuable and having moral rights. Intuitively, it seems that value is one thing, and rights are another. It does not seem incoherent to say that some things (e.g., mountains, rivers, redwood trees) are inherently valuable and yet are not the sorts of things which can have moral rights. Nor does it seem incoherent to ascribe inherent value to some things which are not individuals, e.g., plant or animal species, though it may well be incoherent to ascribe moral rights to such things.

In short, the concept of inherent value seems to create at least as many problems as it solves. If inherent value is based on some natural property, then why not try to identify that property and explain its moral significance, without appealing to inherent value? And if it is not based on any natural property, then why should we believe in it? That it may enable us to avoid some of the problems faced by the utilitarian is not a sufficient reason, if it creates other problems which are just as serious.

Is There a Sharp Line?

Perhaps the most serious problems are those that arise when we try to apply the strong animal rights position to animals other than normal, mature mammals. Regan's theory requires us to divide all living things into two categories: those which have the same inherent value and the same basic moral rights that we do, and those which have no inherent value and presumably no moral rights. But wherever we try to draw the line, such a sharp division is implausible.

It would surely be arbitrary to draw such a sharp line between normal, mature mammals and all other living things. Some birds (e.g., crows, magpies, parrots, mynahs) appear to be just as mentally sophisticated as most mammals and thus are equally strong candidates for inclusion under the subject-of-a-life criterion. Regan is not in fact advocating that we draw the line here. His claim is only that normal mature mammals are clear cases, while other cases are less clear. Yet, on his theory, there must be such a sharp line *somewhere*, since there are no degrees of inherent value. But why should we believe that there is a sharp line between creatures that are subjects-of-a-life and creatures that are not? Isn't it more likely that "subjecthood" comes in degrees, that some creatures have only a little self-awareness, and only a little capacity to anticipate the future, while some have a little more, and some a good deal more?

Should we, for instance, regard fish, amphibians, and reptiles as subjects-of-a-life? A simple yes-or-no answer seems inadequate. On the one hand, some of their behavior is difficult to explain without the assumption that they have sensations, beliefs, desires, emotions, and memories; on the other hand, they do not seem to exhibit very much self-awareness or very much conscious anticipation of future events. Do they have enough mental sophistication to count as subjects-of-a-life? Exactly how much is enough?

It is still more unclear what we should say about insects, spiders, octopi, and other invertebrate animals which have brains and sensory organs but whose minds (if they have minds) are even more alien to us than those of fish or reptiles. Such creatures are probably sentient. Some people doubt that they can feel pain, since they lack certain neurological structures which are crucial to the processing of pain impulses in vertebrate animals. But this argument is inconclusive, since their nervous systems might process pain in ways different from ours. When injured, they sometimes act as if they are in pain. On evolutionary grounds, it seems unlikely that highly mobile creatures with complex sensory systems would not have developed a capacity for pain (and pleasure), since such a capacity has obvious survival value. It must, however, be admitted that we do not *know* whether spiders can feel pain (or something very like it), let alone whether they have emotions, memories, beliefs, desires, self-awareness, or a sense of the future.

Even more mysterious are the mental capacities (if any) of mobile microfauna. The brisk and efficient way that paramecia move about in their incessant search for food *might* indicate some kind of sentience, in spite of their lack of eyes, ears, brains, and other organs associated with sentience in more complex organisms. It is conceivable—though not very probable—that they, too, are subjects-of-a-life.

The existence of a few unclear cases need not pose a serious problem for a moral theory, but in this case, the unclear cases constitute most of those with which an adequate theory of animal rights would need to deal. The subject-of-a-life criterion can provide us with little or no moral guidance in our interactions with the vast majority of animals. That might be acceptable if it could be supplemented with additional principles which would provide such guidance. However, the radical dualism of the theory precludes supplementing it in this way. We are forced to say that either a spider has the same right to life as you and I do, or it has no right to life whatever—and that only the gods know which of these alternatives is true.

Regan's suggestion for dealing with such unclear cases is to apply the "benefit of the doubt" principle. That is, when dealing with beings that may or may not be subjects-of-a-life, we should act as if they are.[6] But if we try to apply this principle to the entire range of doubtful cases, we will find ourselves with moral obligations which we cannot possibly fulfill. In many climates, it is virtually impossible to live without swatting mosquitoes and exterminating cockroaches, and not all of us can afford to hire someone to sweep the path before we walk, in order to make sure that we do not step on ants. Thus, we are still faced with the daunting task of drawing a sharp line somewhere on the continuum of life forms—this time, a line demarcating the limits of the benefit of the doubt principle.

The weak animal rights theory provides a more plausible way of dealing with this range of cases, in that it allows the rights of animals of different kinds to vary in strength. . . .

Why Are Animal Rights Weaker than Human Rights?

How can we justify regarding the rights of persons as generally stronger than those of sentient beings which are not persons? There are a plethora of bad justifications, based on religious premises or false or unprovable claims about the differences between human and non-human nature. But there is one difference which has a clear moral relevance: people are at least sometimes capable of being moved to action or inaction by the force of reasoned argument. Rationality rests upon other mental capacities, notably those which Regan cites as criteria for being a subject-of-a-life. We share these capacities with many other animals. But it is not just because we are subjects-of-a-life that we are both able and morally compelled to recognize one another as beings with equal basic moral rights. It is also because we are able to "listen to reason" in order to settle our conflicts and cooperate in shared projects. This capacity, unlike the others, may require something like a human language.

Why is rationality morally relevant? It does not make us "better" than other animals or more "perfect." It does not even automatically make us more intelligent. (Bad reasoning reduces our effective intelligence rather than increasing it.) But it is morally relevant insofar as it provides greater possibilities for cooperation and for the nonviolent resolution of problems. It also makes us more dangerous than non-rational beings can ever be. Because we are potentially more dangerous and less predictable than wolves, we need an articulated system of morality to regulate our conduct. Any human morality, to be workable in the long run, must recognize the equal moral status of all persons, whether through the postulate of equal basic moral rights or in some other way. The recognition of the moral equality of other persons is the price we must each pay for their recognition of our moral equality. Without this mutual recognition of moral equality, human society can exist only in a state of chronic and bitter conflict. The war between the sexes will persist so long as there is sexism and male domination; racial conflict will never be eliminated so long as there are racist laws and practices. But, to the extent that we achieve a mutual recognition of equality, we can hope to live together, perhaps as peacefully as wolves, achieving (in part) through explicit moral principles what they do not seem to need explicit moral principles to achieve.

Why not extend this recognition of moral equality to other creatures, even though they cannot do the same for us? The answer is that we cannot. Because we cannot reason with most non-human animals, we cannot always solve the problems which they may cause without harming them—although we are always obligated to try. We cannot negotiate a treaty with the feral cats and foxes, requiring them to stop preying on endangered native species in return for suitable concessions on our part.

> if rats invade our houses . . . we cannot reason with them, hoping to persuade them of the injustice they do us. We can only attempt to get rid of them.[7]

Aristotle was not wrong in claiming that the capacity to alter one's behavior on the basis of reasoned argument is relevant to the full moral status which he accorded to free men. Of course, he was wrong in his other premise, that women and slaves by their nature cannot reason well enough to function as autonomous moral agents. Had that premise been true, so would his conclusion that women and slaves are not quite the moral equals of free men. In the case of most non-human animals, the corresponding premise is true. If, on the other hand, there are animals with whom we can (learn to) reason, then we are obligated to do this and to regard them as our moral equals.

Thus, to distinguish between the rights of persons and those of most other animals on the grounds that only people can alter their behavior on the basis of reasoned argument does not commit us to a perfectionist theory of the sort Aristotle endorsed. There is no excuse for refusing to recognize the moral equality of some people on the grounds that we don't regard them as quite as rational as we are, since it is perfectly clear that most people can reason well enough to determine how to act so as to respect the basic rights of others (if they choose to), and that is enough for moral equality.

But what about people who are clearly not rational? It is often argued that sophisticated mental capacities such as rationality cannot be essential for the possession of equal basic moral rights, since nearly everyone agrees that human infants and mentally incompetent persons have such rights, even though they may lack those sophisticated mental capacities. But this argument is inconclusive, because there are powerful practical and emotional reasons for protecting non-rational human beings, reasons which are absent in the case of most non-human animals. Infancy and mental incompetence are human conditions which all of us either have experienced or are likely to experience at some time. We also protect babies and mentally incompetent people because we care for them. We don't normally care for animals in the same way, and when we do—e.g., in the case of much-loved pets—we may regard them as having special rights by virtue of their relationship to us. We protect them not only for their sake but also for our own, lest we be hurt by harm done to them. Regan holds that such "side-effects" are irrelevant to moral rights, and perhaps they are. But in ordinary usage, there is no sharp line between moral rights and those moral protections which are not rights. The extension of strong moral protections to infants and the mentally impaired in no way proves that non-human animals have the same basic moral rights as people.

Why Speak of "Animal Rights" at All?

If, as I have argued, reality precludes our treating all animals as our moral equals, then why should we still ascribe rights to them? Everyone agrees that animals are entitled to some protection against human abuse, but why speak of animal *rights* if we are not prepared to accept most animals as our moral equals? The weak animal rights position may seem an unstable compromise between the bold claim that animals have the same basic moral rights that we do and the more common view that animals have no rights at all.

It is probably impossible to either prove or disprove the thesis that animals have moral rights by producing an analysis of the concept of a moral right and checking to see if some or all animals satisfy the conditions for having rights. The concept of a moral right is complex, and it is not clear which of its strands are essential. Paradigm rights holders, i.e., mature and mentally competent persons, are *both* rational and morally autonomous beings and sentient subjects-of-a-life. Opponents of animal rights claim that rationality and moral autonomy are essential for the possession of rights, while defenders of animal rights claim that they are not. The ordinary concept of a moral right is probably not precise enough to enable us to determine who is right on purely definitional grounds.

If logical analysis will not answer the question of whether animals have moral rights, practical considerations may, nevertheless, incline us to say that they do. The most plausible alternative to the view that animals have moral rights is that, while they do not have *rights*, we are, nevertheless, obligated not to be cruel to them. Regan argues persuasively that the injunction to avoid being cruel to animals is inadequate to express our obligations towards animals, because it focuses on the mental states of those who cause animal suffering, rather than on the harm done to the animals themselves . . . . Cruelty is inflicting pain or suffering and either taking pleasure in that pain or suffering or being more or less indifferent to it. Thus, to express the demand for the decent treatment of animals in terms of the rejection of cruelty is to invite the too easy response that those who subject animals to suffering are not being cruel because they regret the suffering they cause but sincerely believe that what they do is justified. The injunction to avoid cruelty is also inadequate in that it does not preclude the killing of animals—for any reason, however trivial—so long as it is done relatively painlessly.

The inadequacy of the anti-cruelty view provides one practical reason for speaking of animal rights. Another practical reason is that this is an age in which nearly all significant moral claims tend to be expressed in terms of rights. Thus, the denial that animals have rights, however carefully qualified, is likely to be taken to mean that we may do whatever we like to them, provided that we do not violate any human rights. In such a context, speaking of the rights of animals may be the only way to persuade many people to take seriously protests against the abuse of animals.

Why not extend this line of argument and speak of the rights of trees, mountains, oceans, or anything else which we may wish to see protected from destruction? Some environmentalists have not hesitated to speak in this way, and, given the importance of protecting such elements of the natural world, they cannot be blamed for using this rhetorical device. But, I would argue that moral rights can meaningfully be ascribed only to entities which have some capacity for sentience. This is because moral rights are protections designed to protect rights holders from harms or to provide them with benefits which matter *to them*. Only beings capable of sentience can be harmed or benefited in ways which matter to them, for only such beings can like or dislike what happens to them or prefer some conditions to others. Thus, sentient animals, unlike mountains, rivers, or species, are at least logically possible candidates for moral rights. This fact, together with the need to end current abuses of animals— e.g., in scientific research . . . —provides a plausible case for speaking of animal rights.

Conclusion

I have argued that Regan's case for ascribing strong moral rights to all normal, mature mammals is unpersuasive because (1) it rests upon the obscure concept of inherent value, which is defined only in negative terms, and (2) it seems to preclude any plausible answer to questions about the moral status of the vast majority of sentient animals . . .

The weak animal rights theory asserts that (1) any creature whose natural mode of life includes the pursuit of certain satisfactions has the right not to be forced to exist without the opportunity to pursue those satisfactions; (2) that any creature which is capable of pain, suffering, or frustration has the right that such experiences not be deliberately inflicted upon it without some compelling reason; and

(3) that no sentient being should be killed without good reason. However, moral rights are not an all-or-nothing affair. The strength of the reasons required to override the rights of a non-human organism varies, depending upon—among other things—the probability that it is sentient and (if it is clearly sentient) its probable degree of mental sophistication.

Notes

1. Tom Regan, *The Case for Animal Rights* (Berkeley: University of California Press, 1983). All page references are to this edition.
2. For instance, Peter Singer, although he does not like to speak of rights, includes all sentient beings under the protection of his basic utilitarian principle of equal respect for like interests. (Animal Liberation [New York: Avon Books, 1975], p. 3.)
3. The capacity for sentience, like all of the mental capacities mentioned in what follows, is a disposition. Dispositions do not disappear whenever they are not currently manifested. Thus, sleeping or temporarily unconscious persons or non-human animals are still sentient in the relevant sense (i.e., still capable of sentience), so long as they still have the neurological mechanisms necessary for the occurrence of experiences.
4. It is possible, perhaps probable that some non-human animals—such as cetaceans and anthropoid apes—should be regarded as persons. If so, then the weak animal rights position holds that these animals have the same basic moral rights as human persons.
5. See R. G. Frey, *Interests and Rights: The Case Against Animals* (Oxford: Oxford University Press, 1980).
6. See, for instance, p. 319, where Regan appeals to the benefit of the doubt principle when dealing with infanticide and late-term abortion.
7. Bonnie Steinbock, "Speciesism and the Idea of Equality," *Philosophy* 53 (1978): 253.

Study Questions

1. How does Warren distinguish the strong animal rights position and the weak one?
2. Do all human beings deserve the same rights?
3. Do all nonhuman animals deserve the same rights?
4. According to Warren, why do mountains not have rights?

H. The Environment

CHAPTER 38

We Are What We Eat

Tom Regan

In the next selection Tom Regan, whose work we read previously, considers a variety of moral issues related to our environment. How do our actions affect the earth and the other creatures with whom we share it?

The concerns of environmental ethics might begin with the food on our plate. If "we are what we eat," that food should tell us a good deal about what we are, both individually and as a nation. Those of us who live in the United States are blessed with abundant food supplies and, thanks to modern transportation systems, agricultural innovations, and competitive retail stores, we are able to select what we eat from a wide variety of tasty foods available throughout the year at low cost—at least the costs are low when compared with prices elsewhere! Popular national wisdom has it that we are the best fed, as well as the best dressed and housed, people in the world. Are we? And at what costs to the environment and others with whom we share it?

Some of the worries about our food concern the methods used to produce it. Modern agriculture is increasingly monocultural and chemically intensive. It is monocultural because a particular crop, say wheat or corn, soybeans or barley, is grown on the same land year after year; crops are not rotated, nor is acreage allowed to lie fallow so that the earth might renew itself. It is chemically intensive because of extensive use of fertilizers, herbicides, nematicides, pesticides, and the like. Though this form of agriculture has doubtless produced many benefits, it also leaves many serious questions in its wake.

From Tom Regan, ed., *New Introductory Essays in Environmental Ethics*. Copyright © 1984. Reprinted by permission of the author.

One concerns pesticide residue in the food itself. At present there are approximately 400 different pesticides in agricultural use. Three different government agencies—the Environmental Protection Agency (EPA), the United States Department of Agricultural (USDA), and the Food and Drug Administration (FDA)—are charged with insuring that pesticide residue in food, including pesticides known to be carcinogens, do not exceed the "tolerance levels" set by the government. Some critics of government policies and efficiency are skeptical, however, perhaps none more so than Lewis Regenstein who, in his recent book *America the Poisoned*, states that

> a review of the government's policy in setting and enforcing tolerance levels of toxic pesticides leads to the inescapable conclusions that the program exists primarily to insure the public that it is being protected from harmful chemical residues. In fact, the program, as currently administered, does little to minimize or even monitor the amount of poisons in our food, and serves the interests of the users and producers of pesticides rather than those of the public.[1]

If Regenstein is right, the food we eat could be poisoning us to death.

In addition to pesticide residue in our food serious worries also arise concerning the contamination of our water supplies from runoffs of pesticides and other chemicals commonly used in agriculture. Almost 50 percent of Americans use water from underground reservoirs, and approximately 40 percent of the water used in farm irrigation systems comes from this source. The purity of this water, which does not pass through filtration systems, is seriously jeopardized by the presence of toxic chemicals, including those employed as agricultural pesticides. Dibromochloropropane (DBCP), for example, widely used as a pesticide in California before it was banned in 1977, was found in half the irrigation and drinking wells surveyed in the San Joaquin Valley *two years later*. DBCP is a known carcinogen. Even water that comes from aboveground sources (lakes, rivers, streams, and the like) and that passes through municipal filtration systems is not always free from toxic chemicals, including pesticide residue from agricultural use perhaps hundreds of miles away. "The drinking water of every major American city," writes Regenstein, "contains dozens of cancer-causing chemicals and other toxins,"[2] a number of which can be traced to the chemically intensive methods used to produce the food on our plate.

Pesticides, of course, and the other chemicals essential to monocultural agriculture do not occur in nature but are the products of the petrochemical industry. The food on our plate is, therefore, causally related to that industry and, in this respect, is indirectly related to the pollution caused by petrochemical plants. That pollution, critics like Regenstein claim, besides adversely affecting the quality of the water we drink and the food we eat, also impacts detrimentally, directly and indirectly, on the quality of the air we breathe. Directly, quality is affected by petrochemical plants by way of their release into the air of toxic substances, some of which are causally implicated in increased incidences of respiratory diseases, such as emphysema and bronchitis, as well as a variety of cancers, especially lung cancer. Indirectly, the petrochemical industry, pesticides, and the food on our plate are a party to a decline in air quality because industry runs on electrical power that is frequently generated by methods that are themselves detrimental to the quality of the air we breathe.

The phenomenon known as acid rain illustrates the tangled web of cause and effect. The chemistry seems fairly simple. Sulphur oxides and nitrogen oxides emitted into the air form acids when they combine with water vapor. These acids in turn fall to the earth when it rains or snows with the result that both land and water acidity increase. The acidity of rain falling in some parts of the United States, for example, is estimated by an EPA study to have increased fiftyfold in the last twenty-five years and is sometimes over 100 times more acidic than normal rainfall. Though estimates vary, perhaps as much as 80 percent of the sulphur emissions that are the first link in the chain of events that culminate in acid rain result from human activities. Along with the increase in the acidity of rain there is a predictable increase in the incidence of acute and chronic respiratory ailments, and there are also serious reasons to question the continued fertility of the earth itself. Even the products of human creation—buildings, monuments, and the like—are not immune to acid rain. To cite just one example: In 1883 Cleopatra's Needle, a granite obelisk, after spending some thirty-five centuries in the Egyptian desert, was placed in New York City's Central Park. Exposed to the scorching sun, to wind, to sand, the obelisk withstood the rigors of its desert environment for 3,500 years—better than it has its New York home, where in just 100 years it has lost several inches of its granite, in part because of the chemical fallout of acid rain. Human creations, our *urban* environment, not just nature and our bodies, can feel the bite of the acid rain.

Older coal-burning power plants along the Ohio River are among the principal causes of acid rain. But pollution travels, and the areas most affected by acid rain are across state and even national boundaries. "Dead" lakes—absent any plant or aquatic life—are found throughout the northeastern United States and southeastern Canada. A thousand lakes "dead" in Wisconsin, perhaps 10,000 endangered. There are "dead" lakes in Colorado and California, and in other countries, such as Sweden, which has lost approximately 15,000 lakes. Some experts predict that 50,000 or more lakes in Canada and the United States will "die" in the next fifteen years, all as a result of acid rain. How long the surrounding vegetation can withstand this onslaught and what the long-term effects for the earth's fertility will be is anyone's guess. Might the food on our plate turn out to be causally linked with forces which, if allowed to continue, will threaten the very possibility of growing food in the future?

The mention of the future takes us a step beyond concerns we are likely to have about our own health. Barring a catastrophic nuclear war, we will not be the last generation on this earth; an indefinite number of future generations will come after us. The effects of those practices we allow at present, including the effects of pesticides in the food chain and the petrochemical industry's contamination of the air, are likely to be here after we are gone. "Dead" lakes are likely to be here, and so is drinking water that is hazardous to anyone's health. The underground sources of water, mentioned earlier, move beneath the surface of the earth at a snail's pace. Some of the water we drink from these sources today fell as rain over a hundred years ago, and today's rain, absorbed into underground aquifers, may not resurface until the twenty-second century. With the increase in acid rain attributable to human activities, including the power plants that produce the energy to fuel the petrochemical plants that produce the pesticides that are used to produce the food on our plate, and even ignoring, if we may, the many other sources of chemical contamination of the earth's water supplies, are we doing what we should with respect to generations yet unborn? Would we be doing it if, instead of relying on power from coal we rely instead on nuclear plants, given the serious problems *for them*, our descendants, posed by storing nuclear wastes? The food on our plate that we eat today—does it include a message from future persons, condemning us for a failure of moral will and vision to act now to protect the vital interests of generations yet to come?

Except for descendants of the Marquis de Sade, few people are likely to look with enthusiasm on pollution of any kind. It is, as some have said, a *public evils* problem: *public* because pollution travels and, in doing so, harms, or puts at risk of harm, people in general (the "public at large"); *evil* because the effects of pollution on those who are exposed are either actually or potentially harmful. Few of us, then, are likely to be in favor of pollution as such, since this is tantamount to harming, or putting at risk of harm, people in general (perhaps even ourself!). If we consider matters from a political point of view (not "political" in the sense of this or that actual political party, but theoretically—from, that is, the point of view of those who aspire to say what is *the best* political arrangement under which persons can live), how should we deal with this public evils problem? To choose among the options is a daunting challenge. Some political theories will allow a lot of pollution; some might disallow any at all; in between these two extremes are subtly differing conceptions of the ideal state and their respective policies regarding pollution. That there is pollution in America at all, and that the history of the food on our plate involves the use of pesticides and other chemicals that everyone must agree *can* pollute and that some claim *do* pollute, tells us something about the political arrangements under which we in fact live. Should we tolerate pollutants? Should we be less concerned than we are? Or should we restrict their presence, possibly to the extent of banning them altogether? When we think about the food we eat, can we rationally avoid asking these questions? And once they are asked, can we rationally refuse to expend the effort to answer them as best we can?

Unless we happen to be one of the estimated 20 to 25 million people who are practicing vegetarians in the United States, that food on our plate is likely to include meat. Part of the national wisdom about Americans being "the best fed people in the world" includes our access to flesh foods—chicken, steak, ham, ribs, burgers, hot dogs, and the like. Not a few critics of the farm animal industry have argued that, from the point of view of our individual health, we would be better off if we ate no or far less meat. A major part of the health risk, so these critics claim, again involves chemicals. Like other forms of contemporary agriculture, farm animal agriculture tends to be chemically intensive, only the food sources receiving the chemicals in this case are not carrots and wheat but are hogs and chickens, cows and turkeys. Raised in close confinement systems or what are called "factory farms," farm animals increasingly live indoors in dense populations or in cages or stalls. These animals are fed a veritable diet of chemicals from birth to death—growth stimulants, for example, and drugs to prevent or control the outbreak of contagious diseases. Residues of these chemicals collect and are stored in various tissues and organs in the animals' bodies. Some are toxic and again pose serious health questions when consumed by humans. Others, such as antibiotics, could lose their restorative properties for people who, in consuming animal flesh or products, also consume unsuspected quantities of these "wonder drugs." That meat on our plate—perhaps there is more to it than meets the eye? . . .

Moral questions about the treatment of animals are by no means restricted to farm or other domesticated varieties. Wild animals also fall within the scope of moral inquiry, a point given sharp focus by the concern many people have in preserving endangered species. That concern often is selective, with a few exotic, mysterious, or symbolic species favored over others (including many species of plants) that are equally endangered. For Americans, the bald eagle gets a resounding "yes!", the snail darter, a politically vociferous "no!" Whatever we might or should say about the selectivity of concern about endangered species, a variety of causes—including, not surprisingly, the chemical contamination of the air, water, and earth to which, as has been noted, the food on our plate is related—place a large number of species at risk. Another, perhaps subtler relationship between our food and endangered species involves the destruction of their natural habitat. One pattern of destruction repeats itself on a global scale. Cities and their populations grow, pushing ever farther out from the center. Former agricultural lands are converted to residential and other urban uses, and wild areas, formerly home to delicately balanced systems of life (ecosystems), are cleared or plowed under to make room for new farms only to have urban growth encroach on agricultural lands again, and so on, and so on. Wild species caught in the spiral of urban expansion are threatened. Some hang on. Others do not.

The pressures of urban growth, then, are a principal contributing cause of endangering species. If this were a case of one good thing winning out over another, we could rest content that a kind of cosmic justice prevails. But there are problems on both sides of the contest as so described. Most of us live in an urban environment—a city or town of one size or another, or the outskirts (the "burbs"). Quite apart from the impact of urban growth on endangered species, how big is too big? Is there, that is, a limit to the size of the urban environment beyond which it is no longer *good for us* to live there? If there is (and many critics of urban and suburban sprawl think so), then we cannot automatically assume that urban growth is "a good thing." Nor can we breezily dismiss questions about what in our urban environments is worth saving when, as we often must, we have to choose between preservation and redevelopment. If there is a limit to how much outward growth of our urban centers we should allow, there are also important questions about which, if any, of our urban landmarks and neighborhoods we should preserve.

The idea that the survival of a species is itself "a good thing" poses fundamental questions of its own. To a large extent the industrial, technological, and agricultural development that has led to and now underlies the variety of foods available to us has proceeded on the tacit assumption that *human interests* are the measure of all things valuable—at least things of the earth. "Anthropocentrism" is the name usually given to this vision of value. To consider seriously that the continued existence of a species is "a good thing" is to force ourselves to question the credentials of anthropocentrism. Is it possible that *species themselves* have a kind of value that is not reducible to the degree to which they serve human interests? Many would deny this. Value, they say, is to be fixed in economic terms, measured by the yardstick of human satisfaction as determined by what we would be willing to pay for that satisfaction. The value of a car, a house, a coat is set by how much we would be willing to pay for it or, if we already are the owner, by how much we would be willing to take in exchange. To speak of "the value of endangered species," then, in such a view, is a roundabout way of referring to how much we would be willing to pay to have them survive. To establish the amount we would be willing to pay might be difficult but, so proponents of an economic theory of value believe, not impossible. *Species as such* have no value, given an economic theory of value, but neither does anything else, neither truth, nor beauty, nor (noneconomic) goodness.

Many people, including many concerned to protect endangered species, reject economic theories of value. Even among those who are of one voice in rejecting such theories, however, serious and possibly divisive questions remain. In what can the (supposed) value of species as such consist, and how does the value of a species, assuming that it has one, correspond to or depart from the value of individual members, assuming that each member has some kind of (noneconomic) value? Or again, if species as such have value that is independent of human interests, including human economic interests, is it possible that we owe it to species themselves to protect them against human agents and forces which, if they were allowed to operate, would bring about the extinction of these species? If, for example, people in certain localities, responding to population pressures, are destroying the natural habitat of the last known representatives of an endangered species—ought we to halt this human encroachment, not in the name of human interests but for the sake of the value of species themselves? Ought we perhaps to do this *no matter what* the costs to the humans most directly involved, those who need new agricultural land to feed the new mouths which otherwise are likely to go hungry? To dismiss this question out of hand is to run the risk of accepting anthropocentrism uncritically.

The food on our plate is, one might say, a symbol of our predecessors' "conquest of nature," a conquest made possible by the widespread acceptance of anthropocentrism. That food, then, should remind us of our debts to them. But it should also occasion our critical curiosity as we assess the anthropocentric moral vision they have passed down to us. To do so, in its way, is to pay the finest tribute to our predecessors, since one ideal they bequeathed to us (one needs only to think of those true revolutionaries, American's Founding Fathers) *is* to be curious, to question the received opinions and common practices of the day. Those opinions and practices operative today are, metaphorically speaking, part of what we eat when we eat as we do. If we are what we eat, then divining the food on our plate does promise to tell us a good deal about what we are, as individuals and as a nation. And perhaps a good deal more about what we can and should be.

Notes

1. Lewis Regenstein, *America the Poisoned* (Washington, DC: Acropolis Books, 1982) p. 86.
2. Ibid., p. 182.

Study Questions

1. What does Regan mean by "We are what we eat"?
2. What is a public evils problem?
3. What is meant by anthropocentrism?
4. What is valuable about the survival of a species?

CHAPTER 39

Philosophical Problems for Environmentalism

Elliott Sober

Elliott Sober is Professor of Philosophy at the University of Wisconsin–Madison. In this essay he explores possible bases for the values implicit in the environmental movement.

I. Introduction

A number of philosophers have recognized that the environmental movement, whatever its practical political effectiveness, faces considerable theoretical difficulties in justification.[1] It has been recognized that traditional moral theories do not provide natural underpinnings for policy objectives and this has led some to skepticism about the claims of environmentalists, and others to the view that a revolutionary reassessment of ethical norms is needed. In this chapter, I will try to summarize the difficulties that confront a philosophical defense of environmentalism. I also will suggest a way of making sense of some environmental concerns that does not require the wholesale jettisoning of certain familiar moral judgments.

Preserving an endangered species or ecosystem poses no special conceptual problem when the instrumental value of that species or ecosystem is known. When we have reason to think that some natural object represents a resource to us, we obviously ought to take that fact into account in deciding what to do. A variety of potential uses may be under discussion, including food supply, medical

From Bryan G. Norton, ed., *The Preservation of Species,* 1986 by Princeton University Press, 1988 paperback edition. Reprinted by permission of Princeton University Press.

applications, recreational use, and so on. As with any complex decision, it may be difficult even to agree on how to compare the competing values that may be involved. Willingness to pay in dollars is a
familiar least common denominator, although it poses a number of
problems. But here we have nothing that is specifically a problem for
environmentalism.

The problem for environmentalism stems from the idea that species and ecosystems ought to be preserved for reasons additional to
their known value as resources for human use. The feeling is that
even when we cannot say what nutritional, medicinal, or recreational
benefit the preservation provides, there still is a value in preservation. It is the search for a rationale for this feeling that constitutes the
main conceptual problem for environmentalism.

The problem is especially difficult in view of the holistic (as
opposed to individualistic) character of the things being assigned
value. Put simply, what is special about environmentalism is that it values the preservation of species, communities, or ecosystems, rather
than the individual organisms of which they are composed. "Animal
liberationists" have urged that we should take the suffering of sentient animals into account in ethical deliberation.[2] Such beasts are
not mere things to be used as cruelly as we like no matter how trivial
the benefit we derive. But in "widening the ethical circle," we are simply including in the community more individual organisms whose
costs and benefits we compare. Animal liberationists are extending
an old and familiar ethical doctrine—namely, utilitarianism—to
take account of the welfare of other individuals. Although the practical consequences of this point of view may be revolutionary, the theoretical perspective is not at all novel. If suffering is bad, then it is bad
for any individual who suffers.[3] Animal liberationists merely remind
us of the consequences of familiar principles.

But trees, mountains, and salt marshes do not suffer. They do
not experience pleasure and pain, because, evidently, they do not
have experiences at all. The same is true of species. Granted, individual organisms may have mental states; but the species—taken
to be a population of organisms connected by certain sorts of
interactions (preeminently, that of exchanging genetic material in
reproduction)—does not. Or put more carefully, we might say that
the only sense in which species have experiences is that their member organisms do: the attribution at the population level, if true, is
true simply in virtue of its being true at the individual level. Here is a
case where reductionism is correct.

So perhaps it is true in this reductive sense that some species experience pain. But the values that environmentalists attach to preserving species do not reduce to any value of preserving organisms. It is in this sense that environmentalists espouse a holistic value system. Environmentalists care about entities that by no stretch of the imagination have experiences (e.g., mountains). What is more, their position does not force them to care if individual organisms suffer pain, so long as the species is preserved. Steel traps may outrage an animal liberationist because of the suffering they inflict, but an environmentalist aiming just at the preservation of a balanced ecosystem might see here no cause for complaint. Similarly, environmentalists think that the distinction between wild and domesticated organisms is important, in that it is the preservation of "natural" (i.e., not created by the "artificial interference" of human beings) objects that matters, whereas animal liberationists see the main problem in terms of the suffering of any organism—domesticated or not. And finally, environmentalists and animal liberationists diverge on what might be called the $n + m$ *question*. If two species—say blue and sperm whales—have roughly comparable capacities for experiencing pain, an animal liberationist might tend to think of the preservation of a sperm whale as wholly on an ethical par with the preservation of a blue whale. The fact that one organism is part of an endangered species while the other is not does not make the rare individual more intrinsically important. But for an environmentalist, this holistic property—membership in an endangered species—makes all the difference in the world: a world with n sperm and m blue whales is far better than a world with $n + m$ sperm and 0 blue whales. Here we have a stark contrast between an ethic in which it is the life situation of individuals that matters, and an ethic in which the stability and diversity of populations of individuals are what matter.[4]

Both animal liberationists and environmentalists wish to broaden our ethical horizons—to make us realize that it is not just human welfare that counts. But they do this in very different, often conflicting, ways. It is no accident that at the level of practical politics the two points of view increasingly find themselves at loggerheads. This practical conflict is the expression of a deep theoretical divide.

II.   The Ignorance Argument

"Although we might not now know what use a particular endangered species might be to us, allowing it to go extinct forever closes off the possibility of discovering and exploiting a future use." According to this point of view, our ignorance of value is turned into a reason for action. The scenario envisaged in this environmentalist argument is not without precedent; who could have guessed that penicillin would be good for something other than turning out cheese? But there is a fatal defect in such arguments, which we might summarize with the phrase *out of nothing, nothing comes:* rational decisions require assumptions about what is true and what is valuable (in decision-theoretic jargon, the inputs must be probabilities and utilities). If you are completely ignorant of values, then you are incapable of making a rational decision, either for or against preserving some species. The fact that you do not know the value of a species, by itself, cannot count as a reason for wanting one thing rather than another to happen to it.

And there are so many species. How many geese that lay golden eggs are there apt to be in that number? It is hard to assign probabilities and utilities precisely here, but an analogy will perhaps reveal the problem confronting this environmentalist argument. Most of us willingly fly on airplanes, when safer (but less convenient) alternative forms of transportation are available. Is this rational? Suppose it were argued that there is a small probability that the next flight you take will crash. This would be very bad for you. Is it not crazy for you to risk this, given that the only gain to you is that you can reduce your travel time by a few hours (by not going by train, say)? Those of us who not only fly, but congratulate ourselves for being rational in doing so, reject this argument. We are prepared to accept a small chance of a great disaster in return for the high probability of a rather modest benefit. If this is rational, no wonder that we might consistently be willing to allow a species to go extinct in order to build a hydroelectric plant.

That the argument from ignorance is no argument at all can be seen from another angle. If we literally do not know what consequences the extinction of this or that species may bring, then we should take seriously the possibility that the extinction may be beneficial as well as the possibility that it may be deleterious. It may sound deep to insist that we preserve endangered species precisely because we do not know why they are valuable. But ignorance on a scale like this cannot provide the basis for any rational action.

Rather than invoke some unspecified future benefit, an environmentalist may argue that the species in question plays a crucial role in stabilizing the ecosystem of which it is a part. This will undoubtedly be true for carefully chosen species and ecosystems, but one should not generalize this argument into a global claim to the effect that *every* species is crucial to a balanced ecosystem. Although ecologists used to agree that the complexity of an ecosystem stabilizes it, this hypothesis has been subject to a number of criticisms and qualifications, both from a theoretical and an empirical perspective.[5] And for certain kinds of species (those which occupy a rather small area and whose normal population is small) we can argue that extinction would probably not disrupt the community. However fragile the biosphere may be, the extreme view that everything is crucial is almost certainly not true.

But, of course, environmentalists are often concerned by the fact that extinctions are occurring now at a rate much higher than in earlier times. It is mass extinction that threatens the biosphere, they say, and this claim avoids the spurious assertion that communities are so fragile that even one extinction will cause a crash. However, if the point is to avoid a mass extinction of species, how does this provide a rationale for preserving a species of the kind just described, of which we rationally believe that its passing will not destabilize the ecosystem? And, more generally, if mass extinction is known to be a danger to us, how does this translate into a value for preserving any particular species? Notice that we have now passed beyond the confines of the argument from ignorance; we are taking as a premise the idea that mass extinction would be a catastrophe (since it would destroy the ecosystem on which we depend). But how should that premise affect our valuing the California condor, the blue whale, or the snail darter?

III.   The Slippery Slope Argument

Environmentalists sometimes find themselves asked to explain why each species matters so much to them, when there are, after all, so many. We may know of special reasons for valuing particular species, but how can we justify thinking that each and every species is important? "Each extinction impoverishes the biosphere" is often the answer given, but it really fails to resolve the issue. Granted, each extinction impoverishes, but it only impoverishes a little bit. So if it is the *wholesale* impoverishment of the biosphere that matters, one would apparently have to concede that each extinction matters a little, but only a little. But environmentalists may be loathe to concede this, for if they concede that each species matters only a little, they seem to be inviting the wholesale impoverishment that would be an unambiguous disaster. So they dig in their heels and insist that each species matters a lot. But to take this line, one must find some other rationale than the idea that mass extinction would be a great harm. Some of these alternative rationales we will examine later. For now, let us take a closer look at the train of thought involved here.

Slippery slopes are curious things: if you take even one step onto them, you inevitably slide all the way to the bottom. So if you want to avoid finding yourself at the bottom, you must avoid stepping onto them at all. To mix metaphors, stepping onto a slippery slope is to invite being nickeled and dimed to death.

Slippery slope arguments have played a powerful role in a number of recent ethical debates. One often hears people defend the legitimacy of abortions by arguing that since it is permissible to abort a single-celled fertilized egg, it must be permissible to abort a foetus of any age, since there is no place to draw the line from 0 to 9 months. Antiabortionists, on the other hand, sometimes argue in the other direction: since infanticide of newborns is not permissible, abortion at any earlier time is also not allowed, since there is no place to draw the line. Although these two arguments reach opposite conclusions about the permissibility of abortions, they agree on the following idea: since there is no principled place to draw the line on the continuum from newly fertilized egg to foetus gone to term, one must treat all these cases in the same way. Either abortion is always permitted or it never is, since there is no place to draw the line. Both sides run their favorite slippery slope arguments, but try to precipitate slides in opposite directions.

Starting with 10 million extant species, and valuing overall diversity, the environmentalist does not want to grant that each species matters only a little. For having granted this, commercial expansion and other causes will reduce the tally to 9,999.999. And then the argument is repeated, with each species valued only a little, and diversity declines another notch. And so we are well on our way to a considerably impoverished biosphere, a little at a time. Better to reject the starting premise—namely, that each species matters only a little—so that the slippery slope can be avoided.

Slippery slopes should hold no terror for environmentalists, because it is often a mistake to demand that a line be drawn. Let me illustrate by an example. What is the difference between being bald and not? Presumably, the difference concerns the number of hairs you have on your head. But what is the precise number of hairs marking the boundary between baldness and not being bald? There is no such number. Yet, it would be a fallacy to conclude that there is no difference between baldness and hairiness. The fact that you cannot draw a line does not force you to say that the two alleged categories collapse into one. In the abortion case, this means that even if there is no precise point in foetal development that involves some discontinuous, qualitative change, one is still not obliged to think of newly fertilised eggs and foetuses gone to term as morally on a par. Since the biological differences are ones of degree, not kind, one may want to adopt the position that the moral differences are likewise matters of degree. This may lead to the view that a woman should have a better reason for having an abortion, the more developed her foetus is. Of course, this position does not logically follow from the idea that there is no place to draw the line; my point is just that differences in degree do not demolish the possibility of there being real moral differences.

In the environmental case, if one places a value on diversity, then each species becomes more valuable as the overall diversity declines. If we begin with 10 million species, each may matter little, but as extinctions continue, the remaining ones matter more and more. According to this outlook, a better and better reason would be demanded for allowing yet another species to go extinct. Perhaps certain sorts of economic development would justify the extinction of a species at one time. But granting this does not oblige one to conclude that the same sort of decision would have to be made further down the road. This means that one can value diversity without being obliged to take the somewhat exaggerated position that each species, no matter how many there are, is terribly precious in virtue of its contribution to that diversity.

Yet, one can understand that environmentalists might be reluctant to concede this point. They may fear that if one now allows that most species contribute only a little to overall diversity, one will set in motion a political process that cannot correct itself later. The worry is that even when the overall diversity has been drastically reduced, our ecological sensitivities will have been so coarsened that we will no longer be in a position to realize (or to implement policies fostering) the preciousness of what is left. This fear may be quite justified, but it is important to realize that it does not conflict with what was argued above. The political utility of making an argument should not be confused with the argument's soundness.

The fact that you are on a slippery slope, by itself, does not tell you whether you are near the beginning, in the middle, or at the end. If species diversity is a matter of degree, where do we currently find ourselves—on the verge of catastrophe, well on our way in that direction, or at some distance from a global crash? Environmentalists often urge that we are fast approaching a precipice; if we are, then the reduction in diversity that every succeeding extinction engenders should be all we need to justify species preservation.

Sometimes, however, environmentalists advance a kind of argument not predicated on the idea of fast approaching doom. The goal is to show that there is something wrong with allowing a species to go extinct (or with causing it to go extinct), even if overall diversity is not affected much. I now turn to one argument of this kind.

IV. Appeals to What Is Natural

I noted earlier that environmentalists and animal liberationists disagree over the significance of the distinction between wild and domesticated animals. Since both types of organisms can experience pain, animal liberationists will think of each as meriting ethical consideration. But environmentalists will typically not put wild and domesticated organisms on a par. Environmentalists typically are interested in preserving what is natural, be it a species living in the wild or a wilderness ecosystem. If a kind of domesticated chicken were threatened with extinction, I doubt that environmental groups would be up in arms. And if certain unique types of human environments—say urban slums in the United States—were "endangered," it is similarly unlikely that environmentalists would view this process as a deplorable impoverishment of the biosphere.

The environmentalist's lack of concern for humanly created organisms and environments may be practical rather than principled. It may be that at the level of values, no such bifurcation is legitimate, but that from the point of view of practical political action, it makes sense to put one's energies into saving items that exist in the wild. This subject has not been discussed much in the literature, so it is hard to tell. But I sense that the distinction between wild and domesticated has a certain theoretical importance to many environmentalists. They perhaps think that the difference is that we created domesticated organisms which would otherwise not exist, and so are entitled to use them solely for our own interests. But we did not create wild organisms and environments, so it is the height of presumption to expropriate them for our benefit. A more fitting posture would be one of "stewardship": we have come on the scene and found a treasure not of our making. Given this, we ought to preserve this treasure in its natural state.

I do not wish to contest the appropriateness of "stewardship." It is the dichotomy between artificial (domesticated) and natural (wild) that strikes me as wrong-headed. I want to suggest that to the degree that "natural" means anything biologically, it means very little ethically. And, conversely, to the degree that "natural" is understood as a normative concept, it has very little to do with biology.

Environmentalists often express regret that we human beings find it so hard to remember that we are part of nature—one species among many others—rather than something standing outside of nature. I will not consider here whether this attitude is cause for complaint; the important point is that seeing us as part of nature rules out the environmentalist's use of the distinction between artificial-domesticated and natural-wild described above. *If we are part of nature, then everything we do is part of nature, and is natural in that primary sense.* When we domesticate organisms and bring them into a state of dependence on us, this is simply an example of one species exerting a selection pressure on another. If one calls this "unnatural," one might just as well say the same of parasitism or symbiosis (compare human domestication of animals and plants and "slave-making" in the social insects).

The concept of naturalness is subject to the same abuses as the concept of normalcy. *Normal* can mean *usual* or it can mean *desirable.* Although only the total pessimist will think that the two concepts are mutually exclusive, it is generally recognized that the mere fact that something is common does not by itself count as a reason for thinking that it is desirable. This distinction is quite familiar now in popular discussions of mental health, for example. Yet, when it comes to environmental issues, the concept of naturalness continues to live a double life. The destruction of wilderness areas by increased industrialization is bad because it is unnatural. And it is unnatural because it involves transforming a natural into an artificial habitat. Or one might hear that although extinction is a natural process, the kind of mass extinction currently being precipitated by our species is unprecedented, and so is unnatural. Environmentalists should look elsewhere for a defense of their policies, lest conservation simply become a variant of uncritical conservatism in which the axiom "Whatever is, is right" is modified to read "Whatever is (before human beings come on the scene), is right."

This conflation of the biological with the normative sense of "natural" sometimes comes to the fore when environmentalists attack animal liberationists for naive do-goodism. Callicott writes:

> . . . the value commitments of the humane movement seem at bottom to betray a world-denying or rather a life-loathing philosophy. The natural world as actually constituted is one in which one being lives at the expense of others. Each organism, in Darwin's metaphor, struggles to maintain its own organic integrity. . . . To live is to be anxious about life, to feel pain and pleasure in a fitting mixture, and sooner or later to die. That is the way the system works. *If nature as a whole is good, then pain and death are also good.* Environmental ethics in general require people to play fair in the natural system. The neo-Benthamites have in a sense taken the uncourageous approach. People have attempted to exempt themselves from the life death reciprocities of natural processes and from ecological limitations in the name of a prophylactic ethic of maximizing rewards (pleasure) and minimizing unwelcome information (pain). To be fair, the humane moralists seem to suggest that we should attempt to project the same values into the nonhuman animal world and to widen the charmed circle—no matter that it would be biologically unrealistic to do so or biologically ruinous if, per impossible, such an environmental ethic were implemented.
> There is another approach. Rather than imposing our alienation from nature and natural processes and cycles of life on other animals, we human beings could reaffirm our participation in nature by accepting life as it is given without a sugar coating. . . .[6]

On the same page, Callicott quotes with approval Shepard's remark that "the humanitarian's projection onto nature of illegal murder and the rights of civilized people to safety not only misses the point but is exactly contrary to fundamental ecological reality: the structure of nature is a sequence of killings."[7]

Thinking that what is found in nature is beyond ethical defect has not always been popular. Darwin wrote:

> . . . That there is much suffering in the world no one disputes.
> Some have attempted to explain this in reference to man by imagining that it serves for his moral improvement. But the number of men in the world is as nothing compared with that of all other sentient beings, and these often suffer greatly without any moral improvement. A being so powerful and so full of knowledge as a God who could create the universe, is to our finite minds omnipotent and omniscient, and it revolts our understanding to suppose that his benevolence is not unbounded, for what advantage can there be in the sufferings of millions of the lower animals throughout almost endless time?

> This very old argument from the existence of suffering against
> the existence of an intelligent first cause seems to me a strong one;
> whereas, as just remarked, the presence of much suffering agrees well
> with the view that all organic beings have been developed through
> variation and natural selection.[8]

Darwin apparently viewed the quantity of pain found in nature
as a melancholy and sobering consequence of the struggle for existence. But once we adopt the Panglossian attitude that this is the best
of all possible worlds ("there is just the right amount of pain," etc.),
a failure to identify what is natural with what is good can only seem
"world-denying," "life-loathing," "in a sense uncourageous," and
"contrary to fundamental ecological reality."

Earlier in his essay, Callicott expresses distress that animal liberationists fail to draw a sharp distinction "between the very different
plights (and rights) of wild and domestic animals."[9] Domestic animals are creations of man, he says. "They are living artifacts, but artifacts nevertheless. . . . There is thus something profoundly incoherent
(and insensitive as well) in the complaint of some animal liberationists that the 'natural behavior' of chickens and bobby calves is cruelly
frustrated on factory farms. It would make almost as much sense to
speak of the natural behavior of tables and chairs."[10] Here again we
see teleology playing a decisive role: wild organisms do not have the
natural function of serving human ends, but domesticated animals
do. Cheetahs in zoos are crimes against what is natural; veal calves in
boxes are not.

The idea of "natural tendency" played a decisive role in pre-
Darwinian biological thinking. Aristotle's entire science—both his
physics and his biology—is articulated in terms of specifying the natural tendencies of kinds of objects and the interfering forces that can
prevent an object from achieving its intended state. Heavy objects in
the sublunar sphere have location at the center of the earth as their
natural state; each tends to go there, but is prevented from doing so.
Organisms likewise are conceptualized in terms of this natural state
model:

> . . . [for] any living thing that has reached its normal development
> and which is unmutilated, and whose mode of generation is not spon-
> taneous, the most natural act is the production of another like itself,
> an animal producing an animal, a plant a plant. . . .[11]

But many interfering forces are possible, and in fact the occurrence
of "monsters" is anything but uncommon. According to Aristotle,

mules (sterile hybrids) count as deviations from the natural state. In fact, females are monsters as well, since the natural tendency of sexual reproduction is for the offspring to perfectly resemble the father, who, according to Aristotle, provides the "genetic instructions" (to put the idea anachronistically) while the female provides only the matter.

What has happened to the natural state model in modern science? In physics, the idea of describing what a class of objects will do in the absence of "interference" lives on: Newton specified this "zero-force state" as rest or uniform motion, and in general relativity, this state is understood in terms of motion along geodesics. But one of the most profound achievements of Darwinian biology has been the jettisoning of this kind of model. It isn't just that Aristotle was wrong in his detailed claims about mules and women; the whole structure of the natural state model has been discarded. Population biology is not conceptualized in terms of positing some characteristic that all members of a species would have in common, were interfering forces absent. Variation is not thought of as a deflection from the natural state of uniformity. Rather, variation is taken to be a fundamental property in its own right. Nor, at the level of individual biology, does the natural state model find an application. Developmental theory is not articulated by specifying a natural tendency and a set of interfering forces. The main conceptual tool for describing the various developmental pathways open to a genotype is the norm of reaction. The norm of reaction of a genotype within a range of environments will describe what phenotype the genotype will produce in a given environment. Thus, the norm of reaction for a corn plant genotype might describe how its height is influenced by the amount of moisture in the soil. The norm of reaction is entirely silent on which phenotype is the "natural" one. The idea that a corn plant might have some "natural height," which can be, augmented or diminished by "interfering forces" is entirely alien to post-Darwinian biology.

The fact that the concepts of natural state and interfering force have lapsed from biological thought does not prevent environmentalists from inventing them anew. Perhaps these concepts can be provided with some sort of normative content; after all, the normative idea of "human rights" may make sense even if it is not a theoretical underpinning of any empirical science. But environmentalists should not assume that they can rely on some previously articulated scientific conception of "natural."

V.   Appeals to Needs and Interests

The version of utilitarianism considered earlier (according to which something merits ethical consideration if it can experience pleasure and/or pain) leaves the environmentalist in the lurch. But there is an alternative to Bentham's hedonistic utilitarianism that has been thought by some to be a foundation for environmentalism. Preference utilitarianism says that an object's having interests, needs, or preferences gives it ethical status. This doctrine is at the core of Stone's affirmative answer to the title question of his book *Should Trees Have Standing?*[12] "Natural objects can communicate their wants (needs) to us, and in ways that are not terribly ambiguous. . . . The lawn tells me that it wants water by a certain dryness of the blades and soil— immediately obvious to the touch—the appearance of bald spots, yellowing, and a lack of springiness after being walked on." And if plants can do this, presumably so can mountain ranges, and endangered species. Preference utilitarianism may thereby seem to grant intrinsic ethical importance to precisely the sorts of objects about which environmentalists have expressed concern.

The problems with this perspective have been detailed by Sagoff.[13] If one does not require of an object that it have a mind for it to have wants or needs, what is required for the possession of these ethically relevant properties? Suppose one says that an object needs something if it will cease to exist if it does not get it. Then species, plants, and mountain ranges have needs, but only in the sense that automobiles, garbage dumps, and buildings do too. If everything has needs, the advice to take needs into account in ethical deliberation is empty, unless it is supplemented by some technique for weighing and comparing the needs of different objects. A corporation will go bankrupt unless a highway is built. But the swamp will cease to exist if the highway is built. Perhaps one should take into account all relevant needs, but the question is how to do this in the event that needs conflict.

Although the concept of need can be provided with a permissive, all-inclusive definition, it is less easy to see how to do this with the concept of want. Why think that a mountain range "wants" to retain its unspoiled appearance, rather than house a new amusement park?[14] Needs are not at issue here, since in either case, the mountain continues to exist. One might be tempted to think that natural objects like mountains and species have "natural tendencies," and that the concept of want should be liberalized so as to mean that natural objects "want" to persist in their natural states. This Aristotelian view, as I argued in the previous section, simply makes no sense. Granted, a commercially undeveloped mountain will persist in this state, unless it is commercially developed. But it is equally true that a commercially untouched hill will become commercially developed, unless something causes this not to happen. I see no hope for extending the concept of wants to the full range of objects valued by environmentalists.

The same problems emerge when we try to apply the concepts of needs and wants to species. A species may need various resources, in the sense that these are necessary for its continued existence. But what do species want? Do they want to remain stable in numbers, neither growing nor shrinking? Or since most species have gone extinct, perhaps what species really want is to go extinct, and it is human meddlesomeness that frustrates this natural tendency? Preference utilitarianism is no more likely than hedonistic utilitarianism to secure autonomous ethical status for endangered species.

Ehrenfeld describes a related distortion that has been inflicted on the diversity/stability hypothesis in theoretical ecology.[15] If it were true that increasing the diversity of an ecosystem causes it to be more stable, this might encourage the Aristotelian idea that ecosystems have a natural tendency to increase their diversity. The full realization of this tendency—the natural state that is the goal of ecosystems—is the "climax" or "mature" community. Extinction diminishes diversity, so it frustrates ecosystems from attaining their goal. Since the hypothesis that diversity causes stability is now considered controversial (to say the least), this line of thinking will not be very tempting. But even if the diversity/stability hypothesis were true, it would not permit the environmentalist to conclude that ecosystems have an interest in retaining their diversity.

Darwinism has not banished the idea that parts of the natural world are goal-directed systems, but has furnished this idea with a natural mechanism. We properly conceive of organisms (or genes, sometimes) as being in the business of maximizing their chances of survival and reproduction. We describe characteristics as adaptations—as devices that exist for the furtherance of these ends. Natural selection makes this perspective intelligible. But Darwinism is a profoundly individualistic doctrine. Darwinism rejects the idea that species, communities, and ecosystems have adaptations that exist for their own benefit. These higher-level entities are not conceptualized as goal-directed systems; what properties of organization they possess are viewed as artifacts of processes operating at lower levels of organization. An environmentalism based on the idea that the ecosystem is directed toward stability and diversity must find its foundation elsewhere.

VI.   Granting Wholes Autonomous Value

A number of environmentalists have asserted that environmental values cannot be grounded in values based on regard for individual welfare. Aldo Leopold wrote in *A Sand County Almanac* that "a thing is right when it tends to preserve the integrity, stability, and beauty of the biotic community. It is wrong when it tends otherwise."[16] Callicott develops this idea at some length, and ascribes to ethical environmentalism the view that "the preciousness of individual deer, *as of any other specimen*, is inversely proportional to the population of the species."[17] In his *Desert Solitaire,* Edward Abbey notes that he would sooner shoot a man than a snake.[18] And Garrett Hardin asserts that human beings injured in wilderness areas ought not to be rescued: making great and spectacular efforts to save the life of an individual "makes sense only when there is a shortage of people. I have not lately heard that there is a shortage of people."[19] The point of view suggested by these quotations is quite clear. It isn't that preserving the integrity of ecosystems has autonomous value, to be taken into account just as the quite distinct value of individual human welfare is. Rather, the idea is that the only value is the holistic one of maintaining ecological balance and diversity. Here we have a view that is just as monolithic as the most single-minded individualism; the difference is that the unit of value is thought to exist at a higher level of organization.

It is hard to know what to say to someone who would save a mosquito, just because it is rare, rather than a human being, if there were a choice. In ethics, as in any other subject, rationally persuading another person requires the existence of shared assumptions. If this monolithic environmentalist view is based on the notion that ecosystems have needs and interests, and that these take total precedence over the rights and interests of individual human beings, then the discussion of the previous sections is relevant. And even supposing that these higher-level entities have needs and wants, what reason is there to suppose that these matter and that the wants and needs of individuals matter not at all? But if this source of defense is jettisoned, and it is merely asserted that only ecosystems have value, with no substantive defense being offered, one must begin by requesting an argument: *why* is ecosystem stability and diversity the only value?

Some environmentalists have seen the individualist bias of utilitarianism as being harmful in ways additional to its impact on our perception of ecological values. Thus, Callicott writes:

> On the level of social organization, the interests of society may not always coincide with the sum of the interests of its parts. Discipline, sacrifice, and individual restraint are often necessary in the social sphere to maintain social integrity as within the bodily organism. A society, indeed, is particularly vulnerable to disintegration when its members become preoccupied totally with their own particular interest, and ignore those distinct and independent interests of the community as a whole. One example, unfortunately, our own society, is altogether too close at hand to be examined with strict academic detachment. The United States seems to pursue uncritically a social policy of reductive utilitarianism, aimed at promoting the happiness of all its members severally. Each special interest accordingly clamors more loudly to be satisfied while the community as a whole becomes noticeably more and more infirm economically, environmentally, and politically.[20]

Callicott apparently sees the emergence of individualism and alienation from nature as two aspects of the same process. He values "the symbiotic relationship of Stone Age man to the natural environment" and regrets that "civilization has insulated and alienated us from the rigors and challenges of the natural environment. The hidden agenda of the humane ethic," he says, "is the imposition of the anti-natural prophylactic ethos of comfort and soft pleasure on an even wider scale. The land ethic, on the other hand, requires a shrinkage, if at all possible, of the domestic sphere; it rejoices in a recrudescence of the wilderness and a renaissance of tribal cultural experience."[21]

Callicott is right that "strict academic detachment" is difficult here. The reader will have to decide whether the United States currently suffers from too much or too little regard "for the happiness of all its members severally" and whether we should feel nostalgia or pity in contemplating what the Stone Age experience of nature was like.

VII.   The Demarcation Problem

Perhaps the most fundamental theoretical problem confronting an environmentalist who wishes to claim that species and ecosystems have autonomous value is what I will call the *problem of demarcation*. Every ethical theory must provide principles that describe which objects matter for their own sakes and which do not. Besides marking the boundary between these two classes by enumerating a set of ethically relevant properties, an ethical theory must say why the properties named, rather than others, are the ones that count. Thus, for example, hedonistic utilitarianism cites the capacity to experience pleasure and/or pain as the decisive criterion; preference utilitarianism cites the having of preferences (or wants, or interests) as the decisive property. And a Kantian ethical theory will include an individual in the ethical community only if it is capable of rational reflection and autonomy. Not that justifying these various proposed solutions to the demarcation problem is easy; indeed, since this issue is so fundamental, it will be very difficult to justify one proposal as opposed to another. Still, a substantive ethical theory is obliged to try.

Environmentalists, wishing to avoid the allegedly distorting perspective of individualism, frequently want to claim autonomous value for wholes. This may take the form of a monolithic doctrine according to which the only thing that matters is the stability of the ecosystem. Or it may embody a pluralistic outlook according to which ecosystem stability and species preservation have an importance additional to the welfare of individual organisms. But an environmentalist theory shares with all ethical theories an interest in not saying that everything has autonomous value. The reason this position is proscribed is that it makes the adjudication of ethical conflict very difficult indeed. (In addition, it is radically implausible, but we can set that objection to one side.)

Environmentalists, as we have seen, may think of natural objects, like mountains, species, and ecosystems, as mattering for their own sake, but of artificial objects, like highway systems and domesticated animals, as having only instrumental value. If a mountain and a highway are both made of rock, it seems unlikely that the difference between them arises from the fact that mountains have wants, interests, and preferences, but highway systems do not. But perhaps the place to look for the relevant difference is not in their present physical composition, but in the historical fact of how each came into existence. Mountains were created by natural processes, whereas highways are humanly constructed. But once we realize that organisms construct their environments in nature, this contrast begins to cloud. Organisms do not passively reside in an environment whose properties are independently determined. Organisms transform their environments by physically interacting with them. An anthill is an artifact just as a highway is. Granted, a difference obtains at the level of whether conscious deliberation played a role, but can one take seriously the view that artifacts produced by conscious planning are thereby *less* valuable than ones that arise without the intervention of mentality.[22] As we have noted before, although environmentalists often accuse their critics of failing to think in a biologically realistic way, their use of the distinction between "natural" and "artificial" is just the sort of idea that stands in need of a more realistic biological perspective.

My suspicion is that the distinction between natural and artificial is not the crucial one. On the contrary, certain features of environmental concerns imply that natural objects are exactly on a par with certain artificial ones. Here the intended comparison is not between mountains and highways, but between mountains and works of art. My goal in what follows is not to sketch a substantive conception of what determines the value of objects in these two domains, but to motivate an analogy.

For both natural objects and works of art, our values extend beyond the concerns we have for experiencing pleasure. Most of us value seeing an original painting more than we value seeing a copy, even when we could not tell the difference. When we experience works of art, often what we value is not just the kinds of experiences we have, but, in addition, the connections we usually have with certain real objects. Routley and Routley have made an analogous point about valuing the wilderness experience: a "wilderness experience machine" that caused certain sorts of hallucinations would be no substitute for actually going into the wild.[23] Nor is this fact about our valuation limited to such aesthetic and environmentalist contexts. We love various people in our lives. If a molecule-for-molecule replica of a beloved person were created, you would not love that individual, but would continue to love the individual to whom you actually were historically related. Here again, our attachments are to objects and people as they really are, and not just to the experiences that they facilitate.

Another parallel between environmentalist concerns and aesthetic values concerns the issue of context. Although environmentalists often stress the importance of preserving endangered species, they would not be completely satisfied if an endangered species were preserved by putting a number of specimens in a zoo or in a humanly constructed preserve. What is taken to be important is preserving the species in its natural habitat. This leads to the more holistic position that preserving ecosystems, and not simply preserving certain member species, is of primary importance. Aesthetic concerns often lead in the same direction. It was not merely saving a fresco or an altar piece that motivated art historians after the most recent flood in Florence. Rather, they wanted to save these works of art in their original ("natural") settings. Not just the painting, but the church that housed it; not just the church, but the city itself. The idea of objects residing in a "fitting" environment plays a powerful role in both domains.

Environmentalism and aesthetics both see value in rarity. Of two whales, why should one be more worthy of aid than another, just because one belongs to an endangered species? Here we have the $n + m$ question mentioned in Section I. As an ethical concern, rarity is difficult to understand. Perhaps this is because our ethical ideas concerning justice and equity (note the word) are saturated with individualism. But in the context of aesthetics, the concept of rarity is far from alien. A work of art may have enhanced value simply because there are very few other works by the same artist, or from the same historical period, or in the same style. It isn't that the price of the item may go up with rarity; I am talking about aesthetic value, not monetary worth. Viewed as valuable aesthetic objects, rare organisms may be valuable because they are rare.

A disanalogy may suggest itself. It may be objected that works of art are of instrumental value only, but that species and ecosystems have intrinsic value. Perhaps it is true, as claimed before, that our attachment to works of art, to nature, and to our loved ones extends beyond the experiences they allow us to have. But it may be argued that what is valuable in the aesthetic case is always the relation of a valuer to a valued object.[24] When we experience a work of art, the value is not simply in the experience, but in the composite fact that we and the work of art are related in certain ways. This immediately suggests that if there were no valuers in the world, nothing would have value, since such relational facts could no longer obtain. So, to adapt Routley and Routley's "last man argument," it would seem that if an ecological crisis precipitated a collapse of the world system, the last human being (whom we may assume for the purposes of this example to be the last valuer) could set about destroying all works of art, and there would be nothing wrong in this.[25] That is, if aesthetic objects are valuable only in so far as valuers can stand in certain relations to them, then when valuers disappear, so does the possibility of aesthetic value. This would deny, in one sense, that aesthetic objects are intrinsically valuable: it isn't they, in themselves, but rather the relational facts that they are part of, that are valuable.

In contrast, it has been claimed that the "last man" would be wrong to destroy natural objects such as mountains, salt marshes, and species. (So as to avoid confusing the issue by bringing in the welfare of individual organisms, Routley and Routley imagine that destruction and mass extinctions can be caused painlessly, so that there would be nothing wrong about this undertaking from the point of view of the nonhuman organisms involved.) If the last man ought to preserve these natural objects, then these objects appear to have a kind of autonomous value; their value would extend beyond their possible relations to valuers. If all this were true, we would have here a contrast between aesthetic and natural objects, one that implies that natural objects are more valuable than works of art.

Routley and Routley advance the last man argument as if it were decisive in showing that environmental objects such as mountains and salt marshes have autonomous value. I find the example more puzzling than decisive. But, in the present context, we do not have to decide whether Routley and Routley are right. We only have to decide whether this imagined situation brings out any relevant difference between aesthetic and environmental values. Were the last man to look up on a certain hillside, he would see a striking rock formation next to the ruins of a Greek temple. Long ago the temple was built from some of the very rocks that still stud the slope. Both promontory and temple have a history, and both have been transformed by the biotic and the abiotic environments. I myself find it impossible to advise the last man that the peak matters more than the temple. I do not see a relevant difference. Environmentalists, if they hold that the solution to the problem of demarcation is to be found in the distinction between natural and artificial, will have to find such a distinction. But if environmental values are aesthetic, no difference need be discovered.

Environmentalists may be reluctant to classify their concern as aesthetic. Perhaps they will feel that aesthetic concerns are frivolous. Perhaps they will feel that the aesthetic regard for artifacts that has been made possible by culture is antithetical to a proper regard for wilderness. But such contrasts are illusory. Concern for environmental values does not require a stripping away of the perspective afforded by civilization; to value the wild, one does not have to "become wild" oneself (whatever that may mean). Rather, it is the material comforts of civilization that make possible a serious concern for both aesthetic and environmental values. These are concerns that can become pressing in developed nations in part because the populations of those countries now enjoy a certain substantial level of prosperity. It would be the height of condescension to expect a nation experiencing hunger and chronic disease to be inordinately concerned with the autonomous value of ecosystems or with creating and preserving works of art. Such values are not frivolous, but they can become important to us only after certain fundamental human needs are satisfied. Instead of radically jettisoning individualist ethics, environmentalists may find a more hospitable home for their values in a category of value that has existed all along.

Notes

1. Mark Sagoff, "On Preserving the Natural Environment," *Yale Law Review* 84 (1974): 205–38; J. Baird Callicott, "Animal Liberation: A Triangular Affair," *Environmental Ethics* 2 (1980): 311–38; and Bryan Norton, "Environmental Ethics and Nonhuman Rights," *Environmental Ethics* 4 (1982): 17–36.

2. Peter Singer, *Animal Liberation* (New York: Random House, 1975), has elaborated a position of this sort.

3. Occasionally, it has been argued that utilitarianism is not just *insufficient* to justify the principles of environmentalism but is actually mistaken in holding that pain is intrinsically bad. Callicott writes: "I herewith declare in all soberness that I see nothing wrong with pain. It is a marvelous method, honed by the evolutionary process, of conveying important organic information. I think it was the late Alan Watts who somewhere remarks that upon being asked if he did not think there was too much pain in the world replied, 'No, I think there's just enough' " ("A Triangular Affair," p. 333). Setting to one side the remark attributed to Watts, I should point out that pain can be intrinsically bad and still have some good consequences. The point of calling pain intrinsically bad is to say that one essential aspect of experiencing it is negative.

4. A parallel with a quite different moral problem will perhaps make it clearer how the environmentalist's holism conflicts with some fundamental ethical ideas. When we consider the rights of individuals to receive compensation for harm, we generally expect that the individuals compensated must be one and the same as the individuals harmed. This expectation runs counter to the way an affirmative action program might be set up, if individuals were to receive compensation simply for being members of groups that have suffered certain kinds of discrimination, whether or not they themselves were victims of discrimination. I do not raise this example to suggest that a holistic conception according to which groups have entitlements is beyond consideration. Rather, my point is to exhibit a case in which a rather common ethical idea is individualistic rather than holistic.

5. David Ehrenfeld, "The Conservation of Non-Resources," *American Scientist* 64 (1976): 648–56. For a theoretical discussion see Robert M. May, *Stability and Complexity in Model Ecosystems* (Princeton: Princeton University Press, 1973).
6. Callicott, "A Triangular Affair," pp. 333–34 (my emphasis).
7. Paul Shepard, "Animal Rights and Human Rites." *North American Review* (Winter 1974): 35–41.
8. Charles Darwin, *The Autobiography of Charles Darwin* (London: Collins, 1876, 1958), p. 90.
9. Callicott, "A Triangular Affair," p. 330.
10. Callicott, "A Triangular Affair," p. 330.
11. Aristotle, *De Anima*, 415a26.
12. Christopher Stone, *Should Trees Have Standing?* (Los Altos, Calif.: William Kaufmann, 1972), p. 24.
13. Sagoff, "Natural Environment," pp. 220–24.
14. The example is Sagoff's, "Natural Environment," pp. 220–24.
15. Ehrenfeld, "The Conservation of Non-Resources," pp. 651–52.
16. Aldo Leopold, *A Sand County Almanac* (New York: Oxford University Press, 1949), pp. 224–25.
17. Callicott, "A Triangular Affair," p. 326 (emphasis mine).
18. Edward Abbey, *Desert Solitaire* (New York: Ballantine Books, 1968), p. 20.
19. Garrett Hardin, "The Economics of Wilderness," *Natural History* 78 (1969): 176.
20. Callicott, "A Triangular Affair," p. 323.
21. Callicott, "A Triangular Affair," p. 335.
22. Here we would have an inversion, not just a rejection, of a familiar Marxian doctrine—the labor theory of value.
23. Richard Routley and Val Routley, "Human Chauvinism and Environmental Ethics," *Environmental Philosophy, Monograph Series 2*, edited by D. S. Mannison, M. A. McRobbie, and R. Routley (Philosophy Department, Australian National University, 1980) p. 154.
24. Donald H. Regan, "Duties of Preservation," *The Preservation of Species*, ed. B. Norton (Princeton: Princeton University Press, 1986), pp. 195–220.
25. Routley and Routley, "Human Chauvinism," pp. 121–22.

Study Questions

1. What is a "slippery slope argument"?
2. According to Sober, what is the moral significance of the distinction between wild and domesticated animals?
3. According to Sober, what is "the demarcation problem"?
4. Do you find any relevant differences between aesthetic and environmental values?

I. Affirmative Action

CHAPTER 40

Two Concepts of Affirmative Action
Steven M. Cahn

In the essay that follows, I seek to analyze the issues in the dispute over affirmative action. Your conclusion may differ from mine, but I hope you find that the article contributes toward an increased understanding of this complex matter.

In March 1961, less than two months after assuming office, President John F. Kennedy issued Executive Order 10925, establishing the President's Committee on Equal Employment Opportunity. Its mission was to end discrimination in employment by the government and its contractors. The order required every federal contract to include the pledge that "The contractor will not discriminate against any employe[e] or applicant for employment because of race, creed, color, or national origin. The contractor will take affirmative action to ensure that applicants are employed, and that employe[e]s are treated during employment, without regard to their race, creed, color, or national origin."

Here, for the first time in the context of civil rights, the government called for "affirmative action." The term meant taking appropriate steps to eradicate the then widespread practices of racial, religious, and ethnic discrimination.[1] The goal, as the President stated, was "equal opportunity in employment." In other words, *procedural* affirmative action, as I shall call it, was instituted to ensure that applicants for positions would be judged without any consideration of their race, religion, or national origin. These criteria were declared irrelevant. Taking them into account was forbidden.

From *Academe*, 83. Copyright © 1997 by Steven M. Cahn. Reprinted with minor revisions by permission of the author.

The Civil Rights Act of 1964 restated and broadened the application of this principle. Title VI declared that "No person in the United States shall, on the ground of race, color or national origin, be excluded from participation in, be denied the benefits of, or be subjected to discrimination under any program or activity receiving Federal financial assistance."

Before one year had passed, however, President Lyndon B. Johnson argued that fairness required more than a commitment to such procedural affirmative action. In his 1965 commencement address at Howard University, he said, "You do not take a person who for years has been hobbled by chains and liberate him, bring him up to the starting line of a race and then say, 'you're free to compete with all the others,' and still justly believe that you have been completely fair."

Several months later, President Johnson issued Executive Order 11246, stating that "It is the policy of the Government of the United States to provide equal opportunity in Federal employment for all qualified persons, to prohibit discrimination in employment because of race, creed, color or national origin, and to promote the full realization of equal employment opportunity through a positive, continuing program in each department and agency." Two years later the order was amended to prohibit discrimination on the basis of sex.

While the aim of President Johnson's order is stated in language similar to that of President Kennedy's, President Johnson's abolished the Committee on Equal Employment Opportunity, transferred its responsibilities to the Secretary of Labor, and authorized the Secretary to "adopt such rules and regulations and issue such orders as he deems necessary and appropriate to achieve the purposes thereof."

Acting on this mandate, the Department of Labor in December 1971, during the administration of President Richard M. Nixon, issued Revised Order No. 4, requiring all federal contractors to develop "an acceptable affirmative action program," including "an analysis of areas within which the contractor is deficient in the utilization of minority groups and women, and further, goals and timetables to which the contractor's good faith efforts must be directed to correct the deficiencies." Contractors were instructed to take the term "minority groups" to refer to "Negroes, American Indians, Orientals, and Spanish Surnamed Americans." (No guidance was given as to whether having only one parent, grandparent, or great-grandparent from a group would suffice to establish group membership.) The concept of "underutilization," according to the Revised Order, meant "having fewer minorities or women in a particular job classification than would reasonably be expected by their availability." "Goals" were not to be "rigid and inflexible quotas," but "targets reasonably attainable by means of applying every good faith effort to make all aspects of the entire affirmative action program work."[2]

Such preferential affirmative action, as I shall call it, requires that attention be paid to the same criteria of race, sex, and ethnicity that procedural affirmative action deems irrelevant. Is such use of these criteria justifiable in employment decisions?[3]

Return to President Johnson's claim that a person hobbled by discrimination cannot in fairness be expected to be competitive. How are we to determine which specific individuals are entitled to a compensatory advantage? To decide each case on its own merits would be possible, but this approach would undermine the argument for instituting preferential affirmative action on a group basis. For if some members of a group are able to compete, why not others? Thus defenders of preferential affirmative action maintain that the group, not the individual, is to be judged. If the group has suffered discrimination, then all its members are to be treated as hobbled runners.

Note, however, that while a hobbled runner, provided with a sufficient lead in a race, may cross the finish line first, giving that person an edge prevents the individual from being considered as fast a runner as others. An equally fast runner does not need an advantage to be competitive. This entire racing analogy thus encourages stereotypical thinking. For example, recall those men who played in baseball's Negro Leagues. That these athletes were barred from competing in the Major Leagues is the greatest stain on the history of the sport. While they suffered discrimination, these players were as proficient as their counterparts in the Major Leagues. They needed only to be judged by the same criteria as all others, and ensuring such equality of consideration is the essence of procedural affirmative action.

Granted, if individuals are unprepared or ill-equipped to compete, then they ought to be helped to try to achieve their goals. But such aid is appropriate for all who need it, not merely for members of particular racial, sexual, or ethnic groups.

Victims of discrimination deserve compensation. Former players in the Negro Leagues ought to receive special consideration in the arrangement of pension plans and any other benefits formerly denied these athletes due to unfair treatment. The case for such compensation, however, does not imply that present black players vying for jobs in the Major Leagues should be evaluated in any other way than their performance on the field. To assume their inability to compete is derogatory and erroneous.

Such considerations have led recent defenders of preferential affirmative action to rely less heavily on any argument that implies the attribution of noncompetitiveness to an entire population.[4] Instead, the emphasis has been placed on recognizing the benefits society is said to derive from encouraging expression of the varied experiences, outlooks, and values of members of different groups.

This approach makes a virtue of what has come to be called "diversity."[5] As a defense of preferential affirmative action, diversity has at least two advantages. First, those previously excluded are now included not as a favor to them but as a means of enriching all. Second, no one is viewed as hobbled; each competes on a par, although with varied strengths.

Note that diversity requires preferential hiring. Those who enhance diversity are to be preferred to those who do not. Those preferred, however, are not being chosen because of their deficiency; the larger group is deficient, lacking diversity.

What does it mean to say that a group lacks diversity? Or to put the question another way, could we decide, for example, which member of a ten-person group to eliminate in order to decrease most markedly its diversity?

So stated, the question is reminiscent of a provocative puzzle in *The Tyranny of Testing*, a 1962 book by the scientist Banesh Hoffman. In this attack on the importance placed on multiple-choice tests, he quotes the following letter to the editor of the *Times* of London:

> Sir—Among the "odd one out" type of questions which my son had to answer for a school entrance examination was: "Which is the odd one out among cricket, football, billiards, and hockey?" [In England "football" refers to the game Americans call "soccer," and "hockey" here refers to "field hockey."] The letter continued: I said billiards because it is the only one played indoors. A colleague says football because it is the only one in which the ball is not struck by an implement. A neighbour says cricket because in all the other games the object is to put the ball into a net. . . . Could any of your readers put me out of my misery by stating what is the correct answer . . . ?

A day later the *Times* printed the following two letters:

> Sir.—"Billiards" is the obvious answer . . . because it is the only one of the games listed which is not a team game.

> Sir.—football is the odd one out because . . . it is played with an inflated ball as compared with the solid ball used in each of the other three.

Hoffman then continued his own discussion:

> When I had read these three letters it seemed to me that good cases had been made for football and billiards, and that the case for cricket was particularly clever . . . At first I thought this made hockey easily the worst of four choices and, in effect, ruled it out. But then I realized that the very fact that hockey was the only one that could be thus ruled out gave it so striking a quality of separateness as to make it an excellent answer after all—perhaps the best. Fortunately, for my peace of mind, it soon occurred to me that hockey is the only one of the four games that is played with a curved implement.

The following day the *Times* published yet another letter, this from a philosophically sophisticated thinker.

> Sir.—[The author of the original letter] . . . has put his finger on what has long been a matter of great amusement to me. Of the four—cricket, football, billiards, hockey—each is unique in a multitude of respects. For example, billiards is the only one played with more than one ball at once, the only one played on a green cloth and not on a field. . . . It seems to me that those who have been responsible for inventing this kind of brain teaser have been ignorant of the elementary philosophical fact that every thing is at once unique and a member of a wider class.

With this sound principle in mind, return to the problem of deciding which member of a ten-person group to eliminate in order to decrease most markedly its diversity. Unless the sort of diversity is specified, the question has no rational answer.

In searches for college and university faculty members, we know what sorts of diversity are typically of present concern: race, sex, and certain ethnicities. Why should these characteristics be given special regard?

Consider, for example, other nonacademic respects in which prospective faculty appointees can differ: age, religion, nationality, regional background, economic class, social stratum, military experience, bodily appearance, physical soundness, sexual orientation, marital status, ethical standards, political commitments, and cultural values. Why should we not seek diversity of these sorts?

To some extent schools do. Many colleges and universities indicate in advertisements for faculty positions that the schools seek veterans or persons with disabilities. The City University of New York requires all searches to give preference to individuals of Italian-American descent.

The crucial point is that the appeal to diversity never favors any particular candidate. Each one adds to some sort of diversity but not another. In a department of ten, one individual might be the only Black, another the only woman, another the only bachelor, another the only veteran, another the only one over fifty, another the only Catholic, another the only Republican, another the only Scandinavian, another the only socialist, and the tenth the only Southerner.

Suppose the suggestion is made that the sorts of diversity to be sought are those of groups that have suffered discrimination. This approach leads to another problem, clearly put by John Kekes:

> It is true that American blacks, Native Americans, Hispanics, and women have suffered injustice as a group. But so have homosexuals, epileptics, the urban and the rural poor, the physically ugly, those whose careers were ruined by McCarthyism, prostitutes, the obese, and so forth . . .
>
> There have been some attempts to deny that there is an analogy between these two classes of victims. It has been said that the first were unjustly discriminated against due to racial or sexual prejudice and that this is not true of the second. This is indeed so. But why should we accept the suggestion . . . that the only form of injustice relevant to preferential treatment is that which is due to racial or sexual prejudice? Injustice occurs in many forms, and those who value justice will surely object to all of them.[6]

Kekes's reasoning is cogent. In addition, another difficulty looms for the proposal to seek diversity only of groups that have suffered discrimination. For diversity is supposed to be valued not as compensation to the disadvantaged but as a means of enriching all.

Consider a department in which most of the faculty members are women. In certain fields, for example, nursing and elementary education, such departments are common. If diversity by sex is of value, then such a department, when making its next appointment, should prefer a man. Yet men as a group have not been victims of discrimination. To achieve valued sorts of diversity, the question is not which groups have been discriminated against, but which valued groups are not represented. The question thus reappears as to which sorts of diversity are to be most highly valued. I know of no compelling answer.

Seeking to justify preferential affirmative action in terms of its contribution to diversity raises another difficulty. For preferential affirmative action is commonly defended as a temporary rather than a permanent measure.[7] Preferential affirmative action to achieve diversity, however, is not temporary.

Suppose it were. Then once an institution had appointed an appropriate number of members of a particular group, preferential affirmative action would no longer be in effect. Yet the institution may later find that it has too few members of that group. Because lack of valuable diversity is presumably no more acceptable at one time than another, preferential affirmative action would have to be reinstituted. Thereby it would in effect become a permanent policy.

Why do so many of its defenders wish it to be only transitional? They believe the policy was instituted in response to irrelevant criteria for appointment having mistakenly been treated as relevant. To adopt any policy that continues to treat essentially irrelevant criteria as relevant is to share the guilt of those who discriminated originally. Irrelevant criteria should be recognized as such and abandoned as soon as feasible.

Some defenders of preferential affirmative action argue, however, that an individual's race, sex, or ethnicity is germane to fulfilling the responsibilities of a faculty member. They believe, therefore, that preferential affirmative action should be a permanent feature of search processes, because it takes account of criteria that should be considered in every appointment.

At least three reasons have been offered to justify the claim that those of a particular race, sex, or ethnicity are well-suited to be faculty members: first, they would be especially effective teachers of any student who shares their race, sex, or ethnicity;[8] second, they would be particularly insightful researchers because of their experiencing the world from distinctive standpoints;[9] third, they would be role models, demonstrating that those of a particular race, sex, or ethnicity can be effective faculty members.[10]

Consider each of these claims in turn. As to the presumed teaching effectiveness of the individuals in question, no empirical study supports the claim.[11] But assume compelling evidence were presented. It would have no implications for individual cases. A particular person who does not share race, sex, or ethnicity with students might teach them superbly. An individual of the students' own race, sex, or ethnicity might be ineffective. Regardless of statistical correlations, what is crucial is that individuals be able to teach effectively all sorts of students, and seeking individuals who give evidence of satisfying this criterion is entirely consistent with procedural affirmative action. But knowing an individual's race, sex, or ethnicity does not reveal whether that person will be effective in the classroom.

Do members of a particular race, sex, or ethnicity share a distinctive intellectual perspective that enhances their scholarship? Celia Wolf-Devine has aptly described this claim as a form of "stereotyping" that is "demeaning." As she puts it, "A Hispanic who is a Republican is no less a Hispanic, and a woman who is not a feminist is no less a woman."[12] Furthermore, are Hispanic men and women supposed to have the same point of view in virtue of their common ethnicity, or are they supposed to have different points of view in virtue of their different genders?

If our standpoints are thought to be determined by our race, sex, and ethnicity, why not also by the numerous other significant respects in which people differ, such as age, religion, sexual orientation, and so on? Because each of us is unique, can anyone else share my point of view?

That my own experience is my own is a tautology that does not imply the keenness of my insight into my experience. The victim of a crime may as a result embrace an outlandish theory of racism. But neither who you are nor what you experience guarantees the truth of your theories.

To be an effective researcher calls for discernment, imagination, and perseverance. These attributes are not tied to one's race, sex, ethnicity, age, or religion. Black scholars, for example, may be more inclined to study Black literature than are non-Black scholars. But some non-Black literary critics are more interested in and more knowledgeable about Black literature than are some Black literary critics. Why make decisions based on fallible racial generalizations when judgments of individual merit are obtainable and more reliable?

Perhaps the answer lies in the claim that only those of a particular race, sex, or ethnicity can serve as role models, exemplifying to members of a particular group the possibility of their success. Again, no empirical study supports the claim, but it has often been taken as self-evident that, for instance, only a woman can be a role model for a woman, only a Black for a Black, and only a Catholic for a Catholic. In other words, the crucial feature of a person is supposed to be not what the person does but who the person is.

The logic of the situation, however, is not so clear. Consider, for example, a Black man who is a Catholic. Presumably he serves as a role model for Blacks, men, and Catholics. Does he serve as a role model for Black women, or can only a Black woman serve that purpose? Does he serve as a role model for all Catholics or only for those who are Black? Can I serve as a role model for anyone else, because no one else shares all my characteristics? Perhaps I can serve as a role model for everyone else, because everyone else belongs to at least one group to which I belong.

Putting aside these conundrums, the critical point is supposed to be that in a field in which discrimination has been rife, a successful individual who belongs to the discriminated group demonstrates that members of the group can succeed in that field. Obviously success is possible without a role model, for the first successful individual had none. But suppose persuasive evidence were offered that a role model, while not necessary, sometimes is helpful, not only to those who belong to the group in question but also to those prone to believe that no members of the group can perform effectively within the field. Role models would then both encourage members of a group that had suffered discrimination and discourage further discrimination against the group.

To serve these purposes, however, the person chosen would need to be viewed as having been selected by the same criteria as all others. If not, members of the group that has suffered discrimination as well as those prone to discriminate would be confirmed in their common view that members of the group never would have been chosen unless membership in the group had been taken into account. Those who suffered discrimination would conclude that it still exists, while those prone to discriminate would conclude that members of the group lack the necessary attributes to compete equally.

How can we ensure that a person chosen for a position has been selected by the same criteria as all others? Preferential affirmative action fails to serve the purpose, because by definition it differentiates among people on the basis of criteria other than performance. The approach that ensures merit selection is procedural affirmative action. It maximizes equal opportunity by demanding vigilance against every form of discrimination.

The policy of appointing others than the best qualified has not produced a harmonious society in which prejudice is transcended and all enjoy the benefits of self-esteem. Rather, the practice has bred doubts about the abilities of those chosen while generating resentment in those passed over.

Procedural affirmative action had barely begun before it was replaced by preferential affirmative action. The difficulties with the latter are now clear. Before deeming them necessary evils in the struggle to overcome pervasive prejudice, why not try scrupulous enforcement of procedural affirmative action? We might thereby most directly achieve that equitable society so ardently desired by every person of good will.

Notes

1. A comprehensive history of one well-documented case of such discrimination is Dan A. Oren, *Joining the Club: A History of Jews and Yale* (New Haven and London: Yale University Press, 1985). Prior to the end of World War II, no Jew had ever been appointed to the rank of full professor in Yale College.
2. 41 C.F.R. 60-2.12. The Order provides no suggestion as to whether a "good faith effort" implies only showing preference among equally qualified candidates (the "tiebreaking" model), preferring a strong candidate to an even stronger one (the "plus factor" model), preferring a merely qualified candidate to a strongly qualified candidate (the "trumping" model), or canceling a search unless a qualified candidate of the preferred sort is available (the "quota" model).

   A significant source of misunderstanding about affirmative action results from both the government's failure to clarify which type of preference is called for by a "good faith effort" and the failure on the part of those conducting searches to inform applicants which type of preference is in use. Regarding the latter issue, see my "Colleges Should Be Explicit About Who Will Be Considered for Jobs," *The Chronicle of Higher Education, 35* (30), 1989, reprinted in *Affirmative Action and the University: A Philosophical Inquiry,* Steven M. Cahn (ed.), (Philadelphia: Temple University Press, 1993), pp. 3–4.
3. Whether their use is appropriate in a school's admission and scholarship decisions is a different issue, involving other considerations, and I shall not explore that subject in this article.
4. See, for example, Leslie Pickering Francis, "In Defense of Affirmative Action," in Cahn, op. cit., especially pp. 24–26. She raises concerns about unfairness to those individuals forced by circumstances not of their own making to bear all the costs of compensation, as well as injustices to those who have been equally victimized but are not members of specified groups.
5. The term gained currency when Justice Lewis Powell, in his pivotal opinion in the Supreme Court's 1978 *Bakke* decision, found "the attainment of a diverse student body" to be a goal that might justify the use of race in student admissions. An incisive analysis of that decision is Carl Cohen, *Naked Racial Preference* (Lanham, MD: Madison Books, 1995), pp. 55–80.

6. Cahn, op. cit., p. 151.
7. Consider Michael Rosenfeld, *Affirmative Action and Justice: A Philosophical and Constitutional Inquiry* (New Haven and London: Yale University Press, 1991), p. 336: "Ironically, the sooner affirmative action is allowed to complete its mission, the sooner the need for it will altogether disappear."
8. See, for example, Francis, op. cit., p. 31.
9. See, for example, Richard Wasserstrom, "The University and the Case for Preferential Treatment," *American Philosophical Quarterly*, 13(4), 1976, pp. 165–70.
10. See, for example, Joel J. Kupperman, "Affirmative Action: Relevant Knowledge and Relevant Ignorance," in Cahn, op. cit., pp. 181–88.
11. Consider Judith Jarvis Thomson, "Preferential Hiring," *Philosophy and Public Affairs*, 2(4), 1973, p. 368: "I do not think that as a student I learned any better, or any more, from the women who taught me than from the men, and I do not think that my own women students now learn any better or any more from me than they do from my male colleagues."
12. Cahn, op. cit., p. 230.

Study Questions

1. Explain the distinction Cahn draws between procedural and preferential affirmative action.
2. Does preferential affirmative action imply that on occasion a highly qualified candidate should be passed over in favor of one who is not as highly qualified?
3. According to Cahn, why does the appeal to diversity never favor any particular candidate?
4. Are one's sex, race, or ethnicity germane to fulfilling the responsibilities of a faculty member?

CHAPTER 41

What Good Am I?

Laurence Thomas

Laurence Thomas is Professor of Philosophy and of Political Science at Syracuse University. He explains why he believes in the importance of appointing women and members of minorities to college and university faculties. He suggests that their absence results from the insincerity of those who talk about equality but fail to act in accord with this ideal.

What good am I as a black professor? The raging debate over affirmative action surely invites me to ask this searching question of myself, just as it must invite those belonging to other so-called suspect categories to ask it of themselves. If knowledge is color blind, why should it matter whether the face in front of the classroom is a European white, a Hispanic, an Asian, and so on? Why should it matter whether the person is female or male?

One of the most well-known arguments for affirmative action is the role-model argument. It is also the argument that I think is the least satisfactory—not because women and minorities do not need role models—everyone does—but because as the argument is often presented, it comes dangerously close to implying that about the only thing a black, for instance, can teach a white is how not to be a racist. Well, I think better of myself than that. And I hope that all women and minorities feel the same about themselves. . . .

But even if the role-model argument were acceptable in some version or the other, affirmative action would still seem unsavory, as the implicit assumption about those hired as affirmative action

---

appointments is that they are less qualified than those who are not. For, so the argument goes, the practice would be unnecessary if, in the first place, affirmative action appointees were the most qualified for the position, since they would be hired by virtue of their merits. I call this the counterfactual argument from qualifications.

Now, while I do not want to say much about it, this argument has always struck me as extremely odd. In a morally perfect world, it is no doubt true that if women and minorities were the most qualified they would be hired by virtue of their merits. But this truth tells me nothing about how things are in this world. It does not show that biases built up over decades and centuries do not operate in the favor of, say, white males over nonwhite males. It is as if one argued against feeding the starving simply on the grounds that in a morally perfect world starvation would not exist. Perhaps it would not. But this is no argument against feeding the starving now.

It would be one thing if those who advance the counterfactual argument from qualifications addressed the issue of built-up biases that operate against women and minorities. Then I could perhaps suppose that they are arguing in good faith. But for them to ignore these built-up biases in the name of an ideal world is sheer hypocrisy. It is to confuse what the ideal should be with the steps that should be taken to get there. Sometimes the steps are very simple or, in any case, purely procedural: instead of A, do B; or perform a series of well-defined steps that guarantee the outcome. Not so with nonbiased hiring, however, since what is involved is a change in attitude and feelings—not even merely a change in belief. After all, it is possible to believe something quite sincerely and yet not have the emotional wherewithal to act in accordance with that belief. . . .

The philosophical debate over affirmative action has stalled . . . because so many who oppose it, and some who do not, are unwilling to acknowledge the fact that sincere belief in equality does not entail a corresponding change in attitude and feelings in day-to-day interactions with women and minorities. Specifically, sincere belief does not eradicate residual and, thus, unintentional sexist and racist attitudes.[1] So, joviality among minorities may be taken by whites as the absence of intellectual depth or sincerity on the part of those minorities, since such behavior is presumed to be uncommon among high-minded intellectual whites. Similarly, it is a liability for academic women to be too fashionable in their attire, since fashionably attired women are often taken by men as aiming to be seductive.

Lest there be any misunderstanding, nothing I have said entails that unqualified women and minorities should be hired. I take it to be obvious, though, that whether someone is the best qualified is often a judgment call. On the other hand, what I have as much as said is that there are built-up biases in the hiring process that disfavor women and minorities and need to be corrected. I think of it as rather on the order of correcting for unfavorable moral headwinds. It is possible to be committed to gender and racial equality and yet live a life in which residual, and thus unintentional, sexism and racism operate to varying degrees of explicitness.

I want to return now to the question with which I began this essay: What good am I as a black professor? I want to answer this question because, insofar as our aim is a just society, I think it is extremely important to see the way in which it does matter that the person in front of the class is not always a white male, notwithstanding the truth that knowledge, itself, is color blind.

Teaching is not just about transmitting knowledge. If it were, then students could simply read books and professors could simply pass out tapes or lecture notes. Like it or not, teachers are the object of intense emotions and feelings on the part of students [who are] solicitous of faculty approval and affirmation. Thus, teaching is very much about intellectual affirmation; and there can be no such affirmation of the student by the mentor in the absence of deep trust between them, be the setting elementary or graduate school. Without this trust, a mentor's praise will ring empty; constructive criticism will seem mean spirited; and advice will be poorly received, if sought after at all. A student needs to be confident that he can make a mistake before the professor without being regarded as stupid in the professor's eyes and that the professor is interested in seeing beyond his weaknesses to his strengths. Otherwise, the student's interactions with the professor will be plagued by uncertainty; and that uncertainty will fuel the self-doubts of the student.

Now, the position that I should like to defend, however, is not that only women can trust women, only minorities can trust minorities, and only whites can trust whites. That surely is not what we want. Still, it must be acknowledged, first of all, that racism and sexism have very often been a bar to such trust between mentor and student, when the professor has been a white male and the student has been either a woman or a member of a minority group. Of course, trust between mentor and student is not easy to come by in any case. This, though, is compatible with women and minorities having even greater problems if the professor is a white male.

Sometimes a woman professor will be necessary if a woman student is to feel the trust of a mentor that makes intellectual affirmation possible; sometimes a minority professor will be necessary for a minority student; indeed, sometimes a white professor will be necessary for a white student. (Suppose the white student is from a very sexist and racist part of the United States, and it takes a white professor to undue the student's biases.)

Significantly, though, in an academy where there is gender and racial diversity among the faculty, that diversity alone gives a woman or minority student the hope that intellectual affirmation is possible. This is so even if the student's mentor should turn out to be a white male. For part of what secures our conviction that we are living in a just society is not merely that we experience justice, but that we see justice around us. A diverse faculty serves precisely this end in terms of women and minority students believing that it is possible for them to have an intellectually affirming mentor relationship with a faculty member regardless of the faculty's gender or race.

Naturally, there are some women and minority students who will achieve no matter what the environment. Harriet Jacobs and Frederick Douglass were slaves who went on to accomplish more than many of us will who have never seen the chains of slavery. Neither, though, would have thought their success a reason to leave slavery intact. Likewise, the fact that there are some women and minorities who will prevail in spite of the obstacles is no reason to leave the status quo in place.

There is another part of the argument. Where there is intellectual affirmation, there is also gratitude. When a student finds that affirmation in a faculty member, a bond is formed, anchored in the student's gratitude, that can weather almost anything. Without such ties there could be no "ole boy" network—a factor that is not about racism, but a kind of social interaction running its emotional course. When women and minority faculty play an intellectually affirming role in the lives of white male students, such faculty undermine a nonracist and nonsexist pattern of emotional feelings that has unwittingly served the sexist and racist end of passing the intellectual mantle from white male to white male. For what we want, surely, is not just blacks passing the mantle to blacks, women to women, and white males to white males, but a world in which it is possible for all to see one another as proper recipients of the intellectual mantle. Nothing serves this end better than the gratitude between mentor and student that often enough ranges over differences between gender and race or both.

Ideally, my discussion of trust, intellectual affirmation, and gratitude should have been supplemented with a discussion of nonverbal behavior. For it seems to me that what has been ignored . . . is the way in which judgments are communicated not simply by what is said but by a vast array of nonverbal behavior. Again, a verbal and sincere commitment to equality, without the relevant change in emotions and feelings, will invariably leave nonverbal behavior intact. Mere voice intonation and flow of speech can be a dead giveaway that the listener does not expect much of substance to come from the speaker. Anyone who doubts this should just remind her- or himself that it is a commonplace to remark to someone over the phone that he sounds tired or "down" or distracted, where the basis for this judgment, obviously, can only be how the individual sounds. One can get the clear sense that one called at the wrong time just by the way in which the other person responds or gets involved in the conversation. So, ironically, there is a sense in which it can be easier to convince ourselves that we are committed to gender and racial equality than it is to convince a woman or a minority person, for the latter see and experience our nonverbal behavior in a way that we ourselves do not. Specifically, it so often happens that a woman or minority can see that a person's nonverbal behavior belies their verbal support of gender and racial equality in faculty hiring—an interruption here, or an all-too-quick dismissal of a remark there. And this is to say nothing of the ways in which the oppressor often seems to know better than the victim how the victim is affected by the oppression that permeates her or his life, an arrogance that is communicated in myriad ways. This is not the place, though, to address the topic of social justice and nonverbal behavior.[2]

Before moving on let me consider an objection to my view. No doubt some will balk at the very idea of women and minority faculty intellectually affirming white male students. But this is just so much nonsense on the part of those [who are] balking. For I have drawn attention to a most powerful force in the lives of all individuals, namely, trust and gratitude; and I have indicated that just as these feelings have unwittingly served racist and sexist ends, they can serve ends that are morally laudable. Furthermore, I have rejected the idea, often implicit in the role-model argument, that women and minority faculty are only good for their own kind. What is more, the position I have advocated is not one of subservience in the least, as I have spoken of an affirming role that underwrites an often unshakable debt of gratitude.

So, to return to the question with which I began this essay: I matter as a black professor and so do women and minority faculty generally, because collectively, if not in each individual case, we represent the hope, sometimes in a very personal way, that the university is an environment where the trust that gives rise to intellectual affirmation and the accompanying gratitude is possible for all, and between all peoples. Nothing short of the reality of diversity can permanently anchor this hope for ourselves and posterity. . . .

I do not advocate the representation of given viewpoints or the position that the ethnic and gender composition of faculty members should be proportional to their numbers in society. The former is absurd because it is a mistake to insist that points of view are either gender- or color-coded. The latter is absurd because it would actually entail getting rid of some faculty, since the percentage of Jews in the academy far exceeds their percentage in the population. If one day this should come to be true of blacks or Hispanics, they in turn would be fair game. . . .

[T]he continued absence of any diversity whatsoever draws attention to itself. My earlier remarks about nonverbal behavior taken in conjunction with my observations about trust, affirmation, and gratitude are especially apropos here. The complete absence of diversity tells departments more about themselves than no doubt they are prepared to acknowledge.

I would like to conclude with a concrete illustration of the way in which trust and gratitude can make a difference in the academy. As everyone knows, being cited affirmatively is an important indication of professional success. Now, who gets cited is not just a matter of what is true and good. On the contrary, students generally cite the works of their mentors and the work of others introduced to them by their mentors; and, on the other hand, mentors generally cite the work of those students of theirs for whom they have provided considerable intellectual affirmation. Sexism and racism have often been obstacles to faculty believing that women and minorities can be proper objects of full intellectual affirmation. It has also contributed to the absence of women and minority faculty which, in turn, has made it well-nigh impossible for white male students to feel an intellectual debt of gratitude to women and minority faculty. Their presence in the academy cannot help but bring about a change with regard to so simple a matter as patterns of citation, the professional ripple effect of which will be significant beyond many of our wildest dreams.

If social justice were just a matter of saying or writing the correct words, then equality would have long ago been a *fait accompli* in the academy. For I barely know anyone who is a faculty member who has not bemoaned the absence of minorities and women in the academy, albeit to varying degrees. So, I conclude with a very direct question: Is it really possible that so many faculty could be so concerned that women and minorities should flourish in the academy, and yet so few do? You will have to forgive me for not believing that it is. For as any good Kantian knows, one cannot consistently will an end without also willing the means to that end. Onora O'Neill writes, "Willing, after all, is not just a matter of wishing that something were the case, but involves committing oneself to doing something to bring that situation about when opportunity is there and recognized. Kant expressed this point by insisting that rationality requires that whoever wills some end wills the necessary means insofar as these are available."[3] If Kant is right, then much hand-wringing talk about social equality for women and minorities can only be judged insincere.

Notes

1. For a most illuminating discussion along this line, see Adrian M. S. Piper's very important essay, "Higher-Order Discrimination," in Owen Flanagan and Amelie Oksenberg Rorty, eds., *Identity, Character, and Morality: Essays in Moral Psychology* (Cambridge, MA: MIT Press, 1990).
2. For an attempt, see my "Moral Deference," *Philosophical Forum* 24, no. 1–3 (1992–1993): pp. 233–50.
3. Onora O'Neill, *Constructions of Reason: Explorations of Kant's Practical Philosophy* (Cambridge University Press, 1989), p. 90.

Study Questions

1. What is the role-model argument?
2. What does Thomas mean by "unintentional sexist and racist attitudes"?
3. According to Thomas, does an effective mentor need to be of the same race or sex as the student?
4. Do Thomas's arguments in favor of appointing women and minorities also imply the importance of adding members of any other specific groups to the faculty?

CHAPTER 42

Truth in Advertising

Tom L. Beauchamp

Tom L. Beauchamp (pronounced "Beecham") is Professor of Philosophy
at Georgetown University. He points out that advertisements for faculty
positions rarely contain specific information about the role of affirmative action in the appointment process, thereby perhaps deceiving
applicants. Academics thus appear reluctant to reveal policies they
claim to be appropriate, a situation Beauchamp describes as "a moral
embarrassment."

. . . [W]riters about preferential treatment in academia have generally
overlooked what seems to me today's most interesting moral problem
about preferential appointments. This problem can be introduced
through a story from a nonacademic setting told by Bob Woodward
in his recent book, *The Commanders*. Woodward reports an encounter
between White House Chief of Staff John Sununu and Secretary of
Defense Richard Cheney. Sununu, an outspoken critic of all policies
involving minority and gender quotas, is said to have told Cheney that
he "wanted 30 percent of the remaining 42 top jobs in the Defense
Department to be filled by women and minorities."[1] This certainly
looks like a quota, and the White House chief of staff seems to be
defending rival objectives that cannot be reconciled, although each
is suited for a different political context. One can tone down the
language of "quotas" by speaking of hopes, objectives, guidelines,
and the like, but cosmetic changes of wording only thinly obscure

From Tom L. Beauchamp, "Quotas by Any Name: Some Problems of Affirmative Action
in Faculty Appointments," in Steven M. Cahn, ed., *Affirmative Action and the University: A
Philosophical Inquiry.* Reprinted by permission of Temple University Press. Copyright ©
1993 by Temple University Press. All Rights Reserved.

any policy established to recruit minorities and women in which the goals are made explicit by numbers. . . .

Many of my colleagues and acquaintances in academia seem much like Woodward's Sununu. They eschew talk of quotas and condemn reverse discrimination. . . . However, the behavior and stated goals of these same parties [are] considerably softer than their apparent outrage over the injustice of quotas.

This softening of otherwise severe principle occurs as soon as they glimpse an injustice close at home, that is, in their own departments. Here they readily support the vigorous recruitment of minorities and women, and if they believe there is some sort of statistical imbalance (e.g., "we only have one woman in a department of twenty-three), they often have no reservations about setting aside the next one, two, or three positions for targeted groups, perhaps even including a policy of one-year contracts for white males until the appropriate persons can be recruited. . . .

The point is that departments commonly act, in setting out their goals, in ways that suggest department members willingly endorse what either is or has a strong family resemblance to a quota. In my experience only the rare department now insists that race and sex be considered irrelevant in making appointments. Moreover, university administrators, often more energetically than faculty, support particular percentages or numbers of faculty to be appointed from minority groups and women. . . .

It would be difficult, I suspect, for many members of academic departments to articulate the full set of reasons underlying their beliefs about affirmative action. Many of us are more like the ambivalent Sununu than we imagine: We believe we know what is best for our departments, although we cannot articulate why it is best without at the same time admitting that deep problems of potential injustice (reverse discrimination, for example) haunt our favored guidelines.

Such ambivalence and uncertainty also spill over to another level, generating moral problems of truthfulness in advertising positions.[2] Once it has been determined that "almost certainly" a woman or a minority group member will be hired, departments place advertisements that include lines such as the following (which come at the end of a general, purely academic description of the position):

> Women and minority-group candidates are especially encouraged to apply. The University of X is an equal opportunity, affirmative action employer.

Advertisements rarely if ever contain more information about affirmative action objectives than this, although often more information might be disclosed that would be of material relevance to applicants. The following are examples of facts or objectives that might be disclosed: A department may have reserved its position for a woman or minority; the chances may be overwhelming that only a minority group member will be hired; the interview team may have decided in advance that only women will be interviewed; the advertised position may be the result of a university policy that offers an explicit incentive (perhaps a new position) to a department if a minority representative is appointed; and so on.

In the full complexity of departmental deliberation, the reasoning involved is generally more arcane and the reasons never entirely shared across the group. Perhaps an interview team will have decided to allocate roughly three-quarters of its interview slots for women, contingent on the quality of the applicants. If so, there is a slender possibility that a white male will be hired, but it is remote. Such objectives are now widely adopted, but they are rarely advertised so as to reveal the true recruitment goals. This incompleteness in advertising sometimes stems from fear of legal liability but more often from fear of departmental embarrassment and harm either to reputation or to future recruiting efforts.

The greater moral embarrassment, however, is that we academics fear making public what we believe to be morally commendable and mandatory in our recruiting efforts. There is something deeply wrong in this circumstance, one that virtually every academic department now faces. The situation is reminiscent of the moral embarrassment of assisted suicide in medicine. There is mounting evidence in medical journals and commentary that many forms of assisted suicide have been going on for a long time in medicine, although no practitioner would advertise his or her practice in such terms, and, until recently, medical codes, judicial councils, and the like considered the topic taboo. The policy and practice of physician-assisted suicide is still condemned in every medical code of ethics that mentions the subject and in an abundance of state laws. As a consequence, some physicians routinely refer patients to the Hemlock Society rather than to the care of another physician.

It is an embarrassment to medicine that a practice so widespread is underground—little discussed, never publicly announced, and generally condemned in the profession. In academic appointments our recruitment embarrassment is even more difficult to explain.

Our recruitment practices are rarely condemned, but they are also rarely acknowledged in a public form by even their most enthusiastic adherents. This situation is particularly striking, inasmuch as the justification for this special form of treatment, which makes recruitment far more difficult than it otherwise would be, is precisely that it is a morally praiseworthy endeavor.

I believe these endeavors often are morally praiseworthy. They are honest, open-in-the-department, fair attempts to shape the character of an institution for the better. Among the many problems, however, is that a loss of quality or some form of reverse discrimination does occasionally enter the appointment process. But there is also a need to distinguish between real and apparent reverse discrimination. Sometimes faculty are appointed through affirmative action who appear to be displacing better applicants, but the appearance is itself the result of discriminatory perceptions of the person's qualifications. Apparent reverse discrimination is then nullified by a deeper problem of discrimination. In these cases it would be unreasonable to expect faculty to agree over where to place the actual pattern of discrimination. As with so many problems in the moral life, we can only ask that faculty struggle conscientiously with the real problems.

Notes

1. Bob Woodward, *The Commanders* (New York: Simon and Schuster, 1991), p. 72.
2. On this topic, see Steven M. Cahn, "Colleges Should Be Explicit about Who Will Be Considered for Jobs," *Chronicle of Higher Education*, April 5, 1989, p. B3.

Study Questions

1. What does Beauchamp mean by "reverse discrimination"?
2. In what way does he believe reverse discrimination may enter the appointment process?
3. Why are academics reluctant to state explicitly the role of affirmative action in the appointment process?
4. If a candidate who was chosen in part because of considerations of affirmative action seeks assurance that affirmative action played no role in the selection process, what reply should the candidate receive?

J. Academia

CHAPTER 43

Consensual Sex on Campus

Leslie Pickering Francis

Leslie Pickering Francis is Professor of Philosophy at the University of
Utah. She defends a ban on even consensual faculty-student relationships so long as the student is under the direct supervision of the professor. In her view such relationships distract from teaching, learning, and
research; threaten equality of educational opportunity; and too often
proceed without informed consent.

Joan is a graduate student at a top-tier university in her field. She is
about to take her comprehensives and begin work on a cutting-edge
dissertation. She's highly regarded by the faculty in her department:
their rising star. The department is recruiting a new faculty member
in her field; the top candidate is a man who, the professional gossip goes, just has been unfairly denied tenure at unquestionably the
best department in the country. Joan meets the candidate during the
interviews and they hit it off, both intellectually and socially. Joan
learns that he is in the process of a painful divorce; he is sad because
the tenure denial and move prevent him from remaining as involved
in the lives of his two young children. Joan looks forward eagerly to
his arrival and to her ability to work with him. This story has many
beginnings, but it also has many endings.

Ending One. The candidate arrives on campus and becomes Joan's
dissertation chair. Although it's clear that under other circumstances
they might have become romantically involved, it remains unspoken
between them that this would not be a good idea because of their
professional relationship. Her chair publishes a brilliant book and
becomes the object of much professional attention. When Joan goes

From Leslie Pickering Francis, *Sexual Harassment as an Ethical Issue in Academic Life.*
Copyright © 2001 by Rowman & Littlefield. Reprinted by permission of Rowman &
Littlefield.

on the job market, however, she finds herself fighting the suspicion that she and her chair have been having an affair, which is the reason she is so highly regarded by her department. The suspicions are based on what has by now become professional gossip that her chair's departure from his first institution was clouded by an affair with a student. Joan gets a series of temporary jobs and eventually leaves the field. (Or Joan gets a job at a small school too far away to have heard the professional gossip. Or, Joan gets a job at another research university, at a department willing to ignore the gossip. . . .)

Ending Two. Joan and her professor fall in love and are married within six months after his arrival on campus. At first, they experience domestic bliss; Joan works excitedly on her dissertation, gives department dinner parties, and enjoys her status as [an] almost-peer. Their mutual interest in the field and the particular topics on which they are working give the pair subjects for endless hours of conversation. The professor publishes a brilliant book that makes him famous; although no one else knows this, Joan is the author of at least half the book. One child later, Joan finishes her dissertation and reconsiders her professional future. Her institution does not hire its own graduates, and her husband does not want to move. After three years of teaching on a temporary basis for the university's extension program, Joan goes to law school. (Or Joan takes a job at the community college down the road. Or Joan goes on the job market, receives the job of her dreams, and she and her husband commute between universities one thousand miles apart. Or another top research university in the field offers them both "real" jobs, Joan on [a] tenure track and her husband with tenure, and they live happily ever after. . . .)

Ending Three. Joan and her professor begin a passionate affair. At first it is wonderful. Joan makes great progress on her dissertation. Then the affair goes sour. The professor becomes very critical of Joan's work. It's hard to tell which happened first, the end of the affair or the dissatisfaction with Joan's work. Joan herself begins to lose confidence in her abilities. Joan seeks a replacement as her dissertation chair and finds someone who is interested in the area but not an expert. At first, things improve and Joan believes she is beginning to do good work again. Then the new chair becomes very critical of her work, and Joan suspects it is because of derogatory remarks by Joan's first chair. Joan eventually is told that it is unlikely she will be able to complete a dissertation that meets the standards of her department. (Or after the relationship sours, Joan files a complaint of sexual harassment with the university's office of equal opportunity.

The complaint charges that the relationship had been unwelcome from the beginning, that Joan had felt pressured to enter into it and had been afraid that the professor would refuse to work with her unless she gave into his demands. The complaint is investigated but found to have no merit because the relationship was voluntary, and the EEOC office defers to the judgment of departments about the academic qualifications of their students. Or the complaint is investigated and the story comes out that the reason the professor was not given tenure at his former institution is that he had been notorious for having sex with graduate students. Joan is vindicated, but with a reputation as a troublemaker has great difficulty finding a job in the field. . . .)

These stories are all true enough, based on composites of the lives of people I have known, the backgrounds of many academic marriages, and the sad stories of failed careers and acrimonious litigation. What do they show about sexual relationships between faculty and students from varying moral points of view? . . . Viewpoints here range from the position that Joan and the professor are both adults with rights to enter into relationships of their own choosing, to the position that all faculty-student relationships and many other relationships should be prohibited because of the power imbalance and opportunity for exploitation they embody. . . . I defend the moderate view that sexual relationships within universities should be prohibited when one of the parties has direct supervisory authority over the other and should be strongly discouraged when there are significant power imbalances between the two. . . .

Consensual Relations

. . . [Sexual] assaults, threats, and even offers are wrong because they interfere with choice about important, intimate relationships. A policy that seriously limited consensual sexual relationships on campus also would interfere significantly with the liberty to enter into relationships. How, then, could such a policy be defended in the context of a commitment to autonomy about intimate relationships? Joan and her professor, for example, have the moral and the legal right to their intimate associations. As the policy from Wellesley College—interestingly enough, an undergraduate institution—puts it: "When there is no supervisory relation between students, or between faculty members; or between faculty and staff members, or between staff members—any recommendations by the

College concerning sexual relations would constitute an intolerable invasion of privacy." . . . Privacy and associational liberty are the core of the argument for a permissive policy about sexual relationships on campus, but several other moral considerations also lend support to such a policy.

A corollary of the value of autonomy is opposition to paternalism. The critique of consensual sexual relationships between professionals and those who receive their services typically invokes paternalism, as demonstrated in the following way. The professional has experience and skills not possessed by those seeking his services: patients or clients. He is in a position of trust; they are in a position of reliance and dependency, often exacerbated by the life events—an illness, a divorce—that led them to seek professional services in the first place. The best way to protect vulnerable clients from abusive professionals is a prophylactic ban on sexual relationships, even apparently consensual relationships. This critique is, quite frankly, paternalistic in its assumptions about the recipients of professional services. . . . My fictitious graduate student, Joan, for example, might argue that a ban on professor-student relationships is an insult to her independence; she is perfectly able to make decisions about her personal relationships without any help from authoritarian protectionism. She might add that to the extent that such bans are seen as protecting her from her professors, rather than her professors from her, they are particularly demeaning to her.

A further, related concern about any bans on consensual relationships on campus is that they affect women unequally. . . . If faculty demographics are largely male and graduate-student populations increasingly female, bans may preclude women students from a particularly desirable source of satisfying relationships. Or they may force women already in relationships to choose schooling at a different institution or in a different field. At the very least, a ban on consensual relationships between faculty and the students they supervise would force Joan to a hard choice: either seeking a new, possibly less intellectually appropriate advisor or sacrificing the relationship.

These considerations make the case for a permissive policy a very powerful one. It is supported by respect for the autonomy and the equality of women in the academic community. Why, then, have the calls for bans on consensual relationships, in the academy and in other professional relationships, been so persistent and so increasingly accepted? Are any of the arguments powerful enough to override the case for permissiveness? . . .

The first problem of consensual sexual relationships is distraction from teaching, learning, and research. Such distraction may affect the parties to the relationship and those who observe it. . . .

These educational effects of romantic relationships also are exacerbated when one of the parties is the centerpiece of the setting: the senior professor in a laboratory or the instructor in a class. Even apart from the conflicts of interest and power imbalances discussed later, romantic interest on the part of a professor might take his or her own mind away from instruction. The student who is the object of affection might find it more difficult to concentrate. Other students also might be distracted if the relationship is in any way obvious or even known. It is more likely that educational quality would suffer in a small discussion section, a seminar, or a smaller research setting than it would in a large lecture. Both small and large settings might be negatively affected when one of the participants occupies a privileged position vis-à-vis the instructor. Behavior that overtly indicates a sexual relationship in an instructional or research setting is problematic because it interferes with core functions of the academy, the development and transmission of knowledge. Overt expression of a sexual relationship in class is inappropriate and should be regulated by the university in the same way that the university should restrict sexualization as a form of gender harassment.

Another difficulty with consensual sexual relations on campus is that a romantic relationship can create a conflict of interest that impairs the quality of professional services. At universities the most likely conflict is with evaluative functions: grading, awarding fellowships or scholarships, or making decisions about tenure or promotion. In other professions, the case for prohibition rests centrally on the nexus between the delivery of the professional services and the sex. Psychiatrists cannot treat their lovers. Dermatologists can, maybe, if the professional relationship is short-lived and does not involve confidences that could be exploited. Divorce lawyers should not become romantically involved with their clients during the divorce proceedings: Romantic involvement gives the lawyer a personal stake in the outcome and may compromise the client's position as well.[1] In education, it seems that there is a nexus between evaluation and affection. The teacher who is also a lover will both want his beloved to do well and be obligated to judge work impartially. He may find it very difficult to demand excellence from his lover—or, bending over backward trying to be fair, he may judge his lover too harshly. In either case, other students may reasonably fear that evaluations of their work are compromised by the professorial confusion. . . .

Ironically, the impact of such conflicts of interest is probably the worst at the highest academic levels, where relationships are likely to occur; arguably taking an introductory logic class with machine-graded exams is more like filing routine legal documents or taking off a wart than like psychiatry. Such tasks are more mechanical, and so the difficulties raised by a mixture of personal and professional involvement might be less severe. One of the features of academic life, particularly at the graduate-student level and beyond, however, is the mixture of the personal and the professional. Small departments or laboratories become the centers of social lives. Although, there certainly are advantages to this mixture, the conflicts of interest generated where there are direct supervisory relationships seem highly likely to impair the quality of the professional judgments rendered in important academic matters.

In sum, educational quality can be impaired in several ways by consensual relationships. First, if the relationships are overt enough to be distracting, quality may suffer. . . . Second, if the relationships create conflicts of interest because of the supervisory or evaluative responsibilities of one of the parties, the relationship has the potential to impair the quality of the resulting judgments that affect all students. In either case, the knowledge functions of the academy are impaired. . . .

Impaired Consent

A third issue about consensual relationships on campus is the genuineness of the consent. Many writers argue that either the characteristics of one of the parties to the relationship (a gullible student) or the structure of the relationship (a powerful professor importuning a powerless student) mean that even a clear "yes" is not what it seems. This argument is most likely to be made about faculty-student sex, but it might also be made about other relationships in which there is an imbalance of power. Arguing that such a "yes" does not mean "yes" requires an account of what makes consent genuine. Medical ethics literature contains significant discussion of the nature of genuinely informed consent. There are important analogies between the physician-patient relationship and the professor-student relationship for purposes of analyzing problems with consent: the potential vulnerability of the student or patient, the power structure of the relationship, and even possibly the major life-significance of the choice at issue. The medical analogy therefore, is an appropriate framework for analyzing consent in romantic relationships on campus. . . .

For consent to be informed, the patient's level of understanding must be such that she can give an account of the options available to her and what their likely consequences would be. A student considering entering a romantic relationship, by analogy, would need to know what her choices are (enter the relationship, do not enter the relationship, or possibly delay entering the relationship). She also would need to understand what the likely consequences are of each of these options: Is the professor married? Is the relationship likely to be a fling or a long-term affair? How will she feel if the relationship ends despite her wishes to continue it? Because it involves difficult-to-predict factors—how will the relationship develop? how will she feel if things go badly from her perspective? what will be the effects on her education?—levels of understanding are likely to be limited, especially for students who have not had previous serious romantic relationships. . . .

Another set of problematic factors in medicine is the coercive aspects of the patient's situation. The overwhelming nature of illness can make patients particularly vulnerable and is a reason for caution in making important decisions. Students too may feel overwhelmed by the life-decisions they face about fields of study, jobs, or careers. Another aspect of patient vulnerability is being torn from familiar surroundings and familiar systems of support; patients in hospitals or nursing homes may suffer particularly from the effects of dislocation. Students also may be dislocated; an undergraduate, living away from home for the first time, faces new responsibilities and decisions without familiar landmarks. The comparative powerlessness of patients in medical institutions is another noteworthy concern; feminist bioethics writers point out the disparities in information, understanding, and dependency that affect a patient's medical decision making.[2] Although they are not physically dependent in the way patients are, students are powerless vis-à-vis faculty in some ways analogous to the powerlessness of patients vis-à-vis physicians. There are imbalances in information between students and faculty. Faculty can manipulate information, for example, about the nature or importance of courses or fields of study. Faculty who have the power to evaluate students literally can make or break careers. Although colleges are not institutions in the same way hospitals are,[3] they may feel like them sometimes; particularly at small, residential campuses, students' lives may be spent in a confined setting for long periods. There even may be analogies between economic coercion in medicine and in education. Medical expenses may be more catastrophic, less predictable, and less voluntary than educational expenses, but educational expenses in today's world are comparatively huge. A student who fears that continued scholarship support or job recommendations are dependent on the good opinion of faculty may feel just as vulnerable as a patient who faces major medical expenses. . . .

Conclusion

Consensual relationships on campus should be permitted when they do not threaten the educational or opportunity mission of the campus. However . . . where a student is under the direct supervision of a faculty member . . . consensual relationships should be prohibited. This would mean the prohibition of consensual relationships while a student is in the faculty member's class; while the faculty member has responsibility for the student in an extramural program (such as a study-abroad program); and while the faculty member serves on a supervisory committee, awards committee, or as a program director.

Some of these prohibitions will be relatively short-lived and hence minimally burdensome on relationships; quarters or semesters do end eventually. Others, such as Ph.D. supervision, are typically lengthy and may place significant burdens on relationships. Others, even though short-lived, may be unavoidable, as when a spouse in a program needs to take a required course taught by her spouse. Because of these burdens, universities should strive to help the people in the relationship make alternative arrangements so that one party is not supervising the other, such as appointing a new committee for a graduate student, reassigning evaluative functions, or even granting a special exception for a student to take a required course pass-fail if there is simply no other choice.

The university should also prohibit such relationships in other types of campus sexual relationships, involving those in supervisory positions over their partners. Faculty should not be able to vote on the tenure or promotion of those with whom they are romantically involved. Nor should employment supervisors be involved with those whose work they directly evaluate. These prohibitions are typically in force in nonacademic employment relationships, because of the potential for unfairness. As with faculty-student relationships, universities should strive to arrange alternatives in these cases; tenure decisions can be made in the absence of the department member with a conflict, and workplace lines of evaluation can sometimes be reconfigured.

Finally, other consensual relationships on campus should be permitted. Personal relationships are important, and such relationships do not threaten the educational or the opportunity mission of the academy. Caution is appropriate, particularly where there are imbalances in power, as with a faculty member and an undergraduate not in the faculty member's class or a student whom the faculty member mentors. When there are such imbalances, there may be reason for concern about the quality of the consent, and relationships that are not genuinely consensual are impermissible harassment on this basis. Those in the more powerful positions who are able to recognize these risks should enter into such relationships with particular caution.

Notes

1. Several state bar associations prohibit any sexual relationships between a lawyer and a client that did not predate the lawyer-client relationship; see Minnesota Rule 1.8(k), Oregon DR 5–110, West Virginia Rule 1.8(g), Wisconsin Rule 1.8(k). Florida establishes a rebuttable presumption that sexual relationships with a client are exploitative and subject the lawyer to discipline. Florida Rule 4–8.4(1). California, the first state to address sexual relationships between lawyers and clients, prohibits coercive relationships or relationships that compromise the quality of legal services. California Rule 3–120.

2. See, for example, Susan Sherwin, *No Longer Patient: Feminist Ethics and Health Care.* Philadelphia: Temple University Press, 1992.

3. For a discussion of the concept of a total institution, see Erving Goffman, *Asylums: Essays on the Social Situation of Mental Patients and Other Inmates.* Garden City, NY: Anchor Books, 1961.

Study Questions

1. Can you imagine a fourth ending to the story of Joan that is more plausible than the three that are given?
2. Does the physician-patient relationship offer a useful analogy to the professor-student relationship?
3. Is a prohibition on consensual relationships between a professor and a student in the professor's class significantly different from a prohibition on consensual relationships between a judge and a party to a case the judge is deciding?
4. If, as Francis says, a faculty member should be cautious in having a relationship with a student not in the professor's class, what steps would constitute sufficient caution?

CHAPTER 44

The Letter Writer's Dilemma

George Sher

George Sher is Professor of Philosophy at Rice University. He considers the moral dilemma faced by a professor who is asked to write a letter of recommendation for a less than stellar student. Sher suggests how to compose a letter that avoids a candid assessment, while not asserting falsehoods. His essay also displays how humor can play a role in considering a serious moral problem.

At one point he uses the term "moral luck," referring to the situation in which assessing a person's action depends on factors beyond the agent's control. For instance, judging a driver who fails to check car brakes is affected by whether an accident occurs.

Mr. Adam Pendicks has asked me to write in support of his application to your institution, and I am obliged to do so. Adam is a sixth-year graduate student in philosophy here at Ragland University, where he has compiled a satisfactory though undistinguished record. Overall, I would place him in the third quartile of the students in our program.

Adam is currently writing a dissertation under my supervision on a variation of a possible objection to a potential difficulty with a defense of the killing/letting-die distinction that two philosophers, Benson Hedges and the late Arve Suissinnen, once deployed, the former in the middle 1960s and the latter in the early 80s. Although the Suissinnen-Hedges line has not achieved wide currency—no one, to my knowledge, has actually said anything about it—a careful refutation of the variant of the possible objection to the potential

From George Sher, "Global Norming: An Inconvenient Truth," in Robert B. Talisse and Maureen Eckert, eds., *A Teacher's Life: Essays for Steven M. Cahn*. Copyright © 2009 by Lexington Books. Reprinted by permission of Rowman & Littlefield and with minor changes by the author.

difficulty that Adam discusses would nevertheless be an incremental addition to our understanding of the topic. Although Adam has now completed drafts of five of his seven chapters, the dissertation won't be in any shape to defend by this coming September, and I'm not sure about the following September either. There is, however, a probability greater than zero that some of it will eventually be published.

Adam is sometimes helpful in discussions. I rarely have to explain things to him more than twice, and when he manages to avoid irrelevancy, his points can be helpful targets for others. I think of him more as a student than a colleague.

Adam's social skills, like those of many in our profession, leave something to be desired. He is, however, a well-meaning person whose inappropriate laughter and other gaffes are rarely held against him. For the most part, he fulfills his duties adequately. Any department that hires him will gain a faculty member who will meet with his classes. I recommend him with all the enthusiasm his candidacy deserves.

The department in which I teach has just been conducting a job search, so I have just finished reading about 150 sets of letters of recommendation, not one of which is anything like this letter for Adam Pendicks. Over the years, I have read many other letters, and have written many myself, and not one of them was anything like this letter either. Yet many graduate students do of course rank in the third quartile—a full quarter do—and not a few are socially maladroit, derivative in their thinking, and/or at best indifferently dependable. Since most faculty members are at least decent people, and since a good number are admirable human beings, their routine willingness to omit some facts and to stretch others beyond the breaking point can hardly be attributed to a simple lack of veracity. Its source, rather, is a tension, often severe, between two different and equally legitimate moral demands, one the duty to tell the truth and the other the obligation to do one's best to get jobs for one's students. The basic difficulty is that it is logically impossible both to tell the full truth and to write a letter that will get a student a job that he would not get if the full truth were told.

Although this is hardly a tragic choice, I do think it is a genuine moral dilemma. I think, that is, that those who must write on behalf of their students are sometimes in a position in which anything they do will be at least somewhat wrong. When a faculty member's being in this position is not due to any prior wrongdoing or negligence on his part, it is a case of bad moral luck.

There are of course some who believe neither in moral dilemmas nor in moral luck. To these optimistic souls, keeping your nose clean means never having to say you're sorry. Applied to the case at hand, what their position comes to is either that (1) anyone who now must either violate his duty of veracity or fail to fulfill his obligation to a student must previously have created the problem by doing something he shouldn't or that (2) our obligations to our students never require that we distort the truth or omit important facts, or that (3) we owe our students plenty of distorting and omitting, but doing these things in letters of recommendation is not wrong. To bring out the full scope of the letter-writer's plight, and also to score some general points against the optimistic dilemma-denier, I now want to argue against each claim.

Consider first the proposal that whenever everything a recommender can do would be wrong, he must have put himself in this position through some previous moral lapse. This proposal concedes that letters of recommendations may confront us with genuine dilemmas, but denies that these are ever unavoidable. But where, exactly, has Adam's adviser gone wrong?

There are a number of possible places, some further in the past than others. Early on, the adviser may have fallen short by entering a profession that generates obligations that regularly conflict with the duty of veracity. More recently, he may have erred by accepting employment at an institution whose students are not strong enough to win every competition on their merits. Still more recently, he may have gone wrong by agreeing to supervise a weak student or by subsequently agreeing to write on that student's behalf. But none of this is at all plausible. Locating the wrong act at the point where the adviser entered academic life is silly because the academy is at least no more morally tainted than any other institution and is probably less tainted than most. Criticizing him for joining an institution that enrolls students whose prospects will be harmed by truthful letters is unreasonable both because every graduate program has such students and because jobs at the places with the fewest such students are beyond the reach of most job-seekers. Identifying his moral lapse with his agreement to take on a weak student is objectionable both because we often cannot tell how our advisees will pan out and because anyone who avoids weak students to keep his hands clean merely shifts the moral burden to his colleagues. And, finally, to say that the adviser should not have agreed to write on behalf of his weak student is merely to relocate the dilemma, for anyone who takes on an advisee has already undertaken a de facto commitment to write on that student's behalf.

Given all this, those who claim that letters of recommendation never confront us with moral dilemmas may retreat to their second option. They may argue not that any apparent dilemmas can be traced to earlier moral lapses, but rather that we are never obligated to distort or omit important truths to further our students' prospects for employment. But how, exactly, is this last claim to be defended in its turn? The argument can hardly be that we can't be obligated to distort the truth because distorting the truth is wrong, since whether distorting the truth in this context is wrong is just what is at issue. Moreover, although it sounds good to say that Adam's adviser did the right thing by telling the full truth, it doesn't sound quite as good to say that he did the right thing by writing a letter that he knew full well would doom Adam's chances for employment. This last claim would certainly be hard for Adam to swallow ("with supporters like that . . . "), and given that none of us actually writes such letters despite the students' near universal willingness to waive access, the rest of us evidently find it hard to swallow too. There is, to be sure, the occasional maverick who prefaces his recommendations with the disclaimer that unlike his weak and compromised colleagues, he intends to write only the plain and unvarnished truth and hopes his students will not be harmed by his stubborn integrity. However, remarkably, the students on behalf of whom such letters are written turn out to be just as uniformly superior as all the others.

Given all this, those who deny that letters of recommendation confront us with dilemmas may find it advisable to retreat once more. Instead of maintaining either that anyone who has only wrong options has only himself to blame or that our obligations to our students never require that we distort or omit important truths, he may take the position that we often *are* required to distort or omit but that doing so in letters of recommendation is not wrong. Of all the strategies for denying that recommendations confront us with genuine dilemmas, this is the one that seems the most promising. One obvious thing that can be said for it is that even when the currency is very inflated, some letters remain clearly stronger than others, and so real distinctions can still be made. A different but related point is that the need to convey real information has led to the development of a kind of code which any veteran letter-reader can decipher. Taken together, these facts suggest that instead of distorting or omitting important truths, hyperbolic letters may convey accurate information non-literally. Because there's nothing wrong with expressing oneself non-literally as long as the message is clear, we may after all seem capable of fulfilling all our obligations without violating our duty to be honest.

But I don't think we can get off the hook quite this easily; for precisely because we know that our inflated letters will automatically be downgraded, we also know that keeping our students competitive means inflating our letters further to withstand the inevitable downgrading. If "he is among the finest minds of his generation" will be translated as "he is competitive with some of the better students at very good institutions," then we cannot set him apart from the competition without touting his virtues in even more effusive terms ("the very finest mind," "many a generation"). Instead of having to abuse the truth in plain language, we now have to abuse it in recommendationese, but nothing else has changed. As I have said, the basic problem is that it is logically impossible both to tell the full truth and to write a letter that will get a student a job that he would not get if the full truth were told.

So what's a professor to do? In a word, what we all do: compromise. To serve both masters, we must make concessions to each. To do what we can for our weaker students, we can try to write letters that will not disqualify them outright and that may be overlooked if their other letters come in stronger, while to preserve at least a tenuous connection to the truth, we can avoid saying things that are flatly false while playing up every scrap of positive information that is even marginally relevant. Like democracy, it's the worst way of doing things except for all the others.

Over the years, I have witnessed many impressive efforts to airbrush students whose prospects would be damaged by a candid assessment, and in the spirit of professional solidarity, I want to share some of what I've learned. To keep a weak student in the game, a letter-writer can do any or all of the following. First, he can discuss at great length the interest and importance of the problem to which his student is proposing an uninteresting and unimportant answer. Second, he can magnify the student's accomplishments by defining his specialty narrowly enough to guarantee that he will be one of the best at it. Third, he can finesse the all-important question of how this student stacks up against others by comparing him to weaker past students of whom few readers will have heard. Fourth, he can make the student sound good by saying positive things that somehow sound like they're job-related but really aren't. Finally, he can bring his letter to a satisfying conclusion by ending with a resounding but meaningless expression of support. When these techniques are used together, and when they're backed by strategic omissions as required, they are virtually certain to locate any letter squarely in the no-man's land between truth and falsity.

Let me end with an example. I began with a letter that gave Adam Pendicks no chance of being hired. Here, by contrast is one that gives him a fighting chance.

> Mr. Adam Pendicks has asked me to write in support of his applica-tion to your institution, and I am delighted to do so. Adam is a sixth-year graduate student in philosophy here at Ragland University, where he is working on the later stages of a dissertation on the moral importance of the act/omission distinction. This distinction occupies a strategic position in both theoretical and applied ethics. Within the theoretical realm, the distinction raises fascinating questions about the scope and nature of moral responsibility, and disagreements about its importance can be seen to underlie many of the disputes between consequential-ists and their opponents. On a more applied level, some version of the distinction informs many common beliefs about end-of-life decisions, famine relief, and other topics of pressing practical importance. Given all this, it is obviously crucial to gain a clearer understanding of the distinction, and that is precisely what Mr. Pendicks's project is intended to yield. He is already one of the world's two leading experts on the line of inquiry that he is pursuing, and he will in due time be recognized as the single leading expert.
>
> To convey a sense of the regard in which Adam is held here, it may be helpful to compare him to some of our other recent graduates. As far as I can judge, the consensus in our department is that Adam is somewhat better than Waxie Links, formerly of the Friendship Institute and now at Fulham A&M, that he's probably also better than Bibi Freund, who recently received a tenure-track appointment at Land O' Lakes University, but that he ranks just a touch below Lance Puller of Snake State. Adam is an enthusiastic contributor to the life of our close-knit community whose infectious laugh will be greatly missed when he leaves. I am pleased to recommend him warmly.

Isn't that better?

Study Questions

1. If a professor sends a letter of recommendation that omits important information, has the professor acted ethically?
2. If Sher's revised letter leads the members of a department to appoint the candidate he recommends, but those members subsequently are disappointed with the candidate's performance, should they blame themselves entirely or, instead, should they hold Sher partly responsible?
3. Would it be inappropriate for a professor to include in a letter of recommendation the following truthful remark: "This candidate is not among the best students I have taught, nor among the worst"?
4. Would it be useless for a professor to send an honest reference letter that began: "This is a candid recommendation. As such, it necessarily contains criticism as well as praise. Please read it in the spirit in which it is written"?

K. Life and Death

CHAPTER 45

The Trolley Problem

Judith Jarvis Thomson

A hypothetical moral puzzle that has attracted much attention from contemporary ethical theorists is known as "the trolley problem." Here it is explained by Judith Jarvis Thomson, whose work we read previously.

Some years ago Philippa Foot drew attention to an extraordinarily interesting problem.[1] Suppose you are the driver of a trolley. The trolley rounds a bend, and there come into view ahead five track workmen, who have been repairing the track. The track goes through a bit of a valley at that point, and the sides are steep, so you must stop the trolley if you are to avoid running the five men down. You step on the brakes, but alas they don't work. Now you suddenly see a spur of track leading off to the right. You can turn the trolley onto it, and thus save the five men on the straight track ahead. Unfortunately, Mrs. Foot has arranged that there is one track workman on that spur of track. He can no more get off the track in time than the five can, so you will kill him if you turn the trolley onto him. Is it morally permissible for you to turn the trolley?

Everybody to whom I have put this hypothetical case says, Yes, it is. Some people say something stronger than that it is morally *permissible* for you to turn the trolley: They say that morally speaking, you must turn it—that morality requires you to do so. Others do not agree that morality requires you to turn the trolley, and even feel a certain discomfort at the idea of turning it. But everybody says that it is true, at a minimum, that you *may* turn it—that it would not be morally wrong for you to do so.

From *The Yale Law Journal*, 94 (1985) by permission of *The Yale Law Journal* and William S. Hein Company.

Now consider a second hypothetical case. This time you are to imagine yourself to be a surgeon, a truly great surgeon. Among other things you do, you transplant organs, and you are such a great surgeon that the organs you transplant always take. At the moment you have five patients who need organs. Two need one lung each, two need a kidney each, and the fifth needs a heart. If they do not get those organs today, they will all die; if you find organs for them today, you can transplant the organs and they will all live. But where to find the lungs, the kidneys, and the heart? The time is almost up when a report is brought to you that a young man who has just come into your clinic for his yearly check-up has exactly the right blood-type, and is in excellent health. Lo, you have a possible donor. All you need do is cut him up and distribute *his* parts among the five who need them. You ask, but he says, "Sorry. I deeply sympathize, but no." Would it be morally permissible for you to operate anyway? Everybody to whom I have put this second hypothetical case says, No, it would not be morally permissible for you to proceed.

Here then is Mrs. Foot's problem: *Why* is it that the trolley driver may turn his trolley, though the surgeon may not remove the young man's lungs, kidneys, and heart? In both cases, one will die if the agent acts, but five will live who would otherwise die—a net saving of four lives. What difference in the other facts of these cases explains the moral difference between them? I fancy that the theorists of tort and criminal law will find this problem as interesting as the moral theorist does.

Note

1. See Philippa Foot, "The Problem of Abortion and the Doctrine of the Double Effect," in *Virtues and Vices, and Other Essays in Moral Philosophy* (Berkeley and Los Angeles: University of California Press, 1978), p. 19.

Study Questions

1. Can you imagine another hypothetical case akin to that of the trolley?
2. How do you believe the trolley case differs from that of the surgeon?
3. Do you believe that turning the trolley is morally permissible?
4. Do you believe that not turning the trolley is morally permissible?

CHAPTER 46

Turning the Trolley

Judith Jarvis Thomson

More than two decades after publishing a lengthy discussion of the trolley problem from which the previous selection was excerpted, Judith Jarvis Thomson returned to the problem. Influenced by the work of a doctoral student, she offered a surprising solution that casts doubt on a widely accepted assumption critical to the case.

I

In an article provoked by Foot's, I suggested that we should take our eyes off the driver; we should eliminate him. (Make him have dropped dead of a heart attack.) Then let us imagine the situation to be as in the case I will call Bystander's Two Options. A bystander happens to be standing by the track, next to a switch that can be used to turn the tram off the straight track, on which five men are working, onto a spur of track to the right on which only one man is working. The bystander therefore has only two options:

> Bystander's Two Options: he can
> (i) do nothing, letting five die, or
> (ii) throw the switch to the right, killing one.

Most people say that he may choose option (ii). . . .

II

A few years ago, an MIT graduate student, Alexander Friedman, devoted a chapter of his thesis to a discussion of the most interesting

From Judith Jarvis Thomson, "Turning the Trolley," *Philosophy & Public Affairs* 36 (2008). Reprinted by permission of John Wiley & Sons. The principles are renumbered.

solutions to the trolley problem on offer in the literature.[1] He did a very good job: he showed clearly that none of them worked. What was especially interesting, though, was what he concluded. He said: the reason why no adequate solution has been found is that something went wrong at the outset. He said: it just isn't true that the bystander may choose option (ii) in Bystander's Two Options. . . .

Friedman therefore said that we should see the (so-called) trolley problem "for what it really is—a very intriguing, provocative, and eye-opening non-problem."

Well, there's an unsettling idea! But if you mull over Friedman's unsettling idea for a while, then perhaps it can come to seem worth taking very seriously. So let us mull over it.

III

Here is a case that I will call Bystander's Three Options. The switch available to this bystander can be thrown in two ways. If he throws it to the right, then the trolley will turn onto the spur of track to the right, thereby killing one workman. If he throws it to the left, then the trolley will turn onto the spur of track to the left. The bystander himself stands on that left-hand spur of track, and will himself be killed if the trolley turns onto it. Or, of course, he can do nothing, letting five workmen die. In sum,

> Bystander's Three Options: he can
>   (i)   do nothing, letting five die, or
>   (ii) throw the switch to the right, killing one, or
>   (iii) throw the switch to the left, killing himself.

What is your reaction to the bystander's having the following thought? "Hmm. I want to save those five workmen. I can do that by choosing option (iii), that is by throwing the switch to the left, saving the five but killing myself. I'd prefer not dying today, however, even for the sake of saving five. So I'll choose option (ii), saving the five but killing the one on the right-hand track instead."

I hope you will agree that choosing (ii) would be unacceptable on the bystander's part. If he *can* throw the switch to the left and turn the trolley onto himself, how dare he throw the switch to the right and turn the trolley onto the one workman? The bystander doesn't feel like dying today, even for the sake of saving five, but we can assume, and so let us assume, that the one workman also doesn't feel like dying today, even if the bystander would thereby save five.

Let us get a little clearer about why this bystander must not choose option (ii). He wants to save the five on the straight track ahead. That would be good for them, and his saving them would be a good deed on his part. But his doing that good deed would have a cost: his life or the life of the one workman on the right-hand track. What the bystander does if he turns the trolley onto the one workman is to make the one workman pay the cost of his good deed because he doesn't feel like paying it himself.

Compare the following possibility. I am asked for a donation to Oxfam. I want to send them some money. I am able to send money of my own, but I don't feel like it. So I steal some from someone else and send *that* money to Oxfam. That is pretty bad. But if the bystander proceeds to turn the trolley onto the one on the right-hand track in Bystander's Three Options, then what he does is markedly worse, because the cost in Bystander's Three Options isn't money, it is life.

In sum, if A wants to do a certain good deed, and can pay what doing it would cost, then—other things being equal—A may do that good deed only if A pays the cost himself. In particular, here is a . . . *ceteris paribus* [other things being equal] principle:

> *First Principle:* A must not kill B to save five if he can instead kill himself to save the five.

So the bystander in Bystander's Three Options must not kill the one workman on the right-hand track in furtherance of his good deed of saving the five since he can instead save the five by killing himself. Thus he must not choose option (ii).

On the other hand, morality doesn't require him to choose option (iii). If A wants to do a certain good deed, and discovers that the only permissible means he has of doing the good deed is killing himself, then he may refrain from doing the good deed. In particular, here is a second *ceteris paribus* principle:

> *Second Principle:* A may let five die if the only permissible means he has of saving them is killing himself.

So the bystander in Bystander's Three Options may choose option (i).

Let us now return to Bystander's Two Options. We may imagine that the bystander in this case can see the trolley headed for the five workmen, and wants to save them. He thinks: "Does this switch allow for me to choose option (iii), in which I turn the trolley onto myself? If it does, then I must not choose option (ii), in which I turn the trolley onto the one workman on the right-hand track, for as the *First Principle* says, I must prefer killing myself to killing him. But I don't want to kill myself, and if truth be told, I wouldn't if I could. So if the switch does allow for me to choose option (iii), then I have to forgo my good deed of saving the five: I have to choose option (i)—thus I have to let the five die. As, of course, the *Second Principle* says I may."

As you can imagine, he therefore examines the switch *very* carefully. Lo, he discovers that the switch doesn't allow him to choose option (iii). "What luck," he thinks, "I can't turn the trolley onto myself. So it's perfectly all right for me to choose option (ii)!" His thought is that since he can't himself pay the cost of his good deed, it is perfectly all right for him to make the workman on the right-hand track pay it—despite the fact that he wouldn't himself pay it if he could.

I put it to you that that thought won't do. Since he wouldn't himself pay the cost of his good deed if he could pay it, there is no way in which he can decently regard himself as entitled to make someone else pay it.

Of how many of us is it true that if we could permissibly save five only by killing ourselves, then we would? Doing so would be altruism, for as the *Second Principle* says, nobody is required to do so, and doing so would therefore be altruism; moreover, doing so would be doing something for others at a major cost to oneself, and doing so would therefore be major altruism. Very few of us would. Then very few of us could decently regard ourselves as entitled to choose option (ii) if we were in the bystander's situation in Bystander's Two Options.

Note

1. A. W. Friedman. *Minimizing Harm: Three Problems in Moral Theory.* Unpublished doctoral dissertation, Department of Linguistics and Philosophy, Massachusetts Institute of Technology (2002).

Study Questions

1. Do you believe Bystander's turning the trolley is morally acceptable?
2. Do you believe Bystander's not turning the trolley is morally acceptable?
3. Is your judgment affected by which role in the story you imagine yourself playing?
4. Would your judgment be different if turning the trolley saved the lives of many more people?

CHAPTER 47

Death

Thomas Nagel

Is death an evil? If so, why? These profound questions are explored here by Thomas Nagel, whose work we read previously.

If death is the unequivocal and permanent end of our existence, the question arises whether it is a bad thing to die.

There is conspicuous disagreement about the matter: some people think death is dreadful; others have no objection to death *per se*, though they hope their own will be neither premature nor painful. Those in the former category tend to think those in the latter are blind to the obvious, while the latter suppose the former to be prey to some sort of confusion. On the one hand it can be said that life is all we have and the loss of it is the greatest loss we can sustain. On the other hand it may be objected that death deprives this supposed loss of its subject, and that if we realize that death is not an unimaginable condition of the persisting person, but a mere blank, we will see that it can have no value whatever, positive or negative.

Since I want to leave aside the question whether we are, or might be, immortal in some form, I shall simply use the word "death" and its cognates in this discussion to mean *permanent* death, unsupplemented by any form of conscious survival. I want to ask whether death is in itself an evil; and how great an evil, and of what kind, it might be. The question should be of interest even to those who believe in some form of immortality, for one's attitude toward immortality must depend in part on one's attitude toward death.

If death is an evil at all, it cannot be because of its positive features, but only because of what it deprives us of. I shall try to deal with the difficulties surrounding the natural view that death is an evil because it brings to an end all the goods that life contains. We need not give an account of these goods here, except to observe that some of them, like perception, desire, activity, and thought, are so general as to be constitutive of human life. They are widely regarded as formidable benefits in themselves, despite the fact that they are conditions of misery as well as of happiness, and that a sufficient quantity of more particular evils can perhaps outweigh them. That is what is meant, I think, by the allegation that it is good simply to be alive, even if one is undergoing terrible experiences. The situation is roughly this: There are elements which, if added to one's experience, make life better; there are other elements which, if added to one's experience, make life worse. But what remains when these are set aside is not merely *neutral*: it is emphatically positive. Therefore life is worth living even when the bad elements of experience are plentiful, and the good ones too meager to outweigh the bad ones on their own. The additional positive weight is supplied by experience itself, rather than by any of its contents.

I shall not discuss the value that one person's life or death may have for others, or its objective value, but only the value it has for the person who is its subject. That seems to me the primary case, and the case which presents the greatest difficulties. Let me add only two observations. First, the value of life and its contents does not attach to mere organic survival: almost everyone would be indifferent (other things equal) between immediate death and immediate coma followed by death twenty years later without reawakening. And second, like most goods, this can be multiplied by time: more is better than less. The added quantities need not be temporally continuous (though continuity has its social advantages). People are attracted to the possibility of long-term suspended animation or freezing, followed by the resumption of conscious life, because they can regard it from within simply as a *continuation* of their present life. If these techniques are ever perfected, what from outside appeared as a dormant interval of three hundred years could be experienced by the subject as nothing more than a sharp discontinuity in the character of his experiences. I do not deny, of course, that this has its own disadvantages. Family and friends may have died in the meantime; the language may have changed; the comforts of social, geographical, and cultural familiarity would be lacking. Nevertheless these inconveniences would not obliterate the basic advantage of continued, though discontinuous, existence.

If we turn from what is good about life to what is bad about death, the case is completely different. Essentially, though there may be problems about their specification, what we find desirable in life are certain states, conditions, or types of activity. It is *being* alive, *doing* certain things, having certain experiences, that we consider good. But if death is an evil, it is the *loss of life*, rather than the state of being dead, or nonexistent, or unconscious, that is objectionable.[1] This asymmetry is important. If it is good to be alive, that advantage can be attributed to a person at each point of his life. It is a good of which Bach had more than Schubert, simply because he lived longer. Death, however, is not an evil of which Shakespeare has so far received a larger portion than Proust. If death is a disadvantage, it is not easy to say when a man suffers it.

There are two other indications that we do not object to death merely because it involves long periods of nonexistence. First, as has been mentioned, most of us would not regard the *temporary* suspension of life, even for substantial intervals, as in itself a misfortune. If it ever happens that people can be frozen without reduction of the conscious lifespan, it will be inappropriate to pity those who are temporarily out of circulation. Second, none of us existed before we were born (or conceived), but few regard that as a misfortune. I shall have more to say about this later.

The point that death is not regarded as an unfortunate *state* enables us to refute a curious but very common suggestion about the origin of the fear of death. It is often said that those who object to death have made the mistake of trying to imagine what it is like to *be* dead. It is alleged that the failure to realize that this task is logically impossible (for the banal reason that there is nothing to imagine) leads to the conviction that death is a mysterious and therefore terrifying prospective *state*. But this diagnosis is evidently false, for it is just as impossible to imagine being totally unconscious as to imagine being dead (though it is easy enough to imagine oneself, from the outside, in either of those conditions). Yet people who are averse to death are not usually averse to unconsciousness (so long as it does not entail a substantial cut in the total duration of waking life).

If we are to make sense of the view that to die is bad, it must be on the ground that life is a good and death is the corresponding deprivation or loss, bad not because of any positive features but because of the desirability of what it removes. We must now turn to the serious difficulties which this hypothesis raises, difficulties about loss and privation in general, and about death in particular.

Essentially, there are three types of problem. First, doubt may be raised whether *anything* can be bad for a man without being positively unpleasant to him: specifically, it may be doubted that there are any evils which consist merely in the deprivation or absence of possible goods, and which do not depend on someone's *minding* that deprivation. Second, there are special difficulties, in the case of death, about how the supposed misfortune is to be assigned to a subject at all. There is doubt both as to *who* its subject is, and as to *when* he undergoes it. So long as a person exists, he has not yet died, and once he has died, he no longer exists; so there seems to be no time when death, if it is a misfortune, can be ascribed to its unfortunate subject. The third type of difficulty concerns the asymmetry, mentioned above, between our attitudes to posthumous and prenatal nonexistence. How can the former be bad if the latter is not?

It should be recognized that if these are valid objections to counting death as an evil, they will apply to many other supposed evils as well. The first type of objection is expressed in general form by the common remark that what you don't know can't hurt you. It means that even if a man is betrayed by his friends, ridiculed behind his back, and despised by people who treat him politely to his face, none of it can be counted as a misfortune for him so long as he does not suffer as a result. It means that a man is not injured if his wishes are ignored by the executor of his will, or if, after his death, the belief becomes current that all the literary works on which his fame rests were really written by his brother, who died in Mexico at the age of 28. It seems to me worth asking what assumptions about good and evil lead to these drastic restrictions.

All the questions have something to do with time. There certainly are goods and evils of a simple kind (including some pleasures and pains) which a person possesses at a given time simply in virtue of his condition at that time. But this is not true of all the things we regard as good or bad for a man. Often we need to know his history to tell whether something is a misfortune or not; this applies to ills like deterioration, deprivation, and damage. Sometimes his experiential *state* is relatively unimportant—as in the case of a man who wastes his life in the cheerful pursuit of a method of communicating with asparagus plants. Someone who holds that all goods and evils must be temporally assignable states of the person may of course try to bring difficult cases into line by pointing to the pleasure or pain that more complicated goods and evils cause. Loss, betrayal, deception, and ridicule are on this view bad because people suffer when they learn of them. But it should be asked how our ideas of human value would have to be constituted to accommodate these cases directly instead. One advantage of such an account might be that it would enable us to explain *why* the discovery of these misfortunes causes suffering—in a way that makes it reasonable. For the natural view is that the discovery of betrayal makes us unhappy because it is bad to be betrayed—not that betrayal is bad because its discovery makes us unhappy.

It therefore seems to me worth exploring the position that most good and ill fortune has as its subject a person identified by his history and his possibilities, rather than merely by his categorical state of the moment—and that while this subject can be exactly located in a sequence of places and times, the same is not necessarily true of the goods and ills that befall him.[2]

These ideas can be illustrated by an example of deprivation whose severity approaches that of death. Suppose an intelligent person receives a brain injury that reduces him to the mental condition of a contented infant, and that such desires as remain to him can be satisfied by a custodian, so that he is free from care. Such a development would be widely regarded as a severe misfortune, not only for his friends and relations, or for society, but also, and primarily, for the person himself. This does not mean that a contented infant is unfortunate. The intelligent adult who has been *reduced* to this condition is the subject of the misfortune. He is the one we pity, though of course he does not mind his condition—there is some doubt, in fact, whether he can be said to exist any longer.

The view that such a man has suffered a misfortune is open to the same objections which have been raised in regard to death. He does not mind his condition. It is in fact the same condition he was in at the age of three months, except that he is bigger. If we did not pity him then, why pity him now; in any case, who is there to pity? The intelligent adult has disappeared, and for a creature like the one before us, happiness consists in a full stomach and a dry diaper.

If these objections are invalid, it must be because they rest on a mistaken assumption about the temporal relation between the subject of a misfortune and the circumstances which constitute it. If, instead of concentrating exclusively on the oversized baby before us, we consider the person he was, and the person he *could* be now, then his reduction to this state and the cancellation of his natural adult development constitute a perfectly intelligible catastrophe.

This case should convince us that it is arbitrary to restrict the goods and evils that can befall a man to nonrelational properties ascribable to him at particular times. As it stands, that restriction excludes not only such cases of gross degeneration, but also a good deal of what is important about success and failure, and other features of a life that have the character of processes. I believe we can go further, however. There are goods and evils which are irreducibly relational; they are features of the relations between a person, with spatial and temporal boundaries of the usual sort, and circumstances which may not coincide with him either in space or in time. A man's life includes much that does not take place within the boundaries of his body and his mind, and what happens to him can include much that does not take place within the boundaries of his life. These boundaries are commonly crossed by the misfortunes of being deceived, or despised, or betrayed. (If this is correct, there is a simple account of what is wrong with breaking a deathbed promise. It is an injury to the dead man. For certain purposes it is possible to regard time as just another type of distance.) The case of mental degeneration shows us an evil that depends on a contrast between the reality and the possible alternatives. A man is the subject of good and evil as much because he has hopes which may or may not be fulfilled, or possibilities which may or may not be realized, as because of his capacity to suffer and enjoy. If death is an evil, it must be accounted for in these terms, and the impossibility of locating it within life should not trouble us.

When a man dies we are left with his corpse, and while a corpse can suffer the kind of mishap that may occur to an article of furniture, it is not a suitable object for pity. The man, however, is. He has lost his life, and if he had not died, he would have continued to live it, and to possess whatever good there is in living. If we apply to death the account suggested for the case of dementia, we shall say that although the spatial and temporal locations of the individual who suffered the loss are clear enough, the misfortune itself cannot be so easily located. One must be content just to state that his life is over and there will never be any more of it. That *fact*, rather than his past or present condition, constitutes his misfortune, if it is one. Nevertheless if there is a loss, someone must suffer it, and *he* must have existence and specific spatial and temporal location even if the loss itself does not. The fact that Beethoven had no children may have been a cause of regret to him, or a sad thing for the world, but it cannot be described as a misfortune for the children that he never had. All of us, I believe, are fortunate to have been born. But unless good and ill can be assigned to an embryo, or even to an unconnected pair of gametes, it cannot be said that not to be born is a misfortune. (That is a factor to be considered in deciding whether abortion and contraception are akin to murder.)

This approach also provides a solution to the problem of temporal asymmetry, pointed out by Lucretius. He observed that no one finds it disturbing to contemplate the eternity preceding his own birth, and he took this to show that it must be irrational to fear death, since death is simply the mirror image of the prior abyss. That is not true, however, and the difference between the two explains why it is reasonable to regard them differently. It is true that both the time before a man's birth and the time after his death are times when he does not exist. But the time after his death is time of which his death deprives him. It is time in which, had he not died then, he would be alive. Therefore any death entails the loss of *some* life that its victim would have led had he not died at that or any earlier point. We know perfectly well what it would be for him to have had it instead of losing it, and there is no difficulty in identifying the loser.

But we cannot say that the time prior to a man's birth is time in which he would have lived had he been born not then but earlier. For aside from the brief margin permitted by premature labor, he *could* not have been born earlier: anyone born substantially earlier than he was would have been someone else. Therefore the time prior to his birth is not time in which his subsequent birth prevents him from living. His birth, when it occurs, does not entail the loss to him of any life whatever.

The direction of time is crucial in assigning possibilities to people or other individuals. Distinct possible lives of a single person can diverge from a common beginning, but they cannot converge to a common conclusion from diverse beginnings. (The latter would represent not a set of different possible lives of one individual, but a set of distinct possible individuals, whose lives have identical conclusions.) Given an identifiable individual, countless possibilities for his continued existence are imaginable, and we can clearly conceive of what it would be for him to go on existing indefinitely. However inevitable it is that this will not come about, its possibility is still that of the continuation of a good for him, if life is the good we take it to be.[3]

We are left, therefore, with the question whether the nonrealization of this possibility is in every case a misfortune, or whether it depends on what can naturally be hoped for. This seems to me the most serious difficulty with the view that death is always an evil. Even if we can dispose of the objections against admitting misfortune that is not experienced, or cannot be assigned to a definite time in the person's life, we still have to set some limits on *how* possible a possibility must be for its nonrealization to be a misfortune (or good fortune, should the possibility be a bad one). The death of Keats at 24 is generally regarded as tragic; that of Tolstoy at 82 is not. Although they will both be dead for ever, Keats' death deprived him of many years of life which were allowed to Tolstoy; so in a clear sense Keats' loss was greater (though not in the sense standardly employed in mathematical comparison between infinite quantities). However, this does not prove that Tolstoy's loss was insignificant. Perhaps we record an objection only to evils which are gratuitously added to the inevitable; the fact that it is worse to die at 24 than at 82 does not imply that it is not a terrible thing to die at 82, or even at 806. The question is whether we can regard as a misfortune any limitation, like mortality, that is normal to the species. Blindness or near-blindness is not a misfortune for a mole, nor would it be for a man if that were the natural condition of the human race.

The trouble is that life familiarizes us with the goods of which death deprives us. We are already able to appreciate them, as a mole is not able to appreciate vision. If we put aside doubts about their status as goods and grant that their quantity is in part a function of their duration, the question remains whether death, no matter when it occurs, can be said to deprive its victim of what is in the relevant sense a possible continuation of life.

The situation is an ambiguous one. Observed from without, human beings obviously have a natural lifespan and cannot live much longer than a hundred years. A man's sense of his own experience, on the other hand, does not embody this idea of a natural limit. His existence defines for him an essentially open-ended possible future, containing the usual mixture of goods and evils that he has found so tolerable in the past. Having been gratuitously introduced to the world by a collection of natural, historical, and social accidents, he finds himself the subject of a *life*, with an indeterminate and not essentially limited future. Viewed in this way, death, no matter how inevitable, is an abrupt cancellation of indefinitely extensive possible goods. Normality seems to have nothing to do with it, for the fact that we will all inevitably die in a few score years cannot by itself imply that it would not be good to live longer. Suppose that we were all inevitably going to die in *agony*—physical agony lasting six months. Would inevitability make *that* prospect any less unpleasant? And why should it be different for a deprivation? If the normal lifespan were a thousand years, death at 80 would be a tragedy. As things are, it may just be a more widespread tragedy. If there is no limit to the amount of life that it would be good to have, then it may be that a bad end is in store for us all.

Notes

1. It is sometimes suggested that what we really mind is the process of *dying*. But I should not really object to dying if it were not followed by death.
2. It is certainly not true in general of the things that can be said of him. For example, Abraham Lincoln was taller than Louis XIV. But when?
3. I confess to being troubled by the above argument, on the ground that it is too sophisticated to explain the simple difference between our attitudes to prenatal and posthumous nonexistence. For this reason I suspect that something essential is omitted from the account of the badness of death by an analysis which treats it as a deprivation of possibilities. My suspicion is supported by the following suggestion of Robert Nozick. We could imagine discovering that people developed from individual spores that had existed indefinitely far in advance of their birth. In this fantasy, birth never occurs naturally more than a hundred years before the permanent end of the spore's existence. But then we discover a way to trigger the premature batching of these spores, and people are born who have thousands of years of active life before them. Given such a situation, it would be possible to imagine *oneself* having come into existence thousands of years previously. If we put aside the question whether this would really be the same person, even given the identity of the spore, then the consequence appears to be that a person's birth at a given time *could* deprive him of many earlier years of possible life. Now while it would be cause for regret that one had been deprived of all those possible years of life by being born too late, the feeling would differ from that which many people have about death. I conclude that something about the future *prospect* of permanent nothingness is not captured by the analysis in terms of denied possibilities. If so, then Lucretius' argument still awaits an answer. I suspect that it requires a general treatment of the difference between past and future in our attitudes toward our own lives. Our attitudes toward past and future pain are very different, for example. Derek Parfit's unpublished writings on this topic have revealed its difficulty to me.

Study Questions

1. If death is not an evil for a person who dies, does it follow that death is not an evil for anyone?
2. Do you agree with Nagel that a man who devotes himself to cheerful pursuit of a method of communicating with asparagus plants has wasted his life?
3. Do you agree with Nagel that all of us are fortunate to have been born?
4. If we accept without regret not having lived in the past before we were born, should we also accept without regret not living in the future after we die?

L.   The Meaning of Life

CHAPTER 48

The Meaning of Life

Richard Taylor

Richard Taylor (1919–2003) was Professor of Philosophy at the University of Rochester. In this selection he finds that life's meaning is not bestowed on us but comes from within ourselves.

The question whether life has any meaning is difficult to interpret, and the more you concentrate your critical faculty on it the more it seems to elude you, or to evaporate as any intelligible question. You want to turn it aside, as a source of embarrassment, as something that, if it cannot be abolished, should at least be decently covered. And yet I think any reflective person recognizes that the question it raises is important, and that it ought to have a significant answer.

If the idea of meaningfulness is difficult to grasp in this context, so that we are unsure what sort of thing would amount to answering the question, the idea of meaninglessness is perhaps less so. If, then, we can bring before our minds a clear image of meaningless existence, then perhaps we can take a step toward coping with our original question by seeing to what extent our lives, as we actually find them, resemble that image, and draw such lessons as we are able to from the comparison.

Meaningless Existence

A perfect image of meaninglessness, of the kind we are seeking, is found in the ancient myth of Sisyphus. Sisyphus, it will be remembered, betrayed divine secrets to mortals, and for this he was condemned by the gods to roll a stone to the top of a hill, the stone then immediately to roll back down, again to be pushed to the top by Sisyphus, to roll down once more, and so on again and again, *forever*. Now in this we have the picture of meaningless, pointless toil, of a meaningless existence that is absolutely *never* redeemed. It is not even redeemed by a death that, if it were to accomplish nothing more, would at least bring this idiotic cycle to a close. If we were invited to imagine Sisyphus struggling for a while and accomplishing nothing, perhaps eventually falling from exhaustion, so that we might suppose him then eventually turning to something having some sort of promise, then the meaninglessness of that chapter of his life would not be so stark. It would be a dark and dreadful dream, from which he eventually awakens to sunlight and reality. But he does not awaken, for there is nothing for him to awaken to. His repetitive toil is his life and reality, and it goes on forever, and it is without any meaning whatever. Nothing ever comes of what he is doing, except simply, more of the same. Not by one step, nor by a thousand, nor by ten thousand does he even expiate by the smallest token the sin against the gods that led him into this fate. Nothing comes of it, nothing at all.

This ancient myth has always enchanted people, for countless meanings can be read into it. Some of the ancients apparently thought it symbolized the perpetual rising and setting of the sun, and others the repetitious crashing of the waves upon the shore. Probably the commonest interpretation is that it symbolizes our eternal struggle and unquenchable spirit, our determination always to try once more in the face of overwhelming discouragement. This interpretation is further supported by that version of the myth according to which Sisyphus was commanded to roll the stone *over* the hill, so that it would finally roll down the other side, but was never quite able to make it.

I am not concerned with rendering or defending any interpretation of this myth, however. I have cited it only for the one element it does unmistakably contain, namely, that of a repetitious, cyclic activity that never comes to anything. We could contrive other images of this that would serve just as well, and no myth-makers are needed to supply the materials of it. Thus, we can imagine two persons transporting a stone—or even a precious gem, it does not matter—back and forth, relay style. One carries it to a near or distant point where it is received by the other; it is returned to its starting point, there to be recovered by the first, and the process is repeated over and over.

Except in this relay nothing counts as winning, and nothing brings the contest to any close; each step only leads to a repetition of itself. Or we can imagine two groups of prisoners, one of them engaged in digging a prodigious hole in the ground that is no sooner finished than it is filled in again by the other group, the latter then digging a new hole that is at once filled in by the first group, and so on and on endlessly.

Now what stands out in all such pictures as oppressive and dejecting is not that the beings who enact these roles suffer any torture or pain, for it need not be assumed that they do. Nor is it that their labors are great, for they are no greater than the labors commonly undertaken by most people most of the time. According to the original myth, the stone is so large that Sisyphus never quite gets it to the top and must groan under every step, so that his enormous labor is all for nought. But this is not what appalls. It is not that his great struggle comes to nothing, but that his existence itself is without meaning. Even if we suppose, for example, that the stone is but a pebble that can be carried effortlessly, or that the holes dug by the prisoners are but small ones, not the slightest meaning is introduced into their lives. The stone that Sisyphus moves to the top of the hill, whether we think of it as large or small, still rolls back every time, and the process is repeated forever. Nothing comes of it, and the work is simply pointless. That is the element of the myth that I wish to capture.

Again, it is not the fact that the labors of Sisyphus continue forever that deprives them of meaning. It is, rather, the implication of this: that they come to nothing. The image would not be changed by our supposing him to push a different stone up every time, each to roll down again. But if we supposed that these stones, instead of rolling back to their places as if they had never been moved, were assembled at the top of the hill and there incorporated, say, in a beautiful and enduring temple, then the aspect of meaninglessness would disappear. His labors would then have a point, something would come of them all, and although one could perhaps still say it was not worth it, one could not say that the life of Sisyphus was devoid of meaning altogether. Meaningfulness would at least have made an appearance, and we could see what it was.

That point will need remembering. But in the meantime, let us note another way in which the image of meaninglessness can be altered by making only a very slight change. Let us suppose that the gods, while condemning Sisyphus to the fate just described, at the same time, as an afterthought, waxed perversely merciful by implanting in him a strange and irrational impulse; namely, a compulsive impulse to roll stones. We may if we like, to make this more graphic, suppose they accomplish this by implanting in him some substance that has this effect on his character and drives. I call this perverse, because from our point of view there is clearly no reason why anyone should have a persistent and insatiable desire to do something so pointless as that. Nevertheless, suppose that is Sisyphus' condition. He has but one obsession, which is to roll stones, and it is an obsession that is only for the moment appeased by his rolling them—he no sooner gets a stone rolled to the top of the hill than he is restless to roll up another.

Now it can be seen why this little afterthought of the gods, which I called perverse, was also in fact merciful. For they have by this device managed to give Sisyphus precisely what he wants—by making him want precisely what they inflict on him. However it may appear to us, Sisyphus' fate now does not appear to him as a condemnation, but the very reverse. His one desire in life is to roll stones, and he is absolutely guaranteed its endless fulfillment. Where otherwise he might profoundly have wished surcease, and even welcomed the quiet of death to release him from endless boredom and meaninglessness, his life is now filled with mission and meaning, and he seems to himself to have been given an entry to heaven. Nor need he even fear death, for the gods have promised him an endless opportunity to indulge his single purpose, without concern or frustration. He will be able to roll stones *forever*.

What we need to mark most carefully at this point is that the picture with which we began has not really been changed in the least by adding this supposition. Exactly the same things happen as before. The only change is in Sisyphus' view of them. The picture before was the image of meaningless activity and existence. It was created precisely to be an image of that. It has not lost that meaninglessness, it has now gained not the least shred of meaningfulness. The stones still roll back as before, each phase of Sisyphus' life still exactly resembles all the others, the task is never completed, nothing comes of it, no temple ever begins to rise, and all this cycle of the same pointless thing over and over goes on forever in this picture as in the other. The *only* thing that has happened is this: Sisyphus has been reconciled to it, and indeed more, he has been led to embrace it. Not, however, by reason or persuasion, but by nothing more rational than the potency of a new substance in his veins.

The Meaninglessness of Life

I believe the foregoing provides a fairly clear content to the idea of meaninglessness and, through it, some hint of what meaningfulness, in this sense might be. Meaninglessness is essentially endless pointlessness, and meaningfulness is therefore the opposite. Activity, and even long, drawn out and repetitive activity, has a meaning if it has some significant culmination, some more or less lasting end that can be considered to have been the direction and purpose of the activity. But the descriptions so far also provide something else; namely, the suggestion of how an existence that is objectively meaningless, in this sense, can nevertheless acquire a meaning for him whose existence it is.

Now let us ask: Which of these pictures does life in fact resemble? And let us not begin with our own lives, for here both our prejudices and wishes are great, but with the life in general that we share with the rest of creation. We shall find, I think, that it all has a certain pattern, and that this pattern is by now easily recognized.

We can begin anywhere, only saving human existence for our last consideration. We can, for example, begin with any animal. It does not matter where we begin, because the result is going to be exactly the same.

Thus, for example, there are caves in New Zealand, deep and dark, whose floors are quiet pools and whose walls and ceilings are covered with soft light. As you gaze in wonder in the stillness of these caves it seems that the Creator has reproduced there in microcosm the heavens themselves, until you scarcely remember the enclosing presence of the walls. As you look more closely, however, the scene is explained. Each dot of light identifies an ugly worm, whose luminous tail is meant to attract insects from the surrounding darkness. As from time to time one of these insects draws near it becomes entangled in a sticky thread lowered by the worm, and is eaten. This goes on month after month, the blind worm lying there in the barren stillness waiting to entrap an occasional bit of nourishment that will only sustain it to another bit of nourishment until. . . . Until what? What great thing awaits all this long and repetitious effort and makes it worthwhile? Really nothing. The larva just transforms itself finally to a tiny winged adult that lacks even mouth parts to feed and lives only a day or two. These adults, as soon as they have mated and laid eggs, are themselves caught in the threads and are devoured by the cannibalistic worms, often without having ventured into the day, the only point to their existence having now been fulfilled. This has been going on for millions of years, and to no end other than that the same meaningless cycle may continue for another millions of years.

All living things present essentially the same spectacle. The larva of a certain cicada burrows in the darkness of the earth for seventeen years, through season after season, to emerge finally into the daylight for a brief flight, lay its eggs, and die—this all to repeat itself during the next seventeen years, and so on to eternity. We have already noted, in another connection, the struggles of fish, made only that others may do the same after them and that this cycle, having no other point than itself, may never cease. Some birds span an entire side of the globe each year and then return, only to insure that others may follow the same incredibly long path again and again. One is led to wonder what the point of it all is, with what great triumph this ceaseless effort, repeating itself through millions of years, might finally culminate, and why it should go on and on for so long, accomplishing nothing, getting nowhere. But then you realize that there is no point to it at all, that it really culminates in nothing, that each of these cycles, so filled with toil, is to be followed only by more of the same. The point of any living thing's life is, evidently, nothing but life itself.

This life of the world thus presents itself to our eyes as a vast machine, feeding on itself, running on and on forever to nothing. And we are part of that life. To be sure, we are not just the same, but the differences are not so great as we like to think; many are merely invented, and none really cancels the kind of meaninglessness that we found in Sisyphus and that we find all around, wherever anything lives. We are conscious of our activity. Our goals, whether in any significant sense we choose them or not, are things of which we are at least partly aware and can therefore in some sense appraise. More significantly, perhaps, we have a history, as other animals do not, such that each generation does not precisely resemble all those before. Still, if we can in imagination disengage our wills from our lives and disregard the deep interest we all have in our own existence, we shall find that they do not so little resemble the existence of Sisyphus. We toil after goals, most of them—indeed every single one of them—of transitory significance and, having gained one of them, we immediately set forth for the next, as if that one had never been, with this next one being essentially more of the same. Look at a busy street any day, and observe the throng going hither and thither. To what? Some office or shop, where the same things will be done today as were done yesterday, and are done now so they may be repeated tomorrow. And if we think that, unlike Sisyphus, these labors do have a point, that they culminate in something lasting and, independently of our own deep interests in them, very worthwhile, then we simply have not considered the thing closely enough. Most such effort is directed only to the establishment and perpetuation of home and family; that is, to the begetting of others who will follow in our steps to do more of the same. Everyone's life thus resembles one of Sisyphus's climbs to the summit of his hill, and each day of it one of his steps; the difference is that whereas Sisyphus himself returns to push the stone up again, we leave this to our children. We at one point imagined that the labors of Sisyphus finally culminated in the creation of a temple, but for this to make any difference it had to be a temple that would at least endure, adding beauty to the world for the remainder of time. Our achievements, even though they are often beautiful, are mostly bubbles; and those that do last, like the sand-swept pyramids, soon become mere curiosities while around them the rest of human-kind continues its perpetual toting of rocks, only to see them roll down. Nations are built upon the bones of their founders and pioneers, but only to decay and crumble before long, their rubble then becoming the foundation for others directed to exactly the same fate. The picture of Sisyphus is the picture of existence of the individual man, great or unknown, of nations, of the human race, and of the very life of the world.

On a country road one sometimes comes upon the ruined hulks of a house and once extensive buildings, all in collapse and spread over with weeds. A curious eye can in imagination reconstruct from what is left a once warm and thriving life, filled with purpose. There was the hearth, where a family once talked, sang, and made plans; there were the rooms, where people loved, and babes were born to a rejoicing mother; there are the musty remains of a sofa, infested with bugs, once bought at a dear price to enhance an ever-growing comfort, beauty, and warmth. Every small piece of junk fills the mind with what once, not long ago, was utterly real, with children's voices, plans made, and enterprises embarked upon. That is how these stones of Sisyphus were rolled up, and that is how they became incorporated into a beautiful temple, and that temple is what now lies before you. Meanwhile other buildings, institutions, nations, and civilizations spring up all around, only to share the same fate before long. And if the question "What for?" is now asked, the answer is clear: so that just this may go on forever.

The two pictures—of Sisyphus and of our own lives, if we look at them from a distance—are in outline the same and convey to the mind the same image. It is not surprising, then, that we invent ways of denying it, our religions proclaiming a heaven that does not crumble, their hymnals and prayer books declaring a significance to life of which our eyes provide no hint whatever.[1] Even our philosophies portray some permanent and lasting good at which all may aim, from the changeless forms invented by Plato to the beatific vision of St. Thomas and the ideals of permanence contrived by the moderns. When these fail to convince, then earthly ideals such as universal justice and brotherhood are conjured up to take their places and give meaning to our seemingly endless pilgrimage, some final state that will be ushered in when the last obstacle is removed and the last stone pushed to the hilltop. No one believes, of course, that any such state will be final, or even wants it to be in case it means that human existence would then cease to be a struggle; but in the meantime such ideas serve a very real need.

The Meaning of Life

We noted that Sisyphus' existence would have meaning if there were some point to his labors, if his efforts ever culminated in something that was not just an occasion for fresh labors of the same kind. But that is precisely the meaning it lacks. And human existence resembles his in that respect. We do achieve things—we scale our towers and raise our stones to the hilltops—but every such accomplishment fades, providing only an occasion for renewed labors of the same kind.

But here we need to note something else that has been mentioned, but its significance not explored, and that is the state of mind and feeling with which such labors are undertaken. We noted that if Sisyphus had a keen and unappeasable desire to be doing just what he found himself doing, then, although his life would in no way be changed, it would nevertheless have a meaning for him. It would be an irrational one, no doubt, because the desire itself would be only the product of the substance in his veins, and not any that reason could discover, but a meaning nevertheless.

And would it not, in fact, be a meaning incomparably better than the other? For let us examine again the first kind of meaning it could have. Let us suppose that, without having any interest in rolling stones, as such, and finding this, in fact, a galling toil, Sisyphus did nevertheless have a deep interest in raising a temple, one that would be beautiful and lasting. And let us suppose he succeeded in this, that after ages of dreadful toil, all directed at this final result, he did at last complete his temple, such that now he could say his work was done, and he could rest and forever enjoy the result. Now what? What picture now presents itself to our minds? It is precisely the picture of infinite boredom! Of Sisyphus doing nothing ever again, but contemplating what he has already wrought and can no longer add anything to, and contemplating it for an eternity! Now in this picture we have a meaning for Sisyphus' existence, a point for his prodigious labor, because we have put it there; yet, at the same time, that which is really worthwhile seems to have slipped away entirely. Where before we were presented with the nightmare of eternal and pointless activity, we are now confronted with the hell of its eternal absence.

Our second picture, then, wherein we imagined Sisyphus to have had inflicted on him the irrational desire to be doing just what he found himself doing, should not have been dismissed so abruptly. The meaning that picture lacked was no meaning that he or anyone could crave, and the strange meaning it had was perhaps just what we were seeking.

At this point, then, we can reintroduce what has been until now, it is hoped, resolutely pushed aside in an effort to view our lives and human existence with objectivity; namely, our own wills, our deep interest in what we find ourselves doing. If we do this we find that our lives do indeed still resemble that of Sisyphus, but that the meaningfulness they thus lack is precisely the meaningfulness of infinite boredom. At the same time, the strange meaningfulness they possess is that of the inner compulsion to be doing just what we were put here to do, and to go on doing it forever. This is the nearest we may hope to get to heaven, but the redeeming side of that fact is that we do thereby avoid a genuine hell.

If the builders of a great and flourishing ancient civilization could somehow return now to see archaeologists unearthing the trivial remnants of what they had once accomplished with such effort—see the fragments of pots and vases, a few broken statues, and such tokens of another age and greatness—they could indeed ask themselves what the point of it all was, if this is all it finally came to. Yet, it did not seem so to them then, for it was just the building, and not what was finally built, that gave their life meaning. Similarly, if the builders of the ruined home and farm that I described a short while ago could be brought back to see what is left, they would have the same feelings.

What we construct in our imaginations as we look over these decayed and rusting pieces would reconstruct itself in their very memories, and certainly with unspeakable sadness. The piece of a sled at our feet would revive in them a warm Christmas. And what rich memories would there be in the broken crib? And the weed-covered remains of a fence would reproduce the scene of a great herd of livestock, so laboriously built up over so many years. What was it all worth, if this is the final result? Yet, again, it did not seem so to them through those many years of struggle and toil, and they did not imagine they were building a Gibraltar. The things to which they bent their backs day after day, realizing one by one their ephemeral plans, were precisely the things in which their wills were deeply involved, precisely the things in which their interests lay, and there was no need then to ask questions. There is no more need of them now—the day was sufficient to itself, and so was the life.

This is surely the way to look at all of life—at one's own life, and each day and moment it contains; of the life of a nation; of the species; of the life of the world; and of every thing that breathes. Even the glow worms I described, whose cycles of existence over the millions of years seem so pointless when looked at by us, will seem entirely different to us if we can somehow try to view their existence from within. Their endless activity, which gets nowhere, is just what it is their will to pursue. This is its whole justification and meaning. Nor would it be any salvation to the birds who span the globe every year, back and forth, to have a home made for them in a cage with plenty of food and protection, so that they would not have to migrate anymore. It would be their condemnation, for it is the doing that counts for them, and not what they hope to win by it. Flying these prodigious distances, never ending, is what it is in their veins to do, exactly as it was in Sisyphus's veins to roll stones, without end, after the gods had waxed merciful and implanted this in him.

You no sooner drew your first breath than you responded to the will that was in you to live. You no more ask whether it will be worthwhile, or whether anything of significance will come of it, than the worms and the birds. The point of living is simply to be living, in the manner that it is your nature to be living. You go through life building your castles, each of these beginning to fade into time as the next is begun; yet it would be no salvation to rest from all this. It would be a condemnation, and one that would in no way be redeemed were you able to gaze upon the things you have done, even if these were beautiful and absolutely permanent, as they never are. What counts is that you should be able to begin a new task, a new castle, a new bubble. It counts only because it is there to be done and you have the will to do it. The same will be the life of your children, and of theirs; and if the philosopher is apt to see in this a pattern similar to the unending cycles of the existence of Sisyphus, and to despair, then it is indeed because the meaning and point he is seeking is not there—but mercifully so. The meaning of life is from within us, it is not bestowed from without, and it far exceeds in both its beauty and permanence any heaven of which men have ever dreamed or yearned for.

Note

1. A popular Christian hymn, sung often at funerals and typical of many hymns, expresses this thought:

> *Swift to its close ebbs out life's little day;*
> *Earth's joys grow dim, its glories pass away:*
> *Change and decay in all around I see:*
> *O thou who changest not, abide with me.*

Study Questions

1. Can a life be enjoyed yet meaningless?
2. Can a life be immoral yet meaningful?
3. If you find meaning in a task, can you be mistaken?
4. Would Taylor agree with Thomas Nagel's claim in the previous article that a man who devotes himself to cheerful pursuit of a method of communicating with asparagus plants has wasted his life?

CHAPTER 49

Meaning in Life

Susan Wolf

Susan Wolf is Professor of Philosophy at the University of North Carolina at Chapel Hill. She defends the view that not all lives are meaningful but only those in which a person actively engages in projects of worth. So, unlike Taylor, Wolf would not find meaning in the life of Sisyphus, even if his fondest desire was to roll stones up hills.

A meaningful life is, first of all, one that has within it the basis for an affirmative answer to the needs or longings that are characteristically described as needs for meaning. I have in mind, for example, the sort of questions people ask on their deathbeds, or simply in contemplation of their eventual deaths, about whether their lives have been (or are) worth living, whether they have had any point, and the sort of questions one asks when considering suicide and wondering whether one has any reason to go on. These questions are familiar from Russian novels and existentialist philosophy, if not from personal experience. Though they arise most poignantly in times of crisis and intense emotion, they also have their place in moments of calm reflection, when considering important life choices. Moreover, paradigms of what are taken to be meaningful and meaningless lives in our culture are readily available. Lives of great moral or intellectual accomplishment—Gandhi, Mother Teresa, Albert Einstein—come to mind as unquestionably meaningful lives (if any are); lives of waste and isolation—Thoreau's "lives of quiet desperation," typically anonymous to the rest of us, and the mythical figure of Sisyphus—represent meaninglessness.

From "Happiness and Meaning: Two Aspects of the Good Life," *Social Philosophy & Policy,* Vol. 24, 1997. Reprinted with the permission of Cambridge University Press.

To what general characteristics of meaningfulness do these images lead us and how do they provide an answer to the longings mentioned above? Roughly, I would say that meaningful lives are lives of active engagement in projects of worth. Of course, a good deal needs to be said in elaboration of this statement. Let me begin by discussing the two key phrases, "active engagement" and "projects of worth."

A person is actively engaged by something if she is gripped, excited, involved by it. Most obviously, we are actively engaged by the things and people about which and whom we are passionate. Opposites of active engagement are boredom and alienation. To be actively engaged in something is not always pleasant in the ordinary sense of the word. Activities in which people are actively engaged frequently involve stress, danger, exertion, or sorrow (consider, for example: writing a book, climbing a mountain, training for a marathon, caring for an ailing friend). However, there is something good about the feeling of engagement: one feels (typically without thinking about it) especially alive.

That a meaningful life must involve "projects of worth" will, I expect, be more controversial, for the phrase hints of a commitment to some sort of objective value. This is not accidental, for I believe that the idea of meaningfulness, and the concern that our lives possess it, are conceptually linked to such a commitment.[1] Indeed, it is this linkage that I want to defend, for I have neither a philosophical theory of what objective value is nor a substantive theory about what has this sort of value. What is clear to me is that there can be no sense to the idea of meaningfulness without a distinction between more and less worthwhile ways to spend one's time, where the test of worth is at least partly independent of a subject's ungrounded preferences or enjoyment.

Consider first the longings or concerns about meaning that people have, their wondering whether their lives are meaningful, their vows to add more meaning to their lives. The sense of these concerns and resolves cannot fully be captured by an account in which what one does with one's life doesn't matter, as long as one enjoys or prefers it. Sometimes people have concerns about meaning despite their knowledge that their lives to date have been satisfying. Indeed, their enjoyment and "active engagement" with activities and values they now see as shallow seems only to heighten the sense of meaninglessness that comes to afflict them. Their sense that their lives so far have been meaningless cannot be a sense that their activities have not been chosen or fun. When they look for sources of meaning or ways to add meaning to their lives, they are searching for projects whose justifications lie elsewhere.

Second, we need an explanation for why certain sorts of activities and involvements come to mind as contributors to meaningfulness while others seem intuitively inappropriate. Think about what gives meaning to your own life and the lives of your friends and acquaintances. Among the things that tend to come up on such lists, I have already mentioned moral and intellectual accomplishments and the ongoing activities that lead to them. Relationships with friends and relatives are perhaps even more important for most of us. Aesthetic enterprises (both creative and appreciative), the cultivation of personal virtues, and religious practices frequently loom large. By contrast, it would be odd, if not bizarre, to think of crossword puzzles, sitcoms, or the kind of computer games to which I am fighting off addiction as providing meaning in our lives, though there is no question that they afford a sort of satisfaction and that they are the objects of choice. Some things, such as chocolate and aerobics class, I choose even at considerable cost to myself (it is irrelevant that these particular choices may be related); so I must find them worthwhile in a sense. But they are not the sorts of things that make life worth living.[2]

"Active engagement in projects of worth," I suggest, answers to the needs an account of meaningfulness in life must meet. If a person is or has been thus actively engaged, then she does have an answer to the question of whether her life is or has been worthwhile, whether it has or has had a point. When someone looks for ways to add meaning to her life, she is looking (though perhaps not under this description) for worthwhile projects about which she can get enthused. The account also explains why some activities and projects but not others come to mind as contributors to meaning in life. Some projects, or at any rate, particular acts, are worthwhile but too boring or mechanical to be sources of meaning. People do not get meaning from recycling or from writing checks to Oxfam and the ACLU. Other acts and activities, though highly pleasurable and deeply involving, like riding a roller coaster or meeting a movie star, do not seem to have the right kind of value to contribute to meaning.

Bernard Williams once distinguished categorical desires from the rest. Categorical desires give us reasons for living—they are not premised on the assumption that we will live. The sorts of things that give meaning to life tend to be objects of categorical desire. We desire them, at least so I would suggest, because we think them worthwhile.

They are not worthwhile simply because we desire them or simply because they make our lives more pleasant.

Roughly, then, according to my proposal, a meaningful life must satisfy two criteria, suitably linked. First, there must be active engagement, and second, it must be engagement in (or with) projects of worth. A life is meaningless if it lacks active engagement with anything. A person who is bored or alienated from most of what she spends her life doing is one whose life can be said to lack meaning. Note that she may in fact be performing functions of worth. A housewife and mother, a doctor, or a busdriver may be competently doing a socially valuable job, but because she is not engaged by her work (or, as we are assuming, by anything else in her life), she has no categorical desires that give her a reason to live. At the same time, someone who is actively engaged may also live a meaningless life, if the objects of her involvement are utterly worthless. It is difficult to come up with examples of such lives that will be uncontroversial without being bizarre. But both bizarre and controversial examples have their place. In the bizarre category, we might consider pathological cases: someone whose sole passion in life is collecting rubber bands, or memorizing the dictionary, or making handwritten copies of *War and Peace*. Controversial cases will include the corporate lawyer who sacrifices her private life and health for success along the professional ladder, the devotee of a religious cult, or—an example offered by Wiggins[3]—the pig farmer who buys more land to grow more corn to feed more pigs to buy more land to grow more corn to feed more pigs.

We may summarize my proposal in terms of a slogan: "Meaning arises when subjective attraction meets objective attractiveness." The idea is that in a world in which some things are more worthwhile than others, meaning arises when a subject discovers or develops an affinity for one or typically several of the more worthwhile things and has and makes use of the opportunity to engage with it or them in a positive way.

Notes

1. This point is made by David Wiggins in his brilliant but difficult essay "Truth, Invention, and the Meaning of Life," *Proceedings of the British Academy*, vol. 62 (1976).
2. Woody Allen appears to have a different view. His list of the things that make life worth living at the end of *Manhattan* includes, for example "the

crabs at Sam Woo's," which would seem to be on the level of chocolates. On the other hand, the crabs' appearance on the list may be taken to show that he regards the dish as an accomplishment meriting aesthetic appreciation, where such appreciation is a worthy activity in itself; in this respect, the crabs might be akin to other items on his list such as the second movement of the *Jupiter Symphony*, Louis Armstrong's recording of "Potatohead Blues," and "those apples and pears of Cèzanne." Strictly speaking, the appreciation of great chocolate might also qualify as such an activity.

3. See Wiggins, "Truth, Invention, and the Meaning of Life," p. 342.

Study Questions

1. Based on the examples she provides, what does Wolf mean by "a project of worth"?
2. How would Wolf decide whether some activity was a project of worth?
3. In your view, are the lives of a college professor, a professional golfer, a janitor, and a hobo equally meaningful?
4. Would studying certain subjects add more meaning to life than studying other subjects?

CHAPTER 50

Meaningful Lives?

Christine Vitrano

Christine Vitrano is Assistant Professor of Philosophy at Brooklyn College of The City University of New York. She considers the views of a meaningful life offered by both Richard Taylor and Susan Wolf, but finds neither convincing.

Richard Taylor and Susan Wolf offer contrasting visions of a meaningful life. I find each account partially persuasive, but neither entirely satisfactory.

For Wolf, a meaningful life is one in which you are actively engaged in projects of worth. To be engaged is to be "gripped, excited, involved."[1] If you find your life dreary, then it is not meaningful.

Enjoying activities, however, does not by itself render them meaningful; they also need to be worthwhile. As she says, "When someone looks for ways to add meaning to her life, she is looking . . . for worthwhile projects about which she can get enthused" and "whose justifications lie elsewhere," specifically in "objective value."

According to Wolf, worthwhile activities include "[r]elationships with friends and relatives . . . [a]esthetic enterprises (both creative and appreciative), the cultivation of personal virtues, and religious practices." Specific examples include "writing a book, climbing a mountain, training for a marathon." Among the activities that lack such worth are solving crossword puzzles, watching sitcoms, playing computer games, and eating chocolate, as well as "collecting rubber bands, or memorizing the dictionary, or making handwritten copies of *War and Peace*." Controversial cases are the paths of the "corporate

---

lawyer who sacrifices her private life and health for success along the professional ladder, the devotee of a religious cult, or . . . the pig farmer who buys more land to grow more corn to feed more pigs to buy more land to grow more corn to feed more pigs."

An obvious problem with Wolf's position is that by her own admission she has "neither a philosophical theory of what objective value is nor a substantive theory about what has that sort of value." She relies on supposedly shared intuitions regarding the worth of various activities, but to assume such agreement is unjustified. Some people appreciate an activity Wolf disparages, yet dismiss one she values highly. For example, spending thousands of hours training for a marathon strikes many as wearisome; they may be far more engaged by computer games. On the other hand, grappling with a New York Times Sunday Magazine crossword puzzle is a popular intellectual challenge, holding far more appeal for most than reading an article on metaethics, a subject Wolf finds fascinating.

She might respond to these observations by claiming that the problem with crossword puzzles lies not in their essential unimportance but in their use as mere pastimes. In other words, even those who enjoy solving them don't take them seriously.

This reply, however, only deepens Wolf's difficulty because the same activity could be judged as meaningful or meaningless depending on why a person engages in it. Consider, for instance, a physicist who does scientific research because of the enjoyment it brings but is devoted to chess problems for their intellectual challenge. For that scholar, pursuing physics would be meaningless, but composing and solving chess problems would be meaningful—hardly the conclusion Wolf is seeking.

Furthermore, suppose that in order to distract myself from the monotony of caring for my two children, I read an article on metaphysics. Why should the motive affect the worthiness of the activity?

Because Wolf's position is weakened by her commitment to an objective value that she cannot explain, we might drop that aspect of her position and accept Richard Taylor's view that a meaningful life is one that affords you long-term satisfaction, regardless of the activities you choose. Thus the life of Sisyphus would be meaningful if Sisyphus relished rolling stones up hills.

But why call such a life meaningful? Why not just describe it as pleasant, enjoyable, or happy? Declaring it meaningful neither clarifies any issue nor solves any problem.

Taylor correctly claims that Sisyphus would be happy were he contented with his life, but meaningfulness means more than contentment. Wolf emphasizes that point but cannot say what more is required. Thus neither position is convincing.

In sum, we can appropriately characterize lives as long or short, moral or immoral, as well as successful or unsuccessful in various respects, including accumulating business profits, creating artistic works, or maintaining loving relationships. To ask whether a life is meaningful, however, is to pose a question that incorporates an enigmatic term. Searching for the right answer leads only to frustration.

Note

1. All quotations are from the preceding article by Susan Wolf.

Study Questions

1. What is Vitrano's objection to Wolf's account of a meaningful life?
2. What is Vitrano's objection to Taylor's account of a meaningful life?
3. Does Vitrano believe a life is either meaningful or meaningless?
4. Do you believe a life is either meaningful or meaningless?

Index

Note: Page numbers followed by an italicized letter *n* indicate material found in notes.